Dylan on Dylan

Dylan on Dylan

The Essential Interviews

Edited by Jonathan Cott

HODDER &
STOUGHTON

A CIP catalogue record for this title
is available from the British Library

ISBN 0 340 92312 1
ISBN 978 0 340 923122

Endpapers: © Michael Ochs Archives/Redferns (front),
© Richard Mitchell/Rex Features (back).

Printed and bound by Clays Ltd, St Ives plc

Hodder Headline's policy is to use papers that are natural, renewable
and recyclable products and made from wood grown in sustainable
forests. The logging and manufacturing processes are expected to
conform to the environmental regulations of the country of origin.

Hodder and Stoughton Ltd
A division of Hodder Headline
338 Euston Road
London NW1 3BH

Contents

Introduction

"No single event can awaken within us a stranger
totally unknown to us. To live is to be slowly born."

—Antoine de Saint-Exupéry, *Flight to Arras*

It may have been a slow time coming, but one day in 1960, when he was nineteen years old, Robert Allen Zimmerman of Duluth and Hibbing, Minnesota—the elder of two sons of Abraham and Beatrice Zimmerman—decided to make a name for himself, as well as a nascent identity, a self, and a fantasticated life story nearer to his heart's desire. (This may have been a slow but not totally calculated decision: As he told *People* magazine in 1975, "I didn't consciously pursue the Bob Dylan myth. It was given to me by God. Inspiration is what we're looking for. You just have to be receptive to it.")

"Bob Dylan," he volunteered to his early interviewers, was raised in Gallup, New Mexico—he often said, "I don't have a family, I'm all alone"—and was a child of the open road, having run away from home seven times—at ten, twelve, thirteen, fifteen, fifteen-and-a-half, seventeen, and eighteen. His peregrinations took him to North and South Dakota, Kansas, Texas, California (where at age ten, he claimed to have seen Woody Guthrie perform in Burbank), and even Mexico, thumbing rides and riding freight trains. "I danced my way from the Indian festivals in Gallup, New Mexico/To the Mardi Gras in New Orleans, Louisiana," he wrote in his early autobiographical sketch "My Life in a Stolen Moment." He traveled with a carnival "off and on for six years," he confided to the folksinger Cynthia Gooding in 1962. "I was clean-up boy. I was mainliner on the Ferris wheel. Do the shoreline thing. Use to do all kinds of stuff like that." As he told the *New York Herald Tribune* in 1965, "My past is so complicated you wouldn't believe it, man."

His life story changed as he proceeded onward in his journey, as, remarkably, did his physiognomy and everyday appearance. Like the Greek sea deity Proteus, who in order to elude his pursuers continually shape-shifted from dragon to lion to fire to flood—uttering prophecies along the way—Bob Dylan, in his early days, had, according to the folksinger Eric von Schmidt, "the most incredible way of changing shape, changing size, changing looks. The whole time . . . he wore the same thing, his blue jeans and cap. And sometimes he would look big and muscular, and the next day he'd look like a little gnome, and one day he'd be kind of handsome and virile, and the following day he'd look like a thirteen-year-old child. It was really strange." (One thinks of the advice once given by the ancient Greek elegiac poet Theognis: "Present a different aspect of yourself to each of your friends. . . . Follow the example of the octopus with its many coils which assumes the appearance of the stone to which it is going to cling. Attach yourself to one on one day and, another day, change color. Cleverness is more valuable than inflexibility.")

You would also never know what his voice was going to sound like. One of the other fascinating, if obvious, things about Bob Dylan's chameleonic personality was the way the timbre of his voice would change from one record or period of his life to another—as if his voice, too, couldn't stand having just one unvarying sound. When he first arrived in New York City, he was singing like a hillbilly, "like a dog with his leg caught in barbed wire," as someone remarked at the time. And as years went by, Dylan's voice would veer from, in his words, "that thin . . . wild mercury sound . . . metallic and bright gold" of *Blonde on Blonde* (1966) to the insouciant country sound, which Dylan attributes to his having stopped smoking cigarettes, of *Nashville Skyline* (1969) to the openheartedness, gentleness, vulnerability, and anger of *Blood on the Tracks* (1975) to the haunting timbral admixture of sandpaper and sherry of *Time Out of Mind* (1997).

The French poet Arthur Rimbaud's "I is another" became Dylan's self-defining (selves-defining) modus vivendi. Reading a newspaper account of himself, he once remarked, "God, I'm glad I'm not me." When asked by a reporter the reason for his wearing a wig and a fake beard at a 2003 Newport Folk Festival concert, Dylan replied, "Is that me who you saw up there?" In a 1977 interview I conducted with him about his film *Renaldo and Clara*, Dylan explained to me, "There's Renaldo, there's a guy in whiteface singing on the stage, and then there's Ronnie Hawkins playing Bob Dylan. Bob Dylan is listed in the credits as playing Renaldo, yet Ronnie Hawkins is listed as playing Bob Dylan." "So Bob Dylan," I surmised, "may or may not be in the film." "Exactly." "But Bob Dylan made the film." "Bob Dylan didn't make it," he told me. "I made it."

He even explored and confessed to the more particulated (some might say self-splitting) nature of his being. "Have you ever felt like a couple?" the playwright and actor Sam Shepard once asked him. "A couple?" Dylan responded. "You mean two? Yeah. All the time. Sometimes I feel like ten couples." And as he informed *Newsweek*'s David Gates: "I don't think I'm tangible to myself. I mean, I think one thing today and I think another thing tomorrow. I change during the course of a day. I wake and I'm one person, and when I go to sleep I know for certain I'm somebody else. I don't know *who* I am most of the time. It doesn't even matter to me." (One thinks of the Buddhist notion that the ego isn't an entity but rather a process in time, as well as of Virginia Woolf's comment in *Orlando* that "a biography is considered complete if it merely accounts for six or seven selves, whereas a person may well have as many thousand.")

Throughout his career he has played off his role of "Bob Dylan"—"I have my Bob Dylan mask on, I'm masquerading," he told a Halloween concert audience in 1964—against the silent center of his inner life. At a 1986 press conference he said, "I'm only Bob Dylan when I have to be." When asked who he was the rest of the time, he replied, "Myself." In an interview with Clinton Heylin, Cesar Diaz, who spent five years working with Dylan as a guitar tech in almost daily proximity to him, said: "I'd been searching the same guy for years and years. I'd get a glimpse of the guy once in a while. . . . He actually put his cards down a couple of times. . . . You would have to be with him, and be there at that right moment when he just opens up and says, 'Okay, I'm just Bob and Bob has no last name.' " And when the mask comes off, as it does in his astonishing song "Abandoned Love," his life and his world become transparent both to himself and to us:

> Everybody's wearing a disguise
> To hide what they've got left behind their eyes
> But me, I can't cover what I am
> Wherever the children go I'll follow them.

The legendary American pianist William Kapell, who died at the age of thirty-one in a 1953 plane crash, once wrote to a friend: "The only moments I have when I play that are worth anything to me are when I can blissfully ignore the people I am supposed to be entertaining. No me; no silly public to amuse; only the heart and the soul, the world, the birds, storms, dreams, sadness, heavenly serenity. *Then* I am an artist worthy of the name. . . . Until it happens, or if it doesn't happen, I am miserable."

Like Kapell, Bob Dylan is one of a number of creative artists who has throughout his life been chary of courting and rewarding his fans' sometimes fanatical adulation. As the psychologist Jeffrey Satinover presciently wrote: "Once the star is established, his fans will tear him to pieces should ever he fail to carry for them the projected childhood Self. A recent example from pop culture is the fans' vituperative reaction to Bob Dylan's unexpected changes of style. Once a narcissistic complementation has been set up between any leader and his following, he is as bound as they. The rigidity of the relationship and the strength of the forces maintaining the status quo stem from the mutual common individual fear of fragmentation." His sense of other people's "wanting my soul," as he confessed to Nat Hentoff, has often encouraged Dylan to disappear into himself and to become a stranger to others (and perhaps sometimes to himself as well).

"A stranger in a strange land," Bob Dylan calls himself in his song "You Changed My Life." (An "equivocal stranger," like Herman Melville's Confidence Man.) Elusive, oblique, mercurial, and always in motion, he has resisted in both his life and his work being categorized, encapsulated, finalized, conventionalized, canonized, and deified. "Greed and lust I can understand," he once said, "but I can't understand the values of definition and confinement. Definition destroys." He has therefore always been wary of being entrapped in the amber of interviewers' idées fixes or projected fantasies about himself, of their attempt to pry into and unravel his private life, to murder and to dissect his creative processes.

In *Inter Views*, a fascinating book of conversations with Laura Pozzo, the imaginal psychologist James Hillman expresses his own distrust of the interview form in terms that Bob Dylan might well assent to: "Interviews belong to an ego genre: one ego asking another ego. So one thinks one has to proceed in terms of 'I answer a question' and 'stick to the topic,' 'the given subject,' and one tries to say it . . . you know, nicely, tightly, rationally. 'Directed thinking' it's called in psychiatry. All ego. Now, the kind of psychology that I want to do is not addressed to the ego. It is to evoke imagination, it's to be extremely complex, it's to talk with emotion and from emotion and to emotion; so how can you, in an interview, bring in that complexity? How can you speak to the whole psyche at the same time?"

How does one, therefore, go about interviewing someone as mutable and multiple as Bob Dylan—a person who once sang, "Don't ask me nothin' about nothin'/I might just tell you the truth" ("Outlaw Blues"), someone who doesn't give himself (or his self) up lightly?

Mikal Gilmore, who conducted four interviews with Dylan, comments: "His reputation precedes him, more than anybody I've ever encountered. And like so many others, I've seen varying documentations of what that reputation is based on. In his appearance in *Don't Look Back*, he has a conversation with a young man who's referred to as a science student, and he asks Dylan what's his attitude when he first meets somebody, and Dylan says, 'I don't like them.' And in that and other documentations both in film and on the page you expect someone who can be pretty sharp and acerbic. But in my initial meeting with him I was relieved early on in our conversation. There were moments when some of that pride and flair could rise up. But on that occasion he was generous and relaxed.

"The first time I talked to him was between the release of *Infidels* and *Biograph* when I was working at the *Los Angeles Herald-Examiner*. I was initially supposed to see him at his house out in Malibu, but he ended up just coming over to my apartment in West Hollywood. It was a nervous-making prospect having him visit me at my place. I anticipated an hour's length conversation but he stayed for four or five hours, just sitting on my sofa. We had a couple of beers, and I found him amazingly gracious and relaxed, maybe because it was the change of environment that didn't focus on his world so much—it may be that he might have been more guarded if someone came to his home. I talked to him several times after that over the years, and that was pretty much my experience except for one occasion when we got into an argument about something, but even then, at the end of that moment, he lapsed back into being the gracious host.

"I've always felt that there are parts of himself that he doesn't give up easily, if at all, in an interview. I don't think he gives it up even in *Chronicles*, which is an autobiography of the mind. There are parts of his experience and frame of mind that he doesn't go into readily—he may eventually, though I don't think he has yet. But it must not be easy facing questions asking you to analyze yourself and your work and how you've measured up in cultural expectations, because not only can that be so grueling personally, but it must take a toll on one's will to be an artist."

Robert Hilburn, who has interviewed Dylan ten times for *The Los Angeles Times*, remarks: "Elvis Presley and Bob Dylan were the two people I was most nervous about ever meeting because they were such heroes of mine. And I had seen *Don't Look Back* and read about how he was difficult and mysterious and manipulative in interviews. So you bring a nervousness to an interview with him, thinking, My goodness, if I say the wrong thing we're not going to connect. So I think the writer brings a lot of preconceptions to it that sometimes make it difficult to have a conversation with him.

"In his mind, he's seen himself misused in the press, with people misunderstanding or trying to label and categorize him, so that he's a little bit suspicious of the whole interview and media process. And if you come to him with a lot of nervousness, you can almost freeze as an interviewer. You really want to ask certain questions and your focus is on that. But Dylan will often reject those questions. And you have to step back and say, Okay, what does he want to talk about, and then let him find a comfort zone or a topic he's happy with, and then keep going down that path. But as an interviewer you have to make that kind of transition. There's a generosity and straightforwardness about him, and a hidden intelligence that you don't often notice when you're talking to him. You have to get back to the tape and listen to it when the interview is done to discover it because your nervousness has hidden it from you when you were speaking to him.

"He once told me that from his point of view the hard thing was that people often asked him questions he hadn't ever thought about and wanted an answer right then. And he didn't want to give a shallow reply, so sometimes he'd be hesitant or pause, and if he saw that there was no way to do it, he'd just want to move on to something else. A lot of times interviewers try to keep him on that question, and that's why he sometimes starts playing games just to try to get past that.

"He also once told me that he doesn't like interviews because he often didn't know what he should say until he was driving away. So I mentioned to him that he could call me at the paper the next day if he thought of something. And so he did call—it was a Saturday—and he had a couple of things he had written down, like Johnny Carson jokes, and one of them was: 'The country is so confused these days they don't know whether to follow the president or the Green Bay Packers.' So he'd thought about those lines and called back to say them for my article.

"If he can talk about things he feels comfortable about, you don't need to pull or prod him, he'll just start talking. You simply have to relax and let him take the reins a bit. The *Don't Look Back* thing really does hang over him, but that's not the way he always is. Sometimes you just want to give him a hug when he does feel comfortable and starts talking in a meaningful way. And I really treasure those moments and his warmth a lot."

Those of us fortunate enough to have been invited to interview Bob Dylan were usually forewarned to expect a hyperequivocal, trickster-like character, someone ineluctably prone to caustic put-ons and put-downs. In fact, he is—as most of the interviews in this collection make clear—at once obviously reluctant, self-protecting, and self-concealing but equally often a stunningly direct, heartfelt, epiphanic, poetic, and, most important, *playful* expositor of his munificent and inspiring thought-dreams. "I don't know whether to do a serious interview or carry on in that absurdist way we talked last night," Paul J. Robbins says to Dylan at the outset of his 1965 *Los Angeles Free Press* conversation. To which Dylan replies: "It'll be the same thing anyway, man." As Johan Huizinga points out in his classic study of the culture of play, *Homo Ludens*, "The significance of play . . . is by no means defined or exhausted by calling it 'not earnest,' or 'not serious.' Play is a thing by itself. The play-concept as such is of a higher order than is seriousness. For seriousness seeks to exclude play, whereas play can very well include seriousness."

The word *interview* itself is derived from the French *entrevoir* (to see between), which conveys the meaning of "to foresee, to glimpse, to sense, or to have an idea or feeling of." Certainly in an illuminating interview the act of glimpsing and sensing requires, on the part of both interviewer and interviewee, a delicate balance between "seeing between" and "seeing through," a balance between openness and a respect for the mysteries and boundaries of personality. And you cannot engage in this kind of interchange without admiring and delighting in the work of the person you are conversing with, which has not always been the underlying concern of some of Bob Dylan's interlocutors.

We are all "prisoners in a world of mystery," as Dylan sings in "Highlands," one of his most memorable songs ("Well my heart's in the Highlands wherever I roam/That's where I'll be when I get called home"). But I believe we can share our dreams and sense of mystery and home in a true meeting, as sometimes occurs in many of the conversations collected here. From the more than two hundred newspaper, magazine, book, radio, and television interviews Bob Dylan has given over a forty-two-year period (from 1962 to 2004), we have chosen thirty-one that best chart the many stages and illuminate the many sides of Bob Dylan's ongoing journey, allowing us to see between, into, and through a remarkable artist who once doffed his hat to us, singing: "Everything I'm a-sayin'/You can say it just as good" ("One Too Many Mornings").

Jonathan Cott

1. Radio Interview with Cynthia Gooding, WBAI (New York)

1962

Bob Dylan, you must be twenty years old now.

Yeah, I must be twenty . . .

In Minneapolis you were thinking of being a rock & roll singer?

At that time I was sort of doing nothing, I was working, I guess, I was making pretend I was going to school out there—I'd just come in from South Dakota, that was about three years ago . . . yeah, I'd come in from Sioux Falls, that was the only place you didn't have to go too far to find the Mississippi River—it runs right through the town.

Have you sung at any of the coffee houses [in Greenwich Village]?

Yeah, I sang at the Gaslight. That was a long time ago . . . I used to play down at the Wha?, too. I sang down there during the afternoons, played my harmonica for this guy there . . . he used to give me a dollar . . . play with him every day from two o'clock in the afternoon. Play till 8:30 at night. . . . He gave me a dollar, plus a cheeseburger.

What got you off rock & roll and onto folk music?

Well I never got onto that—they were just sorta, I don't know. I wasn't calling it anything, I wasn't singing rock & roll. I was singing

1

Muddy Waters songs, I was writing songs, and I was singing Woody Guthrie songs and also Hank Williams songs . . . Johnny Cash . . .

I heard you doing Johnny Cash.

These are French ones [cigarettes]?

No, they're healthy ones.

My record for Columbia is coming out in March.

What's it going to be called?

Bob Dylan, I think.

This is one of the fastest rises in folksingers.

Yeah, but I really don't think of myself as a folksinger thing . . . [I don't] play in places across the country, you know, I'm not on the circuit or anything. I'm not a folksinger so . . . I play a little, once in a while. But I like more than just folk music too. I sing more than just folk music . . . as such people label folk music "folk music" . . . yeah, I like folk music . . . like Hobart Smith's stuff. I don't sing much of that, and when I do it's a modified version or something . . . it's more of a old-time jazz thing. Jelly Roll Morton 'n' stuff like that.

I'd like you to sing songs from your short history.

Short history?

[To listeners] He's got a list of songs pasted to his guitar.

Well, I don't know all of these songs, it's just a list of what other people gave me. I gathered them on, I copied the best songs I could find. So I don't know a lot of these. Gives me something to do on the stage.

Like something to look at.

[Sings a blues]

That's a great song, how much of it is yours?

I don't know, I can't remember. My hands are cold, it's a pretty cold studio.

You're a very good friend of John Lee Hooker's? . . . Howlin' Wolf. You're a friend of Woody Guthrie . . .

Yeah.

Which ones of his do you like the best, which ones are the best?

Depends. . . . Which one do you want to hear? [*Sings "Hard Travelin'"*]

Tell me about the songs you've written, that you sing.

Those are . . . I don't claim they're folk songs or anything. I just call them contemporary songs I guess. A lot of people paint if they got something they want to say, other people write plays, write songs . . . same place. Wanna hear one?

Why, yes!

I got a new one, it's called "Emmett Till." I stole the melody from Len Chandler. He's a folksinger, uses a lot of funny chords. He got me to using some of these funny chords, trying to teach me new chords. He played me these, said, "Don't they sound nice?" So I said, "They sure do." So I stole it, the whole thing. [*Sings "Emmett Till"*]

It's one of the best contemporary ballads I ever heard. It's tremendous.

You like it?

Oh, yes.

I just wrote it last week, I think.

I don't get a chance much to play. Let me play you a plain ordinary one. Broke my fingernail . . . [*Plays "Standing on the Highway Trying to Bum a Ride"*]

You know, the eight of diamonds is delay, and the ace of spades is death.

Yeah.

So that sort of goes in with the two roads, doesn't it?

I learned that in the carnival. I used to travel with the carnival.

Oh, you can read cards too?

Um . . . I can't read cards, I really believe in palm reading. But for a bunch of personal things, personal experiences, I don't believe too much in the cards. I like to think I don't believe too much in the cards.

So you won't go too far out of your way to have them read. . . . How long were you with the carnival?

I was with the carnival off and on for six years.

What were you doing?

Just about everything. I was clean-up boy. I was mainliner on the Ferris wheel. Do the shoreline thing. Use to do all kinds of stuff like that.

Didn't that interfere with your schooling?

Well, I skipped a lot of things and I didn't go to school for a bunch of years, skipped this, skipped that . . . ha ha! It all came out even, though [*laughs*].

2. Radio Interview with Studs Terkel, WFMT (Chicago)

MAY 1963

Bob Dylan was a young folk poet at the time I spoke with him, one of the most exciting singers of songs around—rumpled trousers, curly hair, wearing a skipper's cap, twenty-two years old. He can't be pigeonholed. Bob Shelton of *The New York Times* writes: "His lyrics mix a sermon out of Woody Guthrie's conversational folksay with a dash of Rimbaud's demonic imagery and even a bit of Yevtushenko's social criticism. Whether his verse is free or rhymed, whether the mood is somber, crusading, satiric, subject to the fanciful, Mr. Dylan's words and melodies sparkle with the light of an inspired poet." He is an American original.

Where did you come from, Cotton-Eyed Joe?

The beginning was there in Minnesota. But that was the beginning before the beginning. I don't know how I come to songs, you know. It's not up to me to explain—I don't really go into myself that deep, I just go ahead and do it. I'm just sort of trying to find a place to pound my nails.

Woody Guthrie, is he a factor in your life?

Oh yeah. Woody's a big factor. I feel lucky just to know Woody. I'd heard of Woody, I knew of Woody. I saw Woody once, a long, long time ago in Burbank, California, when I was just a little boy. I don't even remember seeing him, but I heard him play. I must have been about ten. My uncle took me.

What was it that stuck in your mind?

It stuck in my mind that he was Woody, and everybody else I could see around me was just everybody else.

If I may venture an opinion, that could apply to you, too, Bob. Unique. It's hard to separate you from the songs you sing. You write most of the songs you sing, don't you?

Yeah, I write all my songs now.

There's one song, the only way I can describe it is as a great tapestry — "A Hard Rain's A-Gonna Fall."

I'll tell you how I come to write that. Every line in that really is another song. Could be used as a whole song, every single line. I wrote that when I didn't know how many other songs I could write. That was during October of last year and I remember sitting up all night with a bunch of people someplace. I wanted to get the most down that I knew about into one song, so I wrote that. It was during the Cuba trouble, that blockade, I guess is the word. I was a little worried, maybe that's the word.

You're right. Each one of the lines, each one of the images could be a song in itself. You know why I asked you to sing that live? I have this letter from a kid who's about your age, he's twenty-one. He was wondering what this new generation is really thinking of. We hear so much. At the very end he says, "America's heard the story of the bright, straight-A student, the fraternity-leading good guy Charlie. But there's a quiet group that remains. One that has no overwhelming crusade that is outwardly on the make, but one that is uneasily discontented. Thoughtfully or restless, young people of this sort may eventually determine future directions. . . . Outwardly we seem to be cool, but there's a rage inside us."

I've got a friend who wrote a book called *One Hundred Dollar Misunderstanding*. I don't know if it's around Chicago. It's about this straight-A college kid, you know, fraternity guy, and a fourteen-year-old Negro prostitute. And it's got two dialogues in the same book. A dialogue is one chapter and the other chapter follows with just exactly what he's thinking and what he does. The next chapter is her view of him. The whole books goes like that. This guy Robert Gover wrote it. That would explain a lot too. That's one of the hippest things nowadays, I guess. I mean, it actually comes out and states something that's actually true, that everybody thinks about. I don't know if this fellow who wrote the letter was thinking crusades. This guy who wrote it, you can't label him. That's the word. You understand what I mean?

I follow you, I think. Back in the 1930s there were young people feeling passionately under one label or another. They were pigeonholed. What you stand for, it seems to me, and the fellow who wrote this letter and the guy who wrote that book, they belong to nobody but themselves. But we know some-thing is there. Outwardly cool . . . I suppose you have to be that because the chips on the table are so blue.

Maybe it's just the time, now is the time maybe you have to belong to yourself. I think maybe in 1930, from talking with Woody and Pete Seeger and some other people I know, it seems like everything back then was good and bad and black and white and whatever, you only had one or two. When you stand on one side and you know people are either for you or against you, with you or behind you or whatever you have. Nowa-days it's just, I don't know how it got that way but it doesn't seem so simple. There are more than two sides, it's not black and white anymore.

"A Hard Rain's A-Gonna Fall" — I think it will be a classic. Even though it may have come out of your feelings about atomic rain . . .

No, no, it wasn't atomic rain. Somebody else thought that too. It's not atomic rain, it's just a hard rain. It's not the fallout rain, it isn't that at all. I just mean some sort of end that's just gotta happen which is very easy to see but everybody doesn't really think about is overlooking it. It's bound to happen. Although I'm not talking about that hard rain meaning atomic rain, it seems to me like the bomb is a god in some sort of a way, more of a god and people will worship it actually. You have to be nice to it, you know. You have to be careful what you say about it. People work on it, they go six days a week and work on it, you have people designing it, you know, it's a whole new show.

These are all pretty good people too in everyday life.

Yeah, I don't believe they're bad people. Just like the guy that killed this fella hitchhiking through Alabama. The guy that killed him. I forget his name.

It might have been the storekeeper. We don't know if he did it, but this is the fellow—

Yeah, who might have killed him. Even if it's not him, if it's somebody else that actually shot the bullet. There's nothing more awful, I mean, shot right in the back. I seen so many people before I got to New York, that are good people, that maybe are poor, and there are other people telling them why they're poor, and who made it so that they are poor. To take their minds off of that they are poor, they have to pick a scapegoat—

But do you believe, Bob, in good and evil. There is a basic good—

Oh, I'm sure.

Obviously you do from the songs you write. One of the lines of the song that got me . . . earlier you said things are not quite as simple as they were. "The executioner's face is always well hidden." That's on the button.

Yeah, oh golly. All over the place it's hidden.

It's so impersonal today. You said it's gonna happen. What's gonna happen?

What's gonna happen, there's got to be an explosion of some kind. The hard rain that's gonna fall. In the last verse when I say, "When the pellets of poison are flooding the waters," that means all the lies, you know, all the lies that people get told on their radios and in their newspapers. All you have to do is think for a minute. They're trying to take people's brains away. Which maybe has been done already. I hate to think it's been done. All the lies I consider poison.

I'll be fifty-one soon. My generation has had it. I'm talking about you now and your friends, nineteen, twenty, twenty-one. How many feel as you do?

Oh, there's an awful lot of them. Well, I don't know, you said my friends—

I don't mean just your circle, 'cause you've traveled a good deal.

I can tell you something about my friends, I can tell you about people I growed up with, that I knowed since I been four and five. These same kind of people I knew when I was ten and twelve. Little small-town people. This was in Hibbing, Minnesota, and some other places I lived before I finally split for good. These people were my friends. I went to school with them, I lived with them, I played with them, I ate with them. We did good things, bad things, we went through all kinds of things together. As I stand here right now, the last time I saw any of them was maybe two or three years ago, and you know, either me or them has changed.

What's happened to them?

They still seem to be the same old way. Like when they seen me, they heard I was in New York and they have words like—I can just tell by their whole conversation it's not a free feeling that they have. They still have a feeling that's tied up, where it's tied up in the town, in their parents, in the newspapers that they read which go out to maybe five thousand people. They don't have to go out of town, their world's very small. You don't have to, really. If you leave one town into another town it's the same thing. I'm not putting them down. It's just my road and theirs, it's different. Like a lot of them are married, maybe some are going to school. Some are working, you know, just working. They're still there. They're not thinking about the same things I'm thinking about.

They're not thinking what you're thinking. You spoke of those poison pellets on the water. Maybe it hit them too . . . ?

Oh, yeah. It hit me, too. I just got out of it. I just got out of it, that's all.

You were ten years old when you saw Woody, and it was about five years ago that you took to the guitar and singing.

No, about five years ago I just sort of never really did go back home. I've been in New York City for the past almost two years. Before that I was just all around the country, to the southlands, and I was in Mexico for a while.

You've been influenced not only by people like Woody but by blues singers as well.

Oh yeah. Big Joe Williams, I think you might know him. He lives here. I guess.

Yeah, he does. I know him.

He's an old friend of mine.

You also take traditional songs and make them your own.

Not anymore [*laughs*].

You did "Man of Constant Sorrow," the white spiritual. You took that and made it something wholly different. But not anymore, you say?

Two or three years ago I was singing folk songs that I'd learned. Now I don't sing any of them anymore.

Has it occurred to you that your own songs might be considered folk songs? We always have this big argument: What is a folk song? I think "Hard Rain" certainly will be one, if time is the test.

Yeah, yeah, time will be the test.

It seems you can write about any subject under the sun.

Anything worth thinking about is worth singing.

Any subject. A love song, let's say, like "Boots of Spanish Leather." There we have a song of a lover's farewell. This is far, far removed from the June-moon-spoon-theme way of writing. I suppose it's difficult for you to answer, Bob: What led you to the idea of writing these songs? Was it always with you?

Yeah, it's always been with me. I can't really say what led me to them. I'm one of these people that think everybody has certain gifts, you know, when they're born, and you got enough trouble just trying to find out what it is. I used to play the guitar when I was ten, you know. So I figured maybe my thing is playing the guitar, maybe that's my little gift. Like somebody can make a cake, or somebody else can saw a tree down, and other people write. Nobody's really got the right to say that any one of these gifts are any better than any other body's. That's just the way they're distributed out. I had seen that this is exactly what my gift is, maybe I got a better gift. But as of right now, I haven't found out what it is. I don't call it a gift, it's only my way of trying to explain something that is very hard to explain.

There's a piece you wrote called "My Life in a Stolen Moment." You say, "I wrote my first song for my mother and I titled it 'Mother.' I wrote that in fifth grade and my teacher gave me a B+. I sat in a science class and flunked out for refusing to watch a rabbit die."

That's my college days. I only was there for about four months. But I really did get to see it. If I talk about college I ain't talking about 'em just from anything people have told me. I was actually there. I seen what goes on. I started smoking at eleven years old, I stopped once to catch my breath. I don't remember my parents singing too much, at least I don't remember swapping any songs with them. I just write. I've been writing for a long time.

Some will say: Listen to Bob Dylan, he's talking street mountain talk now, though he's a literate man, see.

[*Laughs*] I don't think I am.

How do you answer when they say it?

I got no answer. If they want to think I'm literate, it's okay by me.

Probably it's just easier for you to express your feelings this way. I suppose the influence of a great many singers—

Woody.

Woody, the fact that Woody, more than college, was the big influence on you. Did Woody hear you sing some of these songs?

Every time I go sing these songs I wrote for Woody, he always wants to hear "A Song for Woody." Even when he was in the hospital [*laughs*]. He always wants to hear that.

The tribute of a young folk poet to an older one who has meant so much to him. Do you remember the words to that one?

Yeah, but I never sing it. Only to Woody.

I'm thinking of the Irish antiwar song "Johnny I Hardly Knew You." You're saying the same thing in your own way.

Somebody's come to the end of one road and actually knows it's the end of one road and knows there's another road there, but doesn't exactly know where it is, and knows he can't go back on this one road.

He knows there's something else.

He's got all kinds of stuff which just doesn't add up, you know, all kinds of thoughts in the head, all about teachers and school, and all about hitchhikers around the country, all about—these are friends of mine, too, you know, college kids going to college. These are people that I knew. Every one of them is sort of a symbol, I guess, for all kinds of people like that. In New York it's a different world, you know, especially 'cause I never been to New York before and I'm still carrying their small-town memories with me, so I decided I oughta write it all down. The road is very hard to find now. Maybe sometimes I wish this was 19–something else.

Nineteen thirties?

Before that. You know like I was talking about pounding a nail in a board, it seems like there's a board there and all the nails are pounded in all over the place, you know, and every new person that comes to pound in a nail finds that there's one less space, you know. I hope we haven't got to the end of the space yet.

You're looking for a fresh piece of wood?

No, I'm content with the same old piece of wood, I just want to find another place to pound in a nail.

Isn't that what most of them are looking for? A place to pound a nail?

Yeah. Some of the people are the nails.

You mean they're being pounded [laughs].

Yeah.

Your new album has "Oxford Town" in it. That deals with the James Meredith case. Was he one of the nails?

Yeah, it deals with the Meredith case [James Meredith was denied entrance to the University of Mississippi], but then again it doesn't. Music, my writing, is something special, not sacred. Like this guitar, I don't consider sacred. This guitar could bust and break, it's pretty old now. I could still get another one. It's a tool for me, that's all it is. It's like anybody else has a tool. Some people saw the tree down, you know, or some people spit tacks. When I go to saw the tree down, I cut myself on the saw. When I spit tacks, I swallow the tacks. I've just sort of got this here tool and that's all I use it as, as a tool. My life is the street where I walk. That's my life. Music, guitar, that's my tool, you know.

3. "The Crackin', Shakin', Breakin', Sounds" by Nat Hentoff, *The New Yorker*

OCTOBER 24, 1964

The word "folk" in the term "folk music" used to connote a rural, homogeneous community that carried on a tradition of anonymously created music. No one person composed a piece; it evolved through generations of communal care. In recent years, however, folk music has increasingly become the quite personal—and copyrighted—product of specific creators. More and more of them, in fact, are neither rural nor representative of centuries-old family and regional traditions. They are often city-bred converts to the folk style; and, after an apprenticeship during which they try to imitate rural models from the older approach to folk music, they write and perform their own songs out of their own concerns and preoccupations. The restless young, who have been the primary support of the rise of this kind of folk music over the past five years, regard two performers as their preeminent spokesmen. One is the twenty-three-year-old Joan Baez. She does not write her own material and she includes a considerable proportion of traditional, communally created songs in her programs. But Miss Baez does speak out explicitly against racial prejudice and militarism, and she does sing some of the best of the new topical songs. Moreover, her pure, penetrating voice and her open, honest manner symbolize for her admirers a cool island of integrity in a society that the folk-song writer Malvina Reynolds has characterized in one of her songs as consisting of "little boxes" ("And the boys go into business/And marry and raise a family/In boxes made of ticky tacky/And they all look the same."). The second—and more influential—demiurge of the folk-music microcosm is Bob Dylan, who is also twenty-three. Dylan's impact has been the greater because he is a writer of songs as well as a performer. Such compositions of his as "Blowin' in the Wind," "Masters of War," "Don't Think Twice, It's All Right," and "Only a Pawn in Their Game" have become part of the repertoire of many other performers, including Miss Baez, who has explained, "Bobby is expressing what I—and many other young people— feel, what we want to say. Most of the 'protest' songs about the bomb and race prejudice and conformity are stupid. They have no beauty. But Bobby's songs are powerful as poetry and powerful as music. And oh, my God, how that boy can sing!" Another reason for Dylan's impact is the singular force of his personality. Wiry, tense, and boyish, Dylan looks and acts like a fusion of Huck Finn and a young Woody Guthrie. Both onstage and off, he appears to be just barely able to contain his prodigious energy. Pete Seeger, who, at forty-five, is one of the elders of American folk music, recently observed, "Dylan may well become the country's most creative troubadour—if he doesn't explode."

Dylan is always dressed informally—the possibility that he will ever be seen in a tie is as remote as the possibility that Miss Baez will perform in an evening gown—and his possessions are few, the weightiest of them being a motorcycle. A wanderer, Dylan is often on the road in search of more experience. "You can find out a lot about a small town by hanging around its poolroom," he says. Like Miss Baez, he prefers to keep most of his time for himself. He works only occasionally, and during the rest of the year he travels or briefly stays in a house owned by his manager, Albert Grossman, in Bearsville, New York—a small town adjacent to Woodstock and about a hundred miles north of New York City. There Dylan writes songs, works on poetry, plays, and novels, rides his motorcycle, and talks with his friends. From time to time, he comes to New York to record for Columbia Records.

A few weeks ago, Dylan invited me to a recording session that was to begin at seven in the evening in a Columbia studio on Seventh Avenue near Fifty-second Street. Before he arrived, a tall, lean, relaxed man in his early thirties came in and introduced himself to me as Tom Wilson, Dylan's recording producer. He was joined by two engineers, and we all went into the control room. Wilson took up a post at a long, broad table, between the engineers, from which he looked out into a spacious studio with a tall thicket of microphones to the left and, directly in front, an enclave containing a music stand, two microphones, and an upright piano, and set off by a large screen, which would partly shield Dylan as he sang for the purpose of improving the quality of the sound. "I have no idea what he's going to record tonight," Wilson told me. "It's all to be stuff he's written in the last couple of months."

I asked if Dylan presented any particular problems to a recording director.

"My main difficulty has been pounding mike technique into him," Wilson said. "He used to get excited and move around a lot and then lean in too far, so that the mike popped. Aside from that, my basic problem with him has been to create the kind of setting in which he's relaxed. For instance, if that screen should bother him, I'd take it away, even if we have to lose a little quality in the sound." Wilson looked toward the door. "I'm somewhat concerned about tonight. We're going to do a whole album in one session. Usually, we're not in such a rush, but this album has to be ready for Columbia's fall sales convention. Except for special occasions like this, Bob has no set schedule of recording dates. We think he's important enough to record whenever he wants to come to the studio."

Five minutes after seven, Dylan walked into the studio, carrying a battered guitar case. He had on dark glasses, and his hair, dark-blond and curly, had obviously not been cut for some weeks; he was dressed in blue jeans, a black jersey, and desert boots. With him were half a dozen friends, among them Jack Elliott, a folk singer in the Woody Guthrie tradition, who was also dressed in blue jeans and desert boots, plus a brown cowboy shirt and a jaunty cowboy hat. Elliott had been carrying two bottles of Beaujolais, which he now handed to Dylan, who carefully put them on a table near the screen. Dylan opened the guitar case, took out a looped-wire harmonica holder, hung it around his neck, and then walked over to the piano and began to play in a rolling, honky-tonk style.

"He's got a wider range of talents than he shows," Wilson told me. "He kind of hoards them. You go back to his three albums. Each time, there's a big leap from one to the next—in material, in performance, in everything."

Dylan came into the control room, smiling. Although he is fiercely accusatory toward society at large while he is performing, his most marked offstage characteristic is gentleness. He speaks swiftly but softly, and appears persistently anxious to make himself clear. "We're going to make a good one tonight," he said to Wilson. "I promise." He turned to me and continued, "There aren't any finger-pointing songs in here, either. Those records I've already made, I'll stand behind them; but some of that was jumping into the scene to be heard and a lot of it was because I didn't see anybody else doing that kind of thing. Now a lot of people are doing finger-pointing songs. You know—pointing to all the things that are wrong. Me, I don't want to write *for* people anymore. You know—be a spokesman. Like I once wrote about Emmett Till in the first person, pretending I was him. From now on, I want to write from inside me, and to do that I'm going to have to get back to writing like I used to when I was ten—having everything come out naturally. The way I like to write is for it to come out the way I walk or talk." Dylan frowned. "Not that I even walk or talk yet like I'd like to. I don't carry myself yet the way Woody, Big Joe Williams, and Lightnin' Hopkins have carried themselves. I hope to someday, but they're older. They got to where music was a tool for them, a way to live more, a way to make themselves feel better. Sometimes I can make myself feel better with music, but other times it's still hard to go to sleep at night."

A friend strolled in, and Dylan began to grumble about an interview that had been arranged for him later in the week. "I hate to say no, because, after all, these guys have a job to do," he said, shaking his head impatiently. "But it bugs me that the first question usually turns out to be 'Are you going down South to take part in any of the civil-rights projects?' They try to fit you into things. Now, I've been down there, but I'm not going down just to hold a picket sign so they can shoot a picture of me. I know a lot of the kids in SNCC—you know, the Student Nonviolent Coordinating Committee. That's the only organization I feel a part of spiritually. The NAACP is a bunch of old guys. I found that out by coming directly in contact with some of the people in it. They didn't understand me. They were looking to use me for something. Man, everybody's hung up. You sometimes don't know if somebody wants you to do something because he's hung up or because he really digs who you are. It's awful complicated, and the best thing you can do is admit it."

Returning to the studio, Dylan stood in front of the piano and pounded out an accompaniment as he sang from one of his own new songs. . . . Another friend of Dylan's arrived, with three children, ranging in age from four to ten. The children raced around the studio until Wilson insisted that they be relatively confined to the control room. By ten minutes to eight, Wilson had checked out the sound balance to his satisfaction, Dylan's friends had found seats along the studio walls, and Dylan had expressed his readiness—in fact, eagerness—to begin. Wilson, in the control room, leaned forward, a stopwatch in his hand. Dylan took a deep breath, threw his head back, and plunged into a song in which he accompanied himself on guitar and harmonica. The first take was ragged; the second was both more relaxed and vivid. At that point, Dylan, smiling, clearly appeared to be confident of his ability to do an entire album in one night. As he moved into succeeding numbers, he relied principally on the guitar for support, except for exclamatory punctuations on the harmonica.

Having glanced through a copy of Dylan's new lyrics that he had handed to Wilson, I observed to Wilson that there were indeed hardly any songs of social protest in the collection.

"Those early albums gave people the wrong idea," Wilson said. "Basically, he's in the tradition of all lasting folk music. I mean, he's not a singer of protest so much as he is a singer of *concern* about people. He doesn't have to be talking about Medgar Evers all the time to be effective. He can just tell a simple little story of a guy who ran off from a woman."

After three takes of one number, one of the engineers said to Wilson, "If you want to try another, we can get a better take."

"No." Wilson shook his head. "With Dylan, you have to take what you can get."

Out in the studio, Dylan, his slight form bent forward, was standing just outside the screen and listening to a playback through earphones. He began to take the earphones off during an instrumental passage, but then his voice came on, and he grinned and replaced them.

The engineer muttered again that he might get a better take if Dylan ran through the number once more.

"Forget it," Wilson said. "You don't think in terms of orthodox recording techniques, when you're dealing with Dylan. You have to learn to be as free on this side of the glass as he is out there."

Dylan went on to record a song about a man leaving a girl because he was not prepared to be the kind of invincible hero and all-encompassing provider she wanted. "It ain't me you're looking for, babe," he sang, with finality.

During the playback, I joined Dylan in the studio. "The songs so far sound as if there were real people in them," I said.

Dylan seemed surprised that I had considered it necessary to make the comment. "There are. That's what makes them so scary. If I haven't been through what I write about, the songs aren't worth anything." He went on, via one of his songs, to offer a complicated account of a turbulent love affair in Spanish Harlem, and at the end asked a friend, "Did you understand it?" The friend nodded enthusiastically. "Well, I didn't," Dylan said, with a laugh, and then became somber. "It's hard being free in a song—getting it all in. Songs are so confining. Woody Guthrie told me once that songs don't have to rhyme—that they don't have to do anything like that. But it's not true. A song has to have some kind of form to fit into the music. You can bend the words and the meter, but it still has to fit somehow. I've been getting freer in the songs I write, but I still feel confined. That's why I write a lot of poetry—if that's the word. Poetry can make its own form."

As Wilson signaled for the start of the next number, Dylan put up his hand. "I just want to light a cigarette, so I can see it there while I'm singing," he said, and grinned. "I'm very neurotic. I need to be secure."

By ten-thirty, seven songs had been recorded.

"This is the fastest Dylan date yet," Wilson said. "He used to be all hung up with the microphones. Now he's a pro."

Several more friends of Dylan's had arrived during the recording of the seven songs, and at this point four of them were seated in the control room behind Wilson and the engineers. The others were scattered around the studio, using the table that held the bottles of Beaujolais as their base. They opened the bottles and every once in a while poured out a drink in a paper cup. The three children were still irrepressibly present, and once the smallest burst suddenly into the studio, ruining a take. Dylan turned to the youngster in mock anger. "I'm gonna rub you out," he said. "I'll track you down and turn you to dust." The boy giggled and ran back into the control room.

As the evening went on, Dylan's voice became more acrid. The dynamics of his singing grew more pronounced, soft, intimate passages being abruptly followed by fierce surges in volume. The relentless, driving beat of his guitar was more often supplemented by the whooping thrusts of the harmonica.

"Intensity, that's what he's got," Wilson said, apparently to himself. "By now, this kid is outselling Thelonious Monk and Miles Davis," he went on, to me. "He's speaking to a whole new generation. And not only here. He's just been in England. He had standing room only in Royal Festival Hall."

Dylan had begun a song called "Chimes of Freedom." One of his four friends in the control room, a lean, bearded man proclaimed, "Bobby's talking for every hung-up person in the whole wide universe." His three companions nodded gravely.

The next composition, "Motorpsycho Nitemare," was a mordantly satirical version of the vintage tale of the farmer, his daughter, and the traveling salesman. There were several false starts, apparently because Dylan was having trouble reading the lyrics.

"Man, dim the lights," the bearded friend counseled Wilson. "He'll get more relaxed."

"Atmosphere is not what we need," Wilson answered, without turning around. "Legibility is what we need."

During the playback, Dylan listened intently, his lips moving, and a cigarette cocked in his right hand. A short break followed, during which Dylan shouted, "Hey, we're gonna need some more wine!" Two of the friends in the studio nodded and left.

After the recording session resumed, Dylan continued to work hard and conscientiously. When he was preparing for a take or listening to a playback, he seemed able to cut himself off completely from the eddies of conversation and humorous byplay stirred up by his friends in the studio. Occasionally, when a line particularly pleased him, he burst into laughter, but he swiftly got back to business.

Dylan started a talking blues—a wry narrative in a sardonic recitative style, which had been developed by Woody Guthrie. "Now I'm a liberal, but to a degree," Dylan was drawling halfway through the song. "I want everybody to be free. But if you think I'll let Barry Goldwater move in next door and marry my daughter, you must think I'm crazy. I wouldn't let him do it for all the farms in Cuba." He was smiling broadly, and Wilson and the engineers were laughing. It was a long song, and toward the end Dylan faltered. He tried it twice more and each time he stumbled before the close.

"Let me do another song," he said to Wilson. "I'll come back to this."

"No," Wilson said. "Finish up this one. You'll hang us up on the order, and if I'm not here to edit, the other cat will get mixed up. Just do an insert of the last part."

"Let him start from the beginning, man," said one of the four friends sitting behind Wilson.

Wilson turned around, looking annoyed. "Why, man?"

"You don't start telling a story with Chapter Eight, man," the friend said.

"Oh, man," said Wilson. "What kind of philosophy is that? We're recording, not writing a biography."

As an obbligato of protest continued behind Wilson, Dylan, accepting Wilson's advice, sang the insert. His bearded friend rose silently and drew a square in the air behind Wilson's head.

Other songs, mostly of love lost or misunderstood, followed. Dylan was now tired, but he retained his good humor. "This last one is called

'My Back Pages,'" he announced to Wilson. It appeared to express his current desire to get away from "finger-pointing" and write more acutely personal material. "Oh, but I was so much older then," he sang as a refrain, "I'm younger than that now."

By one-thirty, the session was over. Dylan had recorded fourteen new songs. He agreed to meet me again in a week or so and fill me in on his background. "My background's not all that important though," he said as we left the studio. "It's what I'm doing now that counts."

Dylan was born in Duluth, on May 24, 1941, and grew up in Hibbing, Minnesota, a mining town near the Canadian border. He does not discuss his parents, preferring to let his songs tell whatever he wants to say about his personal history. "You can stand at one end of Hibbing on the main drag an' see clear past the city limits on the other end," Dylan once noted in a poem, "My Life in a Stolen Moment," printed in the program of a 1963 Town Hall concert he gave. Like Dylan's parents, it appears, the town was neither rich nor poor, but it was, Dylan has said, "a dyin' town." He ran away from home seven times: at ten, at twelve, at thirteen, at fifteen, at fifteen and a half, at seventeen, and at eighteen. His travels included South Dakota, New Mexico, Kansas, and California. In between flights, he taught himself the guitar, which he had begun playing at the age of ten. At fifteen, he was also playing the harmonica and the autoharp, and, in addition, had written his first song, a ballad dedicated to Brigitte Bardot. In the spring of 1960, Dylan entered the University of Minnesota, in Minneapolis, which he attended for something under six months. In "My Life in a Stolen Moment," Dylan has summarized his college career dourly: "I sat in science class an' flunked out for refusin' to watch a rabbit die. I got expelled from English class for using four-letter words in a paper describing the English teacher. I also failed out of communication class for callin' up every day and sayin' I couldn't come. . . . I was kept around for kicks at a fraternity house. They let me live there, an' I did until they wanted me to join." Paul Nelson and Jon Pankake, who edit the *Little Sandy Review*, a quarterly magazine, published in Minneapolis, that is devoted to critical articles on folk music and performers, remember meeting Dylan at the University of Minnesota in the summer of 1960, while he was part of a group of singers who performed at The Scholar, a coffeehouse near the university. The editors, who were students at the university then, have since noted in their publication: "We recall Bob as a soft-spoken, rather unprepossessing youngster . . . well-groomed and neat in the standard campus costume of slacks, sweater, and white oxford sneakers, poplin raincoat, and dark glasses."

Before Dylan arrived at the university, his singing had been strongly influenced by such Negro folk interpreters as Leadbelly and Big Joe Williams. He had met Williams in Evanston, Illinois, during his break from home at the age of twelve. Dylan had also been attracted to several urban-style rhythm-and-blues performers, notably Bo Diddley and Chuck Berry. Other shaping forces were white country-music figures, particularly Hank Williams, Hank Snow, and Jimmie Rodgers. During his brief stay at the University, Dylan became especially absorbed in the recordings of Woody Guthrie, the Oklahoma-born traveler who had created the most distinctive body of American topical folk material to come to light in this century. Since 1954, Guthrie, ill with Huntington's chorea, a progressive disease of the nervous system, had not been able to perform, but he was allowed to receive visitors. In the autumn of 1960, Dylan quit the University of Minnesota and decided to visit Guthrie at Greystone Hospital, in New Jersey. Dylan returned briefly to Minnesota the following May, to sing at a university hootenanny, and Nelson and Pankake saw him again on that occasion. "In a mere half year," they have recalled in the *Little Sandy Review*, "he had learned to churn up exciting, bluesy, hard-driving, harmonica-and-guitar music, and had absorbed during his visits with Guthrie not only the great Okie musician's unpredictable syntax but his very vocal color, diction, and inflection. Dylan's performance that spring evening of a selection of Guthrie . . . songs was hectic and shaky, but it contained all the elements of the now-perfected performing style that has made him the most original newcomer to folk music."

The winter Dylan visited Guthrie was otherwise bleak. He spent most of it in New York, where he found it difficult to get steady work singing. In "Talkin' New York," a caustic song describing his first months in the city, Dylan tells of having been turned away by a coffeehouse owner who told him scornfully, "You sound like a hillbilly. We want folksingers here." There were nights when he slept in the subway, but, eventually he found friends and a place to stay on the Lower East Side, and after he had returned from the spring hootenanny, he began getting more engagements in New York. John Hammond, Director of Talent Acquisition at Columbia Records, who has discovered a sizable number of important jazz and folk performers during the past thirty years, heard Dylan that summer while attending a rehearsal of another folksinger, whom Hammond was about to record for Columbia Records. Impressed by the young man's raw force and by the vivid lyrics of his songs, Hammond auditioned him and immediately signed him to a recording contract. Then, in September 1961, while Dylan was appearing at Gerde's Folk City, a casual refuge for "citybillies" (as the young city singers and musicians are now called in the trade), on West Fourth Street, in Greenwich Village, he was heard by Robert Shelton, the folk-music critic for the *Times*, who wrote of him enthusiastically.

Dylan began to prosper. He enlarged his following by appearing at the Newport and Monterey Folk Festivals and giving concerts throughout the country. There have been a few snags, as when he walked off the Ed Sullivan television show in the spring of 1963 because the Columbia Broadcasting System would not permit him to sing a tart appraisal of the John Birch Society, but on the whole he has experienced accelerating success. His first three Columbia albums—*Bob Dylan*, *The Freewheelin' Bob Dylan*, and *The Times They Are A-Changin'*—have by now reached a cumulative sales figure of nearly four hundred thousand. In addition, he has received large royalties as a composer of songs that have become hits through recordings by Peter, Paul, and Mary, the Kingston Trio, and other performers. At present, Dylan's fees for a concert appearance range from two thousand to three thousand dollars a night. He has sometimes agreed to sing at a nominal fee for new, nonprofit folk societies, however, and he has often performed without charge at civil-rights rallies.

Musically, Dylan has transcended most of his early influences and developed an incisively personal style. His vocal sound is most often characterized by flaying harshness. Mitch Jayne, a member of the Dillards, a folk group from Missouri, has described Dylan's sound as "very much like a dog with his leg caught in barbed wire." Yet Dylan's admirers come to accept and even delight in the harshness, because of the vitality and wit at its core. And they point out that in intimate ballads he is capable of a fragile lyricism that does not slip into bathos. It is Dylan's work as a composer, however, that has won him a wider audience than his singing alone might have. Whether concerned with cosmic specters or personal conundrums, Dylan's lyrics are pungently idiomatic. He has a superb ear for speech rhythms, a generally astute sense of selective detail, and a natural storyteller's command of narrative pacing. His songs sound as if they were being created out of oral street history rather than carefully written in tranquillity. On a stage, Dylan performs his songs as if he had an urgent story to tell. In his work there is little of the polished grace of such carefully trained contemporary minstrels as Richard Dyer-Bennet. Nor, on the other hand, do Dylan's performances reflect the calculated showmanship of Harry Belafonte or of Peter, Paul, and Mary. Dylan off the stage is very much the same as Dylan the performer—restless, insatiably hungry for experience, idealistic, but skeptical of neatly defined causes.

In the past year, as his renown has increased, Dylan has become more elusive. He felt so strongly threatened by his initial fame that he welcomed the chance to use the Bearsville home of his manager as a refuge between concerts, and he still spends most of his time there when he's not traveling. A week after the recording session, he telephoned me from Bearsville, and we agreed to meet the next evening at the Keneret, a restaurant on lower Seventh Avenue in the Village. It specializes in Middle Eastern food, which is one of Dylan's preferences, but it does not have a liquor license. Upon keeping our rendezvous, therefore, we went next door for a few bottles of Beaujolais and then returned to the Keneret. Dylan was as restless as usual, and as he talked, his hands moved constantly and his voice sounded as if he were never quite able to catch his breath.

I asked him what he had meant, exactly, when he spoke at the recording session of abandoning "finger-pointing" songs, and he took a sip of wine, leaned forward and said, "I looked around and saw all these people pointing fingers at the bomb. But the bomb is getting boring, because what's wrong goes much deeper than the bomb. What's wrong is how few people are free. Most people walking around are tied down to something that doesn't let them really *speak*, so they just add their confusion to the mess. I mean, they have some kind of vested interest in the way things are now. Me, I'm cool." He smiled. "You know, Joanie—Joanie Baez—worries about me. She worries about whether people will get control over me and exploit me. But I'm cool. I'm in control, because I don't care about money, and all that. And I'm cool in myself, because I've gone through enough changes so that I know what's real to me and what isn't. Like this fame. It's done something to me. It's O.K. in the Village here. People don't pay attention to me. But in other towns it's funny knowing that people you don't know figure they know *you*. I mean, they think they know everything about you. One thing is groovy, though. I got birthday cards this year from people I'd never heard of. It's weird, isn't it? There are people I've really touched whom I'll never know." He lit a cigarette. "But in other ways being noticed can be a weight. So I disappear a lot. I go to places where I'm not going to be noticed. And I *can*." He laughed. "I have no work to do. I have no job. I'm not committed to anything except making a few records and playing a few concerts. I'm weird that way. Most people, when they get up in the morning, have to do what they *have* to do. I could pretend there were all kinds of things I *had* to do every day. But why? So I do whatever I feel like. I might make movies of my friends around Woodstock one day. I write a lot. I get involved in scenes with people. A lot of scenes are going on with me all the time—here in the Village, in Paris during my trips to Europe, in lots of places."

I asked Dylan how far ahead he planned.

"I don't look past right now," he said. "Now there's this fame business. I know it's going to go away. It has to. This so-called mass fame comes from people who get caught up in a thing for a while and buy the records. Then they stop. And when they stop, I won't be famous anymore."

We became aware that a young waitress was standing by diffidently. Dylan turned to her, and she asked him for his autograph. He signed his name with gusto, and signed again when she asked if he would give her an autograph for a friend. "I'm sorry to have interrupted your dinner," she said, smiling. "But I'm really not."

"I get letters from people—young people—all the time," Dylan continued when she had left us. "I wonder if they write letters like those to other people they don't know. They just want to tell me things, and sometimes they go into their personal hang-ups. Some send poetry. I like getting them—read them all and answer some. But I don't mean I give any people who write to me any *answers* to their problems." He leaned forward and talked more rapidly. "It's like, when somebody wants to tell me what the 'moral' thing is to do, I want them to *show* me. If they have anything to say about morals, I want to know what it is they *do*. Same with me. All I can do is show the people who ask me questions how I live. All I can do is be me. I can't tell them how to change things, because there's only one way to change things, and that's to cut yourself off from all the chains. That's hard for most people to do."

I had Dylan's *The Times They Are A-Changin'* album with me, and I pointed out to him a section of his notes on the cover in which he spoke of how he had always been running when he was a boy—running away from Hibbing and from his parents.

Dylan took a sip of wine. "I kept running because I wasn't free," he said. "I was constantly on guard. Somehow, way back then, I already knew that parents do what they do because they're uptight. They're concerned with their kids in relation to *themselves*. I mean, they want their kids to please them, not to embarrass them—so they can be proud of them. They want you to be what *they* want you to be. So I started running when I was ten. But always I'd get picked up and sent home. When I was thirteen, I was traveling with a carnival through upper Minnesota and North and South Dakota, and I got picked up again. I tried again and again, and when I was eighteen, I cut out for good. I was still running when I came to New York. Just because you're free to move doesn't mean you're free. Finally, I got so far out I was cut off from everybody and everything. It was then I decided there was no sense in running so far and so fast when there was no longer anybody there. It was fake. It was running for the sake of running. So I stopped. I've got no place to run from. I don't have to be anyplace I don't want to be. But I am by no means an example for any kid wanting to strike out. I mean, I wouldn't want a young kid to leave home because I did it, and then have to go through a lot of the things I went through. Everybody has to find his *own* way to be free. There isn't anybody who can help you in that sense. Nobody was able to help me. Like seeing Woody Guthrie was one of the main reasons I came East. He was an idol to me. A couple of years ago, after I'd gotten to know him, I was going through some very bad changes, and I went to see Woody, like I'd go to somebody to confess to. But I couldn't confess to him. It was silly. I did go and talk with him—as much as he could talk—and the talking helped. But basically he wasn't able to help me at all. I finally realized that. So Woody was my last idol."

There was a pause.

"I've learned a lot in these past few years," Dylan said softly. "Like about beauty."

I reminded him of what he had said about his changing criteria of beauty in some notes he did for a Joan Baez album. There he had written that when he first heard her voice, before he knew her, his reaction had been:

"I hate that kind of a sound," said I
"The only beauty's ugly, man
The crackin', shakin', breakin' sounds're
The only beauty I understand."

Dylan laughed. "Yeah," he said. "I was wrong. My hang-up was that I used to try to *define* beauty. Now I take it as it is, however it is. That's why I like Hemingway. I don't read much. Usually I read what people put in my hands. But I do read Hemingway. He didn't have to use adjectives. He didn't really have to define what he was saying. He just said it. I can't do that yet, but that's what I want to be able to do."

A young actor from Julian Beck's and Judith Malina's Living Theatre troupe stopped by the table, and Dylan shook hands with him enthusiastically. "We're leaving for Europe soon," the actor said. "But when we come back, we're going out on the street. We're going to put on plays right on the street, for anyone who wants to watch."

"Hey!" said Dylan, bouncing in his seat. "Tell Julian and Judith that I want to be in on that."

The actor said he would, and took Dylan's telephone number. Then he said, "Bob, are you doing only your own songs now—none of the old folk songs at all?"

"Have to," Dylan answered. "When I'm uptight and it's raining outside and nobody's around and somebody I want is a long way from me—and with someone else besides—I can't sing 'Ain't Got No Use for Your Red Apple Juice.' I don't care how great an old song it is or what its tradition is. I have to make a new song out of what I know and out of what I'm feeling."

The conversation turned to civil rights, and the actor used the term "the Movement" to signify the work of the civil-rights activists. Dylan looked at him quizzically. "I agree with everything that's happening," he said, "but I'm not part of no Movement. If I was, I wouldn't be able to do anything else but in 'the Movement.' I just can't have people sit around and make rules for me. I do a lot of things no Movement would allow." He took a long drink of the Beaujolais. "It's like politics," he went on. "I just can't make it with any organization. I fell into a trap once—last December—when I agreed to accept the Tom Paine Award from the Emergency Civil Liberties Committee. At the Americana Hotel! In the Grand Ballroom! As soon as I got there, I felt uptight. First of all, the people with me couldn't get in. They looked even funkier than I did, I guess. They weren't dressed right, or something. Inside the ballroom, I really got uptight. I began to drink. I looked down from the platform and saw a bunch of people who had nothing to do with my kind of politics. I looked down and I got scared. They were supposed to be on my side, but I didn't feel any connection with them. Here were these people who'd been all involved with the left in the thirties, and now they were support-ing civil-rights drives. That's groovy, but they also had minks and jewels, and it was like they were giving the money out of guilt. I got up to leave, and they followed me and caught me. They told me I had to accept the award. When I got up to make my speech, I couldn't say anything by that time but what was passing through my mind. They'd been talking about Kennedy being killed, and Bill Moore and Medgar Evers and the Buddhist monks in Vietnam being killed. I had to say something about Lee Oswald. I told them I'd read a lot of his feelings in the papers, and I knew he was uptight. Said I'd been uptight, too, so I'd got a lot of his feelings. I saw a lot of myself in Oswald, I said, and I saw in him a lot of the times we're all living in. And, you know, they started booing. They looked at me like I was an animal. They actually thought I was saying it was a good thing Kennedy had been killed. That's how far out they are. I was talking about Oswald. And then I started talking about friends of mine in Harlem— some of them junkies, all of them poor. And I said they need freedom as much as anybody else, and what's anybody doing for *them?* The chairman was kicking my leg under the table, and I told him, 'Get out of here.' Now, what I was supposed to be was a nice cat. I was supposed to say, 'I appreciate your award and I'm a great singer and I'm a great believer in liberals, and you buy my records and I'll support your cause.' But I didn't, and so I wasn't accepted that night. That's the cause of a lot of those chains I was talking about—people wanting to be accepted, people not wanting to be alone. But, after all, what is it to be alone? I've been alone sometimes in front of three thousand people. I was alone that night."

The actor nodded sympathetically.

Dylan snapped his fingers. "I almost forgot," he said. "You know, they were talking about Freedom Fighters that night. I've been in Mississippi, man. I know those people on another level besides civil-rights campaigns. I know them as friends. Like Jim Forman, one of the heads of SNCC. I'll stand on his side any time. But those people that night were actually getting me to look at colored people as colored people. I tell you, I'm never going to have anything to do with any political organization again in my life. Oh, I might help a friend if he was campaigning for office. But I'm not going to be part of any organization. These people at that dinner were the same as everybody else. They're doing their time. They're chained to what they're doing. The only thing is, they're trying to put morals and great deeds on their chains, but basically they don't want to jeopardize their positions. They got their jobs to keep. There's nothing there for me, and there's nothing there for the kind of people I hang around with. The only thing I'm sorry about is that I guess I hurt the collection at the dinner. I didn't know they were going to try to collect money after my speech. I guess I lost them a lot of money. Well, I offered to pay them whatever it was they figured they'd lost because of the way I talked. I told them I didn't care how much it was. I hate debts, especially moral debts. They're worse than money debts."

Exhausted by his monologue, Dylan sank back and poured more Beaujolais. "People talk about trying to change society," he said. "All I know is that so long as people stay so concerned about protecting their status and protecting what they have, ain't nothing going to be done. Oh, there may be some change of levels inside the circle, but nobody's going to learn anything."

The actor left, and it was time for Dylan to head back upstate. "Come up and visit next week," he said to me, "and I'll give you a ride on my motorcycle." He hunched his shoulders and walked off quickly.

4. Interview with Jay Cocks, *The Kenyon Collegian*

NOVEMBER 20, 1964

Wearing high heel boots, a tailored pea-jacket without lapels, pegged dungarees of a kind of buffed azure, large sunglasses with squared edges, his dark, curly hair standing straight up on top and spilling over the upturned collar of his soiled white shirt, he caused a small stir when he got off the plane in Columbus. Businessmen nodded and smirked, the ground crew looked a little incredulous, and a mother put a hand on her child's head and made him turn away. Bob Dylan came into the terminal taking long strides, walking hard on his heels and swaggering just a little. He saw us, smiled a nervous but friendly smile, and came over to introduce himself and his companion, a lanky, unshaven man named Victor who looked like a hip version of Abraham Lincoln. Dave Banks, who had organized the concert and who was Dylan's official reception committee, led Dylan and Victor to baggage claim. Along the way, Victor asked us how far we were from the school and where he and Dylan would be spending the night. Learning that Banks had reserved a room for them in a small motel seven miles from Kenyon, he smiled a little and said, "Tryin' to keep us as far away from the school as you can, huh?"

The trip back from the airport was a quiet one. Both men seemed rather tired, Dylan especially, who was pale and nervous. He said he was right in the middle of a big concert tour which had been on for almost two months, and Victor reminisced about one memorable engagement in Cambridge. "They had this pep rally right before the concert," he said, "and they all came in sweaty and yellin'. Man, the audience was full of football players—*football* players." Banks mentioned that Kenyon hadn't won a single football game all year, and both men seemed enthusiastic. "Yeah? No kidden'?" Dylan said, and Victor flashed a gratified smile. They asked a lot of questions about the college, the *Review*, and girls. Victor was astonished to find the college was so small and that the girls were so far away. "Outside Cleveland?" he commented, "man, that's a *far* away to go for a chick." Dylan nodded sympathetically.

We talked a bit more then about Kenyon. "They really have to wear ties and stuff to the concert," Dylan asked, "ties? Well, I'm gonna tell them they can take them off. That's what I'm gonna do. Rules—man, that's why I never lasted long in college. Too many *rules*." He spoke quietly but with animation, in an unmistakably mid-western accent.

Entering Mt. Vernon, Dylan asked if there was a liquor store around. "Nothin' strong—wine or somethin'. Beaujolais. Chianti's good. Yeah, or Almaden or anything just so it's red and dry."

Banks stopped to get some wine. Dylan was talking faster now, more excitedly, fingering his sideburns and running his hand nervously over the top of his head.

As we came into Gambier, Dylan pressed his face up against the car window. "Wow, great place for a school! Man, if I went here I'd be out in the woods all day gettin' drunk. Get me a chick," (and here he again smiled his nervous smile), "settle down, raise some kids." Banks drove the pair around the campus and stopped at Rosse Hall where the concert was to be given to show them the audio facilities. Victor didn't like the amplifier system ("Man, it's a *phonograph*") and Dylan was worried about making his entrance from the back of the hall and walking all the way to the stage in front. It was finally decided that he would use the classrooms in the basement for a dressing room and come in through the fire exit in front, facing the small College cemetery. "Strange set-up," he kept saying, "really strange set-up." He was pacing up and down, taking quick drags on a Chesterfield. "Look, try and get as many people in here as you can, O.K? Let 'em sit on the floor, just try and let everybody in, O.K.?" Victor mentioned that they were both pretty hungry, so Banks suggested driving back into Mt. Vernon where Dylan wouldn't be recognized; even if he was noticed, Banks said, he would probably be taken for some crazy college student anyway, and the worst that could happen was someone trying to pick a fight. " 'S'all right, man," Dylan said, shrugging his narrow shoulders, "I'm ready for 'em."

Back in Mt. Vernon, both Dylan and Victor were convulsed by the public square. "Hey, man, look at that cat," Dylan said, pointing at a Civil War monument, "who's he?" Victor leaned out the window and squinted: "Don't know—look's like General Custer from here." "Fantastic," Dylan said.

When we finally got to the motel and into the room, Dylan turned on the television and began to tune his Gibson guitar and sing while watching *Wanted: Dead or Alive*. Dave Banks went to take care of the luggage while Victor and I walked to a public phone booth to call out for some food. Dylan only wanted a salad, but Victor told me to order him something else. "Fish or somethin'. And some greens. He's gotta have some greens. Any kind, I don't know." The Rendezvous Restaurant, however, didn't have any greens. Victor smiled, shaking his head. "Wow—we'll just get him that fish plate or whatever it is. No greens—wow." The food would be ready in half-an-hour, so Banks and I left Dylan and Victor in the room watching Steve McQueen tackle some evil-looking Mexicans. Dylan was now completely absorbed in the program; Victor was trying to sleep.

When we returned with the food half-an-hour later, the television was still on, Victor sprawled on his bed, while Dylan clasped and unclasped his hands between his knees. The restaurant had cooked a good meal but had forgotten to include silverware. "Don't make no difference," Dylan and Victor said in chorus, "no difference," so we ate everything from home fried potatoes to salad with our fingers. Dylan poked around at his fried fish platter, but wolfed down the salad. "Greek salad in Mt. Vernon, Ohio," he said, "crazy," wiped his fingers on his azure dungarees, lit a cigarette, and poured himself some more of the Almaden wine. He was interested in the article I was planning to write about him. "There's this one guy who writes for the *Post, The Saturday Evening Post*, you know, named Al Aronowitz. He was going to do this story on me for a year and a half but he couldn't do it. He's really a great guy. He knew it would be cut to shit by the *Post* and he wouldn't get to say what he'd want to be sayin', only what they wanted. And the guy really didn't want me to come out like that, you dig? But we tried to write it anyway, you know, together. I went up to his place one day and we sat down and began to write this story, about me meeting him in Central Park and everything. But we had to stop, because the thing was getting really weird, surrealistic, and the story never got written. The only other cat he won't do a story on is Paul Newman, because he don't want to ruin him by gettin' him all cut up."

While talking he constantly flexed his fingers and crossed and uncrossed his legs. Mentioning Paul Newman got him on the subject of acting. "For me, you know, acting is like the Marx Brothers, somethin' you can't learn. Like the Studio. In the early days it was good, before it became a big fad, but I went there and really got turned off. All these people—actors—they're all themselves, really, tryin' too hard to be someone else. You can't learn to be someone else. It's just gotta be inside. You dig what I'm tryin' to say?"

"Hey, Bob," Victor interrupted, switching off the TV, "we better get movin'." Dylan had been talking for forty-five minutes, and he had wanted to get out to the College before the concert to tune up. On the way, Dylan asked us to lock the door to the classroom he would be using to rehearse. He was worried about people coming in for autographs and an over-enthusiastic group of fans. Banks complied by driving his car across a space of bumpy lawn and up to the side door of the hall, where Victor hustled Dylan out and through the door past three or four gaping couples on their way to collect some early front row seats. We made sure the door was locked, and Victor and I took turns standing guard until Victor decided it was time to rig up the special microphones they had brought along. He went upstairs carrying a suitcase full of tubes and wire, while Dylan, in the next room, tuned up for three minutes by pounding out a wild rock and roll song on a grand piano and singing some gibberish lyrics.

Dave Banks knocked on the door and told Dylan that two people who said they were friends of his were upstairs. They had given their names as Bob and John. "Fantastic," said Dylan. "Hey Victor, go up and bring 'em down quick. Fantastic." I went back to join Dylan, who was pacing around in a circle.

All of a sudden the door crashed open and a soft-faced young man in black boots, trousers, coat, and gloves came running into the room screaming, "Hey Bobby—hiya, baby," his long hair flapping like banners behind him. "Wow, fantastic," Dylan yelled, reeling backwards across the room, laughing and attempting to climb the wall, "whatya doin' here, Bob?"

"Driving out to the coast," said the newcomer, pumping Dylan's hand, "got this car and—hey, you know John. We're drivin' out together." He reintroduced Dylan to a tall, swallow-faced boy who had an expensive Japanese camera hanging around his neck. "Look at this place—I don't believe the set-up. Crazy."

"Yeah, I know. Hey, man, what're ya *doin'*."

"Man, like we have this car belongs to Al, you know, we're goin' out to the Coast. A Cobra—wow. We drove six hundred and fifty miles yesterday in ten hours. Took us thirty-five minutes to get through Pennsylvania. VAROOM—wow!"

Everyone laughed. "Hey listen, man, you gonna be out on the coast, give me a call. I'm gonna do some concert, Joanie and me, so call."

"Yeah, yeah," Bob said. "What's happenin' out there?"

"Oh, Joanie and me's gonna do these concerts. Fantastic number of songs: we'll be out there for a while, but after all this shit we took I don't think it's much use doubling up on the hotel bills anymore, do you?"

"Yeah, yeah," Bob said again. "Listen, did you see the pictures from New York?" Dylan said that he hadn't. "Hey, John, I got 'em in the car. Go out and get 'em." John giggled and went running out. Victor returned from upstairs, reported that the microphones were all fixed and that the hall was about full, and greeted Bob, who said, "Hey, how about all the faggots they've got in this place?" John came back from the car holding some large photographs in his hand which he thrust at Dylan with a smile.

"Hey, these are really great," he said, looking through them. "This one's a little *bizarre* maybe, but I like it." He handed it to me. It was a picture of Bob, his hair trimmed in bangs, standing in front of a feverish abstract mural dressed in a woman's ensemble of matching paisley slacks and blouse, holding a tricycle in his left hand and turning the pedal. John grinned at me.

As the time for Dylan to go on approached, he became more animated, more nervous. He paced and sometimes danced around the room gulping down wine from a small Dixie cup and making large gestures with his hands. Around eight-thirty, Victor handed him his guitar, Dylan placed a black-wire harmonica holder around his neck, played a few chords, blew a few quick notes, and said, "O.K. man, let's go." "Let's go—I'm comin' in through the graveyard, man."

We walked out and around the side of the auditorium, in front of the College cemetery and up some wobbly iron stairs to a fire exit. Several of the people standing near the door caught a glimpse of Dylan and began to nudge one another; one rather pudgy girl wearing an army surplus raincoat and blue tennis shoes even began primping her hair. Victor put his arm on Dylan's shoulder. Dylan nodded, straightened his shoulders, and walked into the hall to enthusiastic applause. He made no introductions, starting immediately to play his first song. But something was wrong with the amplifier system, and the music sounded like mosquitoes caught in a net of Saran Wrap. Dylan finished the number and made a few sly comments while Victor replaced the microphone and someone from the college played with the amplifier system. Seemingly unfazed, Dylan proceeded, with better audio and the audience now completely with him. A predominantly conservative student body applauded at every derogatory mention of prejudice, injustice, segregation, or nuclear warfare. Dylan, who had intended to sing only six songs for the first half, was apparently enjoying himself and added two more to the set. At intermission, he got a big hand.

Downstairs during the intermission, Dylan talked a lot, and drank more wine. He only half-jokingly spoke about the speaker system in the hall, about the songs, and about the audience. There were a lot of people waiting to see him outside, but he was almost too wound up even to cope with friends who were already in the room with him. Victor said that except for the speaker system he thought it was going pretty well, although he was still worried about the crowds that would gather after the concert. "You'll see, man," he said, "you'll see."

For the second half of the concert, almost seventy-five people had left their seats and were sitting on the floor close to the stage. A path had to be cleared before Dylan could get on, but passing by one girl, he reached out, said "Hi" and touched her hair with his hand, which caused the people around her to laugh and applaud, while the girl herself simply—but audibly—sighed. For the rest of the concert she stared straight at Dylan, who by now was a little drunk, although he was performing as well as in the first half. After his last song Victor and I met him just as he got off the stage, and led him to the exit. He had gotten a standing ovation, and while we were persuading him to do an encore he kept repeating "They don't have to do *that*," nodding at the audience. He had unfastened the leather shoulder strap of his guitar, and the pudgy girl in the surplus raincoat rushed up to him, asking for "All I Really Want to Do," fumbling with the leather strap attempting to help him refasten it. He grinned at her, and went back on stage for the encore. Victor sent Bob and John downstairs to guard the entrance to the dressing room, he posted himself by the exit to block the pudgy girl and her companions and detailed me to get Dylan off the stage and through the crowd in the front row. Dylan finished up and, smiling, walked down into the audience and through the exit, Victor and I on either side.

We got him inside just before the crowd. Dylan was happy about the way the concert had gone, poured himself several congratulatory cups of wine and began to wonder about getting out of the building through the crowd and into the car which was waiting outside. He decided finally to wait twenty minutes or so, then make a break for it. At the outside door,

Bob, wearing a pair of dark leather gloves which he kept rubbing together and up and down his thighs, was talking to a tall blonde man who kept repeating, "Listen, Bobby invited me afterwards to . . . " He bent down and began to whisper in Bob's ear. Bob listened for a moment and pushed the man back.

"Listen, man, I don't want to hear about it. Go away."

"But, Bobby . . . "

"Listen, just go away, man. I don't want to talk about it. I don't want to hear about it. Just go away." He turned his attentions to the crowd which now must have been a hundred strong.

Victor meantime was packing the remainder of Dylan's clothes and equipment, and sticking the one surviving bottle of wine into his pocket. He looked tired; Dylan looked exhausted and drunk. "O.K.," Dylan almost sighed, "lead the way." We walked out of the classroom and towards the main door. When the crowd outside saw Dylan coming, many of them came forward to press their faces against the glass. As soon as I opened the door, Dylan stepped out and they all pressed forward.

"Bobby!"

"Hiya, Bobby!"

"Hey Bobby!"

"Hiya, Mr. Dylan."

"Hello, kid," Dylan said to a girl who was squirming against the door, "long time no see." In reply, she giggled and coughed. Walking through the crowd Dylan waved and shook a few hands. Another girl followed him all the way to the car. "I'm Billie Dylan's roommate from State," she announced, "Bob, you remember." Dylan said that he didn't remember. "Billie Dylan. From," the girl said, almost following him into the car. "Oh yeah," Dylan said, not very convincingly, "how is she?" "Great," the girl replied, "she says to tell you hello." "Fantastic," Dylan said. He slammed the door and we began to pull away. "Hey, Bobby, wait a minute," someone said, running frantically alongside the car, "wait a minute." Bob looked around, rubbing his black leather gloves together. It was the blonde man whom he had pushed away a little earlier at the door. "Keep goin'," he said, "Keep drivin'."

The morning was cold. In the frost and dust covering Banks's car, which had been parked outside Dylan's improvised dressing room the night before, we could still see outlines of little inscriptions written by some of the girls all over the hood, roof, and windows: "Bobby," "Bobby," "Bobby Dylan," "Dylan," "Dylan," "Bobby Dylan." No one spoke much during the trip to the airport. Victor looked still asleep, and Dylan a little fuzzy. About ten miles out of Mt. Vernon he folded his arms across his chest and, slinking down as much as he could in the Volkswagen, leaned his head back over the top of the seat and closed his eyes. All of a sudden, asleep, in that early morning, he looked very young.

Victor checked his baggage at the airport and we went for something to eat. Dylan, who looked a little more refreshed, spoke easily and with humor about his upcoming concerts. "Tomorrow we're goin' to Princeton, and Sunday to Bangor, Maine. Man, I don't know what's in Bangor, Maine. It's not a school or anything." I told him I didn't think the Chamber of Commerce had booked him, and he threw back his head and laughed for a long time. "Yeah, the Chamber of Commerce—wow!" For the first time since we had met him the day before he seemed completely at ease. "I'm gonna do these concerts out on the Coast, and Joanie's gonna be with me. Pretty soon we're gonna get billed together." He smiled that friendly vulnerable smile of his, but this time without a trace of nervousness. "I'm gonna be out there for a while."

The flight to New York was announced, and Banks and I walked them to the gate. The businessmen were staring again. When one of them turned to his companion nudging him and pointing at us, Dylan looked over his shoulder and waved. "It's alright man," he said, "I make more money than you do."

Banks thanked them both, and apologized for any embarrassing incidents that might have happened the previous evening. "That's O.K. man," Dylan replied, "wasn't nothin'."

"Look," Victor said, "we'll see you again, huh? If there's a concert somewhere, come back and see us."

We said we would if we could get past the crowds we hadn't thought would be around.

"Well, so long," Dylan said. "And thanks."

Banks and I watched them get on the plane. On their way, they passed two T.W.A. groundcrewmen wearing coveralls and white crash-helmets who turned and stared. One of them came up to us. "Hey, wasn't that that folksinger?"

We said that it was.

"Which one? The short one?"

Banks nodded.

"What's his name?" he asked.

"Bob Dylan," I said.

"Hey," he said, turning to his friend, "that was Bob Dylan."

5. Interview with Paul J. Robbins, L.A. *Free Press*

March 1965

I don't know whether to do a serious interview or carry on in that absurdist way we talked last night.

It'll be the same thing anyway, man.

Yeah, okay . . . If you are a poet and write words arranged in some sort of rhythm, why do you switch at some point and write lyrics in a song so that you're singing the words as part of a Gestalt presence?

Well, I can't define that word poetry, I wouldn't even attempt it. At one time I thought that Robert Frost was poetry, other times I thought that Allen Ginsberg was poetry, sometimes I thought François Villon was poetry—but poetry isn't really confined to the printed page. Hey, then again, I don't believe in saying "Look at that girl walking! Isn't that poetry?" I'm not going to get insane about it. The lyrics to the songs . . . just so happens that it might be a little stranger than in most songs. I find it easy to write songs. I been writing songs for a long time and the words to the songs aren't written out just for the paper; they're written as you can read it, you dig. If you take whatever there is to the song away—the beat, the melody—I could still recite it. I see nothing wrong with songs you can't do that with either—songs that, if you took the beat and the melody away, they wouldn't stand up. Because they're not supposed to do that, you know. Songs are songs . . . I don't believe in expecting too much out of any one thing.

Whatever happened to Blind Boy Grunt?

I was doing that four years ago. Now there's a lot of people writing songs on protest subjects. But it's taken some kind of weird step. Hey, I'd rather listen to Jimmy Reed or Howlin' Wolf, man, or the Beatles, or Françoise Hardy, than I would listen to any protest song singers— although I haven't heard all the protest song singers there are. But the ones I've heard—there's this very emptiness which is like a song written "Let's hold hands and everything will be grand." I see no more to it than that. Just because someone mentions the word "bomb," I'm not going to go "Aalee!" and start clapping.

Is it that they just don't work anymore?

It's not that it don't work, it's that there are a lot of people afraid of the bomb, right. But there are a lot of other people who're afraid to be seen carrying a *Modern Screen* magazine down the street, you know. Lot of people afraid to admit that they like Marlon Brando movies . . . Hey, it's not that they don't work anymore but have you ever thought of a place where they DO work? What exactly DOES work?

They give a groovy feeling to the people who sing them, I guess that's about it. But what does work is the attitude, not the song. And there's just another attitude called for.

Yeah, but you have to be very hip to the fact about that attitude— you have to be hip to communication. Sure, you can make all sorts of protest songs and put them on a Folkways record. But who hears them? The people that do hear them are going to be agreeing with you anyway. You aren't going to get somebody to hear it who doesn't dig it. People don't listen to things they don't dig. If you can find a cat that can actually say "Okay, I'm a changed man because I heard this one thing—or I just saw this one thing. . . ." Hey it don't necessarily happen that way all the time. It happens with a collage of experience which somebody can actually know by instinct what's right and wrong for him to do. Where he doesn't actually have to feel guilty about anything. A lot of people can act out of guilt. They act because they think somebody's looking at *them*. No matter what it is. There's people who do anything because of guilt . . .

And you don't want to be guilty?

It's not that I'm NOT guilty. I'm not any more guilty than you are. Like, I don't consider any elder generation guilty. I mean, they're having these trials at Nuremberg, right? Look at that and you can place it out. Cats say "I had to kill all those people or else they'd kill me." Now, who's to try them for that? Who are these judges that have got the right to try a cat? How do you know they wouldn't do the same thing?

This may be a side trip, but this thing about the Statute of Limitations running out and everybody wants to extend it? You remember, in 'Animal Farm,' what they wrote on the wall? "All animals are equal." But later they added " . . . but some are more equal than others." It's the same thing in reverse. That some are less equal than others. Like Nazis are *really* criminals, so let's *really* get them; change any law just to nail them all.

Yeah, all that shit runs in the same category. Nobody digs revenge, right? But you have cats from Israel who, after *twenty* years, are still trying to catch these cats, who're *old* cats, man, who have escaped. God knows they aren't going to go anywhere, they're not going to do anything. And you have these cats from Israel running around catching them. Spending twenty years out of their lives. You take that job away from them and they're no more or less than a baker. He's got his whole life tied up in one thing. It's a one-thought thing, without anything between: "That's what it is, and I'm going to get it." Anything between gets wiped all away. I can't make that, but I can't really put it down. Hey: I can't put *anything* down, because I don't have to be around any of it. I don't have to put people down which I don't like, because I don't have to be around any of those people. Of course there is the giant great contradiction of What Do You Do. Hey, I don't know what you do, but all I can do is cast aside all the things *not* to do. I don't know where it's at once in a while, all I know is where it's *not* at. And as long as I know that, I don't really have to know, myself, where's it at. Everybody knows where it's at once in a while, but nobody can walk around all the time in a complete Utopia. Dig poetry. You were asking about poetry? Man, poetry is just bullshit, you know? I don't know about other countries, but in this one it's a total massacre. It's not poetry at all. People don't read poetry in this country—if they do, it offends them; they don't dig it. You go to school, man, and what kind of poetry do you read? You read Robert Frost's "The Two Roads," you read T.S. Eliot—you read all that bullshit and that's just bad, man. It's no good. It's not anything hard, it's just soft-boiled egg shit. And then, on top of it, they throw Shakespeare at some kid who can't read Shakespeare in high school, right? Who digs reading *Hamlet*, man? All they give you is *Ivanhoe*, *Silas Marner*, *Tale of Two Cities*—and they keep you away from things which you should do. You shouldn't even be there in school. You should find out from people. Dig! That's where it all starts. In the beginning—like from 13 to 19—that's where all the corruption is. These people all just overlook it, right? There's more V.D. in people 13 to 19 than there is in any other group, but they ain't ever going to say so. They're never going to go into the schools and give shots. But that's where it's at. It's all hype, man.

Relating all this: if you put it in lyrics instead of poetry, you have a higher chance of hitting the people who have to be hit?

I do, but I don't expect anything from it, you dig? All I can do is be me—whoever that is—for those people that I do play to, and not come on with them, tell them I'm something I'm not. I'm not going to tell them I'm the Great Cause Fighter or the Great Lover or the Great Boy Genius or whatever. Because I'm not, man. Why mislead them? That's all just Madison Avenue selling me, but it's not really selling ME, 'cause I was hip to it before I got there.

Which brings up another thing. All the folk magazines and many folk people are down on you. Do they put you down because you changed or . . .

It's that I'm successful and they want to be successful, man. It's jealousy. Hey, anybody, with any kind of knowledge at all would know by instinct what's happening here. Somebody who doesn't know that, is still hung up with success and failure and good and bad . . . maybe he doesn't have a chick all the time . . . stuff like that. But I can't use comments, man. I don't take nothing like that seriously. If somebody praises me and says "How groovy you are!" it doesn't mean nothing to me, because I can usually sense where that person's at. And it's no compliment if someone who's a total freak comes up and says "How groovy you are!" And it's the same if they don't dig me. Other kinds of people don't *have* to say anything because, when you come down to it, it's all what's happening in the moment which counts. Who *cares* about tomorrow and yesterday? People don't live there, they live now.

I have a theory, which I've been picking up and shaking out every so often. When I spoke with the Byrds, they were saying the same thing as I am saying—a lot of people are saying—you're talking it. It's why we have new so-called rock & roll sound emerging, it's a synthesis of all things a . . .

It's further than that, man. People know nowadays more than before. They've had so much to look at by now and know the bullshit of everything. People now don't even care about going to jail. So what? You're still with yourself as much as if you're out on the streets. There's still those who don't care about anything, but I got to think that anybody who doesn't hurt anybody, you can't put that person down, you dig, if that person's happy doing that.

But what if they freeze themselves into apathy? What if they don't care about anything at all anymore?

Whose problem is that? Your problem or theirs? No, it's not that, it's that nobody can learn by somebody else showing them or teaching them. People got to learn by themselves, going through something which relates. Sure, you say how do you make somebody know something . . . people know it by themselves; they can go through some kind of scene with other people and themselves which somehow will come out somewhere and it's grind into them and be them. And all that just comes out of them somehow when they're faced up to the next thing.

It's like taking in until the times comes to put out, right. But people who don't care don't put anything out. It's a whole frozen thing where nothing's happening anywhere; it's just like the maintenance of status quo, of existing circumstances, whatever they are . . .

People who don't care? Are you talking about gas station attendants or a Zen doctor, man? Hey, there's a lot of people who don't care; a lot don't care for different reasons. A lot care about some things and not about others, and some who don't care about anything—it's just up to me not to let them bring me down and not to bring them down. It's like the whole world has a little thing: it's being taught that when you get up in the morning, you have to go out and bring somebody down. You walk down the street and, unless you've brought somebody down, don't come home today, right? It's a circus world.

So who is it that you write and sing for?

Not writing and singing for anybody, to tell you the truth. Hey, really, I don't care what people say. I don't care what they make me seem to be or what they tell other people I am. If I did care about that, I'd tell you; I really have no concern with it. I don't even come in contact with these people. Hey, I dig people, though. But if somebody's going to come up to me and ask me some questions which have been on his mind for such a long time, all I can think of is "Wow, man, what else can be in that person's head besides me? Am I that important, man, to be in a person's head for such a long time he's got to know this answer?" I mean, can that really straighten him out—if I tell him something? Hey, come on . . .

A local disc jockey, Les Claypool, went through a whole thing on you one night, just couldn't get out of it. For maybe 45 minutes, he'd play a side of yours and then an ethnic side in which it was demonstrated that both melodies were the same. After each pair he'd say, "Well, you see what's happening . . . This kid is taking other people's melodies; he's not all that original. Not only that," he'd say, "but his songs are totally depressing and have no hope."

Who's Les Claypool?

A folk jockey out here who has a long talk show on Saturday nights and an hour one each night, during which he plays highly ethnic sides.

He played *those* songs? He didn't play something hopeful?

No, he was loading it to make his point. Anyway, it brings up an expected question: Why do you use melodies that are already written?

I used to do that when I was more or less in folk. I knew the melodies; they were already there. I did it because I liked the melodies. I did it when I really wasn't that popular and the songs weren't reaching that many people, and everybody around dug it. Man. I never introduced a song, "Here's the song I've stole the melody from, someplace." For me it wasn't that important; still isn't that important. I don't care about the melodies, man, the melodies are all traditional anyway. And if anybody wants to pick that out and say "That's Bob Dylan," that's their thing, not mine. I mean if they want to think that. Anybody with any sense at all, man, he says that I haven't any hope . . . Hey, I got *faith*. I know that there are people who're going to know that's total bullshit. I know the cat is just uptight. He hasn't really gotten into a good day and he has to pick on something. Groovy. He has to pick on me? Hey, if he can't pick on me, he picks on someone else, it don't matter. He doesn't step on me, 'cause I don't care. He's not coming up to me on the street and stepping on my head, man. Hey, I've only done that with very few of my songs, anyway. And then when I don't do it, everybody says they're rock & roll melodies. You can't satisfy the people—you just can't. You got to know, man; they just don't care about it.

Why is rock & roll coming in and folk music going out?

Folk music destroyed itself. Nobody destroyed it. Folk music is still here, if you want to dig it. It's not that it's going in or out. It's all the soft mellow shit, man, that's just being replaced by something that people know there is now. Hey, you must've heard rock & roll long before the Beatles, you must've discarded rock & roll around 1960. I did that in 1957. I couldn't make it as a rock & roll singer then. There were too many groups. I used to play piano. I made some records, too.

Okay, you got a lot of bread now. And your way of life isn't like it was four or five years ago. It's much grander. Does that kind of thing tend to throw you off?

Well, the transition never came from working at it. I left where I'm from because there's nothing there. I come from Minnesota, there was nothing there. I'm not going to fake it and say I went out to see the world. Hey, when I left there, man, I knew one thing: I had to get out of there and not come back. Just from my sense I knew there was something more than Walt Disney movies. I was never turned on or off by money. I never considered the fact of money as really that important. I could always play the guitar, you dig, and make friends—or fake friends. A lot of other people do other things and get to eat and sleep that way. Lot of people do a lot of things just to get around. You can find cats who get very scared, right? Who get married and settle down. But, after somebody's got something and sees it all around him, so he doesn't have to sleep out in the cold at night, that's all. The only thing is he don't die. But is he happy? There's nowhere to go. Okay, so I get the money, right? First of all, I had to move out of New York. Because everybody was coming down to see me—people which I didn't really dig. People coming in from weird-ass places. And I would think, for some reason, that I had to give them someplace to stay and all that. I found myself not really being myself but just staying out of things I wanted to go to because people I knew would go there.

Do you find friends—real friends—are they recognizable anymore?

Oh, sure, man, I can tell somebody I dig right away. I don't have to go through anything with anybody. I'm just lucky that way.

Back to protest songs. The IWW's work is over now and the unions are pretty well established. What about the civil rights movement?

Well, it's okay. It's proper. It's not "Commie" anymore. *Harper's Bazaar* can feature it, you can find it on the cover of *Life*. But when you get beneath it, like anything, you find there's bullshit tied up in it. The Negro Civil Rights Movement is proper now, but there's more to it than what's in *Harper's Bazaar*. There's more to it than picketing in Selma, right? There's people living in utter poverty in New York. And then again, you have this big Right to Vote. Which is groovy. You want all these Negroes to vote? Okay, I can't go over the boat and shout "Hallelujah" only because they want to vote. Who're they going to vote for? Just politicians; same as the white people put in their politicians. Anybody that gets into politics is a little greaky anyway. Hey, they're just going to vote, that's all they're going to do. I hate to say it like that, make it sound hard, but it's going to boil down to that.

What about the drive for education?

Education? They're going to school and learn about all the things the white private schools teach. The catechism, the whole thing. What're they going to learn? What's this education? Hey, the cat's much better off never going to school. The only thing against him is he can't be a doctor or a judge. Or he can't get a good job with the salesman's company. But that's the only thing wrong. If you want to say it's good that he gets an education and goes out and gets a job like that, groovy. I'm not going to do it.

In other words, the formal intake of factual knowledge . . .

Hey, I have no respect for factual knowledge, man. I don't care what anybody knows, I don't care if somebody's a walking encyclopedia. Does that make him nice to talk to? Who cares if Washington was even the first president of the United States? You think anybody has actually ever been helped with this kind of knowledge?

Maybe through a test. Well, what's the answer?

There aren't any answers, man. Or any questions. You must read my book . . . there's a little part in there about that. It evolves into a thing where it mentions words like "Answer." I couldn't possibly rattle off the words for these, because you'd have to read the whole book to see these specific words or Question and Answer. We'll have another interview after you read the book.

Yeah, you have a book coming out. What about it? The title?

Tentatively, *Bob Dylan Off the Record*. But they tell me there's already books out with that "off the record" title. The book can't really be titled, that's the kind of book it is. I'm also going to write the reviews for it.

Why write a book instead of lyrics?

I've written some songs which are kind of far out, a long continuation of verses, stuff like that—but I haven't really gotten into writing a completely free song. Hey, you dig something like cut-ups? I mean, like William Burroughs?

Yeah, there's a cat in Paris who published a book with no pagination. The book comes in a box and you throw it in the air and, however it lands, you read it like that.

Yeah, that's where it's at. Because that's what it means, anyway. Okay, I wrote the book because there's a lot of stuff in there I can't possibly sing . . . all the collages. I can't sing it because it gets too long or it goes too far out. I can only do it around a few people who would know. Because the majority of the audience—I don't care where they're from, how hip they are—I think it would just get totally lost. Something that had no rhyme, all cut up, no nothing, except something happening, which is words.

You wrote the book to say something?

Yeah, but certainly not any kind of profound statement. The book don't begin or end.

But you had something to say. And you wanted to say it to somebody.

Yeah, I said it to myself. Only, I'm lucky, because I could put it into a book. Now somebody else is going to be allowed to see what I said to myself.

You have four albums out now, with a fifth any day. Are these albums sequential in the way that you composed and sung them?

Yeah, I've got about two or three albums that I've never recorded, which are lost songs. They're old songs; I'll never record them. Some very groovy songs. Some old songs which I've written and sung maybe once in a concert and nobody else ever heard them. There are a lot of songs which would fill in between the records. It was growing from the first record to the second, then a head change on the third. And the fourth. The fifth I can't even tell you about.

So if I started with Album One, Side One, Band One, I could truthfully watch Bob Dylan grow?

No, you could watch Bob Dylan laughing to himself. Or you could see Bob Dylan going through changes. That's really the most.

What do you think of the Byrds? Do you think they're doing something different?

Yeah, they could. They're doing something really new now. It's like a danceable Bach sound. Like "Bells of Rhymney." They're cutting across all kinds of barriers which most people who sing aren't even hip to. They know it all. If they don't close their minds, they'll come up with something pretty fantastic.

6. Interview with Nora Ephron and Susan Edmiston, *Positively Tie Dream*

AUGUST 1965

This interview took place in late summer of 1965 in the office of Dylan's manager, Albert Grossman. Dylan had just been booed in the historic Forest Hills concert where he abandoned folk purity to the use of electric accompaniment. He was wearing a red-and-navy op-art shirt, a navy blazer, and pointy high-heeled boots. His face, so sharp and harsh when translated through media, was then infinitely soft and delicate. His hair was not bushy or electric or Afro; it was fine-spun soft froth like the foam of a wave. He looked like an underfed angel with a nose from the land of the Chosen People.

Some American folk singers—Carolyn Hester, for example—say that what you're now doing, the new sound, "folk rock," is liberating them.

Did Carolyn say that? You tell her she can come around and see me any time now that she's liberated.

Does labeling, using the term, "folk rock," tend to obscure what's happening?

Yes.

It's like "pop gospel." What does the term mean to you?

47

Yeah, classical gospel could be the next trend. There's country rock, rockabilly. What does it mean to me? Folk rock. I've never even said that word. It has a hard gutter sound. Circusy atmosphere. It's nose-thumbing. Sound like you're looking down on what is . . . fantastic, great music.

The definition most often given of folk rock is the combination of the electronic sound of rock and roll with the meaningful lyrics of folk music? Does that sum up what you're doing?

Yes. It's very complicated to play with electricity. You play with other people. You're dealing with other people. Most people don't like to work with other people, it's more difficult. It takes a lot. Most people who don't like rock & roll can't relate to other people.

You mention the Apollo Theatre in Harlem on one of your album covers. Do you go there often?

Oh, I couldn't go up there. I used to go up there a lot about four years ago. I even wanted to play in one of the amateur nights, but I got scared. Bad things can happen to you. I saw what the audience did to a couple of guys they didn't like. And I would have had a couple things against me right away when I stepped out on the stage.

Who is Mr. Jones in "Ballad of a Thin Man"?

He's a real person. You know him, but not by that name.

Like Mr. Charlie?

No. He's more than Mr. Charlie. He's actually a person. Like I saw him come into the room one night and he looked like a camel. He proceeded to put his eyes in his pocket. I asked this guy who he was and he said, "That's Mr. Jones." Then I asked this cat, "Doesn't he do anything but put his eyes in his pocket?" And he told me, "He puts his nose on the ground." It's all there, it's a true story.

Where did you get that shirt?

California. Do you like it? You should see my others. You can't get clothes like that here. There are a lot of things out there we haven't got here.

Isn't California on the way here?

It's uptight here compared to there. Hollywood I mean. It's not really breathable here. It's like there's air out there. The Sunset Strip can't be compared to anything here, like 42nd Street. The people there look different, they look more like . . . you want to kiss them out there.

Do you spend a lot of time out there?

I don't have much time to spend anywhere: The same thing in England. In England everybody looks very hip East Side. They wear things . . . they don't wear things that bore you. They've got other hang-ups in other directions.

Do you consider yourself primarily a poet?

No. We have our ideas about poets. The word doesn't mean any more than the word "house." There are people who write _po_ems and people who write po_ems_. Other people write _poems_. Everybody who writes poems do you call them a poet? There's a certain kind of rhythm in some kind of way that's visible. You don't necessarily have to write to be a poet. Some people work in gas stations and they're poets. I don't call myself a poet because I don't like the word. I'm a trapeze artist.

What I meant was, do you think your words stand without the music?

They would stand but I don't read them. I'd rather sing them. I write things that aren't songs—I have a book coming out.

What is it?

It's a book of words.

Is it like the back of your albums? It seemed to me that the album copy you write is a lot like the writing of William Burroughs. Some of the accidental sentences —

Cut-ups.

Yes, and some of the imagery and anecdotes. I wondered if you had read anything by him.

I haven't read *Naked Lunch* but I read some of his shorter things in little magazines, foreign magazines. I read one in Rome. I know him. I don't really know him—I just met him once. I think he's a great man.

Burroughs keeps an album, a collection of photographs that illustrate his writing. Do you have anything similar to that?

I do that too. I have photographs of "Gates of Eden" and "It's All Over Now, Baby Blue." I saw them after I wrote the songs. People send me a lot of things and a lot of the things are pictures, so other people must have that idea too. I gotta admit, maybe I wouldn't have chosen them, but I can see what it is about the pictures.

I heard you used to play the piano for Buddy Holly.

No. I used to play the rock & roll piano, but I don't want to say who it was for because the cat will try to get hold of me. I don't want to see the cat. He'll try to reclaim the friendship. I did it a long time ago, when I was seventeen years old. I used to play country piano too.

This was before you became interested in folk music?

Yes. I became interested in folk music because I had to make it somehow. Obviously I'm not a hard-working cat. I played the guitar, that was all I did. I thought it was great music. Certainly I haven't turned my back on it or anything like that. There is—and I'm sure nobody realizes this, all the authorities who write about what it is and what it should be, when they say keep things simple, they should be easily understood—folk music is the only music where it isn't simple. It's never been simple. It's weird, man, full of legend, myth, Bible, and ghosts. I've never written anything hard to understand, not in my head anyway, and nothing as far out as some of the old songs. They were out of sight.

Like what songs?

"Little Brown Dog." "I bought a little brown dog, its face is all gray. Now I'm going to Turkey flying on my bottle." And "Nottemun Town," that's like a herd of ghosts passing through on the way to Tangiers. "Lord Edward," "Barbara Allen," they're full of myth.

And contradictions?

Yeah, contradictions.

And chaos?

Chaos, watermelon, clocks, everything.

You wrote on the back of one album, "I accept chaos but does chaos accept me?"

Chaos is a friend of mine. It's like I accept him, does he accept me?

Do you see the world as chaos?

Truth is chaos. Maybe beauty is chaos.

Poets like Eliot and Yeats—

I haven't read Yeats.

They saw the world as chaos, accepted it as chaos and attempted to bring order from it. Are you trying to do that?

No. It exists and that's all there is to it. It's been here longer than I have. What can I do about it? I don't know what the songs I write are. That's all I do is write songs, right? Write. I collect things too.

Monkey wrenches?

Where did you read about that? Has that been in print? I told this guy out on the coast that I collected monkey wrenches, all sizes and shapes of monkey wrenches, and he didn't believe me. I don't think you believe me either. And I collect the pictures too. Have you talked to Sonny and Cher?

No.

They're a drag. A cat got kicked out of a restaurant and he went home and wrote a song about it.

They say your fan mail has radically increased since you switched sounds.

Yeah. I don't have time to read all of it, but I want you to put that I answer half of it. I don't really. A girl does that for me.

Does she save any for you—any particularly interesting letters?

She knows my head. Not the ones that just ask for pictures, there's a file for them. Not the ones that say, I want to make it with you, they go in another file. She saves two kinds. The violently put-down—

The ones that call you a sellout?

Yeah. Sellout, fink, Fascist, Red, everything in the book. I really dig those. And ones from old friends.

Like, "You don't remember me but I was in the fourth grade with you"?

No, I never had any friends then. These are letters from people who knew me in New York five, six years ago. My first fans. Not the people who call themselves my first fans. They came in three years ago, two years ago. They aren't really my first fans.

How do you feel about being booed at your concert at Forest Hills?

I thought it was great, I really did. If I said anything else I'd be a liar.

And at Newport Folk Festival?

That was different. They twisted the sound. They didn't like what I was going to play and they twisted the sound on me before I began.

I hear you are wearing a sellout jacket?

What kind of jacket is a sellout jacket?

Black leather.

I've had black leather jackets since I was five years old. I've been wearing black leather all my life.

I wonder if we could talk about electronic music and what made you decide to use it.

I was doing fine, you know, singing and playing my guitar. It was a sure thing, don't you understand, it was a sure thing. I was getting very bored with that. I couldn't go out and play like that. I was thinking of quitting. Out front it was a sure thing. I knew what the audience was gonna do, how they would react. It was very automatic. Your mind just drifts unless you can find some way to get in there and remain totally there. It's so much of a fight remaining totally there all by yourself. It takes too much. I'm not ready to cut that much out of my life. You can't have nobody around. You can't be bothered with anybody else's world. And I like people. What I'm doing now—it's a whole other thing. We're not playing rock music. It's not a hard sound. These people call it folk rock—if they want to call it that, something that simple, it's good for selling records. As far as it being what it is, I don't know what it is. I can't call it folk rock. It's a whole way of doing things. It has been picked up on, I've heard songs on the radio that have picked it up. I'm not talking about words. It's a certain feeling, and it's been on every single record I've ever made. That has not changed. I know it hasn't changed. As far as what I was totally, before, maybe I was pushing it a little then. I'm not pushing things now. I know it. I know very well how to do it. The problem of how I want to play something—I know it in front. I know what I am going to say, what I'm going to do. I don't have to work it out. The band I work with—they wouldn't be playing with me if they didn't play like I want them to. I have this song, "Queen Jane Approximately"—

Who is Queen Jane?

Queen Jane is a man.

Was there something that made you decide to change sounds? Your trip to England?

I like the sound. I like what I'm doing now. I would have done it before. It wasn't practical to do it before. I spend most of my time writing. I wouldn't have had the time. I had to get where I was going all alone. I don't know what I'm going to do next. I probably will record with strings some time, but it doesn't necessarily change. It's just a different color. And I know it's real. No matter what anybody says. They can boo till the end of time. I know that the music is real, more real than the boos.

How do you work?

Most of the time I work at night. I don't really like to think of it as work. I don't know how important it is. It's not important to the average cat who works eight hours a day. What does he care? The world can get along very well without it. I'm hip to that.

Sure, but the world can get along without any number of things.

I'll give you a comparison. Rudy Vallee. Now that was a lie, that was a downright lie. Rudy Vallee being popular. What kind of people could have dug him? You know, your grandmothers and mothers. But what kind of people were they? He was so sexless. If you want to find out about those times and you listen to his music you're not going to find out anything about the times. His music was a pipedream. All escapes. There are no more escapes. If you want to find out anything that's happening now, you have to listen to the music. I don't mean the words, although "Eve of Destruction" will tell you something about it. The words are not really gonna tell it, not really. You gotta listen to the Staples Singers, Smokey and the Miracles, Martha and the Vandellas. That's scary to a lot of people. It's sex that's involved. It's not hidden. It's real. You can overdo it. It's not only sex, it's a whole beautiful feeling.

But Negro rhythm and blues has been around underground for at least twelve years. What brought it out now?

The English did that. They brought it out. They hipped everybody. You read an interview asking who the Beatles' favorite singer was and they say Chuck Berry. You never used to hear Chuck Berry records on the radio, hard blues. The English did that. England is great and beautiful, though in other ways kinda messy. Though not outside London.

In what way messy?

There's a snobbishness. What you see people doing to other people. It's not only class. It's not that simple. It's a kind of Queen kind of thing. Some people are royalty and some are not. Here, man, somebody don't like you he tells you. There it's very tight, tight kinds of expressions, their whole tone of speaking changes. It's an everyday kind of thing. But the kids are a whole other thing. Great. They're just more free. I hope you don't think I take this too seriously—I just have a headache.

I think you started out to say that music was more in tune with what's happening than other art forms.

Great paintings shouldn't be in museums. Have you ever been in a museum? Museums are cemeteries. Paintings should be on the walls of restaurants, in dime stores, in gas stations, in men's rooms. Great paintings should be where people hang out. The only thing where it's happening is on radio and records, that's where people hang out. You can't see great paintings. You pay half a million and hang one in your house and one guest sees it. That's not art. That's a shame, a crime. Music is the only thing that's in tune with what's happening. It's not in book form, it's not on the stage. All this art they've been talking about is non-existent. It just remains on the shelf. It doesn't make anyone happier. Just think how many people would really feel great if they could see a Picasso in their daily diner. It's not the bomb that has to go, man, it's the museums.

7. Interview with Joseph Haas, *Chicago Daily News*

NOVEMBER 27, 1965

Bob Dylan, one of the most talented and controversial figures in American entertainment, will perform tonight in the second of two concerts in Arie Crown Theater of McCormick Place. When the twenty-four-year-old performer sings his original compositions, in his highly distinctive way, millions of young people listen—at concerts and on his best-selling long-playing albums and single recordings. Wise parents, who want to understand what the younger generation is thinking, would do well to listen to him, too. Dylan is a difficult performer to classify. Is he a protest singer, leader of the folk-rock cult, a rock'n'roller, or a natural progression in American folk music? He has been called all of these things, and perhaps the wisest course is not to try to classify him at all, but to let him speak for himself, about himself, at length and informally.

Will you sing any of the so-called folk-rock music in your concerts here?

No, it's not folk-rock, it's just instruments . . . It's not folk-rock. I call it the mathematical sound, sort of Indian music. I can't really explain it.

Do you dislike folk-rock groups?

No, no, I like what everybody else does, what a lot of people do. I don't necessarily like the writing of too many songwriters but I like the idea of, look, like they're trying to make it, you know, to say something about the death thing.

Actually I don't know many of them. I'm twenty-four now and most of them playing and listening are teenagers. I was playing rock'n'roll when I was thirteen and fourteen and fifteen, but I had to quit when I was sixteen or seventeen because I couldn't make it that way. The image of the day was Frankie Avalon or Fabian or this whole athletic supercleanness bit, you know, which if you didn't have that, you couldn't make any friends. I played rock'n'roll when I was in my teens. Yeah, I played semi-professionally, piano with rock'n'roll groups. About 1958 or 1959, I discovered Odetta, Harry Belafonte, that stuff, and I became a folk singer.

Did you make this change so you could "make it"?

You couldn't make it livable back then with rock'n'roll. You couldn't carry around an amplifier and electric guitar and expect to survive, it was just too much of a hangup. It cost bread to make enough money to buy an electric guitar, and then you had to make more money to have enough people to play the music. You need two or three to create some conglomeration of sound. So it wasn't an alone kind of thing, you know. When you got other things dragging you down, you're sort of beginning to lose, crash, you know? When somebody's sixteen or twenty-five, who's got the right to lose, to wind up as a pinboy at sixty-five?

By "making it," do you mean making commercial success?

No, no, that's not it, making money. It's being able to be nice and not hurt anybody.

How does your sound differ today?

It differs because it doesn't. I don't know, you see. I don't know exactly what to say rock'n'roll is. I do know that . . . think of it in terms of a whole thing. It's not just pretty words to a tune or putting tunes to words, there's nothing that's exploited. The words and the music, I can hear the sound of what I want to say.

Did you go into the folk field, then, because you had a better chance of "making it"?

No, that was an accidental thing. I didn't go into folk music to make any money, but because it was easy. You could be by yourself, you didn't need anybody. All you needed was a guitar. You didn't need anybody else at all. I don't know what's happened to it now. I don't think it's as good as it used to be. Most of the folk music singers have gone on, they're doing other things. Although there're still a lot of good ones around.

Why did you give up the folk sound?

I've been on too many other streets to just do that. I couldn't go back and just do that. The real folk never seen Forty-second Street, they've never ridden an airplane. They've got their little world, and that's fine.

Why have you begun using the electric guitar?

I don't use it that much, really.

Some people are hurt because you've used one at all.

That's their fault. It would be silly of me to say I'm sorry because I haven't really done anything. It's not really all that serious. I have a hunch the people who feel I betrayed them picked up on me a few years ago and weren't really back there with me at the beginning. Because I still see the people who were with me from the beginning once in a while and they know what I'm doing.

Can you explain why you were booed at the Newport Folk Festival last summer when you came on stage with an electric guitar and began singing your new material?

Like, I don't even know who those people were. Anyway, I think there's always a little boo in all of us. I wasn't shattered by it. I didn't cry. I don't even understand it. I mean, what are they going to shatter, my ego? And it doesn't even exist, they can't hurt me with a boo.

What will you do when the success of your present kind of music fades?

I'm going to say when I stop, it just doesn't matter to me. I've never followed any trend, I just haven't the time to follow a trend. It's useless to even try.

In songs like "The Times They Are A-Changin'" you made a distinction between young and old thinking. You talked about the older generation failing to understand the younger?

That's not what I was saying. It happened maybe that those were the only words I could find to separate aliveness from deadness. It has nothing to do with age.

What can you say about when your first book is coming out?

Macmillan is the publisher, and the title now is *Tarantula*. Right now it's called that but I might change it. It's just a lot of writings. I can't really say what it's about. It's not a narrative or anything like that.

Some stories have said that you plan to give up music, perhaps soon, and devote your time to writing?

When I really get wasted, I'm gonna have to do something, you know. Like I might never write again. I might start painting soon.

Have you earned enough money to have freedom to do exactly what you want?

I wouldn't say that. You got to get up and you got to sleep, and the time in between there you got to do something. That's what I'm dealing with now. I do a lot of funny things. I really have no idea, I can't afford to think tonight, tomorrow, any time. It's really meaningless to me.

Do you live from day to day?

I try to. I try not to make any plans. Every time I go and make plans, nothing really seems to work. I've given up on most of that stuff. I have a concert schedule I keep, but other people get me there. I don't have to do anything.

Do you ever hope to settle down to a normal life, get married, have kids?

I don't hope to be like anybody. Getting married, having a bunch of kids, I have no hopes for it. If it happens, it happens. Whatever my hopes, it never turns out. I don't think anybody's a prophet.

You sound quite pessimistic about everything.

No, not pessimistic. I don't think things can turn out. That's all, and I've accepted it. It doesn't matter to me. It's not pessimism, just a sort of sadness, sort of like not having no hopes.

What about religion or philosophy?

I just don't have any religion or philosophy. I can't say much about any of them. A lot of people do, and fine if they really do follow a certain code. I'm not about to go around changing anything. I don't like anybody to tell me what I have to do or believe, how I have to live. I just don't care, you know. Philosophy can't give me anything that I don't already have. The biggest thing of all, that encompasses it all, is kept back in this country. It's an old Chinese philosophy and religion, it really was one . . . There is a book called the *I-Ching*, I'm not trying to push it, I don't want to talk about it, but it's the only thing that is amazingly true, period, not just for me. Anybody would know it. Anybody that ever walks would know it. It's a whole system of finding out things, based on all sorts of things. You don't have to believe in anything to read it, because beside being a great book to believe in it's also very fantastic poetry.

How do you spend your time when you're not on a concert tour?

I keep a regular bunch of hours. I just do what I have to do, not doing nothing really. I can be satisfied anywhere, I never read too much. Once in a while I write up a bunch of things, and then I record them. I do the normal things.

What about romantic reports about you and Joan Baez?

Oh, man, no, that was a long time ago.

On her latest album, about half of her songs are Dylan songs.

Heaven help her.

What about the story that you changed your name from Bob Zimmerman to Bob Dylan because you admired the poetry of Dylan Thomas?

No, God no. I took the Dylan because I have an uncle named Dillon. I changed the spelling but only because it looked better. I've read some of Dylan Thomas' stuff, and it's not the same as mine. We're different.

What about your family?

Well, I just don't have any family, I'm all alone.

What about a story that you invited your parents to one of your early concerts, paid their way there, and then when they were seated, you said on the stage that you were an "orphan," and then didn't visit them when they were in New York?

That's not true. They came to a concert, they drove there on their own, and I gave them some money. I don't dislike them or anything, I just don't have any contact with them. They live in Minnesota and there's nothing for me in Minnesota. Probably sometimes I'd like to go back for a while. Everybody goes back to where they came from, I guess.

You talk as if you are terribly separated from people.

I'm not disconnected from anything because of a force, just habit. It's just the way I am. I don't know, I have an idea that it's easier to be disconnected than to be connected. I've got a huge hallelujah for all the people who're connected, that's great, but I can't do that. I've been connected so many times. Things haven't worked out right, so rather than break myself up, I just don't get connected.

Are you just trying to avoid being hurt again?

I haven't been hurt at the time, the realization is afterwards. Just looking back on it, thinking about it, it's just like a cold winter.

Do you avoid close relationships with people?

I have relationships with people. People like me, also disconnected, there are a lot of disconnected people. I don't feel alienated, or disconnected, or afraid. I don't feel there's any kind of organization of disconnected people. I just can't go along with any kind of organization. Some day I might find myself all alone in a subway car, stranded when the lights go out, with forty people, and I'll have to get to know them. Then I'll just do what has to be.

8. Television Press Conference, KQED (San Francisco)

DECEMBER 3, 1965

When Bob Dylan's five concerts in the San Francisco Bay Area were scheduled in December 1965, the idea was proposed that he hold a press conference in the studios of KQED, the educational television station.

Dylan accepted and flew out a day early to make it.

He arrived early for the press conference accompanied by Robbie Robertson and several other members of his band, drank tea in the KQED office and insisted that he was ready to talk about "anything you want to talk about." His only request was that he be able to leave at 3 p.m. so that he could rehearse in the Berkeley Community Theater where he was to sing that night.

At the press conference there were all sorts of people. The TV news crews of all the local stations were there; so were reporters for three metropolitan dailies (their stories were subsequently compared to the broadcast of the interview by a University of California journalism department class) plus representatives of several high school papers, and personal friends of Dylan including poet Allen Ginsberg, producer Bill Graham and comedian Larry Hankin.

Thus the questions ranged from standard straight press and TV reporters' questions to teenage fan club questions to in-group personal queries and put ons, to questions by those who really had listened to Dylan's songs.

He sat on a raised platform facing the cameras and the reporters and answered questions over a microphone all the while smoking cigarettes and swinging his leg back and forth. At one point he held up a poster for a benefit that week for the San Francisco Mime Troupe (the first rock dance at the Fillmore Auditorium and one of the first public dances featuring the Jefferson Airplane). At the conclusion of the press conference, he chatted with friends for a while, jumped into a car and went back to Berkeley for the rehearsal. He cut the rehearsal off early to go to the hotel and watch the TV program which was shown that night and repeated the following week.

This is the only full length press conference by Dylan ever televised in its entirety. The transcript was made from an audio tape of the conference, and the only editing has been to take out statements concerning ticket availability and times of the local concerts.

—Ralph J. Gleason

I'd like to know the meaning of the cover photo on your album, 'Highway 61 Revisited'?

What would you like to know about it?

It seems to have some philosophy in it. I'd like to know what it represents to you—you're a part of it . . .

I haven't really looked at it that much.

I've thought about it a great deal.

It was just taken one day when I was sittin' on the steps y'know—I don't really remember too much about it.

I thought the motorcycle was an image in your song-writing. You seem to like that.

Oh, we all like motorcycles to some degree.

Do you think of yourself primarily as a singer or a poet?

Oh, I think of myself more as a song and dance man, y'know.

Why?

Oh, I don't think we have enough time to really go into that.

You were quoted as saying when you're really wasted you may enter into another field. How "wasted" is really wasted and do you foresee it?

No, I don't foresee it, but it's more or less like a ruthless type of feeling. Very ruthless and intoxicated to some degree.

The criticism that you have received for leaving the folk field and switching to folk-rock hasn't seemed to bother you a great deal. Do you think you'll stick to folk-rock or go into more writing?

I don't play folk-rock.

What would you call your music?

I like to think of it more in terms of vision music—it's mathematical music.

Would you say that the words are more important than the music?

The words are just as important as the music. There would be no music without the words.

Which do you do first, ordinarily?

The words.

Do you think there ever will be a time when you will paint or sculpt?

Oh, yes.

Do you think there will ever be a time when you'll be hung as a thief?

You weren't supposed to say that.

Bob, you said you always do your words first and think of it as music. When you do the words can you hear it?

Yes.

The music you want when you do your words?

Yes, oh yes.

Do you hear any music before you have words—do you have any songs that you don't have words to yet?

Ummm, sometimes, on very general instruments, not on the guitar though—maybe something like the harpsichord or the harmonica or autoharp—I might hear some kind of melody or tune which I would know the words to put to. Not with the guitar though. The guitar is too hard an instrument. I don't really hear many melodies based on the guitar.

What poets do you dig?

Rimbaud, I guess; W.C. Fields; the family, you know, the trapeze family in the circus; Smokey Robinson; Allen Ginsberg; Charlie Rich— he's a good poet.

In a lot of your songs you are hard on people — in "Like a Rolling Stone" you're hard on the girl and in "Positively 4th Street" you're hard on a friend. Do you do this because you want to change their lives, or do you want to point out to them the error of their ways?

I want to needle them.

Do you still sing your older songs?

No. No. I just saw a songbook last night, I don't really see too many of those things, but there's a lotta songs in those books I haven't even recorded, y'know. I've just written down, and y'know and put little tunes to and they published them. I haven't sung them, though. A lotta the songs I just don't even know anymore, even the ones I did sing. There doesn't seem to be enough time, y'know.

Did you change your program when you went to England?

No, no, I finished it there. That was the end of my older program. I didn't change it, it was developed and by the time we got there it was all, it was more or less, I knew what was going to happen all the time, y'know. I knew how many encores there was, y'know, which songs they were going to clap loudest and all this kind of things.

In a concert tour like this do you do the same program night after night?

Oh, sometimes it's different. I think we'll do the same one here in this area, though.

In a recent 'Broadside' interview, Phil Ochs said you should do films. Do you have any plans to do this?

I do have plans to make a film but not because anybody said I should do it.

How soon will this be?

Next year probably.

Can you tell us what it will be about?

It'll be just another song.

Who are the people making films that you dig, particularly?

Truffaut. I really can't think of any more people. Italian movie direc-tors, y'know, but not too many people in England and the United States which I really think that I would dig.

You did a Chaplin bit as an exit in a concert once.

I did!!!??? That musta been an accident. Have to stay away from that kind of thing.

What do you think of people who analyze your songs?

I welcome them—with open arms.

The University of California mimeographed all the lyrics from the last album and had a symposium discussing them. Do you welcome that?

Oh, sure. I'm just kinda sad I'm not around to be a part of it.

Josh Dunson in his new book implies that you have sold out to commercial interests and the topical song movement. Do you have any comment, sir?

Well, no comments, no arguments. No, I sincerely don't feel guilty.

Of all the people who record your compositions, who do you feel does the most justice to what you're trying to say?

I think Manfred Mann. They've done the songs—they've done about three or four. Each one of them has been right in context with what the song was all about.

What's your new album about?

Oh, it's about, uh—just about all kinds of different things—rats, balloons. They're about the only thing that comes to my mind right now.

Mr. Dylan, how would you define folk music?

As a constitutional re-play of mass production.

Would you call your songs "folk songs"?

No.

Are protests songs "folk songs"?

I guess, if they're a constitutional re-play of mass production.

Do you prefer songs with a subtle or obvious message?

With a what???

A subtle or obvious message?

Uh—I don't really prefer those kinds of songs at all—"message"—you mean like—what songs with a message?

Well, like "Eve of Destruction" and things like that.

Do I prefer that to what?

I don't know, but your songs are supposed to have a subtle message.

Subtle message???

Well, they're supposed to.

Where'd you hear that?

In a movie magazine?

Oh—Oh God! Well, we won't—we don't discuss those things here.

Are your songs ever about real people?

Sure they are, they're all about real people.

Particular ones?

Particular people? Sure, I'm sure you've seen all the people in my songs—at one time or another.

Who is Mr. Jones?

Mr. Jones, I'm not going to tell you his first name. I'd get sued.

What does he do for a living?

He's a pinboy. He also wears suspenders.

How do you explain your attraction?

Attraction to what?

Your attraction—your popularity—your mass popularity.

No, no. I really have no idea. That's the truth. I always tell the truth. That is the truth.

What are your own personal hopes for the future and what do you hope to change in the world?

Oh, my hopes for the future: to be honest, you know, I don't have any hopes for the future and I just hope to have enough boots to be able to change them. That's all really, it doesn't boil down to anything more than that. If it did, I would certainly tell you.

What do you think of a question and answer session of this type (with you as the principal subject)?

Well, I think we all have different—uh—(I may have dropped an ash on myself somewhere—you'll see in a minute here)—I'm not going to say anything about it though—uh—what was the question?

What are you thinking about right now?

I'm thinking about this ash.

Right before that.

Uh—the ash is creeping up on me somewhere—I've lost—lost touch with myself so I can't tell where exactly it is.

Was that an inadvertent evading of the question?

No, no—

What do you feel about the meaning of this kind of question and answer session?

I just know in my own mind that we all have a different idea of all the words we're using—uh—y'know so I don't really have too much—I really can't take it too seriously because everything—like if I say the word "house"—like we're both going to see a different house. If I just say the word—right? So we're using all these other words like "mass production" and "movie magazine" and we all have a different idea of these words too, so I don't even know what we're saying.

Is it pointless?

No, it's not pointless. It's—it's—you know, if you want to do it, you're there—then that's not pointless. You know, it doesn't hurt me any.

Is there anything in addition to your songs that you want to say to people?

Good luck.

You don't say that in your songs.

Oh, yes I do, every song tails off with "Good luck—I hope you make it."

Why couldn't you—uh—

Who are you? [*Laughter*] Get the camera on this person here.

What do you bother to write the poetry for if we all get different images? If we don't know what you're talking about.

Because I got nothing else to do, man.

Do you have a rhyme for "orange"?

What, I didn't hear that.

A rhyme for "orange."

A-ha . . . just a rhyme for "orange"?

Is it true that you were censored for singing on the Ed Sullivan show, etc., etc.

I'll tell you the rhyme in a minute.

Did they censor you from singing what you wanted on the Ed Sullivan show?

Yes. It was a long time ago.

What did you want to sing?

I don't know. It was some song which I wanted to sing and they said I could sing. There's more to it than just censorship there. They actually said I could sing the song, but when we went through the rehearsal of it, the guy came back afterwards and said that I'd have to change it and he said, "Can't you sing some folk song like the Clancy Brothers do?" And I didn't know any of their songs and so I couldn't get on the program. That's the way it came down.

Have you found that the text of the interviews with you are accurate to the original conversations?

No. That's another reason I don't really give press interviews or anything, because you know, I mean, even if you do something—there are a lot of people here, so they know what's going on—but like if you just do it with one guy or two guys, they just take it all out of context, you know, they just take it, split it up in the middle or just take what they want to use and they even ask you a question and you answer it and then it comes out in print that they just substitute another question for your answer. It's not really truthful, you know, to do that kind of thing, so I just don't do it. That's just a press problem there.

Do you think the entire text of your news conference today should be printed in the newspaper?

Oh no, nothing like that, nothing like that. But this is just for the interview, you know, when they want to do interviews in places like Omaha, or in Cincinnati, man, you know. I don't do it and then they write bad things.

Well, isn't this partly because you are often inaudible? Like, for most of this dialogue you have been inaudible, and now when you are touched person-ally by the misquotation, your voice rises and we can hear you.

Yeah, well, I just realized that maybe the people in the back there can't hear me, that's all.

I was just going to ask you—in your songs you sing out—

Yes I do.

And whether . . .

You see the songs are what I do—write the songs and sing them and perform them. That's what I do. The performing part of it could end, but like I'm going to be writing these songs and singing them and recording them and I see no end, right now. That's what I do—uh—anything else interferes with it. I mean anything else trying to get on top of it making something out of it which it isn't, it just brings me down, and it's not, uh—it just makes it seem all very cheap.

Well, it made me feel like you were almost kind of doing a penance of silence here . . .

No, no.

The first half.

I'm not one of those kind of people at all.

You don't need silence?

No, no silence. It's always silent where I am.

Mr. Dylan, when you're on a concert tour how many people travel in your party?

We travel with about 12 people now.

Do the number of people seem to go with the amount of money you're making?

Oh, yes, of course.

Is that known as Dylan's law?

We have the band, we have five in the group. And we need other things; we have to—it's a lot of electronic equipment now, a lot of different things which have to be taken care of so we need a lot of people. We have three Road Managers and things like that. We don't make any big public presentations though, like we never come into town in limousines or anything like that. We just—uh—go from place to place, you know, and do the shows. That's all.

You fly in your own plane?

Yes, yes.

Do you have to get in a certain type of mood to write your music?

Yeah, I guess so. A certain type of mood, if you want to call it that.

Do you find that you are more creative at a certain time of the day?

Yes, yes, I feel that way.

Like a night writer?

I would say night has nothing to do with it.

Have you ever sung with the Beatles?

No. Well, I think we have messed around in London, but, no I don't think anything serious.

Have you ever played a dance?

No. It's not that kind of music.

It is.

Well, what can I say. You must know more about the music than I do. How long have you been playing it?

Do you find that when you're writing you free-associate often?

No, it's all very clear and simple to me. These songs aren't complicated to me at all. I know what they are all about! There's nothing hard to figure out for me. I wouldn't write anything I can't really see.

I don't mean it that way. I meant when you're creating a song are you doing it on a subliminal level?

No. That's the difference in the songs I write now. In the past year or so—in the last year and a half, maybe two, I don't know—the songs before, up till one of these records, I wrote the fourth record in Greece—there was a change there, but the records before that, I used to know what I wanted to say, before I used to write the song. All the stuff which I had written before which wasn't song, was just on a piece of toilet paper. When it comes out like that it's the kind of stuff I never would sing because people would just not be ready for it. But I just went through that other thing of writing songs and I couldn't write like it anymore. It was just too easy and it wasn't really "right." I would start out, I would know what I wanted to say before I wrote the song and I would say it, you know, and it would never come out exactly the way I thought it would, but it came out, you know, it touched it, but now, I just write a song, like *I know* that it's just going to be all right and I don't really know exactly what it's all about, but I do know the minutes and the layers of what it's all about.

What did you think about your song "It's Alright, Ma (I'm Only Bleeding)"? It happens to be my favorite one.

God bless you, son. I haven't heard it for a long time. I couldn't even sing it for you probably.

How long does it take you to write a . . .

Usually not too long a time, really. I might write all night and get one song out of a lot of different things I write.

How many have you written?

Uh—I guess, well, there's one publisher that's got about a hundred. I've written about fifty others I guess. I got about 150 songs I've written.

Have they all been published?

No, some of the scraps haven't been published. But I find I can't really sing that anyway, because I forget it, so the songs I don't publish, I usually do forget.

Have you ever taken these scraps and made them into a song?

No, I've forgotten the scraps. I have to start over all the time. I can't really keep notes or anything like that.

You can't go back to one of your earlier things and use them in your . . .

No, no. That wouldn't be right either.

On your songs do you get any help from the rest of your entourage?

Robbie [Robertson], the lead guitar player, sometimes we play the guitars together—something might come up—but I know it's going to be right. I'll be just sitting around playing so I can write up some words. I don't get any ideas though of what I want to or what's really going to happen here.

Why do you think you're so popular?

I don't know. I'm not a reporter, I'm not a newsman or anything. I'm not even a philosopher, so I have no idea I would think other people would know, but I don't think I know. You know, when you get too many people talking about the same thing it tends to clutter up things. Everybody asks me that so I realize they must be talking about it, so I'd rather stay out of it and make it easier for them. Then, when they get the answer, I hope they tell me.

Has there been any more booing?

Oh, there's booing—you can't tell where the booings going to come up. Can't tell at all. It comes up in the weirdest, strangest places and when it comes it's quite a thing in itself. I figure there's a little "boo" in all of us.

Bob, where is Desolation Row?

Where? Oh, that's someplace in Mexico. It's across the border. It's noted for its Coke factory. Coca-Cola machines are—sells—sell a lotta Coca-Cola down there.

Where is Highway 61?

Highway 61 exists—that's out in the middle of the country. It runs down to the south, goes up north.

Mr. Dylan, you seem very reluctant to talk about the fact that you're a popular entertainer—a most popular entertainer.

Well, what do you want me to say?

Well, I don't understand why you . . .

Well, what do you want me to say? What do you want me to say, d'you want me to say—who—who—What do you want me to say about it?

You seem almost embarrassed to admit that you're popular.

Well, I'm not embarrassed, I mean, you know—Well, what do you want, exactly—for me to say. You want me to jump up and say "Hallelujah!"—and crash the cameras or do something weird? Tell me, tell me. I'll go along with you, if I can't go along with you, I'll find somebody to go along with you.

I find that you really have no idea as to why you are popular, no thoughts on why you are popular.

I just haven't really struggled for that. It happened, you know? It happened like anything else happens. Just a happening. You don't try to figure out happenings. You dig happenings. So I'm not going to even talk about it.

Do you feel that part of the popularity is because of a kind of identification?

I have no idea. I don't really come too much in contact.

Does it make life more difficult?

No, it certainly doesn't.

Were you surprised the first time the boos came?

Yeah, that was at Newport. Well, I did this very crazy thing. I didn't know what was going to happen, but they certainly booed, I'll tell you that. You could hear it all over the place. I don't know who they were though, and I'm certain whoever it was did it twice as loud as they normally would. They kind of quieted down some at Forest Hills although they did it there, too. They've done it just about all over except in Texas—they didn't boo us in Texas or in Atlanta or in Boston, or in Ohio. They've done it in just about—or in Minneapolis, they didn't do it there. They've done it a lot of other places. I mean, they must be pretty rich, to be able to go someplace and boo. I couldn't afford it if I was in their shoes.

Other than booing, have the audiences changed much? Do they scream and get hysterical and rush on stage?

Oh, sometimes you get people rushing the stage, but you just, y'know—turn 'em off very fast. Kick 'em in the head or something like that. They get the picture.

You said that you don't know why you are so popular. That is in direct opposition to what most people who reach this level of popularity say.

Well, you see, a lot of people start out and they plan to try to be stars, I would imagine, like, however, they have to be stars. I mean I know a lot of those people, you know? And they start out and they go into show business for many, many reasons, to be seen, you know. I started out, you know, like this had nothing to do with it when I started. I started from New York City, you know, and there just wasn't any of that around. It just happened.

Don't misunderstand me, I agree with your right not to have to care, my point is that it would be somewhat disappointing for the people who think that you feel towards them, the way that they feel towards you.

Oh—well, I don't want to disappoint anybody. I mean, tell me what I should say—you know, I'll certainly go along with anything, but I really don't have much of an idea.

You have a poster there.

Yeah, it's a poster somebody gave me. It looks pretty good. The Jefferson Airplane, John Handy, and Sam Thomas and the Mystery Trend and the Great Society and all playing at the Fillmore Auditorium this Friday, December 10th, and I would like to go if I could, but unfortunately, I won't be here, I don't think, but if I was here, I certainly would be there.

What's more important to you: The way that your music and words sound, or the content, the message?

The whole thing while it's happening. The whole total sound of the words, what's really going down is—it either happens or it doesn't happen, you know. That's what I feel is—just the thing, which is happening there at that time. That's what we do, you know? That is the most important thing, there really isn't anything else. I don't know if I answered your question.

You mean it might happen one time, and it might not happen the next?

We've had some bad nights, but we always take good cuts for the records. The records are always made out of good cuts and in person most of the time it does come across. Most of the time we do feel like playing. That's important, to me; the aftermath, and whatever happens before, is not really important to me; just the time on the stage and the time that we're singing the songs and performing them. Or not really performing them even, just letting them be there.

If you were going to sell out to a commercial interest, which one would you choose?

Ladies garments.

Bob, have you worked with any rock & roll groups?

Uh, professionally?

Or just sitting in or on concert tours with them.

No, no, I don't usually play too much.

Do you listen to other people's recordings of your songs?

Sometimes. A few of them I've heard. I don't really come across it that much though.

Is it a strange experience?

No, it's like a, more or less like a, heavenly kind of thing.

What do you think of Joan Baez's interpretations of your earlier songs?

I haven't heard her latest album, or her one before that. I heard one. She does 'em all right, I think.

What about Donovan's "Colors" and his things? Do you think he's a good poet?

Ehh. He's a nice guy, though.

I'm shattered.

Well, you needn't be.

Are there any young folksingers you would recommend that we hear?

I'm glad you asked that. Oh, yeah, there's the Sir Douglas Quintet, I think are probably the best that are going to have a chance of reaching the commercial airways. They already have with a couple of songs.

What about Paul Butterfield?

They're good.

Mr. Dylan, you call yourself a completely disconnected person.

No, I didn't call myself that. They sort of drove those words in my mouth. I saw that paper.

How would you describe yourself. Have you analyzed . . .

I certainly haven't. No.

Mr. Dylan, I know you dislike labels and probably rightfully so, but for those of us well over thirty, could you label yourself and perhaps tell us what your role is?

Well, I'd sort of label myself as "well under thirty." And my role is to just, y'know, to just stay here as long as I can.

Phil Ochs wrote in 'Broadside' that you have twisted so many people's wigs that he feels it becomes increasingly dangerous for you to perform in public.

Well, that's the way it goes, you know. I don't, I can't apologize certainly.

Did you envision the time when you would give five concerts in one area like this within ten days?

No. This is all very new to me.

If you were draftable at present, do you know what your feelings might be?

No. I'd probably just do what had to be done.

What would that be?

Well, I don't know, I never really speak in terms of "what if" y'know, so I don't really know.

Are you going to participate in the Vietnam Day Committee demonstration in front of the Fairmont Hotel tonight.

No, I'll be busy tonight.

You planning any demonstrations?

Well, we thought—one. I don't know if it could be organized in time.

Would you describe it?

Uh—well it was a demonstration where I make up the cards you know, they have—uh—they have a group of protesters here—uh—perhaps carrying cards with pictures of the Jack of Diamonds on them and the Ace of Spades on them. Pictures of mules, maybe words and—oh maybe about 25–30,000 of these things printed up and just picket, carry signs and picket in front of the postoffice.

What words?

Oh, words: "camera," "microphone"—"loose"—just words—names of some famous people.

Do you consider yourself a politician?

Do I consider myself a politician? Oh, I guess so. I have my own party though.

Does it have a name?

No. There's no presidents in the party—there's no presidents, or vice presidents, or secretaries or anything like that, so it makes it kinda hard to get in.

Is there any right wing or left wing in that party?

No. It's more or less in the center—kind of on the Uppity scale.

Do you think your party could end the war with China?

Uh—I don't know. I don't know if they would have any people over there that would be in the same kind of party. Y'know? It might be kind of hard to infiltrate. I don't think my party would ever be approved by the White House or anything like that.

Is there anyone else in your party?

No. Most of us don't even know each other, y'know. It's hard to tell who's in it and who's not in it.

Would you recognize them if you see them?

Oh, you can recognize the people when you see them.

How long do you think it will be before you will finally quit?

Gee, I don't know. I could answer that you know, but it would mean something different probably for everybody, so we want to keep away from those kind of sayings.

What did you mean when you said . . .

I don't know, what things were we talking about?

You said I don't think things can turn out on a . . .

No, no, no—it's not that I don't think things can turn out, I don't think anything you plan ever turns out the way you plan.

Is that your philosophy?

No, no. Doesn't mean anything.

Do you think that it's fun to put on an audience.

I don't know, I've never done it.

You wrote a song called "Mama, You Been On My Mind." Do you sing it in concerts?

No I haven't. No I haven't.

Are the concerts fun still?

Yeah. Concerts are much more fun than they used to be.

Do you consider them more important than your albums, for instance?

No. It's just a kick to do it now. The albums are the most important.

Because they reach more people?

No, because it's all concise, it's very concise, and it's easy to hear the words and everything. There's no chance of the sound interfering, whereas in a concert, we've played some concerts where sometimes they have those very bad halls. You know, microphone systems. So it's not that easy for somebody to just come and listen to a band as if they were listening to one person, you know.

Do you consider your old songs less valid than the ones you are putting out now?

No, I just consider them something else to themselves, you know for another time, another dimension. It would be kind of dishonest for me to sing them now, because I wouldn't really *feel* like singing them.

What is the strangest thing that ever happened to you?

You're gonna get it, man.

What is the weirdest thing that ever happened to you?

I'll talk to you about it, later. I wouldn't do that to you.

What areas in music that you haven't gotten into do you hope to get into.

Writing a symphony—with different melodies and different words, different ideas—all being the same which just roll on top of each other and underneath each other.

Mr. Dylan, when would you know that it was time to get out of the music field into another field?

When I get very dragged.

When you stop making money?

No, when my teeth get better—or God, when something makes a drastic—uh—when I start to itch, y'know? When something just goes to a terrifying turn and I know it's got nothing to do with anything and I know it's time to leave.

You say you would like to write symphonies. Is this in the terms that we think of symphonies?

I'm not sure. Songs are all written as part of a symphony—different melodies, different changes—with words or without them, you know, but the end result being a total . . . I mean they say that my songs are long now, y'know, well sometime it's just gonna come up with the one that's going to be one whole album, consisting of one song. I don't know who's going to buy it. That might be the time to leave.

What's the longest song you've recorded?

I don't know. I don't really check those things, they just turn out long. I guess I've recorded one about 11 or 12 minutes long. "Ballad of Hollis Brown" was pretty long on the second record and "With God on Our Side" was kind of long. But none of them, I don't think, are as much into anything as "Desolation Row" was, and that was long, too. Songs shouldn't seem long, y'know, it just so happens that it looks that way on paper, y'know. The length of it doesn't have anything to do with it.

Doesn't this give you a problem in issuing records?

No, they are just ready to do anything that I put down now, so they don't really care.

What happens if they have to cut a song in half like "Subterranean Home-sick Blues"?

They didn't have to cut that in half.

They didn't have to but they did.

No they didn't.

Yeah?

No. You're talking about "Like a Rolling Stone."

Oh, yeah.

They cut it in half for the disc jockeys. Well, you see, it didn't matter for the disc jockeys if they had it cut in half because the other side was just a continuation on the other side and if anybody was interested they could just turn it over and listen to what really happens, you know. We just made a song the other day which came out ten minutes long, and I thought of releasing it as a single but they would have easily released it and just cut it up but it wouldn't have worked that way so we're not going to turn it out as a single. It's called "Freeze Out" you'll hear it on the next album.

9. Interview with Robert Shelton, from *No Direction Home*

MARCH 1966

> "I have a death thing—I have a suicidal thing, I know. . . .
> If the songs are dreamed, it's like my voice is coming out of
> their dream."
>
> —DYLAN, 1966

> "Judas!"
>
> —HECKLER AT ALBERT HALL, 1966

> "Bob Dylan, go home."
>
> —PARIS JOUR, 1966

In the dark, Lincoln Municipal Airport blended into the surrounding farmland. It was just past the break of midnight on a Saturday in mid-March 1966. As Dylan, The Band, two roadies, and I arrived, runway lights flashed on, tower controllers stirred, and mechanics busied themselves around Dylan's private plane, the two-engine Lockheed Lodestar jet.

Denver was next, then back to New York, then up to the Pacific Northwest, Hawaii, Australia, Scandinavia, Ireland, England, France, then back home. This was the beginning of the end of one of Dylan's many careers. As he walked into the lunch-canteen room, a mechanic in white overalls peered into the night. "It must get lonely out here," Bob said. Both looked at the field. "It does," the mechanic replied, "but it's a job. I just take the hours they give me." "I know how that feels, I really do," Dylan said, as they stared across prairie land.

He had just evaded fifty fans at his hotel, but a half dozen clustered around the plane. He scribbled his autograph a few times. A shy youth, about seventeen, approached. "Mr. Dylan," he said, nervously, "I'm interested in poetry too." "Yeah, is that so?" Dylan replied. "Yes, sir," the boy answered. "I was wondering if you could spare a few minutes, sometime, to read some poems I've written." "Sure," Bob responded. The young man handed Dylan a large envelope that bulged like a football. "Are all these poems?" Dylan asked. "Yes . . . I've been writing more since I began to study your songs." "Well," Dylan said, "thank you. I'll try to read some tonight. Is your address on the envelope? I'll let you know what I think of them." The boy glowed: "That's wonderful. I hope you like them."

Inside the plane, The Band members were dozing off, a pile of slumping bodies. Road managers Bill Avis and Victor Maimudes checked everyone's seat belt. Dylan and I sat face-to-face. On one knee rested a packet of proofs of his book, *Tarantula*. On his other knee was the fan's envelope. I fussed with my tape recorder, cursing the engine noise. His eyes were nearly slits, but he told me he wouldn't have slept even if I hadn't been there. He just had too much to do.

"It takes a lot of medicine to keep up this pace," Dylan said. "It's very hard, man. A concert tour like this has almost killed me. It's been like this since October. . . . It really drove me out of my mind. . . . I'm really going to cut down. Next year, the concert tour is only going to last a month or two. I'm only doing it like this because I want everyone to know what we're doing." Dylan sent a cloud of cigarette smoke over his head, tugged his shirt collar, and continued. "It's just absurd for people to sit around being offended by their own meaninglessness, so that they have to force everything else to come into the hole with them, and die trying. That's the hang-up here. But I'm not involved with that anymore. I've told you that many times. I don't know if you think I'm kidding, or if you think it's a front. I really just don't *care*—honestly just don't *care*—what people say about me. I don't care what people think about me. I don't care what people know about me.

"Playing on the stage is a kick for me, now. It wasn't before, because I knew what I was doing then was just too empty. . . . It was just dead ambassadors who would come and see me and clap and say: 'Oh, groovy, I would like to meet him and have a cocktail. Perhaps I'll bring my son, Joseph, with me.' And the first thing you know you've got about five or six little boys and girls hanging around with Coke bottles and ginger-ale bottles . . . and you're confronted by some ambassador who's got his hand in your pocket trying to shake your spine and give you compliments. I won't let *anybody* backstage anymore. Even to give me a compliment. I just don't care. . . ."

His eyes cleared: "You can't ask me about how I sleep. You can't ask me about how I make it, and you cannot ask me what I think I am doing here. Other than that, we'll just get along fine. You just ask me anything and I will shoot right back . . . Now, we have one thing straight about the book. I'm going to tell Albert we have come to an understanding about the book. I'll give you as much time as I can. I'll come very quickly to the point in all the things that I want done, but you can easily go back on me . . . But I won't forgive you for doing that, man. It's not going to be a biography, because I'm not dead yet. It's going to be a timeless thing, right?

"Nobody knows about me. What do people really know? That my father's name is Zimmerman and my mother's family is middle class? I'm not about to go around telling people that this is false . . . I'm not covering up anything I did before. I'm not going back on anything, any statement or anything I've done. . . . I've given up trying to tell anybody that they are wrong in their thinking about anything, about the world, or me, or whatever. . . . Now, you are not going to say 'authorized by Bob Dylan.' I'll write four sentences on the cover and sign my name, to something like: 'Bob Shelton wrote me up in the *New York Times* five years ago. And he's a nice guy and I like him. And he wrote this book and for that, it is not'—just to make sure it sells in Nebraska and Wyoming—'it's just not chintzy.' " Dylan laughed.

"There is nothing anybody can expose about me. Everybody thinks that there is such an exposé, on millions of little tiny things, like name change. It doesn't really matter to me. Obviously, there are people who like to read that shit. And people might say 'Oh, I don't believe it,' or 'That doesn't matter to me.' But it tickled them, you know." Twisting restlessly, Dylan was getting angry at the hungers of his audience. He seemed to want to *explain* himself. He tried a new beginning: "I think of all that I do as my *writing*. It cheapens it to call it anything else but writing. But there is not a person on the earth who takes it less seriously than I do. I know that it's not going to help me into heaven one little bit. It's not going to keep me out of the fiery furnace. It's not going to extend my life any and it's not going to make me happy."

What did he think would make him happy? I asked. "I'm happy, you know," he said. "I'm happy to just be able to come across things. I don't need to be happy. Happiness is a kind of cheap word. Let's face it, I'm not the kind of cat that's going to cut off an ear if I can't do something. I would commit suicide. I would shoot myself in the brain if things got bad. I would jump from a window. . . . You know, I can think about death openly. It's nothing to fear. It's nothing sacred. I've seen so many people die." I asked: Is life sacred? "Life's not sacred either," Dylan replied. "Look at all the spirits that actually control the atmosphere, which are not living and yet which attract you, as ideas, or like games with the solar system. Or look at the farce of politics, economy, and war."

Another variation on an old theme: inner despair battling outer hope. "It's become so easy for me to do everything, you have no idea, man, everything at my command. I can make money now doing absolutely anything. But I don't want that kind of money. I'm not a millionaire now, in terms of everything I have. But it is really close . . . This next year, I'm going to be a millionaire, but that means nothing. To be a millionaire means that next year you can lose it all. You must realize that I have not copped out on one thing. I mean, I love what I do. I also make money off it—Hey, I sing honest stuff, man, and it's consistent. It's *all* I do. I don't give a damn what anybody says. Nobody can criticize what I do that's going to have any effect on me. I never really read what people say about me. I'm just not interested.

"When I first really knew that I had money that I couldn't see, I looked around to see what a few of my agents were doing with it. First of all, I like chauffeurs. When I came back from England last time, I didn't buy a chauffeur, but I sure rented one. I make no bones about it . . . I *need* the money to *employ* people. It all works hand in hand. If I had no money, I could walk invisible. But it costs me money now to be able to walk *invisible*. That's the *only* reason I need the money. I don't need the money to buy clothes or nothing. . . ." Again his anger mounted. "I'm sick of giving creeps more off my soul. When I lose my teeth tomorrow, they are not going to buy me a new pair of teeth. I don't like little short people who smoke Tiparillo cigarettes and have their pockets turned inside out all the time and wear glasses and who once wanted to be Groucho Marx making all the money off me. And there are a lot of them. . . . All in the music business.

"Oh, if it's not the promoter cheating you, it's the box office cheating you. Somebody is always giving you a hard time. . . . Even the record company figures won't be right. Nobody's going to be straight with you because nobody wants the information out. Do you know that up to a certain point I made more money on a song I wrote if it were on an album by Carolyn Hester, or anybody, than if I did it myself. That's the contract they gave me. Horrible! Horrible! . . .

"I'm not going to be accepted, but I would like to be accepted . . . by the *Hogtown Dispatch* literary crowd, who wear violets in their crotch and make sure that they get on all the movie and TV reviews and also write about the ladies' auxiliary meetings and the PTA gatherings, you know, all in the same column. I would like to be accepted by them people. But I don't think I'm ever going to be. Whereas the Beatles have been." Did he want the Beatles' sort of acceptance? "No, no, no . . . I'm not saying that. I'm just saying the Beatles have arrived, right? In all music forms, whether Stravinsky or Leopold Jake the Second, who plays in the Five Spot, the Black Muslim Twins, or whatever. The Beatles are accepted, and you've got to accept them for what they do. They play songs like 'Michelle' and 'Yesterday.' A lot of smoothness there."

When I told him Joan Baez planned to record "Yesterday" on her next album, Bob responded: "Yeah, it's the thing to do, to tell all the teeny-boppers, 'I dig the Beatles,' and you sing a song like 'Yesterday' or 'Michelle.' Hey, God knows, it's such a cop-out, man, both of those songs. If you go into the Library of Congress, you can find a lot better than that. There are millions of songs like 'Michelle' and 'Yesterday' written in Tin Pan Alley." There aren't millions of songs like his being written by anyone, I suggested. 'I don't know if I fully appreciate that because it's going to get to the point where nobody else is going to be able to sing my songs but me. Like, I'm going to drive myself right out of business. I'll have to put out ten thousand records a year, for God's sake, because nobody will record the songs I write." Did he influence young people because he broke the rules? "It's not a question of breaking the rules, don't you understand? I don't break the rules, because I don't see any rules to break. As far as I'm concerned, there aren't any rules. . . ."

Like Lenny Bruce, he was riffing, in and out of communication, like a jazzman going in and out of a melody line. It was word music, chin music, symbol music. "My thing is with colors. It's not black and white. It's always been with colors, whether with clothes or anything. Color. Now, with something like that driving you, sometimes it gets very fiery red, you understand? And at times it gets very jet black.

"You just have to make it. When I say 'make it,' I don't mean being a popular folk-rock star. Making it means finding your line. Everybody's line is there, someplace. People think they just have to go through living hell on earth, but I don't really believe that attitude. The only people who believe . . . that life is a tragedy, are the people who are simple, closed-minded, who have to make excuses for themselves. Despite everybody who has been born and has died, the world has just gone on. I mean, look at Napoleon—but we went right on. Look at Harpo Marx—the world went around, it didn't stop for a second. It's sad but true. John Kennedy, right?"

Isn't the difference in what people did when they were here on earth? "Don't you see they did *nothing*? Has anybody done anything? Name anybody you think has done something." Shaw, I said. "George Bernard Shaw," Dylan slowly repeated. "Who has he helped?" "He helped a lot of people to use their heads," I replied, adding: "You've helped a lot of people to use their heads and their ears." "Well," Dylan rejoined, "I don't think I have, that's all. It's funny people think I have. I'm certainly not the one to go around saying that that is what I do. . . . At one time I did read a lot of the stuff that was written about me, maybe three or four years ago. Now, I don't even read anything anymore. So I have no idea what people say about me. I really don't. I do know that a lot of people really like me. I know that . . ."

Eight miles high, over the Great Plains, he joggled *Tarantula* on one knee and the Nebraska boy's poems on the other, an unconscious seesaw. Did he think *Tarantula* was going to be accepted by the literary establishment, by serious poets? ". . . I think a poet is anybody who wouldn't call himself a poet . . . When people start calling me a poet, I say: 'Oh, groovy, how groovy to be called a poet!' But it didn't do me any good, I'll tell you that. It didn't make me any happier.

"Hey, I would love to say that I am a poet. I would really like to think of myself as a poet, but I just can't because of all the slobs who are called poets." Who was a poet, then? Allen Ginsberg? "He's a poet," Dylan fired back. "To be a poet does not necessarily mean that you have to write words on a paper. One of those truck drivers at the motel is a poet. He talks like a poet. I mean what else does a poet have to do? Poets—" his voice trailed off inchoately, ideas running too fast for his tongue. "People like Robert Frost poetry about trees and branches, but that isn't what I mean. . . . Allen Ginsberg is the only writer I know. The rest of the writers I don't have that much respect for. If they really want to do it, they're going to have to *sing* it. . . . I wouldn't call myself a poet for any more reason than I would call myself a protest singer. All that would do would put me in a category with a whole lot of people who would just bother me. To tell anybody I'm a poet would just be fooling people. That would put me in a class, man, with people like Carl Sandburg, T. S. Eliot, Stephen Spender, and Rupert Brooke. Hey, name them—Edna St. Vincent Millay and Robert Louis Stevenson and Edgar Allan Poe and Robert Lowell.

"I know two saintly people," Bob continued. "I know just two holy people. Allen Ginsberg is one. The other, for lack of a better term I just want to call 'this person named Sara.' What I mean by 'holy' is crossing all the boundaries of time and usefulness. . . . William Burroughs is a poet, I like all his old books and Jean Genet's old books. Genet's scholastical lectures are just a waste of time, they are just boring. But if we are talking now in terms of writers I think can be called poets, then Allen must be the best. I mean Allen's 'Kaddish,' not 'Howl.' Allen doesn't have to sing 'Kaddish,' man. You understand what I mean? He just has to lay it down. He's the only poet that I know of. He's the only person I respect who writes, that just totally writes. He don't have to do nothing, man. Allen Ginsberg, he's just holy." How is Sara holy? "I don't want to call her 'a girl.' I know it's very corny, but the only thing I can think of is, more or less, 'madonna-like.'"

I was beginning to think he'd forgotten my tape recorder, when he asked: "Are you getting it all? How much tape do you have left? Is it still running?" He plunged on: "Love and sex are things that really hang everybody up. When things aren't going right and you're really nobody, if you don't get laid in one way or another, you get mean, you know. You get cruel. Now, why in the world sex should force this is beyond me. I truthfully can tell you that male and female are not here to have sex, you know, that's not the purpose. I don't believe that that's God's will, that females have been created so that they can be a counterpart of man's urge. There are too many other things that people just won't let themselves be involved in. Sex and love have nothing to do with female and male. It is just whatever two souls happen to be. It could be male and female, and it might not be male and female. It might be female and female or it might be male and male. You can try to pretend that it doesn't happen, and you can make fun of it and be snide, but that's not really the rightful thing. I know, I know."

His verbal floodstream seemed driven by pressure built up during years of talking guardedly for publication. Inevitably, music displaced all other topics, even though he had remarked to me before we got on the plane that "music is only twenty percent of what I am." "I want you to have explanations of my songs in your book," Dylan said. "Things nobody else will ever have." "Such as," I broke in, "who Mr. Jones is to you?" "Well," Bob parried, "I'm not going to tell you that way. I'm going to tell you about the stuff that *I* want to tell you about . . . I could tell you who Mr. Jones is in my life, but, like, everybody has got their Mr. Jones, so I can't really say that he is the same for everyone." Nothing struck me so strongly as this passage in his two-in-the-morning monologue: "Mr. Jones's loneliness can easily be covered up to the point where he can't recognize that he is alone . . . suddenly locked in a room . . . it's not so incredibly absurd, and it's not so imaginative, to have Mr. Jones in a room with three walls with a midget and a geech and a naked man. Plus a voice, a voice coming in his dream. I'm just a voice speaking. Anytime I'm singing about people, and if the songs are dreamed, it's like my voice is coming out of their dream. . . ."

He was speeding along, now attacking some false myths: "I hung around college, but it's a cop-out from life, from experience. A lot of people started out to be lawyers, but I venture to say that one hundred percent of the really groovy lawyers haven't gotten through school the way they ought to. They've always been freaks in their school, and have always had a hard time making it . . . so many lawyers just take people for what they're worth. They all made deals and all are very criminal . . . but doctors, lawyers, all these kinds of people—they're just in it for money . . . and for resentment. They put in their time and they're going to get it back. I agree with them that way. But I'm sure it could be done in other ways, and it's not. . . . I've known people who've been really loaded down with burdens and who have been in the right to collect, and who have been so innocent, that when they got lawyers to get what they deserve . . . Do you follow me? The parties they are suing make deals with their lawyers. Like, it happens all the time, man. How anybody could have respect for lawyers baffles me! I have lawyers working for me I never see. I don't see my lawyers. Anytime they see the chance, they jump on it. . . ."

Did he want to talk about Joan Baez? Would he shed any light on his attitudes *then* toward one of the most intriguing show-business liaisons of the times, or would he bite my head off? "Me and Joan?" Bob asked. "I'll tell you. I hope you do explain it, if you can do this book straight. She brought me up. . . . I rode on her, but I don't think I owe her anything. . . . I want you to print that, because I am not joking. I feel sorry for her, knowing that I don't have to feel sorry for her, or anybody to feel sorry for her. . . . I feel bad for her because she has nobody to turn to that's going to be straight with her. . . . She hasn't got that much in common with the street vagabonds who play insane instruments. She's not that kind of person. Her family is a very gentle kind of family. She's very fragile and very sick and I lived with her and I loved the place. . . . Can you write this in your book? If you can't, man, it's a waste of time. I mean, is your book going to be a mature book, or is this all just a waste of time?" I reassured him.

Dylan's strangely defiant mood seemed to stress his most unappealing, antiheroic side, daring me, it seemed, to take at face value all his negative thinking or self-destructive patterns. I think that he wanted it understood that behind all the applause, there was a lot of pain. He talked of when we had knocked around the Village together. "After Suze moved out of the house . . . I got very, very strung out for a while. I mean, really, very strung out." But, he told me, he'd survived. "I can do anything, knowing in front that it's not going to catch me and pull me . . . 'cause I've been through it once already. I've been through people. A lot of times you get strung out with people. They are just like junk. . . . The same thing, no more, no less. They kill you the same way. . . . They rot you the same way. . . ." I suggested it reminded me of the line in Sartre's *No Exit*: "Hell is other people." Dylan joked: "Whatever it is, man. I don't know Sartre. He's cross-eyed, that's all I know about him. Anybody cross-eyed can't be all bad. . . ." Then he seemed to hit bottom: "I have a death thing, I know. I have a suicidal thing, I know. . . ."

Later, I asked if he wanted to leave all this despair on the record. He said: "I haven't explained those things I said against myself. . . . A lot of people *think* that I shoot heroin. But that's *baby talk*. . . . I do a lot of things. Hey, I'm not going to sit here and lie to you . . . and make you wonder about all the things I do. I do a lot of things, man, which help me. . . . And I'm smart enough to know that I don't depend on them for my existence, you know, and that's all. Man, that's where it lays, like that. . . ."

I'd been thinking then of how one night at the Gaslight Dylan had advised me "to just write about something that is really important to you." At that time, I couldn't envision that it would be about the man who'd given me the advice. Dylan continued: "I can't be hurt, man, if the book is honest. No kidding, I can't be hurt. Hey, I'm trusting you. . . ." We were bitter then because the folk world was so hostile toward his electric merging of folk and rock. "Nobody told me to go electric," Bob said emphatically. "No, I didn't even ask anybody. I asked not a soul, believe me. . . . Hey, I went electric on my second record. Why don't you bring that out in the book?" Dylan reminded me that the *Freewheelin'* album, released in May 1963, had been meant to include "four electric songs. The only reason they cut out the electric ones was because I didn't write them. . . . Columbia still has them. I don't know if they would play them for you, because I know they are trying to retouch them."

Before the Beatles were known in America and before the folk-rock craze of 1965, Dylan had tried to show he was not a performer to pigeon-hole. "I hate all the labels people have put on me . . . because they are labels. It's just that they are ugly, and I know, in my heart, that it's not me. . . .

I have not *arrived* at where I am at now, I have just *returned* to where I am now, knowing it's the only way. What I am doing now is what I must do before I move on."

Dylan dug his heels in about the music world and his early attraction toward folk music: "I hate to say this, because I don't want it to be taken the wrong way, but I latched on, when I got to New York City, because I saw a huge audience was there. People I *knew* I was not taking advantage of. I knew I wasn't going to stay there. I knew it wasn't my thing. Many times I spoiled it. Many times I went against it. Anytime they tried to think I was like them, I knew I wasn't like them. I just told them whatever happened to be in my mind at the time. I didn't have any respect for any of the organizations. In New York City, they are all organizations. I had respect for the people.

"Woody [Guthrie] turned me on romantically. . . . Woody used his own time, in a way nobody else did. He was just a little bit better . . . just a little smarter, because he was from the country. . . . I met Woody and I talked with him. I dug him. I would dig him, I imagine, if he were around today. . . ." He cited some reservations about Guthrie's style, and I asked if Woody's work seemed too simple for him. "No, not simple at all! The fundamental objection is that I can see *why* he wrote what he wrote. I can see him sitting down and writing what he wrote, in a very calm kind of a way. I am *not* putting him down. I am not copping out of my attraction to him and his influence on me. His influence on me was never in inflection or in voice. What drew me to him was that hearing his voice I could tell he was very lonesome, very alone, and very lost out in his time. That's why I dug him."

Dylan stressed that at the height of his involvement in the folk world, he still loved rock 'n' roll. "Suze Rotolo could tell you, because Suze knows more than anybody else that I played, back in 1961 and 1962, when nobody was around, all those Elvis Presley records. She'll tell you how many nights I stayed up and wrote songs and showed them to her and asked her: 'Is this right?' Because I knew her father and mother were associated with unions and she was into this equality-freedom thing long before I was. I checked the songs out with her. . . . Suze is a very talented girl, man, but she is very frightened. . . ."

We talked about *Sing Out!*, the folk-song magazine. In defense of Dylan's changes, I had wrangled with them. He cautioned me against my wasting time with polemics. Dylan: "Don't you understand? If you're smart, you just gotta keep going, you're just not going to stand still. Everyone else is going to die. I don't mean *die*. I mean, they are going to decay and go crazy. If I could help them, I would love to see them straightened out. But I know in my heart that it is impossible to straighten all these people out, because they are all so nine-to-five, and so involved with that life that it is impossible. I don't want nothing to do with it. *Sing Out!* has a big organization . . . they know they control a lot. They have a very big hand in a lot of money. They have an Establishment. The only person in that organization I respect . . . is Moe Asch, who is old and hip. He's the only one who knows that he's not a clown, that the whole world is not a circus. He knows. The rest of the people there don't know it. They have power . . . fake, phony power. . . . They're dumb, man. . . . They're clods. I never signed their petitions. If you're out of it, groovy! But I'm telling you, man, get out of it. It's not that you have to put them down to leave it."

He eyed the boy's poems, knowing he wouldn't read them that night. I told him how touching it was when he told that airport mechanic how lonely it got out there. "Well, I loved him, man," Dylan replied. "He's a poor cat. What's he doing out there in Nebraska? I just wanted to know. Hey, it's lonesome everyplace. The people that can't live with it, that can't accept it . . . They are just going to blow up the world . . . and make things bad for everybody, ony because they feel so out of place. . . . Everybody has that in common—they are all going to die."

10. Interview with Nat Hentoff, *Playboy*

MARCH 1966

As a versatile musicologist and trenchant social commentator, Nat Hentoff brings uniquely pertinent credentials to his role as interviewer of this month's controversial subject, about whom he writes:

"Less than five years ago, Bob Dylan was scuffling in New York—sleeping in friends' apartments on the Lower East Side and getting very occasional singing work at Gerde's Folk City, an unprepossessing bar for citybillies in the Village. With his leather cap, blue jeans and battered desert boots—his unvarying costume in those days—Dylan looked like an updated, undernourished Huck Finn. And like Huck, he had come out of the Midwest; he would have said 'escaped.' The son of Abraham Zimmerman, an appliance dealer, he was raised in Hibbing, Minnesota, a bleak mining town near the Canadian border. Though he ran away from home regularly, young Zimmerman did manage to finish high school, and went on to spend about six months at the University of Minnesota in 1960. By then, he called himself Bob Dylan—in tribute to Dylan Thomas, according to legend; but actually after a gambling uncle whose last name was similar to Dylan.

"In the fall of that year, he came East to visit his idol, Woody Guthrie, in the New Jersey hospital where the Okie folk-singing bard was wasting away with a progressive disease of the nervous system. Dylan stayed and tried to scrape together a singing career. According to those who knew him then, he was shy and stubborn but basically friendly and, beneath the hipster stance, uncommonly gentle. But they argued about his voice. Some found its flat Midwestern tones gratingly mesmeric; others agreed with a Missouri folk singer who had likened the Dylan sound to that of 'a dog with his leg caught in barbed wire.' All agreed, however, that his songs were strangely personal and often disturbing, a pungent mixture of loneliness and defiance laced with traces of Guthrie, echoes of the Negro blues singers and more than a suggestion of country-and-western; but essentially Dylan was developing his own penetratingly distinctive style. Yet the voice was so harsh and the songs so bitterly scornful of conformity, race prejudice and the mythology of the Cold War that most of his friends couldn't conceive of Dylan making it big.

"They were wrong. In September of 1961, a music critic for *The New York Times* caught his act at Gerde's and hailed the scruffy 19-year-old Minnesotan as a significant new voice on the folk horizon. Around the same time, he was signed by Columbia Records, and his first album was released early the next year. Though it was far from a smash hit, concerts and club engagements gradually multiplied; and then Dylan scored his storied triumph at the Newport Folk Festival in 1962. His next LP began to move, and in the spring of 1963 came his first big single: 'Blowin' in the Wind.' That same spring he turned down a lucrative guest shot on *The Ed Sullivan Show* because CBS wouldn't permit him to sing a mordant parody he'd written about the John Birch Society. For the nation's young, the Dylan image began to form: kind of a singing James Dean with overtones of Holden Caulfield; he was making it, but he wasn't selling out. His concerts began to attract overflow crowds, and his songs—in performances by him and other folk singers—were rushing onto the hit charts. One of them, 'The Times They Are A-Changin',' became an anthem for the rebellious young.

"By 1965 he had become a major phenomenon on the music scene. More and more folk performers, from Joan Baez to the Byrds, considered it mandatory to have an ample supply of Dylan songs in their repertoires; in one frantically appreciative month—last August—48 different recordings of Dylan ballads were pressed by singers other than the composer himself. More and more aspiring folk singers—and folk-song writers—have begun to sound like Dylan. The current surge of 'protest' songs by such long-haired, post-beat rock-'n-rollers as Barry McGuire and Sonny and Cher is credited to Dylan. And the newest commercial boom, 'folk-rock,' a fusion of folk-like lyrics with a rock beat and background, is an outgrowth, in large part, of Dylan's recent decision—decried as a 'sellout' by folknik purists—to perform with a rock-and-roll combo rather than continue to accompany himself alone on the guitar. Backed by the big beat of the new group, Dylan tours England with as much tumultuous success as he does America, and the air play for his single records in both countries is rivaled only by that of the Beatles, Herman's Hermits and the Rolling Stones on the Top 40 deejay shows. In the next 18 months, his income—from personal appearances, records and composer's royalties—is expected to exceed $1,000,000.

"Withal, Dylan seems outwardly much the same as he did during lean years in Greenwich Village. His dress is still casual to the point of exoticism; his hair is still long and frizzy, and he is still no more likely to be seen wearing a necktie than a cutaway. But there have been changes. His songs have become increasingly personal—a surrealistic amalgam of Kafkaesque menace, corrosive satire and opaque sensuality. His lyrics are more crowded than ever with tumbling words and restless images, and they read more like free-verse poems than conventional lines. Adults still have difficulty digging his offbeat language—and its message of alienation—but the young continue to tune in and turn on.

"But there are other changes. Dylan has become elusive. He is no longer seen in his old haunts in the Village and on the Lower East Side. With few exceptions, he avoids interviewers, and in public, he is usually seen from afar at the epicenter of a protective coterie of tousle-topped young men dressed like him, and lissome, straight-haired young ladies who also seem to be dressed like him. His home base, if it can be called that, is a house his manager owns near Woodstock, a fashionable artists' colony in New York State, and he also enjoys the run of his manager's apartment on dignified Gramercy Park in New York City. There are tales told of Dylan the motorcyclist, the novelist, the maker of high-camp home movies; but except among his small circle of intimates, the 24-year-old folk hero is inscrutably aloof.

"It was only after a long period of evasion and hesitation that Dylan finally agreed to grant this 'Playboy Interview'—the longest he's ever given. We met him on the 10th floor of the new CBS and Columbia Records building in mid-Manhattan. The room was antiseptic: white walls with black trim, contemporary furniture with severe lines, avant-garde art chosen by committee, everything in order, neat desks, neat personnel. In this sterile setting, slouched in a chair across from us, Dylan struck a refreshingly discordant note—with his untamed brownish-blond mane brushing the collar of his tieless blue plaid shirt, in his black jacket, gray vaudevillian-striped pipestem pants and well-worn blue-suede shoes. Sitting nearby—also long-haired, tieless and black-jacketed, but wearing faded jeans—was a stringy young man whom the singer identified only as Taco Pronto. As Dylan spoke—in a soft drawl, smiling only rarely and fleetingly, sipping tea and chainsmoking cigarettes—his unspeaking friend chuckled and nodded appreciatively from the side lines. Tense and guarded at first, Dylan gradually began to loosen up, then to open up, as he tried to tell us—albeit a bit surrealistically—just where he's been and where he's going. Under the circumstances, we chose to play straight man in our questions, believing that to have done otherwise would have stemmed the freewheeling flow of Dylan's responses."

PLAYBOY: *"Popular songs," you told a reporter last year, "are the only art form that describes the temper of the times. The only place where it's happening is on the radio and records. That's where the people hang out. It's not in books; it's not on the stage; it's not in the galleries. All this art they've been talking about, it just remains on the shelf. It doesn't make anyone happier." In view of the fact that more people than ever before are reading books and going to plays and art galleries, do you think that statement is borne out by the facts?*

DYLAN: Statistics measure quantity, not quality. The people in the statistics are people who are very bored. Art, if there is such a thing, is in the bathrooms; everybody knows that. To go to an art-gallery thing where you get free milk and doughnuts and where there is a rock-and-roll band playing: That's just a status affair. I'm not putting it down, mind you; but I spend a lot of time in the bathroom. I think museums are vulgar. They're all against sex. Anyhow, I didn't say that people "hang out" on the radio, I said they got "hung *up*" on the radio.

PLAYBOY: *Why do you think rock and roll has become such an international phenomenon?*

DYLAN: I can't really think that there *is* any rock and roll. Actually, when you think about it, anything that has no real existence is bound to become an international phenomenon. Anyway, what does it mean, rock and roll? Does it mean Beatles, does it mean John Lee Hooker, Bobby Vinton, Jerry Lewis' kid? What about Lawrence Welk? He must play a few rock-and-roll songs. Are all these people the same? Is Ricky Nelson like Otis Redding? Is Mick Jagger really Ma Rainey? I can tell by the way people hold their cigarettes if they like Ricky Nelson. I couldn't care *less* if somebody likes Ricky Nelson. But I think we're getting off the track here. There *isn't* any Ricky Nelson. There isn't any Beatles; oh, I take that back: there are a lot of beetles. But there isn't any Bobby Vinton. Anyway, the word is not "international phenomenon"; the word is "parental nightmare."

PLAYBOY: *Has jazz lost much of its appeal to the younger generation?*

DYLAN: I don't think jazz has *ever* appealed to the younger generation. Anyway, I don't really know who this younger generation is. I don't think they could get into a jazz club anyway. But jazz is hard to follow; I mean you actually have to *like* jazz to follow it; and my motto is, never follow *anything*. I don't know what the motto of the younger generation is, but I would think they'd have to follow their parents. I mean, what would some parent say to his kid if the kid came home with a glass eye, a Charlie Mingus record and a pocketful of feathers? He'd say, "Who are you following?" And the poor kid would have to stand there with water in his shoes, a bow tie on his ear and soot pouring out of his belly button and say, "Jazz. Father, I've been following jazz." And his father would probably say, "Get a broom and clean up all that soot before you go to sleep." Then the kid's mother would tell her friends, "Our little Donald, he's part of the younger generation, you know."

PLAYBOY: *You used to say that you wanted to perform as little as possible, that you wanted to keep most of your time to yourself. Yet you're doing more concerts and cutting more records every year. Why? Is it the money?*

DYLAN: Everything is changed now from before. Last spring, I guess I was going to quit singing. I was very drained, and the way things were going, it was a very draggy situation—I mean, when you do *Everybody Loves You for Your Black Eye*, and meanwhile the back of your head is caving in. Anyway, I was playing a lot of songs I didn't want to play. I was singing words I didn't really want to sing. I don't mean words like "God" and "mother" and "President" and "suicide" and "meat cleaver." I mean simple little words like "if" and "hope" and "you." But *Like a Rolling Stone* changed it all; I didn't care anymore after that about writing books or poems or whatever. I mean it was something that I myself could dig. It's very tiring having other people tell you how much they dig you if you yourself don't dig you. It's also very deadly entertainmentwise. Contrary to what some scary people think, I don't play with a band now for any kind of propaganda-type or commercial-type reasons. It's just that my songs are pictures and the band makes the sound of the pictures.

PLAYBOY: *Do you feel that acquiring a combo and switching from folk to folk-rock has improved you as a performer?*

DYLAN: I'm not interested in myself as a performer. Performers are people who perform for other people. Unlike actors, I know what I'm saying. It's very simple in my mind. It doesn't matter what kind of audience reaction this whole thing gets. What happens on the stage is straight. It doesn't expect any rewards or fines from any kind of outside agitators. It's ultra-simple, and would exist whether anybody was looking or not.

As far as folk and folk-rock are concerned, it doesn't matter what kind of nasty names people invent for the music. It could be called arsenic music, or perhaps Phaedra music. I don't think that such a word as folk-rock has anything to do with it. And folk music is a word I can't use. Folk music is a bunch of fat people. I have to think of all this as traditional music. Traditional music is based on hexagrams. It comes about from legends, Bibles, plagues, and it revolves around vegetables and death. There's nobody that's going to kill traditional music. All these songs about roses growing out of people's brains and lovers who are really geese and swans that turn into angels—they're not going to die. It's all those paranoid people who think that someone's going to come and take away their toilet paper—*they're* going to die. Songs like *Which Side Are You On?* And *I Love You, Porgy*—they're not folk-music songs; they're political songs. They're already dead. Obviously, death is not very universally accepted. I mean, you'd think that the traditional-music people could gather from their songs that mystery—just plain simple mystery—is a fact, a traditional fact. I listen to the old ballads; but I wouldn't go to a *party* and listen to the old ballads. I could give you descriptive detail of what they do to me, but some people would probably think my imagination had gone mad. It strikes me funny that people actually have the gall to think that I have some kind of fantastic imagination. It gets very lonesome. But anyway, traditional music is too unreal to die. It doesn't need to be protected. Nobody's going to hurt it. In that music is the only true, valid death you can feel today off a record player. But like anything else in great demand, people try to own it. It has to do with a purity thing. I think its meaninglessness is holy. Everybody knows that I'm not a folk singer.

PLAYBOY: *Some of your old fans would agree with you—and not in a complimentary vein—since your debut with the rock-and-roll combo at last year's Newport Folk Festival, where many of them booed you loudly for "selling out" to commercial pop tastes. How do you feel about it?*

DYLAN: I was kind of stunned. But I can't put anybody down for coming and booing; after all, they paid to get in. They could have been maybe a little quieter and not so persistent, though. There were a lot of old people there, too; lots of whole families had driven down from Vermont, lots of nurses and their parents, and well, like they just came to hear some relaxing hoedowns, you know, maybe an Indian polka or two. And just when everything's going all right, here I come on, and the whole place turns into a beer factory. There were a lot of people there who were very pleased that I got booed. I saw them afterward. I do resent somewhat, though, that everybody that booed said they did it because they were old fans.

PLAYBOY: *What about their charge that you vulgarized your natural gifts?*

DYLAN: What can I say? I'd like to *see* one of these so-called fans. I'd like to have him blindfolded and brought to me. It's like going out to the desert and screaming, and then having little kids throw their sandbox at you. I'm only 24. These people that said this—were they Americans?

PLAYBOY: *Americans or not, there were a lot of people who didn't like your new sound. In view of this widespread negative reaction, do you think you may have made a mistake in changing your style?*

DYLAN: A mistake is to commit a misunderstanding. There could be no such thing, anyway, as this action. Either people understand or they *pretend* to understand—or else they really *don't* understand. What you're speaking of here is doing wrong things for selfish reasons. I don't know the word for that, unless it's suicide. In any case, it has nothing to do with my music.

PLAYBOY: *Mistake or not, what made you decide to go the rock-and-roll route?*

DYLAN: Carelessness. I lost my one true love. I started drinking. I wind up in Phoenix. I get a job as a Chinaman. I start working in a dime store, and move in with a 13-year-old girl. Then this big Mexican lady from Philadelphia comes in and burns the house down. I go down to Dallas. I get a job as a "before" in a Charles Atlas "before and after" ad. I move in with a delivery boy who can cook fantastic chili and hot dogs. Then this 13-year-old girl from Phoenix comes and burns the house down. The next thing I know I'm in Omaha. It's so cold there, by this time I'm robbing my own bicycles and frying my own fish. I move in with a high school teacher who also does a little plumbing on the side, who ain't much to look at, but who's built a special kind of refrigerator that can turn newspaper into lettuce. Everything's going good until that delivery boy shows up and tries to knife me. Needless to say, he burned the house down, and I hit the road. The first guy that picked me up asked me if I wanted to be a star. What could I say?

PLAYBOY: *And that's how you became a rock-and-roll singer?*

DYLAN: No, that's how I got tuberculosis.

PLAYBOY: *Let's turn the question around: Why have you stopped composing and singing protest songs?*

DYLAN: I've stopped composing and singing anything that has either a reason to be written or a motive to be sung. Don't get me wrong, now. "Protest" is not my word. I've never thought of myself as such. The word "protest," I think, was made up for people undergoing surgery. It's an amusement-park word. A normal person in his righteous mind would have to have the hiccups to pronounce it honestly. The word "message" strikes me as having a hernia-like sound. It's just like the word "delicious." Also the word "marvelous." You know, the English can say "marvelous" pretty good. They can't say "raunchy" so good, though. Well, we each have our thing. Anyway, message songs, as everybody knows, are a drag. It's only college newspaper editors and single girls under 14 who could possibly have time for them.

PLAYBOY: *You've said you think message songs are vulgar. Why?*

DYLAN: Well, first of all, anybody that's got a message is going to learn from experience that they can't put it into a song. I mean it's just not going to come out the same message. After one or two of these unsuccessful attempts, one realizes that his resultant message, which is not even the same message he thought up and began with, he's now got to stick by it; because, after all, a song leaves your mouth just as soon as it leaves your hands. You've got to respect other people's right to also have a message themselves. Myself, what I'm going to do is rent Town Hall and put about 30 Western Union boys on the bill. I mean, then there'll really be some messages. People will be able to come and hear more messages than they've ever heard before in their life.

PLAYBOY: *But your early ballads have been called "songs of passionate protest." Wouldn't that make them "message" music?*

DYLAN: This is unimportant. Don't you understand? I've been writing since I was eight years old. I've been playing the guitar since I was ten. I was raised playing and writing whatever it was I had to play and write.

PLAYBOY: *Would it be unfair to say that you were motivated commercially rather than creatively in writing the kind of songs that made you popular?*

DYLAN: All right, now, look. It's not all that deep. It's not a complicated thing. My motives, or whatever they are, were never commercial in the money sense of the word. It was more in the don't-die-by-the-hacksaw sense of the word. I never did it for money. It happened, and I let it happen to me. There was no reason *not* to let it happen to me. I couldn't have written before what I write now, anyway. The songs used to be about what I felt and saw. Nothing of my own rhythmic vomit ever entered into it. Vomit is not romantic. I used to think songs are supposed to be romantic. And I didn't want to sing anything that was unspecific. Unspecific things have no sense of time. All of us people have no sense of time; it's a dimensional hangup. Anybody can be specific and obvious. That's always been the easy way. The leaders of the world take the easy way. It's not that it's so difficult to be unspecific and less obvious; it's just that there's nothing, absolutely nothing, to be specific and obvious *about*. My older songs, to say the least, were about nothing. The newer ones are about the same nothing—only as seen inside a bigger thing, perhaps called the nowhere. But this is all very constipated. I *do* know what my songs are about.

PLAYBOY: *And what's that?*

DYLAN: Oh, some are about four minutes; some are about five, and some, believe it or not, are about eleven.

PLAYBOY: *As you know, it's the age group from about 16 to 25 that listens to your songs. Why, in your opinion?*

DYLAN: I don't see what's so strange about an age group like that listening to my songs. I'm hip enough to know that it ain't going to be the 85-to-90-year-olds. If the 85-to-90-year-olds *were* listening to me, they'd know that I can't tell them anything. The 16-to-25-year-olds, they probably know that I can't tell *them* anything either—and they know that *I* know it. It's a funny business. Obviously, I'm not an IBM computer any more than I'm an ashtray. I mean it's obvious to anyone who's ever slept in the back seat of a car that I'm just not a schoolteacher.

PLAYBOY: *Even though you're not a schoolteacher, wouldn't you like to help the young people who dig you from turning into what some of their parents have become?*

DYLAN: Well, I must say that I really don't know their parents. I really don't know if *anybody's* parents are so bad. Now, I hate to come on like a weakling or a coward, and I realize it might seem kind of irreligious, but I'm really not the right person to tramp around the country saving souls. I wouldn't run over anybody that was laying in the street, and I certainly wouldn't become a hangman. I wouldn't think twice about giving a starving man a cigarette. But I'm not a shepherd. And I'm not about to save anybody from fate, which I know nothing about. "Parents" is not the key word here. The key word is "destiny." I can't save them from that.

PLAYBOY: *Still, thousands of young people look up to you as a kind of folk hero. Do you feel some sense of responsibility toward them?*

DYLAN: I don't feel I have any responsibility, no. Whoever it is that listens to my songs owes *me* nothing. How could I possibly have any responsibility to any kind of thousands? What could possibly make me think that I owe anybody anything who just happens to be there? I've never written any song that begins with the words "I've gathered you here tonight . . ." I'm not about to tell anybody to be a good boy or a good girl and they'll go to heaven. I really don't know what the people who are on the receiving end of these songs think of me, anyway. It's horrible. I'll bet Tony Bennett doesn't have to go through this kind of thing. I wonder what Billy the Kid would have answered to such a question.

PLAYBOY: *In their admiration for you, many young people have begun to imitate the way you dress which one adult commentator has called "self-consciously oddball and defiantly sloppy." What's your reaction to that kind of put-down?*

DYLAN: Bullshit. Oh, such bullshit. I know the fellow that said that. He used to come around here and get beat up all the time. He better watch it; some people are after him. They're going to strip him naked and stick him in Times Square. They're going to tie him up, and also put a thermometer in his mouth. Those kind of morbid ideas and remarks are so petty—I mean there's a war going on. People got rickets; everybody wants to start a riot; 40-year-old women are eating spinach by the carload; the doctors haven't got a cure for cancer—and here's some hillbilly talking about how he doesn't like somebody's clothes. Worse than that, it gets printed and innocent people have to read it. This is a terrible thing. And he's a terrible man. Obviously, he's just living off the fat of himself, and he's expecting his kids to take care of him. His kids probably listen to my records. Just because my clothes are too long, does that mean I'm unqualified for what I do?

PLAYBOY: *No, but there are those who think it does—and many of them seem to feel the same way about your long hair. But compared with the shoulder-length coiffures worn by some of the male singing groups these days, your tonsorial tastes are on the conservative side. How do you feel about these far-out hair styles?*

DYLAN: The thing that most people don't realize is that it's warmer to have long hair. Everybody wants to be warm. People with short hair freeze easily. Then they try to hide their coldness, and they get jealous of everybody that's warm. Then they become either barbers or Congressmen. A lot of prison wardens have short hair. Have you ever noticed that Abraham Lincoln's hair was much longer than John Wilkes Booth's?

PLAYBOY: *Do you think Lincoln wore his hair long to keep his head warm?*

DYLAN: Actually, I think it was for medical reasons, which are none of my business. But I guess if you figure it out, you realize that all of one's hair surrounds and lays on the brain inside your head. Mathematically speaking, the more of it you can get out of your head, the better. People who want free minds sometimes overlook the fact that you have to have an uncluttered brain. Obviously, if you get your hair on the outside of your head, your brain will be a little more freer. But all this talk about long hair is just a trick. It's been thought up by men and women who look like cigars—the anti-happiness committee. They're all freeloaders and cops. You can tell who they are: They're always carrying calendars, guns or scissors. They're all trying to get into your quicksand. They think you've got something. I don't know why Abe Lincoln had long hair.

PLAYBOY: *Until your abandonment of "message" songs, you were considered not only a major voice in the student protest movement but a militant champion of the civil rights struggle. According to friends, you seemed to feel a special bond of kinship with the Student Nonviolent Coordinating Committee. Why have you withdrawn from participation in all these causes? Have you lost interest in protest as well as in protest songs?*

DYLAN: As far as SNCC is concerned, I knew some of the people in it, but I only knew them as people, not as of any part of something that was bigger or better than themselves. I didn't even know what civil rights was before I met some of them. I mean, I knew there were

Negroes, and I knew there were a lot of people who don't *like* Negroes. But I got to admit that if I didn't know some of the SNCC people, I would have gone on thinking that Martin Luther King was really nothing more than some underprivileged war hero. I haven't lost any interest in protest since then. I just didn't have any interest in protest to begin with—any more than I did in war heroes. You can't lose what you've never had. Anyway, when you don't like your situation, you either leave it or else you overthrow it. You can't just stand around and whine about it. People just get aware of your noise; they really don't get aware of *you*. Even if they give you what you want, it's only because you're making too much noise. First thing you know, you want something else, and then you want something else, and then you want something else, until finally it isn't a joke anymore, and whoever you're protesting against finally gets all fed up and stomps on everybody. Sure, you can go around trying to bring up people who are lesser than you, but then don't forget, you're messing around with gravity. I don't fight gravity. I do believe in equality, but I also believe in distance.

PLAYBOY: *Do you mean people keeping their racial distance?*

DYLAN: I believe in people keeping everything they've got.

PLAYBOY: *Some people might feel that you're trying to cop out of fighting for the things you believe in.*

DYLAN: Those would be people who think I have some sort of responsibility toward *them*. They probably want me to help them make friends. I don't know. They probably either want to set me in their house and have me come out every hour and tell them what time it is, or else they just want to stick me in between the mattress. How could they possibly understand what I believe in?

PLAYBOY: *Many of your folk-singing colleagues remain actively involved in the fight for civil rights, free speech and withdrawal from Vietnam. Do you think they're wrong?*

DYLAN: I don't think they're wrong, if that's what they see themselves doing. But don't think that what you've got out there is a bunch of little Buddhas all parading up and down. People that use God as a weapon should be amputated upon. You see it around here all the time: "Be good or God won't like you, and you'll go to hell." Things like that. People that march with slogans and things tend to take themselves a little too holy. It would be a drag if they, too, started using God as a weapon.

PLAYBOY: *Do you think it's pointless to dedicate yourself to the cause of peace and racial equality?*

DYLAN: Not pointless to dedicate yourself to peace and racial equality, but rather, it's pointless to dedicate yourself to the *cause*: that's *really* pointless. That's very unknowing. To say "cause of peace" is just like saying "hunk of butter." I mean, how can you listen to anybody who wants you to believe he's dedicated to the hunk and not to the butter? People who can't conceive of how others hurt, they're trying to change the world. They're all afraid to admit that they don't really know each other. They'll all probably be here long after we've gone, and we'll give birth to new ones. But they themselves—I don't think *they'll* give birth to *anything*.

PLAYBOY: *You sound a bit fatalistic.*

DYLAN: I'm not fatalistic. Bank tellers are fatalistic; clerks are fatalistic. I'm a farmer. Who ever heard of a fatalistic farmer? I'm not fatalistic. I smoke a lot of cigarettes, but that doesn't make me fatalistic.

PLAYBOY: *We take it you don't share Pete Seeger's belief that songs can change people, that they can help build international understanding.*

DYLAN: On the international understanding part, that's OK. But you have a translation problem there. Anybody with this kind of a level of thinking has to also think about this translation thing. But I don't believe songs can change people anyway. I'm not Pinocchio. I consider that an insult. I'm not part of that. I don't blame anybody for thinking that way. But I just don't donate any money to them. I don't consider them anything like unhip: they're more in the rubber-band category.

PLAYBOY: *How do you feel about those who have risked imprisonment by burning their draft cards to signify their opposition to U.S. involvement in Vietnam, and by refusing—as your friend Joan Baez has done—to pay their income taxes as a protest against the Government's expenditures on war and weaponry? Do you think they're wasting their time?*

DYLAN: Burning draft cards isn't going to end any war. It's not even going to save any lives. If someone can feel more honest with himself by burning his draft card, then that's great; but if he's just going to feel more important because he does it, then that's a drag. I really don't know too much about Joan Baez and her income-tax problems. The only thing I can tell you about Joan Baez is that she's not Belle Starr.

PLAYBOY: *Writing about "beard-wearing draft-card burners and pacifist income-tax evaders," one columnist called such protesters "no less outside society than the junkie, the homosexual or the mass murderer." What's your reaction?*

DYLAN: I don't believe in those terms. They're too hysterical. They don't describe anything. Most people think that homosexual, gay, queer, queen, faggot are all the same words. Everybody thinks that a junkie is a dope freak. As far as I'm concerned, I don't consider myself outside of anything. I just consider myself *not around.*

PLAYBOY: *Joan Baez recently opened a school in northern California for training of civil rights workers in the philosophy and techniques of nonviolence. Are you in sympathy with that concept?*

DYLAN: If you mean do I agree with it or not, I really don't see anything to be in agreement *with.* If you mean has it got my approval, I guess it does, but my approval really isn't going to do it any good. I don't know about other people's sympathy, but my sympathy runs to the lame and crippled and beautiful things. I have a feeling of loss of power—something like a reincarnation feeling; I don't feel that for mechanical things like cars or schools. I'm sure it's a *nice* school, but if you're asking me would I go to it, I would have to say no.

PLAYBOY: *You seem to take a dim view of schooling in general, whatever the subject.*

DYLAN: I really don't think about it.

PLAYBOY: *Well, have you ever had any regrets about not completing college?*

DYLAN: That would be ridiculous. Colleges are like old-age homes; except for the fact that more people die in colleges than in old-age homes, there's really no difference. People have one great blessing—obscurity—and not really too many people are thankful for it. Everybody is always taught to be thankful for their food and clothes and things like that, but not to be thankful for their obscurity. Schools don't teach that; they teach people to be rebels and lawyers. I'm not going to put down the reading system; that would be too silly. It's just that it really doesn't have too much to teach.

PLAYBOY: *Would you advise young people to skip college, then?*

DYLAN: I wouldn't advise anybody to do anything. I certainly wouldn't advise somebody not to go to college; I just wouldn't pay his *way* through college.

PLAYBOY: *Do the things one learns in college help enrich one's life?*

DYLAN: I don't think anything like that is going to enrich my life, no—not *my* life, anyway. Things are going to happen whether I know why they happen or not. It just gets more complicated when you stick *yourself* into it. You don't find out why things move. You *let* them move; you *watch* them move; you *stop* them from moving; you *start* them moving. But you don't sit around and try to figure out *why* there's movement—unless, of course, you're just an innocent moron, or some wise old Japanese man. Out of all the people who just lay around and ask "Why?", how many do you figure really want to know?

PLAYBOY: *Can you suggest a better use for the four years that would otherwise be spent in college?*

DYLAN: Well, you could hang around in Italy; you could go to Mexico; you could become a dishwasher; you could even go to Arkansas. I don't know; there are thousands of things to do and places to go. Everybody thinks that you have to bang your head against the wall, but it's silly when you really think about it. I mean, here you have fantastic scientists working on ways to prolong human living, and then you have other people who take it for granted that you have to beat your head against the wall in order to be happy. You can't take everything you don't like as a personal insult. I guess you should go where your wants are bare, where you're invisible and not needed.

PLAYBOY: *Would you classify sex among your wants, wherever you go?*

DYLAN: Sex is a temporary thing; sex isn't love. You can get sex anywhere. If you're looking for someone to *love* you, now that's different. I guess you have to stay in college for that.

PLAYBOY: *Do you have any difficulty relating to people—or vice versa?*

DYLAN: Well, sometimes I have the feeling that other people want my *soul*. If I say to them, "I don't *have* a soul," they say, "I know that. You don't have to tell me that. Not me. How dumb do you think I am? I'm your *friend*." What can I say except that I'm sorry and I feel bad? I guess maybe feeling bad and paranoia are the same thing.

PLAYBOY: *Paranoia is said to be one of the mental states sometimes induced by such hallucinogenic drugs as peyote and LSD. Considering the risks involved, do you think that experimentation with such drugs should be part of the growing-up experience for a young person?*

DYLAN: I wouldn't advise anybody to use drugs—certainly not the hard drugs; drugs are medicine. But opium and hash and pot—now, those things aren't drugs; they just bend your mind a little. I think *everybody's* mind should be bent once in a while. Not by LSD, though. LSD is medicine—a different kind of medicine. It makes you aware of the universe, so to speak; you realize how foolish *objects* are. But LSD is not for groovy people; it's for mad, hateful people who want revenge. It's for people who usually have heart attacks. They ought to use it at the Geneva Convention.

PLAYBOY: *Are you concerned, as you approach 30, that you begin to "go square," lose some of your openness to experience, become leery of change and new experiment?*

DYLAN: No. But if it happens, then it happens. What can I say? There doesn't seem to *be* any tomorrow. Every time I wake up, no matter in what position, it's always been today. To look ahead and start worrying about trivial little things I can't really say has any more importance than looking back and *remembering* trivial little things. I'm not going to become any poetry instructor at any girls' school; I know *that* for sure. But that's about *all* I know for sure. I'll just keep doing these different things, I guess.

PLAYBOY: *Such as?*

DYLAN: Waking up in different positions.

PLAYBOY: *What else?*

DYLAN: I'm just like anybody else; I'll try anything once.

PLAYBOY: *Including theft and murder?*

DYLAN: I can't really say that I wouldn't commit theft or murder and expect anybody to really believe me. I wouldn't believe anybody if they told me that.

PLAYBOY: *By their mid-20s, most people have begun to settle into their niche, to find a place in society. But you've managed to remain inner-directed and uncommitted. What was it that spurred you to run away from home six times between the ages of ten and eighteen and finally leave for good?*

DYLAN: It was nothing; it was just an accident of geography. Like if I was born and raised in New York or Kansas City, I'm sure everything would have turned out different. But Hibbing, Minnesota, was just not the right place for me to stay and live. There really was nothing there. The only thing you could do there was be a miner, and even that kind of thing was getting less and less. The mines were just dying, that's all; but that's not their fault. *Everybody* about my age left there. It was no great romantic thing. It didn't take any great amount of thinking or individual genius, and there certainly wasn't any pride in it. I didn't run away from it; I just turned my back on it. It couldn't give me anything. It was very void-like. So leaving wasn't hard at all; it would have been much harder to stay. I didn't want to die there. As I think about it now, though, it wouldn't be such a bad place to go back to and die in. There's no place I feel closer to now, or get the feeling that I'm part of, except maybe New York; but I'm *not* a New Yorker. I'm North Dakota–Minnesota–Midwestern. I'm *that* color. I speak that way. I'm from someplace called Iron Range. My brains and feeling have come from there. I wouldn't amputate on a drowning man; nobody from out there would.

PLAYBOY: *Today, you're on your way to becoming a millionaire. Do you feel in any danger of being trapped by all this affluence—by the things it can buy?*

DYLAN: No, my world is very small. Money can't really improve it any; money can just keep it from being smothered.

PLAYBOY: *As a man with three thriving careers—as a concert performer, recording star and songwriter—do you ever feel boxed in by such noncreative responsibilities?*

DYLAN: No, I've got other people to do that for me. They watch my money; they guard it. They keep their eyes on it at all times; they're supposed to be very smart when it comes to money. They know just what to do with my money. I pay them a lot of it. I don't really speak to them much, and they don't really speak to me at all, so I guess everything is all right.

PLAYBOY: *If fortune hasn't trapped you, how about fame? Do you find that your celebrity makes it difficult to keep your private life intact?*

DYLAN: My private life has been dangerous from the beginning. All this does is add a little atmosphere.

PLAYBOY: *You used to enjoy wandering across the country—taking off on open-end trips, roughing it from town to town, with no particular destination in mind. But you seem to be doing much less of that these days. Why? Is it because you're too well known?*

DYLAN: It's mainly because I have to be in Cincinnati Friday night, and the next night I got to be in Atlanta, and then the next night after that, I have to be in Buffalo. Then I have to write some more songs for a record album.

PLAYBOY: *Do you get the chance to ride your motorcycle much anymore?*

DYLAN: I'm still very patriotic to the highway, but I don't ride my motorcycle too much anymore, no.

PLAYBOY: *How do you get your kicks these days, then?*

DYLAN: I hire people to look into my eyes, and then I have them kick me.

PLAYBOY: *That's how you get your kicks?*

DYLAN: No. Then I *forgive* them; that's where my kicks come in.

PLAYBOY: *You told an interviewer last year, "I've done everything I ever wanted to." If that's true, what do you have to look forward to?*

DYLAN: Salvation. Just plain salvation.

PLAYBOY: *Anything else?*

DYLAN: Praying. I'd also like to start a cookbook magazine. And I've always wanted to be a boxing referee. I want to referee a heavyweight championship fight. Can you imagine that? Can you imagine any fighter in his right mind recognizing me?

PLAYBOY: *If your popularity were to wane, would you welcome being anonymous again?*

DYLAN: You mean welcome it, like I'd welcome some poor pilgrim coming in from the rain? No, I wouldn't welcome it; I'd accept it, though. Someday, obviously, I'm going to *have* to accept it.

PLAYBOY: *Do you ever think about marrying, settling down, having a home, maybe living abroad? Are there any luxuries you'd like to have, say, a yacht or a Rolls-Royce?*

DYLAN: No, I don't think about those things. If I felt like buying anything, I'd buy it. What you're asking me about is the future, *my* future. I'm the last person in the world to ask about my future.

PLAYBOY: *Are you going to be passive and just let things happen to you?*

DYLAN: Well, that's being very philosophical about it, but I guess it's true.

PLAYBOY: *You once planned to write a novel. Do you still?*

DYLAN: I don't think so. All my writing goes into songs now. Other forms don't interest me anymore.

PLAYBOY: *Do you have any unfulfilled ambitions?*

DYLAN: Well, I guess I've always wanted to be Anthony Quinn in *La Strada*. Not always—only for about six years now; it's not one of those childhood-dream things. Oh, and come to think of it, I guess I've always wanted to be Brigitte Bardot, too; but I don't want to think about *that* too much.

PLAYBOY: *Did you ever have the standard boyhood dream of growing up to be President?*

DYLAN: No. When I was a boy, Harry Truman was President; who'd want to be Harry Truman?

PLAYBOY: *Well, let's suppose that you were the President. What would you accomplish during your first thousand days?*

DYLAN: Well, just for laughs, so long as you insist, the first thing I'd do is probably move the White House. Instead of being in Texas, it'd be on the East Side in New York. McGeorge Bundy would definitely have to change his name, and General McNamara would be forced to wear a coonskin cap and shades. I would immediately rewrite *The Star-Spangled Banner*, and little school children, instead of memorizing *America the Beautiful*, would have to memorize *Desolation Row*. And I would immediately call for a showdown with Mao Tse-tung. I would fight him *personally*—and I'd get somebody to film it.

PLAYBOY: *One final question: Even though you've more or less retired from political and social protest, can you conceive of any circumstance that might persuade you to reinvolve yourself?*

DYLAN: No, not unless all the people in the world disappeared.

11. Interview with John Cohen and Happy Traum, *Sing Out!*

OCTOBER/NOVEMBER 1968

. . . JC: *I recall a conversation we had in* 1962 . . . *I don't know if I was seeing something, or wishing something on you—but I had just come back from Kentucky and you showed me "Hard Rain," at Gerde's or upstairs from the Gaslight* . . .

I believe at the time, you were wondering how it fit into music. How I was going to sing it.

JC: *That was my initial reaction. That's really ancient history now because a whole aesthetic, a whole other approach has come into music since then, to make it very possible to sing that kind of song.*

Yes, that's right.

JC: *Before then it wasn't so possible. The question I asked you on seeing this stream of words was, if you were going to write things like that, then why do you need Woody Guthrie? How about Rimbaud? And you didn't know Rimbaud* . . . *yet.*

No, not until a few years ago.

JC: *Back then, you and Allen Ginsberg met.*

Al Aronowitz, a reporter from the *Saturday Evening Post*, introduced me to Allen Ginsberg and his friend Peter Orlovsky, above a bookstore on 8th street, in the fall of '64 or '65. I'd heard his name for many years. At that time these two fellas had just gotten back from a trip to India. Their knapsacks were in the corner and they were cooking a dinner at the time. I saw him again at Washington Square, at a party . . .

JC: *At that time, for you, was there a stronger leaning towards poetry, and the kind of thing that Allen had dealt with? . . . as opposed to what Woody had dealt with.*

Well, the language which they were writing, you could read off the paper, and somehow it would begin some kind of tune in your mind. I don't really know what it was, but you could see it was possible to do more than what . . . not more . . . something different than what Woody and people like Aunt Molly Jackson and Jim Garland did. The subject matter of all their songs wasn't really accurate for me; I could see that they'd written thousands of songs, but it was all with the same heartfelt subject matter . . . whereas that subject matter did not exist then, and I knew it. There was a sort of semi-feeling of it existing, but as you looked around at the people, it didn't really exist the way it probably existed back then, there was no real movement, there was only organized movement. There wasn't any type of movement which was a day by day, livable movement. When that subject matter wasn't there anymore for me, the only thing that was there was the style. The idea of this type of song which you can live with in some kind of way, which you don't feel embarrassed twenty minutes after you've sung it; that type of song where you don't have to question yourself . . . where you're just wasting your time.

JC: *I don't know which was the cart and which was the horse, but people were asking about your music (and Phil Ochs' and others'), "Is this stuff poetry or is this song?"*

Yes, well you always have people asking questions.

JC: *What I'm trying to get at is whether you were reading a lot then, books, literature? Were your thoughts outside of music?*

No, my mind was with the music. I tried to read, but I usually would lay the book down. I never have been a fast reader. My thoughts weren't about reading, no . . . they were just about that feeling that was in the air. I tried to somehow get ahold of that, and write that down, and using my musical training to sort of guide it by, and in the end, have something I could do for a living.

JC: *Training!*

Yes, training. You have to have some. I can remember traveling through towns, and if somebody played the guitar, that's who you went to see. You didn't necessarily go to meet them, you just went necessarily to watch them, listen to them, and if possible, learn how to do something . . . whatever he was doing. And usually at that time it was quite a selfish type of thing. You could see the people, and if you knew you could do what they were doing with just a little practice, and you were looking for something else, you could just move on. But when it was down at the bottom, everyone played the guitar, and when you knew that they knew more than you, well, you just had to listen to everybody. It wasn't necessarily a song; it was technique and style, and tricks and all those combinations which go together—which I certainly spent a lot of hours just trying to do what other people have been doing. That's what I mean by training.

JC: *It's hard for me, because this is an interview and can't be just a conversation . . . like the tape recorder is the third element . . . I can't just say to your face that you did something great, that I admire you . . .*

Well in my mind, let me tell you John, I can see a thousand people who I think are great, but I've given up mentioning names anymore. Every time I tell somebody who I think is pretty good, they just shrug their shoulders . . . and so I now do the same thing. Take a fellow like Doc Watson, the fellow can play the guitar with such ability . . . just like water running. Now where do you place somebody like that in the current flow of music? Now he doesn't use any tricks. But that has to do with age, I imagine, like how long he lives.

JC: *I think it's also got to do with the age he comes from, he doesn't come from yours or mine.*

No, but I'm a firm believer in the longer you live, the better you get.

JC: *But Doc is different from you and me. I know people who hate your voice. They can't stand that sound, that kind of singing, that grating. The existence of your voice and people like you, like Roscoe Holcomb, it challenges their very existence. They can't conceive of that voice in the same breath as their own lives.*

Well my voice is one thing, but someone actually having hate for Roscoe Holcomb's voice, that beautiful high tenor, I can't see that. What's the difference between Roscoe Holcomb's voice and Bill Monroe's?

JC: *I don't think Bill likes Roscoe's voice. Bill sings with such control. Roscoe's voice is so uncontrolled.*

Well Bill Monroe is most likely one of the best, but Roscoe does have a certain untamed sense of control which also makes him one of the best.

JC: *I don't think Doc Watson's voice and your voice are compatible, it doesn't bother me.*

No, no . . . maybe some day, though.

———

JC: *I'd like to talk about the material in the songs.*

All right.

JC: *Well, I mean your music is fine, it's complete . . . but what I'm asking about is the development of your thoughts . . . which could be called "words." That's why I was asking about your poetry and literature. Where do these things come upon a person? Maybe nobody asks you that.*

No, nobody does, but . . . who said that, it wasn't Benjamin Franklin, it was somebody else. No, I think it was Benjamin Franklin. He said (I'm not quoting it right) something like, "For a man to be—(something or other)—at ease, he must not tell all he knows, nor say all he sees." Whoever said that certainly I don't think was trying to cover up anything.

JC: *I once got a fortune cookie that said "Clear water hides nothing."* . . . *Three or four years ago, there was an interview with you in 'Playboy.' One particular thought stuck with me. You said it was very important that Barbara Allen had a rose grow out of her head, and that a girl could become a swan.*

That's for all those people who say, "Why do you write all these songs about mystery and magic and Biblical implications? Why do you do all that? Folk music doesn't have any of that." There's no answer for a question like that, because the people who ask them are just wrong.

JC: *They say that folk music doesn't have this quality. Does rock and roll music have it?*

Well, I don't know what rock and roll music is supposed to represent. It isn't that defined as a music. Rock and roll is dance music, perhaps an extension of the blues forms. It's live music; nowadays they have these big speakers, and they play it so loud that it might seem live. But it's got rhythm . . . I mean if you're riding in your car, rock and roll stations playing, you can sort of get into that rhythm for three minutes—and you lose three minutes. It's all gone by and you don't have to think about anything. And it's got a nice place; in a way this place is not necessarily in every road you turn, it's just pleasant music.

JC: *You're part of it aren't you? Or it's part of you.*

Well, music is a part of me, yes.

JC: *From what I saw in that film 'Eat the Document,' you were really in it.*

I was in it because it's what I've always done. I was trying to make the two things go together when I was on those concerts. I played the first half acoustically, second half with a band, somehow thinking that it was going to be two kinds of music.

JC: *So acoustic would mean "folk" and band would mean "rock and roll" at that moment?*

Yes, rock and roll is working music. You have to work at it. You just can't sit down in a chair and play rock and roll music. You can do that with a certain kind of blues music, you can sit down and play it . . . you may have to lean forward a little.

JC: *Like a ballad, or one of your "dreams"?*

Yes, you can think about it, you don't necessarily have to be in action to think about it. Rock and roll is hard to visualize unless you're actually doing it . . . Actually, too, we're talking about something which is for the most part just a commercial item; it's like boats and brooms, it's like hardware, people sell it, so that's what we're talking about. In the other sense of the way which you'd think about it, it's impossible.

JC: *But the kids who are getting into it today, they don't want to sell brooms.*

It's an interesting field . . .

[*Aside to daughter*] Hello, did you just get home? Well maybe you better ask mamma. How was school? You learn anything? Well that's good. "My shoes hurt right here." Well, we'll see what we can do about it.

JC: *Could we talk about your new record 'John Wesley Harding'?*

There were three sessions: September, October, and December, so it's not even a year old. I know that the concepts are imbedded now, whereas before that record I was just trying to see all of which I could do, trying to structure this and that. Every record was more or less for impact. Why, I did one song on a whole side of an album! It could happen to anybody. One just doesn't think of those things though, when one sees that other things can be done. It was spontaneously brought out, all those seven record albums. It was generously done, the material was all there. Now, I like to think that I can do it, do it better, on my own terms, and I'll do whatever it is I can do. I used to slight it off all the time. I used to get a good phrase or a verse, and then have to carry it to write something off the top of the head and stick it in the middle, to lead this into that. Now as I hear all the old material that was done, I can see the whole thing. I can't see how to perfect it, but I can see what I've done. Now I can go from line to line, whereas yesterday it was from thought to thought. Then of course, there are times you just pick up an instrument—something will come, like a tune or some kind of wild line will come into your head and you'll develop that. If it's a tune on the piano or guitar—you'll just be uuuuhhhh [*hum*] whatever it brings out in the voice, you'll write those words down. And they might not mean anything to you at all, and you just go on, and that will be what happens. Now I don't do that anymore. If I do it, I just keep it for myself. So I have a big lineup of songs which I'll never use. On the new record, it's more concise. Here I am not interested in taking up that much of anybody's time.

JC: *That's why I gave you Kafka's 'Parables and Paradoxes,' because those stories really get to the heart of the matter, and yet you can never really decipher them.*

Yes, but the only parables that I know are the Biblical parables. I've seen others. Khalil Gibran perhaps. . . . It has a funny aspect to it—you certainly wouldn't find it in the Bible—this type of soul. Now Mr. Kafka comes off a little closer to that. Gibran, the words are all mighty but the strength is turned into that of a contrary direction. There used to be this disc jockey, Rosko. I don't recall his last name. Sometimes at night, the radio would be on and Rosko would be reciting this poetry of Khalil Gibran. It was a radiant feeling, coming across it on the radio. His voice was that of the inner voice in the night.

JC: *When did you read the Bible parables?*

I have always read the Bible, though not necessarily always the parables.

JC: *I don't think you're the kind who goes to the hotel, where the Gideons leave a Bible, and you pick it up.*

Well, you never know.

JC: *What about Blake, did you ever read . . . ?*

I have tried. Same with Dante, and Rilke. I understand what's there, it's just that the connection sometimes does not connect . . . Blake did come up with some bold lines though . . .

JC: *A feeling I got from watching the film—which I hadn't considered much before folk music and rock and roll got so mixed together—is about this personal thing of put ons, as a personal relationship. Like with the press, they ask such idiotic questions that they are answered by put ons.*

The only thing there, is that that becomes a game in itself. The only way to not get involved in that is not to do it, because it'll happen every time. It even happens with the housewives who might be asked certain questions.

JC: *It's become a way of imparting information. Like someone will come with an idea, a whole thesis, and then they'll ask, "Is this so?" and you might not have thought about it before, but you can crawl on top of it.*

It's this question and answer business, I can't see the importance of it. There's so many reporters now. That's an occupation in itself. You don't have to be any good at it at all. You get to go to fancy places. It's all on somebody else.

JC: *Ridiculous questions get ridiculous answers, and the ridiculous response becomes the great moment.*

Yes, well you have to be able to do that now. I don't know who started that, but it happens to everybody.

JC: *I wouldn't have mentioned it, but to me, you've moved away from it . . . gotten beyond it.*

I don't know if I've gotten beyond it. I just don't do it anymore, because that's what you end up doing. You end up wondering what you're doing.

JC: *Hey. In the film, was that John Lennon with you in the car, where you're holding your head? He was saying something funny, but it was more than that . . . it was thoughtful.*

He said "Money." . . .

JC: *Do you see the Beatles when you go there or they come here? There seems to be a mutual respect between your musics—without one dominating the other.*

I see them here and there.

JC: *I fear that many of the creative young musicians today may look back at themselves ten years from now and say "We were just under the tent of the Beatles." But you're not.*

Well, what they do . . . they work much more with studio equipment, they take advantage of the new sound inventions of the past year or two. Whereas I don't know anything about it. I just do the songs, and sing them and that's all.

JC: *Do you think they are more British or International?*

They're British I suppose, but you can't say they've carried on with their poetic legacy, whereas the Incredible String Band who wrote this "October Song" . . . that was quite good.

JC: *As a finished thing—or did it reach you?*

As a finished song it's quite good.

JC: *Is there much music now that you hear, that reaches you?*

Those old songs reach me. I don't hear them as often as I used to. But like this other week, I heard on the radio Buell Kazee and he reached me. There's a lot . . . Scrapper Blackwell, Leroy Carr, Jack Dupree, Lonnie Johnson, James Ferris, Jelly Roll Morton, Buddy Bolden, Ian and Sylvia, Benny Ferguson, Tom Rush, Charley Pride, Porter Wagoner, The Clancy Brothers and Tommy Makem . . . Everything reaches me in one way or another.

JC: *How do you view the music business?*

I don't exactly view it at all. Hearing it and doing it, I'll take part in that—but talking about it . . . there's not much I can contribute to it.

JC: *I recall in 'Billboard,' a full page ad of you with electric guitar like in the movie. . . .*

Sure, I was doing that.

JC: *I'm interested in how you talk of it in the past tense, as if you don't know what's coming next.*

Well, I don't in a sense . . . but I've been toying with some ridiculous ideas—just so strange and foreign to me, as a month ago. Now some of the ideas—I'll tell you about them—after we shut off this tape recorder.

———

JC: *I was pleased that you know the music of Dillard Chandler, and that you were familiar with some unaccompanied ballads on a New Lost City Ramblers record. Do you think you'll ever try to write like a ballad?*

Yes, I hope so. Tom Paxton just did one called "The Cardinal," quite interesting . . . it's very clean . . . sings it unaccompanied. The thing about the ballad is that you have to be conscious of the width of it at all times, in order to write one. You could take a true story, write it up as a ballad, or you can write it up in three verses. The difference would be, what are you singing it for, what is it to be used for. The uses of a ballad have changed to such a degree. When they were singing years ago, it would be as entertainment . . . a fellow could sit down and sing a song for a half hour, and everybody could listen, and you could form opinions. You'd be waiting to see how it ended, what happened to this person or that person. It would be like going to a movie. But now we have movies, so why does someone want to sit around for a half hour listening to a ballad? Unless the story was of such a nature that you couldn't find it in a movie. And after you heard it, it would have to be good enough so that you could sing it again tomorrow night, and people would be listening to hear the story again. It's because they want to hear that story, not because they want to check out the singer's pants. Because they would have conscious knowledge of how the story felt and they would be a part of that feeling . . . like they would want to feel it again, so to speak.

JC: *It must be terrific to try to write within those dimensions.*

Well once you set it up in your mind, you don't have to think about it any more. If it wants to come, it will come.

JC: *Take a song like "The Wicked Messenger." Does that fit?*

In a sense, but the ballad form isn't there. Well, the scope is there actually, but in a more compressed sense. The scope opens up, just by a few little tricks. I know why it opens up, but in a ballad in the true sense, it wouldn't open up that way. It does not reach the proportions I had intended for it.

JC: *Have you ever written a ballad?*

I believe on my second record album, "Boots of Spanish Leather."

JC: *Then most of the songs on 'John Wesley Harding,' you don't consider ballads.*

Well I do, but not in the traditional sense. I haven't fulfilled the balladeer's job. A balladeer can sit down and sing three ballads for an hour and a half. See, on the album, you have to think about it after you hear it, that's what takes up the time, but with a ballad, you don't necessarily have to think about it after you hear it, it can all unfold to you. These melodies on the *John Wesley Harding* album lack this traditional sense of time. As with the third verse of "The Wicked Messenger," which opens it up, and then the time schedule takes a jump and soon the song becomes wider. One realizes that when one hears it, but one might have to adapt to it. But we are not hearing anything that isn't there; anything we can imagine is really there. The same thing is true of the song "All Along the Watchtower," which opens up in a slightly different way, in a stranger way, for we have the cycle of events working in a rather reverse order.

———

JC: *One suggested interpretation of "Dear Landlord" is that you wrote it to bring out the line "each one has his own special gift." . . .*

I don't know about that. These songs might lay around in your head for two or three years and you're always writing about something previous. You learn to do that, so that the song would not tend to be a reaction, something contemporary would make it a reaction. I don't know what it seems to explain any more than anyone else. But you always have to consider that I would write the song for somebody else. He might say something, or behave in a certain manner, or come right out and offer information like that. And if it's striking enough, it might find an opening. And don't forget now, John, I'll tell you another discovery that I've made. When the songs are done by anybody on a record, on a strange level the songs are done for somebody, about somebody and to somebody. Usually that person is the somebody who is singing the song. Hear all the records which have ever been made and it kinda comes down to that after a while.

JC: *Could you talk about where you were going when you first started out from home?*

As I think about it, it's confusing to me to think of how I reached whatever place this is. I tend not to wonder about it anyway. It's true I have no goal so to speak. I don't have any more intentions than you do.

JC: *I intend to do my work.*

Yes, me too, and to make the work interesting enough, in order to keep doing it. That's what has kept it up so far. I really can't do it if it's not interesting. My intention would be not to think about it, not to speak about it, or remember any of it that might tend to block it up somehow. I've discovered this from the past anyway. There was one thing I tried to do which wasn't a good idea for me. I tried to write another "Mr. Tambourine Man." It's the only song I tried to write "another one." But after enough going at it, it just began bothering me, so I dropped it. I don't do that anymore.

JC: *A danger of such a position is that you can be accused of only living in the present. People will say you're just living for the minute—with no plan and no care for the past.*

I have more memories for the past than for the future. I wouldn't think about the future. I would only have expectations, and they'd all be very good. For the past I just have those memories. We were just talking of this "past" business the other night. Say this room is empty now except with just myself. Now you enter the room. But you're bound to leave, and when you do what's to guarantee that you've even been in this room. But yet you were in this room, if I want to reconstruct it, sit here for the rest of the day . . . if I take enough notes while you are in the room I could probably sit here for a week, with you in the room . . . something like that anyway.

JC: *It's elusive. Anyway, back to the thought of "each one has his own special gift."*

That would be . . . just a fact.

JC: *But if everybody felt it, perhaps the American army wouldn't be so capable of killing, and Kennedy might not be killed—King might not be killed.*

But we're talking now about things which have always happened since the beginning of time, the specific name or deed isn't any different than that which has happened previous to this. Progress hasn't contributed anything but changing face . . . and changing situations of money, wealth . . . that's not progress really. Progress for disease—that's progress . . . but putting in a new highway through a backyard is getting rid of the old things.

JC: *The real progress each person makes is not going outwards, but going inwards. I have the feeling that a change has come over you . . . you seem to have discovered that same idea.*

Well, I discover ideas here and there, but I can't put them into words.

JC: *You mean, that by the time they are songs, they're said?*

Well, the songs are a funny thing. If I didn't have the recording contract and I didn't have to fulfill a certain amount of records, I don't really know if I'd write down another song as long as I lived. I'm just content enough to play just anything I know. But seeing as how I do have this contract, I figure my obligation is to fill it, not in just recording songs, but the best songs I can possibly record. Believe me, I look around. I don't care if I record my own songs, but I can't sometimes find enough songs to put on an album, so then I've got to do it all with my songs. I didn't want to record this last album. I was going to do a whole album of other people's songs, but I couldn't find enough. The song has to be of a certain quality for me to sing and put on a record. One aspect it would have to have is that it didn't repeat itself. I shy away from those songs which repeat phrases, bars and verses, bridges . . . so right there it leaves out about nine-tenths of all the contemporary material being written, and the folk songs are just about the only ones that don't . . . the narrative ones, or the ones with a chorus like "Ruben's Train." I don't know, maybe then too I'm just too lazy to look hard enough.

JC: *Do you consider that there's been a change of pace in your life over the past three years?*

"Change of pace" if you mean what I was doing before. I was touring for a couple of years. That's a fast pace, plus we were doing a whole show, no other acts. It's pretty straining to do a show like that, plus a lot of really unhealthy situations rise up. I was just going out there performing these songs. Everyone else was having a good time, and I did it enough to know that there must be something else to do.

JC: *In a way, you had the opportunity to move into it and move out of it at your own choice.*

It wasn't my own choice. I was more or less being pushed into it—pushed in and carried out.

[*Enter Happy Traum*]

HT: *Has anyone picked up on your new approach—like on the album, clear songs and very personal, as opposed to the psychedelic sounds?*

I don't know.

HT: *What do you know?*

What I do know is that I put myself out of the songs. I'm not in the songs anymore, I'm just there singing them, and I'm not personally connected with them. I write them all now at a different time than when I record them. It used to be, if I would sing, I'd get a verse and go on and wait for it to come out as the music was there, and sure enough, something would come out, but in the end, I would be deluded in those songs. Besides singing them, I'd be in there acting them out—just pulling them off. Now I have enough time to write the song and not think about being in it. Just write it for somebody else to sing, then do it—like an acetate. At the moment, people are singing a simpler song. It's possible in Nashville to do that.

JC: *I heard "Blowin' in the Wind" played on the radio after the most recent assassination.*

By who?

JC: *It was Muzak style . . . music to console yourself by.*

Airplane style.

JC: *Do you think you'll ever get a job playing for Muzak? The best musicians do that work, Bob.*

Well I'd give it a try if they ask.

JC: *No one calls you into the studio to "Lay down some music" as they say.*

Before I did the new album, I was waiting to meet someone who would figure out what they would want me to do. Does anybody want any songs written about anything? Could Bob be commissioned, by anybody? Nobody came up with anything, so I went ahead and did something else.

JC: *For a while a number of years ago, the songs you were writing, and that others were writing along similar lines, were played a lot on popular radio.*

Today it's not completely disappeared, but it certainly is going in some other direction.

You just about have to cut something tailor-made for the popular radio. You can't do it with just half a mind. You must be conscious of what you're involved in. I get over-anxious when I hear myself on the radio, anyway. I don't mind the record album, but it's the record company, my A & R man, Bob Johnston—he would pick out what's to be played on the radio.

HT: *Did you ever make a song just to be a single?*

Yes I did. But it wasn't very amusing because it took me away from the album. The album commands a different sort of attention than a single does. Singles just pile up and pile up; they're only good for the present. The trend in the old days was that unless you had a hit single, you couldn't do very well with an album. And when you had that album, you just filled it up. But now albums are very important.

JC: *You've tried movies and books . . .*

In both cases, in shallow water.

JC: *In that book of photographs of you that was published, when I finished looking at it, I came away knowing not one bit more than when I started.*

Yes, well what can you know about anybody? Book or photographs, they don't tell you too much about a person.

HT: *For years now, people have been analyzing and pulling apart your songs. People take the lines out of context and use them to illustrate points like on "Quinn the Eskimo" . . . I've heard some kids say that Quinn is the "bringer of drugs." Whatever you meant doesn't matter . . . the kids say "Dylan is really into this drug thing . . . when the drugs come up, everybody is happy." This kind of thing is always happening with all of your songs.*

Well, that's not my concern.

JC: *Many of the songs have set up conditions where people can read whatever they want into them.*

HT: *People pull them apart and analyze them.*

It's not everyone who does that—just a certain kind. People I come in contact with don't have any questions.

HT: *Perhaps that's come back lately in the very spontaneous art, in the whole multi-media kind of thing. Response to impulses . . . you can't respond any other way.*

JC: *I think it's to anyone's favor that they can follow what's on their own mind, what comes from within them, rather than getting swept up in all these other possibilities . . . which might be just a reaction against the analytic approach anyway. There is another way . . . someone might just follow his inner course . . . without being unaware of what is going on. Bob, how do you respond to multi-media?*

When you say multi-media, would that be like the clothes stores?

JC: *Never having been to one, I'll say yes.*

I've never been to one either.

HT: *It's also stage presentations where music, dance, lights and the rest are jumbled together, piled on the viewer, where all the senses are used.*

JC: *In that context of multi-media, where are you?*

Well I'm a very simple man. I take one, maybe two . . . too much just confuses me. I just can't master confusion. If I don't know what's happening and everyone who goes and tells me just says that they don't know what happened any more than I do, and they were there, then I'd say that I didn't know where we were.

HT: *Do you feel the same way about the psychedelic sound on records?*

No, I don't.

HT: *A lot of music today is not only very loud and very fast, but it's structured in such a way that a lot of instruments are playing at once, with a lot of distortion.*

That's fine. A lot of people are playing it.

HT: *You seem to have made a conscious effort away from that on your last record.*

It was a conscious effort just to begin again. It wasn't a conscious effort to go in a certain direction, but rather like put up or shut up, so-to-speak. So that's all.

JC: *I see that picture of Muhammad Ali here. Do you know him?*

No, I've seen him perform a few times.

HT: *Do you follow the fights?*

Not anymore. When he came down to Bleecker Street to read his poetry, you would have wished you were there.

JC: *He really made a point that lasted afterwards—beyond that someone got conked.*

HT: *Not being particularly interested in fighting, what impressed me is how he stayed true to himself—his own stand as a human being was more important to himself than the championship.*

— ⸻ —

JC: *Could you talk about some of the diverse elements which go into making up one of your songs, using a song from which you have some distance?*

Well, there's not much we could talk about—that's the strange aspect about the whole thing. There's nothing you can see. I wouldn't know where to begin.

JC: *Take a song like "I Pity the Poor Immigrant." There might have been a germ that started it.*

Yes, the first line.

JC: *What experience might have triggered that. Like you kicked the cat who ran away, who said "Ouch!" which reminded you of an immigrant.*

To tell the truth, I have no idea how it comes into my mind.

JC: *You've said there was a person usually in it.*

Well, we're all in it. They're not any specific people . . . say, someone kicks the cat, and the cat writes a song about it. It might seem that way, during some of the songs, and in some of the poetry that's being passed around now a days. But it's not really that way.

JC: *You said that often a song is written for a certain person.*

That's for a person, not about him. You know, you might sometimes be with someone who's got no song to sing, and I believe you can help someone out, that's the extent of it really.

JC: *Well, "Quinn the Eskimo" wasn't that way.*

You see, it's all grown so serious, the writing-song business. It's not that serious. The songs don't painfully come out. They come out in a trick or two, or from something you might overhear. I'm just like any other songwriter, you pick up the things that are given to you. "Quinn the Eskimo," I can't remember how that came about. I know the phrase came about, I believe someone was just talking about Quinn, the Eskimo.

JC: *Someone told me there was once a movie with Anthony Quinn playing an Eskimo. Did you know of that?*

I didn't see the movie.

JC: *But that could have triggered it.*

Of course.

JC: *This makes a lot of sense, in the sense that you can travel down a road, and see two signs advertising separate things, but where two words come together, it will make a new meaning which will trigger off something.*

Well, what the songwriter does, is just connect the ends. The ends that he sees are the ones that are given to him and he connects them.

HT: *It seems that people are bombarded all the time with random thoughts and outside impulses, and it takes the songwriter to pick something out and create a song out of them.*

It's like this painter who lives around here—he paints the area in a radius of twenty miles, he paints bright strong pictures. He might take a barn from twenty miles away, and hook it up with a brook right next door, then with a car ten miles away, and with the sky on some certain day, and the light on the trees from another certain day. A person passing by will be painted alongside someone ten miles away. And in the end he'll have this composite picture of something which you can't say exists in his mind. It's not that he started off willfully painting this picture from all his experience . . . That's more or less what I do.

JC: *Which and where is Highway 61?*

I knew at one time, but at this time it seems so far away I wouldn't even attempt it. It's out there, it's a dividing line.

JC: *Is it a physical Highway 61?*

Oh yes, it goes from where I used to live . . . I used to live related to that highway. It ran right through my home town in Minnesota. I traveled it for a long period of time actually. It goes down the middle of the country, sort of southwest.

JC: *I think there is an old blues about Highway 61.*

Same highway, lot of famous people came off that highway.

JC: *Can you keep contact with the young audiences who perhaps buy most of your records?*

That's a vague notion, that one must keep contact with a certain illusion of people which are sort of undefinable. The most you can do is satisfy yourself. If you satisfy yourself then you don't have to worry about remembering anything. If you don't satisfy yourself, and you don't know why you're doing what you do, you begin to lose contact. If you're doing it for *them* instead of you, you're likely not in contact with them. You can't pretend you're in contact with something you're not. I don't really know who I'm in contact with, but I don't think it's important.

JC: *Well, on the airplanes, they have these seven channels of stereo, and your music is marked as "for the kids" rather than anywhere else, and it sort of bothered me. Do you have a chance to meet the kids?*

I always like to meet the kids.

JC: *Do you get a chance?*

Not so much when I'm touring as when I'm not touring. When you're touring, you don't get a chance to meet anybody. I've just been meeting people again in the last few years.

JC: *It's a strange phenomenon, for you reach them the most when you are on tour yet you can't reach them at all.*

Well yes, but the next time I go out, it's going to be a little bit more understandable. Next time out, my hopes are to play the music in a different way.

HT: *How can you get around the problems you encountered last time?*

I'm not really aware of those problems. I know they exist because it was very straining, and that's not the way work should be. But it's a situation that's pretty much all over . . . the screaming. Even some musician like Jimi Hendrix gets people seeing him who aren't coming there to scream—they're coming there to hear him.

HT: *Do you see any way that you can approach your music in a public way, that would give a different perspective to an audience?*

Yes. Just playing the songs. See, the last time we went out, we made too much of a production of the songs. They were all longer, they were all my own songs, not too much thought had gone into the program, it just evolved itself from when I was playing single.

JC: *And the film we've been discussing, is that a fair summary of that kind of a tour?*

Yes it was. I hope people get a chance to see that film.

JC: *Why do you think your music appeals to American Indians?*

I would hope that it appeals to everybody.

JC: *I know suburban people who can't stand it.*

Well, I wish that there was more I could do about that.

JC: *We just heard your record being played at an elegant store in New York City, as the background for people shopping.*

HT: *Pete Seeger told me the 'John Wesley Harding' album is great to skate to. He said some records are good to skate to and some aren't, and that's a good one.*

I'm awfully glad he feels that way about it.

JC: *What is your relationship to student groups, or black militants, like the kids at Columbia or at Berkeley?*

If I met them at all, I would meet them individually; I have no special relationship to any group.

JC: *Do you follow these events, even from a distance, like reading a newspaper?*

Just like anyone else. I know just as much about it as the lady across the street does, and she probably knows quite a bit. Just reading the papers, talking to the neighbors, and so forth.

JC: *These groups feel more about you than they do about the lady next door.*

I can assure you I feel the same thing. There are people who are involved in it and people who are not. You see, to be involved, you just about have to be there, I couldn't think about it any other way.

JC: *Someone like Pete Seeger, who is different from all of us in this room, he reaches out.*

But how much of a part of it is he?

HT: *Do you foresee a time when you're going to have to take some kind of a position?*

No.

HT: *You don't think that events will ever reach you?*

It's not that events won't reach me, it's more a case of what I, myself would reach for. The decisions I would have to make are my own decisions, just like anyone else has to make his own. It doesn't necessarily mean that any position must be taken.

JC: *Although I asked it, this is not really the kind of question I'm really concerned with. After all, if someone asked me, I could only say I do what I can, I sing my own music, and if they like to hear it, well, fine.*

Yes, but I don't know . . . what was the question again? You must define it better.

HT: *I think that every day we get closer to having to make a choice.*

How so?

HT: *I think that events of the world are getting closer to us, they're as close as the nearest ghetto.*

Where's the nearest ghetto?

HT: *Maybe down the block. Events are moving on a mass scale.*

What events?

HT: *War, racial problems, violence in the streets.*

JC: *Here's a funny aspect; we're talking like this here, but in a strange way, Bob has gone further than you or I in getting into such places. I just heard from Izzy Young that the songs they were singing at Resurrection City were "Blowin' in the Wind" and "The Times They Are A-Changin'." So, in a sense by maintaining his own individual position, Bob and his songs are in the ghetto, and the people there are singing them—to them they mean action.*

HT: *Well, the kids at Columbia University are taking a particular stand on what they see as the existing evils. They're trying to get their own say in the world, and in a way trying to overcome the people ruling them, and there are powerful people who are ruling them, and there are powerful people who are running the show. They can be called the establishment, and they are the* same people who make the wars, that build the missiles, that manufacture the instruments of death.

Well, that's just the way the world is going.

HT: *The students are trying to make it go another way.*

Well, I'm for the students of course, they're going to be taking over the world. The people who they're fighting are old people, old ideas. They don't have to fight, they can sit back and wait.

HT: *The old ideas have the guns, though.*

JC: *Perhaps the challenge is to make sure that the young minds growing up remain open enough so that they don't become the establishment they are fighting.*

You read about these rebels in the cartoons, people who were rebels in the twenties, in the thirties, and they have children who are rebels, and they forget that they were rebels. Do you think that those who are rioting today will someday have to hold their kids back from doing the same thing?

———

JC: *Are your day-to-day contacts among the artists, crusaders, business-men or lumberjacks?*

Among the artists and lumberjacks.

JC: *Crusaders?*

Well, you mean the people who are going from here to there, the men in long brown robes and little ivy twines on their head? I know quite a few crusaders but don't have much contact with them.

JC: *How about leaders of the student groups? Do you know Malcolm X, or the kids from SNCC?*

I used to know some of them.

JC: *Social crusaders, someone like Norman Mailer.*

No.

JC: *What about businessmen?*

I get a lot of visitors and see a lot of people, and who's a business-man? I'm sure a whole lot of businessmen have passed by the past few hours, but my recollection really isn't that brilliant.

JC: *Does your management serve as a buffer in translating your artistic works into business?*

I'm just very thankful that my management is there to serve what purpose a management serves. Every artist must have one these days.

——

JC: *Would you talk of any of the positive things that drugs have to offer, how they might have affected your work?*

I wouldn't think they have anything to offer. I'm speaking about drugs in the everyday sense of the word. From my own experience they would have nothing positive to offer, but I'm not speaking for anyone else. Someone else might see them offering a great deal.

JC: *But in the way of insights or new combinations, it never affected you that way?*

No, you get those same insights over a period of time anyway.

——

JC: *For a while you were working on a book, they gave it a name, 'Tarantula.' Have you tried any other writing since then, or did you learn anything from the experience of trying?*

Yes, I do have a book in me, it'll be out sometime. Macmillan will publish it.

JC: *Did you learn from the one you did reject?*

I learned not to do a book like that. That book was the kind of thing where the contract comes in before the book is written, so you have to fulfill the contract.

JC: *In thinking over this interview thus far, it seems like that has happened to you several times over the recent years, not necessarily of your own choosing.*

Yes, that's true. But it happens to other people and they come through. Dostoevsky did it, he had a weekly number of words to get in. I understand Frederick Murrey does it, and John Updike must . . . For someone else it might be exactly what they had always wished.

JC: *In trying to write it, was it a difficulty of structure or concept?*

No, there was no difficulty in writing it at all. It just wasn't a book, it was just a nuisance. It didn't have that certain quality which now I think a book should have. It didn't have any structure at all, it was just one flow. It flowed for ninety pages.

JC: *I'm thinking of a parallel. You know some of these old crazy talking blues? They go on where just the last phrase of a sentence connects up to the next sentence, but the two thoughts aren't related. "Slipping up and down the mantle piece, feet in a bucket of grease, hunting matches, etc." Did it go that way?*

More or less. They were short little lines, nothing within a big framework. I couldn't even conceive of doing anything in a big framework at that time. I was doing something else.

HT: *Do you think future writings will use the poetic form or the novel?*

I think it will have everything in it.

⸻

JC: *Listening to the car radio, I heard that you have a song on the country music stations, "I'll Be Your Baby Tonight." I can't remember the singer's name, but I understand that Burl Ives has also recorded it.*

A lot of people record them, they always do a good job.

JC: *When did you first hear Burl Ives?*

I first heard Burl Ives when I was knee-high to a grasshopper.

JC: *Was that folk music to you when you first heard it?*

Yes, I guess everybody's heard those old Burl Ives records on Decca, with a picture of him in a striped T-shirt, holding a guitar up to his ear, just wailing.

JC: *Did you know that his first recordings were for Moe Asch (of Folkways records)? Alan Lomax had brought him in. Who made the first recordings you are on?*

I recorded with Big Joe Williams.

JC: *Where did this Blind Boy Grunt thing come in?*

Someone told me to come down 'cause they were doing some kind of an album. So I was there and singing this song, and it only had a couple of verses and that's all, so someone in the control booth said "Do some more." I said well, there is no more, I can't sing any more. The fellow says, "If you can't sing, GRUNT." So I said, "Grunt?" Then someone else sitting at a desk to my left says, "What name shall I put down on this record?" and I said, "Grunt." She said, "Just Grunt?" Then the fellow in the control booth said, "Grunt." Somebody came in the door then and said, "Was that Blind Boy Grunt?" and the lady at the desk said, "Yes it was."

JC: *Was this Moe Asch and Marion Distler?*

It could have been.

———

JC: *My last question is really a rehash of one aspect we've already discussed; at the moment, your songs aren't as socially or politically applicable as they were earlier.*

As they were earlier? Could it be that they are just as social and political, only that no one cares to . . . let's start with the question again. [JC *repeats question*] Probably that is because no one cares to see it the way I'm seeing it now, whereas before, I saw it the way they saw it.

HT: *You hear a lot about the word "engaged" artists. Painters, film makers, actors, they're actively involved in current events, through their art.*

Well, even Michelangelo though . . .

HT: *Many artists feel that at this particular time in history, they can't just do their thing without regarding the larger scale around them.*

The thing is, if you can get the scales around you in whatever you create, that's nice. If you physically have to go out there and experience it time and time again, you're talking about something else.

HT: *Probably the most pressing thing going on in a political sense is the war. Now I'm not saying that any artist or group of artists can change the course of the war, but they still feel it their responsibility to say something.*

I know some very good artists who are for the war.

HT: *Well I'm just talking about the ones who are against it.*

That's like what I'm talking about; it's for or against the war. That really doesn't exist. It's not for or against the war. I'm speaking of a certain painter, and he's all for the war. He's just about ready to go over there himself. And I can comprehend him.

Why can't you argue with him?

I can see what goes on in his paintings, and why should I?

HT: *I don't understand how that relates to whether a position should be taken.*

Well, there's nothing for us to talk about really.

JC: *Someone just told me that the poet and artist William Blake harbored Tom Paine when it was dangerous to do so. Yet Blake's artistic production was mystical and introspective.*

HT: *Well, he separated his work from his other activity. My feeling is that with a person who is for the war and ready to go over there, I don't think it would be possible for you and him to share the same basic values.*

I've known him a long time, he's a gentleman and I admire him, he's a friend of mine. People just have their own views. Anyway, how do you know I'm not, as you say, for the war?

JC: *Is this comparable? I was working on a fireplace with an old local stone mason last summer, while running off to sing at the New Politics Convention. When I returned I was chopping rocks with him, and he says, "All the trouble today is caused by people like Martin Luther King." Now I respect that man, not for his comments on Dr. King, but for his work with stone, his outlook on his craft, and on work and life, and in the terms he sees it. It is a dilemma.*

HT: *I think it is the easy way out, to say that. You have to feel strongly about your own ideas, even if you can respect someone else for their ideas. [to Bob] I don't feel that there is much difference between your work now and your earlier work. I can see a continuity of ideas, although they're not politically as black and white as they once were. "Masters of War" was a pretty black and white song. It wasn't too equivocal. You took a stand.*

That was an easy thing to do. There were thousands and thousands of people just wanting that song, so I wrote it up. What I'm doing now isn't more difficult, but I no longer have the capacity to feed this force which is needing all these songs. I know the force exists but my insight has turned into something else. I might meet one person now, and the same thing can happen between that one person (and myself) that used to happen between thousands.

JC: *This leads right to the last statement on my interview list: On your latest album, the focus has become more on the individual, axioms and ideas about living, rather than about society's doings or indictments of groups of people. In other words, it's more of how one individual is to act.*

Yes, in a way . . . in a way. I would imagine that's just the way we grow.

12. Interview with Jann S. Wenner,
ROLLING STONE

NOVEMBER 29, 1969

They say Bob Dylan is the most secretive and elusive person in the entire rock & roll substructure, but after doing this interview, I think it would be closer to the point to say that Dylan, like John Wesley Harding, was "never known to make a foolish move."

The preparations for the interview illustrate this well. About eighteen months ago, I first started writing Bob letters asking for an interview, suggesting the conditions and questions and reasons for it. Then, a little over a year ago, the night before I left New York, a message came from the hotel operator that a "Mr. Dillon" had called.

Two months later, I met Bob for the first time at another hotel in New York: He casually strolled in wearing a sheepskin outfit, leather boots, very well put together but not too tall, y'understand. It was ten a.m., and I rolled out of bed stark naked—sleep that way, y'understand—and we talked for half an hour about doing an interview, what it was for, why it was necessary. Bob was feeling out the situation, making sure it would be cool.

That meeting was in the late fall of 1968. It took eight months—until the end of June this year—to finally get the interview. The meantime was covered with a lot of phone calls, near misses in New York City, Bob's trips to California which didn't take place and a lot of waiting and waiting for that right time when we were both ready for the show.

The interview took place on a Thursday afternoon in New York City at my hotel, right around the corner from the funeral home where Judy Garland was being inspected by ten thousand people, who formed lines around several city blocks. We were removed from all that activity, but somehow it seemed appropriate enough that Judy Garland's funeral coincided with the interview.

Bob was very cautious in everything he said, and took a long time between questions to phrase exactly what he wanted to say, nothing more and sometimes a little less. When I wasn't really satisfied with his answers, I asked the questions another way, later. But Bob was hip.

Rather than edit the interview into tight chunks and long answers, I left in all the pauses, asides and laughs. So, much of the time, it's not what is said, but how it is said, and I think you will dig it more just as it went down.

Why haven't you worked in so long?

Well, uh . . . I do work.

I mean on the road.

On the road . . . I don't know, working on the road . . . well, Jann, I'll tell ya—I was on the road for almost five years. It wore me down. I was on drugs, a lot of things. A lot of things just to keep going, you know? And I don't want to live that way anymore. And uh . . . I'm just waiting for a better time—you know what I mean?

What would you do that would make the tour that you're thinking about doing different from the ones you did do?

Well, I'd like to slow down the pace a little. The one I did do . . . the next show's gonna be a lot different from the last show. The last show, during the first half, of which there was about an hour, I only did maybe six songs. My songs were long, *long* songs. But that's why I had to start dealing with a lot of different methods of keeping myself awake, alert . . . because I had to remember all the words to those songs. Now I've got a whole bag of new songs. I've written 'em for the road, you know. So I'll be doing all these songs on the road. They're gonna sound a lot better than they do on record. My songs always sound a lot better in person than they do on the record.

Why?

Well, I don't know why. They just do.

On 'Nashville Skyline' — who does the arrangements? The studio musicians, or . . .

Boy, I wish you could've come along the last time we made an album. You'd probably enjoyed it . . . 'cause you see right there, you know how it's done. We just take a song; I play it and everyone else just sort of fills in behind it. No sooner you got that done, and at the same time you're doing that, there's someone in the control booth who's turning all those dials to where the proper sound is coming in . . . and then it's done. Just like that.

Just out of rehearsing it? It'll be a take?

Well, maybe we'll take about two times.

When are you going to do another record?

You mean when am I going to *put out* an album?

Have you done another record?

No . . . not exactly. I was going to try and have another one out by the fall.

Is it done in Nashville again?

Well, we . . . I think so . . . I mean it's . . . seems to be as good a place as any.

On 'Nashville Skyline,' do you have any song that you particularly dig? Above the others?

Uh . . . "Tonight I'll Be Staying Here With You." I like "Tell Me That It Isn't True," although it came out completely different than I'd written it. It came out real slow and mellow. I had it written as sort of a jerky, kind of polka-type thing. I wrote it in F. I wrote a lot of songs on this new album in F. That's what gives it kind of a new sound. They're all in F . . . not all of them, but quite a few. There's not many on that album that aren't in F. So you see I had those chords . . . which gives it a certain sound. I try to be a little different on every album.

I'm sure you read the reviews of 'Nashville Skyline.' Everybody remarks on the change of your singing style. . . .

Well, Jann, I'll tell you something. There's not too much of a change in my singing style, but I'll tell you something which is true . . . I stopped smoking. When I stopped smoking, my voice changed . . . so drastically, I couldn't believe it myself. That's true. I tell you, you stop smoking those cigarettes [*laughter*] . . . and you'll be able to sing like Caruso.

How did you make the change . . . or why did you make the change, of producers, from Tom Wilson to Bob Johnston?

Well, I can't remember, Jann. I can't remember . . . all I know is that I was out recording one day, and Tom had always been there—I had no reason to think he wasn't going to be there—and I looked up one day and Bob was there [*laughs*].

There's been some articles on Wilson and he says that he's the one that gave you the rock & roll sound . . . and started you doing rock & roll. Is that true?

Did he say that? Well, if he said it . . . [*laughs*] more power to him [*laughs*]. He did to a certain extent. That is true. He did. He had a sound in mind.

Have you ever thought of doing an album . . . a very arranged, very orchestrated album, you know, with chicks and . . . ?

Gee, I've thought of it . . . I think about it once in a while. Yeah.

You think you might do one?

I do whatever comes naturally. I'd like to do an album like that. You mean using my own material and stuff?

Yeah, using your own material but with vocal background and . . .

I'd like to do it. Who wouldn't?

When did you make the change from John Hammond . . . or what caused the change from John Hammond?

John Hammond. He signed me in 1960. He signed me to Columbia Records. I think he produced my first album. I think he produced my second one, too.

And Tom Wilson was also working at Columbia at the time?

He was . . . you know, I don't recall how that happened . . . or why that switch took place. I remember at one time I was about to record for Don Law. You know Don Law? I was about to record for Don Law, but I never did. I met Don Law in New York, in 1962 . . . and again recently, last year when I did the *John Wesley Harding* album. I met him down in the studio. He came in . . . he's a great producer. He produced many of the earlier records for Columbia and also for labels which they had before—Okeh and stuff like that. I believe he did the Robert Johnson records.

What did you do in the year between 'Blonde on Blonde' and 'John Wesley Harding'?

Well, I was on tour part of that time . . . Australia, Sweden . . . an overseas tour. Then I came back . . . and in the spring of that year, I was scheduled to go out—it was one month off, I had a one-month vacation—I was gonna go back on the road again in July. *Blonde on Blonde* was up on the charts at this time. At that time I had a dreadful motorcycle accident . . . which put me away for a while . . . and I still didn't sense the importance of that accident till at least a year after that. I realized that it was a *real* accident. I mean I thought that I was just gonna get up and go back to doing what I was doing before . . . but I couldn't do it anymore.

What did I do during that year? I helped work on a film . . . which was supposed to be aired on *Stage 67*, a television show which isn't on anymore . . . I don't think it was on for very long.

What change did the motorcycle accident make?

What change? Well . . . it limited me. It's hard to speak about the change, you know? It's not the type of change that one can put into words . . . besides the physical change. I had a busted vertebra; neck vertebrae. And there's really not much to talk about. I don't want to talk about it.

Laying low for a year . . . you must have had time to think. That was the ABC-TV show? What happened to the tapes of that? How come that never got shown?

Well, I could make an attempt to answer that, but . . . [*laughs*] . . . I think my manager could probably answer it a lot better.

What is the nature of your acquaintance with John Lennon?

Oh, I always love to see John. Always. He's a wonderful fellow . . . and I always like to see him.

He said that the first time that you met, in New York, after one of the concerts or something like that, it was a very uptight situation.

It probably was, yes. Like, you know how it used to be for them. They couldn't go out of their room. They used to tell me you could hardly get in to see them. There used to be people surrounding them, not only in the streets, but in the corridors in the hotel. I should say it was uptight.

How often have you seen them subsequently?

Well, I haven't seen them too much recently.

What do you think of the bed-ins for peace? Him and Yoko.

Well, you know . . . everybody's doing what they can do. I don't mind what he does, really . . . I always like to see him.

Do you read the current critics? The music critics, so-called "rock & roll writers"?

Well I try to keep up. I try to keep up to date . . . I realize I don't do a very good job in keeping up to date, but I try to. I don't know half the groups that are playing around now. I don't know half of what I should.

———

I don't want to get nosy or get into your personal life . . . but there was a series recently in the 'Village Voice,' about your growing up, living and going to high school. Did you read that series?

Yeah, I did. At least, I read some of it. But as far as liking it or disliking it, I didn't do neither of those things. I mean it's just publicity from where I am. So if they want to spend six or seven issues writing about me [*laughs*] . . . as long as they get it right, you know, as long as they get it in there, I can't complain.

You must have some feelings about picking up a newspaper that has a hundred thousand circulation and seeing that some guy's gone and talked to your parents and your cousins and uncles . . .

Well, the one thing I did . . . I don't like the way this writer talked about my father who has passed away. I didn't dig him talking about my father and using his name. Now, that's the only thing about the article I didn't dig. But that boy has got some lessons to learn.

What did he say?

That don't matter what he said. He didn't have no right to speak about my father, who has passed away. If he wants to do a story on me, that's fine. I don't care what he wants to say about me. I got the feeling that he was taking advantage of some good people that I used to know and he was making *fun* of a lot of things. I got the feeling he was making fun of quite a *few* things . . . this fellow, Toby. You know what I mean, Jann? Soooo . . . we'll just let that stand as it is . . . for now.

I've gone through all the collected articles that have appeared, all the early ones and Columbia Records' biographies, that's got the story about running away from home at eleven and twelve and thirteen-and-one-half . . . why did you put out that story?

I didn't put out any of those stories!

Well, it's the standard Bob Dylan biography. . . .

Well, you know how it is, Jann . . . If you're sittin' in a room, and you have to have something done . . . I remember once, I was playing at Town Hall, and the producer of it came over with that biography . . . you know, I'm a *songwriter*, I'm not a biography writer, and I need a little help with these things.

So if I'm sitting in a room with some people, and I say "Come on now, I need some help; gimme a biography," so there might be three or four people there and out of those three or four people maybe they'll come up with something, come up with a biography. So we put it down, it reads well, and the producer of the concert is satisfied. In fact, he even gets a kick out of it. You dig what I mean?

But in actuality, this thing wasn't written for hundreds of thousands of people . . . it was just a little game for whoever was going in there and getting a ticket, you know, they get one of these things too. That's just show business. So you do that, and pretty soon you've got a million people who get it on the side. You know? They start thinkin' that it's written all for them. And it's *not* written for them—it was written for someone who bought the ticket to the concert. You got all these other people taking it too seriously. Do you know what I mean? So a lot of things have been blown out of proportion.

At the time when all your records were out, and you were working and everybody was writing stories about you, you let that become your story . . . you sort of covered up your parents, and your old friends . . . you sort of kept people away from them . . .

Did I?

Well, that was the impression it gave . . .

Jann, you know, my best friends . . . you're talking about old friends, and best friends . . . if you want to go by those standards, I haven't seen my best friends for over fifteen years. You know what I mean?

I'm not in the business of covering anything up. If I was from New Jersey, I could make an effort to show people my old neighborhood. If I was from Baltimore, same thing. Well, I'm from the Midwest. Boy, that's two different worlds.

This whole East Coast . . . there are a few *similarities* between the East Coast and the Midwest, and, of course, the people are similar, but it's a big jump. So, I came out of the Midwest, but I'm not interested in leading anybody back there. That's not my game.

Why didn't you publish 'Tarantula'?

Why? Well . . . it's a long story. It begins with when I suddenly began to sell quite a few records, and a certain amount of publicity began to be carried in all the major news magazines about this "rising young star." Well, this industry being what it is, book companies began sending me contracts, *because* I was doing interviews before and after concerts, and reporters would say things like "What else do you write?" And I would say, "Well, I don't write much of anything else." And they would say, "Oh, come on. You must write other things. Tell us something else. Do you write books?" And I'd say, "Sure, I write books."

After the publishers saw that I wrote books, they began to send me contracts . . . Doubleday, Macmillan, Hill and Range [*laughter*] . . . we took the biggest one, and then owed them a book. You follow me?

But there was no book. We just took the biggest contract. Why? I don't know. Why I *did*, I don't know. Why I was *told* to do it, I don't know. Anyway, I owed them a book.

So I sat down, and said, "Wow, I've done many things before, it's not so hard to write a book." So I sat down and wrote them a book in the hotel rooms and different places, plus I got a lot of other papers laying around that other people had written, so I threw it all together in a week and sent it to them.

Well, it wasn't long after that when I got it back to proofread it. I got it back and I said, "My gosh, did I write this? I'm not gonna have this out." Do you know what I mean? "I'm not gonna put this out. The folks back home just aren't going to understand this at all." I said, "Well, I have to do some corrections on this," I told them, and set about correcting it. I told them I was improving it.

Boy, they were hungry for this book. They didn't care what it was. People up there were saying "Boy, that's the second James Joyce," and "Jack Kerouac again," and they were saying "Homer revisited" . . . and they were all just talking through their heads.

They just wanted to sell *books*, that's all they wanted to do. It wasn't about anything . . . and I knew that—I figured they *had* to know that, they were in the business of it. I knew that, and I was just nobody. If I knew it, where were they at? They were just playing with me. My book.

So I wrote a new book. I figured I was satisfied with it and I sent that in. Wow, they looked at that and said, "Well, that's another book." And I said, "Well, but it's better." And they said, "Okay, we'll print this." So they printed that up and sent that back to proofread it. So I proofread it—I just looked at the first paragraph—and knew I just couldn't let that stand. So I took the whole thing with me on tour. I was going to rewrite it all. Carried a typewriter around the world. Trying to meet this deadline which they'd given me to put this book out. They just backed me into a corner. A lot of invisible people. So finally, I had a deadline on it, and was working on it, before my motorcycle accident. And I was studying all kinds of different prints and how I wanted them to print the book, by this time. I also was studying a lot of other poets at this time. . . . I had books which I figured could lead me somewhere . . . and I was using a little bit from everything.

But still, it wasn't any book; it was just to satisfy the publishers who wanted to print something that we had a contract for. Follow me? So eventually, I had my motorcycle accident, and that just got me out of the whole thing, 'cause I didn't care anymore. As it stands now, Jann, I could write a book. But I'm gonna write it first and then give it to them. You know what I mean?

Do you have any particular subject in mind, or plan, for a book?

Do you?

For yours or mine?

[*Laughs*] For any of them.

What writers today do you dig? Like who would you read if you were writing a book? Mailer?

All of them. There's something to be learned from them all.

What about the poets? You once said something about Smokey Robinson.

I didn't mean Smokey Robinson, I meant Arthur Rimbaud. I don't know how I could've gotten Smokey Robinson mixed up with Arthur Rimbaud [*laughter*]. But I did.

Do you see Allen Ginsberg much?

Not at all. Not at all.

Do you think he had any influence on your songwriting at all?

I think he did at a certain period. That period of . . . "Desolation Row," that kind of New York type period when all the songs were just "city songs." His poetry is city poetry. Sounds like the city.

Before, you were talking about touring and using drugs. During that period of songs like "Mr. Tambourine Man" and "Baby Blue," which a lot of writers have connected to the drug experience, not in the sense of them being "psychedelic music," or drug songs, but having come out of the drug experience.

How so?

In terms of perceptions. A level of perceptions . . . awareness of the songs . . .

Awareness of the *minute*. You mean that?

An awareness of the mind.

I would say so.

Did taking drugs influence the songs?

No, not the writing of them, but it did keep me up there to pump 'em out.

Why did you leave the city and city songs for the country and country songs?

The country songs?

The songs . . . you were talking about "Highway 61" being a song of the city, and songs of New York City . . .

What was on that album?

'Highway 61'? "Desolation Row," "Queen Jane" . . .

Well, it was also what the audiences wanted to hear, too . . . don't forget that. When you play every night in front of an audience, you know what they want to hear. It's easier to write songs then. You know what I'm talking about?

Many people — writers, college students, college writers — all felt tremendously affected by your music and what you're saying in the lyrics.

Did they?

Sure. They felt it had a particular relevance to their lives . . . I mean, you must be aware of the way that people come on to you.

Not entirely. Why don't you explain to me?

I guess if you reduce it to its simplest terms, the expectation of your audience — the portion of your audience that I'm familiar with — feels that you have the answer.

What answer?

Like from the film, 'Don't Look Back' — people asking you "Why? What is it? Where is it?" People are tremendously hung up on what you write and what you say. Do you react to that at all? Do you feel responsible to those people?

I don't want to make anybody *worry* about it . . . but boy, if I could ease someone's mind, I'd be the first one to do it. I want to lighten every load. Straighten out every burden. I don't want anybody to be hung up . . . [*laughs*] especially over *me*, or anything I do. That's not the point at all.

Let me put it another way . . . what I'm getting at is that you're an extremely important figure in music and an extremely important figure in the experience of growing up today. Whether you put yourself in that position or not, you're in that position. And you must have thought about it . . . and I'm curious to know what you think about that . . .

What would I think about it? What can I do?

You wonder if you're really that person.

What person?

A great "youth leader" . . .

If I thought I was that person, wouldn't I be out there doing it? Wouldn't I be, if I thought I was meant to do that, wouldn't I be doing it? I don't have to hold back. This Maharishi, he thinks that—right? He's out there doing it. If I thought that, I'd be out there doing it. Don't you agree, right? So obviously, I don't think *that*.

What do you feel about unwillingly occupying that position?

I can see that position filled by someone else. I play music, man. I write songs. I have a certain balance about things, and I believe there should be an order to everything. Underneath it all, I believe, also, that there are people trained for this job that you're talking about—"youth leader" type of thing, you know? I mean, there must be people *trained* to do this type of work. And I'm just one person, doing what I do. Trying to get along . . . staying out of people's hair, that's all.

You've been very reluctant to talk to reporters, the press and so on . . . why is that?

Why would you think?

Well, I know why you won't go on those things.

Well, if you know why, *you tell 'em* . . . 'cause I find it hard to talk about. People don't understand how the press works. People don't understand that they just use you to sell papers. And, in a certain way, that's not *bad* . . . but when they misquote you all the time, and when they just use you to fill in some story and when you read it after, it isn't anything the way you pictured it happening. Well, anyhow, it hurts. It hurts because you think you were just played for a fool. And the more hurts you get, the less you want to do it. Ain't that correct?

Were there any writers that you met that you liked? That you felt did good jobs? Wrote accurate stories . . .

On what?

On you. For instance, I remember two big pieces—one was in 'The New Yorker,' by Nat Hentoff. . . .

Yeah, I like 'em. I like that. In a way, I like 'em all. Whether I feel bad about 'em or not, in a way I like 'em all. I seldom get a kick out of them, Jann, but . . . I mean, I just can't be spending my time reading what people write [*laughter*]. I don't know anybody who can, do you?

How much of the day do you think about songwriting and playing the guitar?

Well, I try to get it when it comes. I play the guitar wherever I find one. But I try to write the song when it comes. I try to get it all . . . 'cause if you don't get it all, you're not gonna get it. So the best kinds of songs you can write are in motel rooms and cars . . . places which are all temporary. 'Cause you're forced to do it. Rather, it lets you go into it.

You go into your kitchen and try to write a song, and you can't write a song—I know people who do this—I know some songwriters who go to work every day, at eight thirty and come home at five. And usually bring something back . . . I mean, that's legal too. It just depends on how you do it. Me, I don't have those kind of things known to me yet, so I just get 'em when they come. And when they don't come, I don't try for it.

What do you look for when you make a record . . . I mean, what qualities do you judge it by when you hear it played back?

Ummmm . . . for the spirit. I like to hear a good lick once in a while. Maybe it's the spirit . . . don't you think so? I mean, if the spirit's not there, it don't matter how good a song it is.

What was the origin of that collection of basement tape songs? Did you write most of those songs, those demos, for yourself?

No, they weren't demos for myself, they were demos of the songs. I was being PUSHED again . . . into coming up with some songs. You know how those things go.

Do you have any artists in mind for any of those particular songs?

No. They were just fun to do. That's all. They were a kick to do. Fact, I'd do it all again. You know . . . that's really the way to do a recording—in a peaceful, relaxed setting—in somebody's basement. With the windows open . . . and a dog lying on the floor.

What is your day-to-day life like?

Hmmmm . . . there's no way I could explain that to you, Jann. Every day is different. Depends on what I'm doing. I may be fiddling around with the car or I may be painting a boat, or . . . possibly washing the windows. I just do what has to be done. I play a lot of music. I'm always trying to put shows together which never come about. I don't know what it is, but sometimes we get together and I say, "Okay, let's take six songs and do 'em up." So we do six songs, we got 'em in, let's say, forty minutes . . . we got a stopwatch timing 'em. But I mean nothing happens to it.

Boy, I hurried . . . I hurried for a long time. I'm sorry I did. All the time you're hurrying, you're not really as aware as you should be. You're trying to make things happen instead of just letting it happen. You follow me?

That's the awkwardness of this interview.

Well, I don't find anything awkward about it. I think it's going real great.

The purpose of any interview is to let the person who's being interviewed unload his head.

Well, that's what I'm doing.

And trying to draw that out is . . .

Boy, that's a good . . . that'd be a great title for a song. "Unload my head. Going down to the store . . . going down to the corner to unload my head." I'm gonna write that up when I get back [*laughter*]. "Going to Tallahassee to unload my head."

You said in one of your songs on 'Highway 61' . . . "I need a dump truck, mama, to unload my head." Do you still need a dump truck or something? [laughter]

What album was that?

It was on 'Highway 61.' What I'm trying to ask is what are the changes that have gone on between the time you did 'Highway 61' and 'Nashville Skyline' or 'John Wesley Harding'?

The changes. I don't think I know exactly what you mean.

How has life changed for you? Your approach to . . . your view of what you do . . .

Not much. I'm still the same person. I'm still uhh . . . going at it in the same old way. Doing the same old thing.

Do you think you've settled down, and slowed down?

I *hope* so. I was going at a tremendous speed at the time of my *Blonde on Blonde* album, I was going at a tremendous speed.

How did you make the change? The motorcycle accident?

I just took what came. That's how I made the changes. I took what came.

What do they come from?

What was what coming from? Well, they come from the same sources that everybody else's do. I don't know if it comes from within oneself any more than it comes from without oneself. Or outside of oneself. Don't you see what I mean? Maybe the inside and the outside are both the same. I don't know. But I feel it just like everyone else. What's that old line—there's a line from one of those old songs . . . "I can recognize it in others, I can feel it in myself." You can't say that's from the inside or the outside, it's like *both*.

Are there any albums or tracks from the albums that you think now were particularly good?

On any of my old albums? As songs or as performances?

Songs.

Oh yeah, quite a few.

Which ones?

Well, if I was performing now . . . if I was making personal appearances, you would know which ones, because I would play them. You know? But I don't know which ones I'd play now. I'd have to pick and choose. Certainly couldn't play 'em all. I like "Maggie's Farm." I always liked "Highway 61 Revisited." I always liked that song. "Mr. Tambourine Man" and "Blowin' in the Wind" and "Girl from the North Country" and "Boots of Spanish Leather" and "Times They Are A-Changin'" . . . I liked "Ramona."

Where did you write "Desolation Row"? Where were you when you wrote that?

I was in the back of a taxicab.

In New York?

Yeah.

During the period where you were recording songs with a rock & roll accompaniment, with a full-scale electric band, of those rock & roll songs that you did, which do you like?

The best rock & roll songs . . . which ones are there?

Uhh . . . "Like a Rolling Stone."

Yeah, I probably liked that the best.

And that was the Tom Wilson record . . . how come you never worked with that collection of musicians again?

Well, Michael Bloomfield, he was touring with Paul Butterfield at that time . . . and I could only get him when I could. So I wouldn't wait on Michael Bloomfield to make my records. He sure does play good, though. I missed having him there, but what could you do?

In talking about the songs as performances, *which of the* performances *that you did, that were recorded . . .*

I like "Like a Rolling Stone" . . . I can hear it now, now that you've mentioned it. I like that sound. You mean, which recorded performances?

Yeah, I mean in your performance *of the song . . .*

Oh . . . I like some of them on the last record, but I don't know, I tend to close up in the studio. I could never get enough presence on me. Never really did sound like me, to me.

There's a cat named Alan Weberman who writes in the 'East Village Other.' He calls himself the world's leading Dylanologist. You know him?

No . . . oh, yes. I did. Is this the guy who tears up all my songs? Well, he oughta take a rest. He's way off. I saw something he wrote about "All Along the Watchtower," and boy, let me tell you, this boy's *off*. Not only did he create some type of fantasy—he had Allen Ginsberg in there—he couldn't even hear the words to the song right. He didn't hear the song right. Can you *believe* that? I mean, this fellow couldn't hear the words . . . or something. I bet he's a hardworking fellow, though. I bet he really does a good job if he could find something to do, but it's too bad it's just my songs, 'cause I don't really know if there's enough material in my songs to sustain someone who is really out to do a big job. You understand what I mean?

I mean, a fellow like that would be much better off writing about Tolstoy, or Dostoevsky, or Freud . . . doing a really big analysis of somebody who has countless volumes of writings. But here's me, just a few records out. Somebody devoting so much time to those few records, when there's such a wealth of material that hasn't even been touched yet, or hasn't even been heard or read . . . that escapes me. Does it escape you?

I understand putting time into it, but I read this, in this *East Village Other*; I read it . . . and it was clever. And I got a kick out of reading it [*laughter*] on some level, but I didn't want to think anybody was taking it too seriously. You follow me?

He's just representative of thousands of people who do take it seriously.

Well, that's their own business. Why don't I put it that way? That's their business and his business. But I'm the source of that and I don't know if it's my business or not, but I'm the source of it. You understand? So I see it a little differently than all of them do.

People in your audience, they obviously take it very seriously, and they look to you for something. . . .

Well, I wouldn't be where I am today without them. So, I owe them my music.

Does the intensity of some of the response annoy you?

No. No, I rather enjoy it.

What do you think your following is like?

Well, I think there are all kinds. You would probably know just as much about that as I would. You know, they're all kinds of people. I remember when I used to do concerts, you couldn't pin 'em down. All the road managers and the sound-equipment carriers and even the truck drivers would notice how different the audiences were, in terms of individual people. Like sometimes I might have a concert and all the same kind of people show up. I mean, what does that mean?

Did you vote for president?

We got down to the polls too late [*laughter*].

People are always asking about what does this song mean and what does that song mean, and a lot of them seem to be based on some real person, just like any kind of fiction. Are there any songs that you can relate to particular people, as having inspired the song?

Not now, I can't.

What do you tell somebody who says, "What is 'Leopard-Skin Pill-Box Hat' about?"

It's just about that. I think that's something I mighta taken out of the newspaper. Mighta seen a picture of one in a department-store window. There's really no more to it than that. I know it can get blown up into some kind of illusion. But in reality, it's no more than that. Just a leopard-skin pill-box. That's *all.*

—

How did you come in contact with the Band?

Well, there used to be this young lady that worked up at Al Grossman's office—her name was Mary Martin, she's from Canada. And she was a rather persevering soul, as she hurried around the office on her job; she was a secretary; did secretarial work and knew all the bands and all the singers from Canada. She was from Canada. Anyway, I needed a group to play electric songs.

Where did you hear them play?

Oh, I never did hear them play. I think the group I wanted was Jim Burton and Joe Osborne. I wanted Jim Burton, and Joe Osborne to play bass, and Mickey Jones. I knew Mickey Jones, he was playing with Johnny Rivers. They were all in California, though. And there was some difficulty in making that group connect. One of them didn't want to fly and Mickey couldn't make it immediately, and I think Jim Burton was playing with a television group at that time.

He used to play with Ricky Nelson?

Oh, I think this was after that. He was playing with a group called the Shindogs, and they were on television. So he was doing that job. Anyway, that was the way it stood, and Mary Martin kept pushing this group who were out in New Jersey—I think they were in Elizabeth, New Jersey, or Hartford, Connecticut, or some town close to around New York. She was pushing them, and she had two of the fellows come up to the office so we could meet. I just asked them if they could do it, and they said they could [*laughs*]. These two said they could. And that was how it started. Easy enough, you know.

How come you never made an album with them?

We tried. We cut a couple sides in the old New York Columbia studios. We cut two or three, and right after "Positively 4th Street," we cut some singles, and they didn't really get off the ground. You oughta hear 'em. You know, you could find 'em. They didn't get off the ground. They didn't even make it on the charts.

Consequently, I've not been back on the charts since the singles. I never did so much care for singles, 'cause you have to pay so much attention to them. Unless you make your whole album full of singles. You have to make them separately. So I didn't really think about them too much that way.

But, playing with the Band was a natural thing. We have a real
different sound. Real different. I heard one of the records recently
. . . it was on a jukebox. "Please Crawl Out Your Window."

That was one of them? What were the others?

There were some more songs out of that same session . . . "Sooner or
Later"—that was on *Blonde on Blonde*. That's one of my favorite songs.

*What role did you play in the 'Big Pink' album, the album they made by
themselves.*

Well, I didn't do anything on that album. They did that with John
Simon.

Did you play piano on it or anything?

No.

*What kind of sound did you hear when you went in to make 'John Wesley
Harding'?*

I heard the sound that Gordon Lightfoot was getting, with Charlie
McCoy and Kenny Buttrey. I'd used Charlie and Kenny both before, and
I figured if he could get that sound, I could. But we couldn't get it [*laughs*]
It was an attempt to get it, but it didn't come off. We got a different
sound . . . I don't know what you'd call that . . . it's a muffled sound.

There used to be a lot of friction in the control booth on these
records I used to make. I didn't know about it; I wasn't aware of them
until recently. Somebody would want to put limiters on this and somebody would want to put an echo on that, someone else would have some
other idea. And myself, I don't know anything about any of this. So I
just have to leave it up in the air. In someone else's hands.

The friction was between the engineer and the producer. . . .

No, the managers and the advisers and the agents.

*Do you usually have sessions at which all these people are there, or do you
prefer to close them up?*

Well, sometimes there's a whole lot of people. Sometimes you can't
even move, there's so many people . . . other times, there's no one. Just
the musicians.

Which is more comfortable for you?

Well, it's much more comfortable when there's . . . oh, I don't know, I could have it both ways. Depends what kind of song I'm gonna do. I might do a song where I *want* all those people around. Then I do another song and have to shut the lights off, you know?

Was "Sad Eyed Lady of the Lowlands" originally planned as a whole side?

It started out as just a little thing. "Sad Eyed Lady of the Lowlands," but I got carried away somewhere along the line. I just sat down at a table and started writing. At the session itself. And I just got carried away with the whole thing. . . . I just started writing and I couldn't stop. After a period of time, I forgot what it was all about, and I started trying to get back to the beginning [*laughs*]. Yeah.

'John Wesley Harding' — why did you call the album that?

Well, I called it that because I had that song, "John Wesley Harding." It didn't mean anything to me. I called it that, Jann, 'cause I had the song "John Wesley Harding," which started out to be a long ballad. I was gonna write a ballad on . . . like maybe one of those old cowboy . . . you know, a real long ballad. But in the middle of the second verse, I got tired. I had a tune, and I didn't want to waste the tune; it was a nice little melody, so I just wrote a quick third verse, and I recorded that.

Why did you choose the name of the outlaw John Wesley Harding?

Well, it fits in tempo. Fits right in tempo. Just what I had at hand.

What other titles did you have for the album?

Not for that one. That was the only title that came up for that one. But for the *Nashville Skyline* one, the title came up *John Wesley Harding, Volume II.* We were gonna do that . . . the record company wanted to call the album *Love Is All There Is.* I didn't see anything wrong with it, but it sounded a little spooky to me. . . .

What about 'Blonde on Blonde'?

Well, I don't even recall exactly how it came up, but I do know it was all in good faith. It has to do with just the word. I don't know who thought of that. *I* certainly didn't.

Of all the albums as albums, excluding your recent ones, which one do you think was the most successful in what it was trying to do? Which was the most fully realized, for you?

I think the second one. The second album I made.

Why?

Well, I felt real good about doing an album with my own material, and I picked a little on it, picked the guitar, and it was a *big* Gibson—I felt real accomplished on that. "Don't Think Twice." Got a chance to do some of that. Got a chance to play in open tuning. . . . "Oxford Town," I believe that's on that album. That's open tuning. I got a chance to do talking blues. I got a chance to do ballads, like "Girl from the North Country." It's just because it had more variety. I felt good at that.

Of the electric ones, which do you prefer?

Well, soundwise, I prefer this last one. 'Cause it's got the sound. See, I'm listening for sound now.

As a collection of songs?

Songs? Well, this last album maybe means more to me, 'cause I did undertake something. In a certain sense. And . . . there's a certain pride in that.

It was more premeditated than the others? I mean, you knew what you were gonna go after?

Right.

Where did the name 'Nashville Skyline' . . .

Well, I always like to tie the name of the album in with some song. Or if not some song, some kind of general feeling. I think that just about fit because it was less in the way, and less specific than any of the other ones on there.

Certainly couldn't call the album *Lay, Lady Lay.* I wouldn't have wanted to call it that, although that name was brought up. It didn't get my vote, but it was brought up. *Peggy Day—Lay, Peggy Day,* that was brought up. A lot of things were brought up. *Tonight I'll Be Staying Here with Peggy Day.* That's another one. Some of the names just didn't seem to fit. *Girl from the North Country.* That was another title which didn't really seem to fit. Picture me on the front holding a guitar and *Girl from the North Country* printed on top [*laughs*]. *Tell Me That It Isn't Peggy Day.* I don't know who thought of that one.

What general thing was happening that made you want to start working with the Band, rather than working solo?

I only worked solo because there wasn't much going on. There wasn't. There were established people around . . . yeah, the Four Seasons . . . there were quite a few other established acts. But I worked alone because it was easier to. Plus, everyone else I knew was working alone, writing and singing. There wasn't much opportunity for groups or bands then—there wasn't. You know that.

When did you decide to get one together, like that? You played at Forest Hills, that was where you first appeared with a band. Why did you feel the time had come?

To do that? Well, because I could *pay* a backing group now. See, I didn't want them to use a backing group unless I could pay them.

Do you ever get a chance to work frequently with the Band? In the country?

Work? Well, *work* is something else. Sure, we're always running over old material. We're always playing, running over old material. New material . . . and different kinds of material. Testing out this and that.

What do you see yourself as—a poet, a singer, a rock & roll star, married man . . .

All of those. I see myself as it all. Married man, poet, singer, song-writer, custodian, gatekeeper . . . all of it. I'll be it all. I feel "confined" when I have to choose one or the other. Don't you?

13. Interview with A. J. Weberman, *East Village Other*

JANUARY 19, 1971

A Dylan Interview Conducted by A. J. Weberman, Dylanologist & Minister of Defense, Dylan Liberation Front

By (of course) A. J. Weberman, Dylanologist

Preface
The following interview is actually a series of conversations I had with Dylan in early January 1971. Since D wouldn't let me record them, I had to reconstruct them through my recollections. When I showed Bob what I had come up with, he said, "There's lies in there & that's sneaky shit talkin to a cat, then writing about it." We corrected my errors over the phone & D gave me some direct quotes (I recorded the phone call & have included parts of it). I think I caught the leap of D's bound to some extent.

Note
D stands for Dylan
CB stands for current bag

I was really fucking hassled the day I met Dylan. Pigs. Heavy shit. I was goin fucking crazy. I made it to the D class that I teach each week at the Alternate U & gave a shirt rap & then said—"Tonight's the field trip to D's pad." About fifty of us headed down 6th Ave. towards MacDougal St. When we got to 4th St. I pointed out the pad D lived in from 62–64 and tried to explain how it related to D's single—POSITIVELY FOURTH STREET—but this drunk wouldn't let me get a word in edgewise. We continued to march & picked up a couple of street kids along the way (that's the dangerous part about doing something like this—like I could trust the people in my class, but these kids were full of undirected violence). Soon we were all standing in front of D's. I began to yell, HEY BOBBY PLEASE CRAWL OUT YOUR WINDOW. Someone else screamed—OPEN THE DOOR BOBBY. The lights started to go on and off and one of D's kids came to the window & started playing with his blocks on the sill, building sort of a wall against us. We stopped yelling. I invited the class into D's lobby in order to show them where D "came down into the lobby to make a small call out" but by this time the class had split into two groups—the hardcore Dylan Liberationists were with me in the hall, while the people with groupie tendencies were standing across the street. Then Eric Williams (DLF) said—"Hey man, I saw someone look out from on top of the stairs for a flash." Dylan was home!

We went outside & I decided to go thru D's garbage with the class, & so they formed a circle around me. David Peel (DLF) pointed out that his garbage bags were green, like his money. My "Garbage Article" had already come out so there was nothing of interest to be found, but we did the thing anyway. Then one of the street kids decided he was gonna enter D's thru a window. I was explaining what we'd do to him if he tried it (I wasn't ready for an illegal demo—yet) when Sharon (DLF—groupie tendencies) comes over and says: "There's someone standing across the street who looks JUST LIKE DYLAN." "Holy shit," I thought. "What the fuck am I going to do? D's caught me red-handed going thru his garbage. He's gonna be pissed off . . . he may get violent. I may have to beat the shit out of that slimy bootlicker here and now." I looked up and saw Bob standing directly across the street from me—he was dressed in denim, wearing rimless glasses, & it looked like smoke was coming out of his head. I just stood there. David Peel came over and pushed me forward. It was like High Noon. "Do not forsake me oh my Dylanology." I eventually walked over to D, who looked like a cross between someone in his "current bag" and a Talmudic scholar, and said, "How are you, man?" "Turn off the tape recorder" (I had one with me & I did). Then D said, "Al, why'd ye bring all these people around my house for?" "It's a field trip for my Dylan class, man . . . but actually it's a demonstration against you and all you've come to represent in rock music." "Alan, let's go talk about this," and he took me by the arm (I knew that very instant he meant to do me harm) & he started putting on the pressure and I had no other choice except but for to go. "Cool it man," I yelled, "that fuckin hurts—no violence—unless you want to fight it out here and now." "Al, did you ever write anything about my Karate? Ever write anything about my race & stuff it in my mailbox?" "I knew you took Karate but I never wrote anything about it . . . your race . . .?" "What race are you, Alan?" "The human race." "And what race were yer parents?" "Well, they considered themselves Jewish, I guess." "You sure you never wrote anything about my race?" "No, man, it ain't yer race I object to, it's yer politics and lifestyle." "Well, I didn't think ya would, Al." "Hey Bob, what do you do with all your money?" "It all goes to Kibbutzim in Israel and Far Rockaway." "But you were one of the first Jews to put down Israel." "Where?" "In the liner notes to ANOTHER SIDE OF D." "Don't remember! . . . You know, Al, you've been in the city too long, the city does something to your thinking—I know how it is."

D sat down on this stoop a few blocks from his pad and we continued the conversation—"What about your cb, Bobby?" He denied it and did something that would make people believe he was telling the truth. But not A. J. Like he says—"We'll fly over the ocean JUST AS THEY SUSPECT" ("Fly over ocean" is a metaphor for D's cb from other contexts). Later on he told me—"Everyone's been asking me about your writing" THE RUMOR. "The man in Dylan would do nearly any task when asked for compensation . . ." just give him his current bag. "From my TOES up to my HEELS" Dig what I mean.

Somewhat taken aback by D's willingness to cooperate, I told him— "Man, but there's all this evidence in your poetry—I could stand here for hours and hours running it all down . . . and then there's all the songs written to you by other poets in yer own language putting you down for your cb." "Al, you've got to keep in mind that my poetry doesn't reflect the way I'm feeling, now, it's like years behind." "Well, bullshit . . ."

So we talked. D said he didn't dig the Panthers because of their position on the Mideast situation—"Little Israel versus all those . . ." I started to explain to D how the Panthers believed that everyone has a right to live: Jews, Arabs AND Palestinian refugees, when this kid from my class come over and says he wants to talk to D. I told him that was cool but to wait until we got done . . . I had something important to say to Bob & I didn't know if I'd ever see him again. (I was seizing the time.) So the punk says—"You're full of shit and so is Dylanology." So I grabbed him by the collar & screamed SPLIT, ASSHOLE! He left but as he was going he yelled out in grade-school intonation—WEBERMAN'S BOOTLEG-GING TARANTULA (D's suppressed novel). Dylan said I only had half of the book—the other half was out in Calif.—& that I should never worry about running out of things to interpret. He said he was gonna invite me up to Woodstock a couple of months ago. I asked, "How come you didn't, how come I had to have a demonstration in front of yer house to get you to negotiate . . . you know how dedicated I am & how well I know your work." "I know, Al, and one day we'll go for a ride together and I'll interpret all my poems for ya." "We ain't goin down by the docks, are we?" "No . . . Al, you scared my tenants yelling like that." "Sorry, man, I didn't mean to grag yer innocent people into it . . . dig like these radical freaks were staying over at The Archives & I told them where you were at & they thought about trashing your place but I told them DON'T DO IT . . . it ain't fair to Dylan's kids." "Al, I know a lot of people who want to hurt you, especially after that 'Garbage' thing—you know, all these college kids come to my garbage & take some of it back to their dorms—you wouldn't like these kids either . . ." "Get a garbage compactor and I'll come around and pick it up once a week." "I don't like machines . . . no, that's not true. "Bob, you wouldn't have me offed, would you?" "You scared?" "Sure I am, this is an oligarchy, the more money you have the more power." "I wouldn't do it, Al, don't worry, it's too late anyway." "I didn't think so, man, it would be like GM offing Nader, but if you do, you BETTER do a good job."

I went on & gave D a rap against Imperialism, Racism & Sexism (he didn't seem like he was listening) and then I told him that NASHVILLE SKYLINE sucked while SELF PORTRAIT was a stone rip-off since many people bought it, played it once, and stuck it on their shelf. Neither album related to objective reality. Dylan responded quietly—"Well, there were 2 good songs on S.P., DAYS OF FORTY-NINE and KOPPER KETTLE . . . and without those 2 lps they'd be no NEW MORNING, anyway I'm just starting to get back on my feet as far as my music goes . . . Al, do you use Amphetamine?" "No, man, the reason I have so much energy is because I'm tuned in to the life force that's trying to assert itself here on earth—I'M ALIVE MAN." "Why worry so much about earth when there's . . ." "What do you want me to worry about: if Mars invades us?" "What drugs do you use, Al?" "Just reefer & caffeine, and you?" "No drugs." "BULLSHIT!" Although I must admit that D's eyes looked normal almost every time we met. "Well, so long, Al, you're an interesting fellow, see you in a few weeks." I gave him the power handshake & he split.

When I got home I was fucking wasted. I was rapping with Harvey, a lawyer friend, when the phone rang—"Hello Al, this is Bob." Suddenly the telephone began to look like my record player. "Want to come over and visit me tomorrow?" "That's like asking a strung-out junkie if he wants a fix." "Al, I wanted to thank you for helping me sell a lot of records—your articles have helped to keep it going." "Yeah, that's one aspect of Dylanology I don't dig . . . but I may cancel it out soon." "Al, do you have a driver's license?" "No, never learned to drive." "Too bad, I know of this chauffeur's job that's open." "Are you trying to buy me out, man? STOP RIGHT HERE. It's im-fucking-possible." "No, no, I wasn't trying to buy you out, I just wanted you to see me from another seat, you've been on the streets too long." "Hey Bob, you know that song CHAMPAGNE, ILLINOIS you wrote and gave to Carl Perkins?" "Yeah, I figured Carl needed a song." "He needed something, anyway, why not write a song called CARBONDALE, ILL. Cause that's where the pigs just murdered this black man who was gonna testify against them . . ." Dylan remained silent. "You there?" "Call me tomorrow." I hung up.

The next day he called me & told me to come over to his midtown studio with a tape deck & an amplifier if I wanted to hear some rare D tapes cause all he had at the studio was a record player. My old lady, Ann, helped me take the stuff uptown & then split cause D said he wanted to see me alone. D began—"I've seen you around a lot, Al." "Bob, let's set up the equipment, okay?" I went over to the speaker and asked him to disconnect it & he started unscrewing the terminal with no lead on it. "Let me do it, man," & I did the thing. (This little bit of play acting and the riff about not having a tape recorder in his studio was a clever ploy designed to convince me D wasn't into recording conversations, but I didn't go for it & maintained my cool when it came to saying self-incriminating things.)

We began—"What do you think of Tim Leary?" Dylan asked. "I think he's great—like he was into revolution all along but felt he could attract a lot of the middle class by talking about it in mystical terms. He's a national hero of Woodstock Nation. What do you think?" "I don't follow politics." "How come I found newspaper in yer garbage, every day?" "It's not my garbage—everyone in my building—we mix all the garbage together." "Sure ye do! . . . hey man, I'll tell you something about yer politics— they're fucking genocidal—cause I talk to a lot of people when I'm out on the streets selling TARANTULA and most of the people I talk to got the impression from that SING OUT! interview that you support the war in Vietnam." "I only did that to get back at the freaks who wouldn't leave me alone & let me do my thing up in Woodstock—every five minutes there was someone at my door. I mean this fame thing got out of hand. I never expected to become this famous. I DON'T DIG IT. Everywhere I go—man, even if I go to some small town somewhere—a bunch of freaks always manage to find me and then they go apeshit." "Get a long-haired wig, they'd never recognize you." "Why don't you buy me one, Al . . ." "Hey man, how come you associated yourself with Cash—that lackey was so conservative at that time you did things together that Nixon later invited him to sing at the White House & Cash still goes out of his way to praise Nixon's genocidal policies at his concerts." "I've heard Cash since I was a kid . . . I love him." "Bob, yer so fucking conservative lately, I'm surprised Nixon didn't invite you to sing fer him." "I am too, man." "Man, almost all the other rock people put you down in their songs—in yer own language—for yer politics." "They're just using my phrasing."

"No, man, they understand what you're saying the same way I do—from studying yer poetry."

"Why don't you ask them about it?" "Man, they'd deny it cause it's a secret language & cause of the controversial nature of you cb which they sing about—anyway it's poetry & it's up to the listener or critic to figure it out." "I deny it's happening and so do they." "Hey, Dylan man, all of you can deny your asses off, but as long as ya don't come up with another system that's more consistent, makes more sense, etc., MINE STANDS, DIG?" "NO."

"And, man, if you really believe in yer current bag and want to continue to remain in it, how come you copped-out on yourself in your poetry? And the poetry is simple enough that many people understand it. Isn't that indicative of a contradiction in yer personality?" Now I had Dylan going. He suddenly became very depressed and didn't say anything. He looked hurt. I almost felt sorry for him. "Hey Bob, you okay, man? Like a lot of these cats are full of shit—putting you down for not doing anything when they don't do shit themselves." "Remember, Al, I'm not like them . . . not fresh out of college . . ." "Man, you've been telling everyone my interpretations are 'way off' . . . let's hear you interpret one of your songs, then I'll interpret it and we'll see whose interpretation is better . . . how about TONIGHT I'LL BE STAYING WITH YOU?" "Okay, but I feel stupid . . . Throw my ticket out the window . . . so we were down in Nashville and the train was leaving and I didn't want to go so I said . . ." "Hey man, didn't you once sing 'You hand in your money' for the line 'You hand in your ticket' (from MR. JONES) at a concert in England?" "Yeah." "So doesn't ticket symbolize money?" "A ticket is anything you want it to be." "You mean your symbolism isn't consistent?" "It's as consistent as me." "So isn't it money?" "It could be." Dylan then changed the subject—"You sure you didn't write any letters about my race?" "No, man, how many times do I have to tell you . . . like every letter I ever wrote you was on Dylan Archives stationery—was that?" "Yes, I got it right here." He couldn't find it. (Since "letter" symbolizes "article" in D's symbology, he may have been referring to part of my *EVO* "garbage article," where, after finding cards and thank-you notes from D's family, I wrote—"Good to see Dylan is still a Zimmerman." What I meant by that was, "Good to see D still associates with middle class, lames like his straight relatives." It was a riff in the Lenny Bruce LIMA OHIO & John Lennon "don't believe in Zimmerman" tradition & not antisemitic.)

"Did you ever write a song to me?" "Absolutely not." "How about Dear Landlord, or was that to Grossman?" "Grossman wasn't in my mind when I wrote it. Only later when people pointed out that the song may have been written for Grossman I thought it could have been . . . it's an abstract song . . . sure as hell wasn't written for you . . . I wasn't aware of you then." "Does Albert still act in your behalf?" "No."

Throughout our conversation the phone rang constantly, and at one point someone came to the door and handed D a fan letter and a book of poems. He read the fan letter right then and there and handed me the book—"Take a look at it—tell me what you think—advise me—you're a knowledgeable cat and I could use some advice—even on politics." "Bullshit." "I should have a book of my poems out in two years & a book containing all my songs should be out soon & I'm planning to release that song you have a rare tape of—SHE'S YOUR LOVER NOW—as a single." "Bullshit . . . what do you think about my work, man?" "Your approach is sincere." "You know, if I lived in another age I might have been a Talmudic scholar." "So would I." "I guess so—you say I'm 'sincere.' Why didn't you say that in the *Rolling Stone* interview instead of saying I was 'way-off'?" "I'm thru with that. The only reason I gave them an interview was because they hounded me for years." "Do you follow the rock criticism scene closely?" "No." "How come I found all those rock papers in yer garbage?" "I only read them when Al Kooper brings them over . . . wanna hear a tape?" He played one cut—it was D singing DON'T YE TELL HENRY, a song the band often does at concerts—this lent support to my theory that D ghosts for the band. "We got a better fidelity version of this tape back in the Archives." Then D offered me all this stuff that would help my "career" as a rock critic; I could sit in on recording sessions, he hinted I could call him up & get info on his new records thusly making my review "straight from the horse's mouth" so to speak. I kind of got the feeling that

I'd get all these privileges if I behaved. FUCK THAT SHIT. "Want to see the rest of the studio?" We walked into this room filled with the band's instruments and D's paintings. They were impressionistic abysslike things. "What do you think of my paintings?" "Stick to poetry." "I paint what's on my mind." "Yeah, empty." For the first time D laughed—IT TAKES A LOT to make Dylan LAUGH—but he could relate to emptiness. Then I decided to lay it on the line—"Dylan, you've got to live up to your responsibility as a culture hero—you're Dylan, man, every freak has a soft spot in their heart for ya, they love ya, you're DYLAN, DYLAN, DYLAN." "I'm not Dylan, you're Dylan." "I know, you're some other man, right?" We went back into the front of the studio—"Want some records, Al?" "No, I get them for free from the record companies." "Want a rare picture of me?" "I told you we got all that shit back in the Archives . . . getting back to the subject at hand, did you ever think that maybe your wealth has corrupted you—you once said that the more of a stake you have in the system the more conservative one becomes—'Relationships of ownership they whisper in the sings,' etc. And man, you used the struggle of black people for a decent life to make you famous, remember BLOWIN IN THE WIND and you ripped the blacks for their music—YOU OWE THEM QUITE A BIT—any truth to what I'm saying, man?" "Could be." Then I began to tell Bob why I feel the way I do about 3rd World Liberation & went into a riff about my visit with a very poor cat in Mexico. "Let's write a song together about your trip & we'll split the royalties." "Send my cut to Caesar Chavez, man." "So you just tell me what happened to you and I'll do the writing." "I was down in Progresso, in the Yucatan, & I stayed with this laborer, a typical third world scene, poverty, famine, disease—like being born in a nitemare—prolonged death agony—anyway, the cat became a 'bracero'—rhymes with sombrero." "And this cat thought the communists were 'little people'—he was brainwashed—his pad was next to a garbage dump. Now we got to convince Amerikans—thru this song—that they should support wars of national liberation." Dylan came up with a song that went like this—"Down in Progresso a bracero lived in a sombrero full of espresso." "What the fuck is this, man? No one is ever gonna be convinced of anything when you write that abstractly." "That's my thing, Al."

"Know anything about the other books being written about me?" "Well, Robert Shelton, Tony Scaduto and Toby Thompson are doing books. I know Tony. He says he's goin around talkin to all yer old friends (Jack Elliott, the McKenzies, etc.) and yer old lovers (Suzie Rotollo, Joanie Baez, etc.) collecting 'information' about you—he said he would have

studied yer lyrics but he knew he couldn't get permission to reprint them."
"That's not the reason—he could have never figured them out—he'll only
come up with rumors." "He did a pretty good job, tho."

"Man, I think you're a fucking reactionary. You don't use your influence to save lives. Look at all the death around us. Look what just happened
in Pakistan—that was the result of capitalism—the people were so poor
they couldn't cope with a natural disaster." "I wonder why the good Lord
wanted all those people to die?" "You don't believe in God . . . !" "I sure
do . . ." "But how about WITH GOD ON OUR SIDE . . . Did ya believe
in God then?" "I must have then too."

"How about using some of your five million dollars to save lives?" "I
don't have that much." "Bullshit, I got inside info, you multi millionaire
PIG. Anyway, you were a self proclaimed millionaire in '65. And you
never do any benefits. Then there's your apolitical lyrics—everyone who
heard NASHVILLE SKYLINE said—'Dylan's in a mellow head; he's singing about love.' You cut your hair, you only help apolitical rock people
with their careers—you're a punk and me and the DLF are going to do a
number on you. We got some shit planned that gonna blow your mind.
Not only that, but everyone in rock with a political consciousness is gonna
come down on you. Lennon has started already by calling you Zimmerman; McGuinn just put you down." "Where?" "In *Creem*." "How?" "By
saying you write BALLAD OF EASY RIDER even tho you told him not
to." "What? Well, I want to know who's gonna do this (getting angry)
cause I'm not gonna take it. I'm gonna get them. I'm gonna get them.
They'll never get out of it. Too bad for them . . . punks!" "Hey Bob, why
not show the people your heart's in the right place and do a benefit for
John Sinclair?" "I'm not about to help Sinclair by doing a concert, nor
am I about to do any concerts at this time, man." "All you got to do is
show up and plunk your guitar a little and a hundred thousand freaks will
come out of their pads and go anywhere you are . . ." "Sorry, Al, I can't
do it. But I will write a song about political prisoners on my next album
. . ." "I don't want any promises for nine months later, I WANT TO SEE
SOME ACTION NOW . . . see, Bob, you set the trends in rock and if you
become like a human being a lot of other performers will go along . . ."

"Al, a lot of the things you do aren't on the up and up. You 'tap'
phones, and ya go thru garbage like a pig." "But I didn't sell the garbage
to LIFE MAGAZINE." "You must get money for your articles." "I'm not
like you man, I send em all out fer free . . . everything should be free . . .
money equals slavery. I'm proud I do it." "No reason not to be, but Al, I'm
gonna write a song about you." "I could use the publicity." "That's one

reason why I wouldn't . . . but I got a good song called PIG." "I can't take that seriously coming from you, multi-millionaire who hoards his bread. No matter how you cut it, when you have all that bread and most people in the world have shit, you're the enemy—THE PIG. Bobby, you're just another capitalist, but instead of producing cars, guns, etc., you produce culture." "That's something." "Sure it is . . . 'Blue moon, you left me standing alone' . . ." "Al, if I was a kid growing up I'd have to look out for you . . . I'd keep my eyes open for you. I'd make sure whatever street I went down I'd have to stand on the other side of the street when you came down, man. Al, why don't you get a guitar and put some of this energy to good use?" "But there's a need for someone like myself—no one else is doing the thing." "But yer so extreme . . ." "Thanks." "Off on one end—there's no one balancing the other end . . . " "How about lame rock critics . . ." "They're in the middle . . ." "Hey Bob, they all say I'm full of shit, Griel Mucus, Richie Goldstein, Christgau . . . they're all CORRUPT."

The sun had set & Dylan's wife had called him for dinner on the phone a couple of times. Bob gave me his phone number and asked me to call him when I'm on the radio or if something comes up. "Ever hear me on the radio, Bob?" "Just a couple of times on Alex Bennett's Show—I dug it when he asked you if you had any personal messages for me. What do you think of Bob Fass?" "He's a revolutionary brother but he don't dig it when I attack you cause you were an old friend of his." "Well, Al, so long, and one more thing—you're not going to get into my life." "Why?" "If you do I might gain a soul." "Is that a threat?"

Talking to Dylan was like talking to a ghost. The old Dylan, full of ideas and stories was gone, replaced with a shell. It was also like talking to a con-man who was really conning himself. I know D's still into his cb & he was trying to cool me out by using his charisma & offering me his "friendship." Trying to co-opt me & the DLF but we will fight on— till we win.

FREE BOB DYLAN
POWER TO THE PEOPLE

14. Interview with Jonathan Cott, ROLLING STONE

JANUARY 26, 1978

We were driving down Sunset Boulevard—Christmastime in L.A.—looking for a place to eat, when Bob Dylan noticed Santa Claus, surrounded by hundreds of stuffed, Day-Glo animals, standing and soliciting on the street. "Santa Claus in the desert," he commented disconcertedly, "it really brings you down."

A few minutes later, we passed a billboard which showed a photo of George Burns pointing to a new album by John Denver and praising it to the skies. "Did you see that movie they appeared in together?" Dylan asked me. "I sort of like George Burns. What was he playing?"

"I saw it on the plane coming out here. He played God," I said.

"That's a helluva role," Dylan replied.

Bob Dylan should know. For years he has been worshiped—and deservedly so. His songs are miracles, his ways mysterious and unfathomable. In words and music, he has reawakened, and thereby altered, our experience of the world. In statement ("He not busy being born is busy dying") and in image ("My dreams are made of iron and steel/With a big bouquet of roses hanging down/From the heavens to the ground") he has kept alive the idea of the poet and artist as *vates*—the visionary eye of the body politic—while keeping himself open to a conception of art that embraces and respects equally Charles Baudelaire and Charley Patton, Arthur Rimbaud and Smokey Robinson.

"Mystery is an essential element in any work of art," says the director Luis Buñuel in a recent *New Yorker* profile by Penelope Gilliatt. "It's usually lacking in film, which should be the most mysterious of all. Most filmmakers are careful not to perturb us by opening the windows of the screen onto their world of poetry. Cinema is a marvelous weapon when it is handled by a free spirit. Of all the means of expression, it is the one that is most like the human imagination. What's the good of it if it apes everything conformist and sentimental in us? It's a curious thing that film can create such moments of compressed ritual. The raising of the everyday to the dramatic."

I happened to read these words during my flight to Los Angeles—having just finished watching "the conventional and sentimental" in-flight movie—hardly knowing then that, just a day later, I would be seeing a film that perfectly embodied Buñuel's notion of the possibilities of cinema.

Renaldo and Clara—an audacious and remarkable four-hour movie that will open in New York and Los Angeles on January 25th and soon thereafter in cities around the country—is Bob Dylan's second film. His first, *Eat the Document*, was a kind of antidocumentary, a night journey through the disjointed landscapes of Dylan's and the Band's 1966 world tour, a magic swirling ship of jump cuts, "ready for to fade." It was a fascinating work, but it came and went after only a few showings.

To remain on a given level, no matter how exalted, is a sin, a spiritual teacher once said. And just as it is impossible for Bob Dylan "to sing the same song the same way twice"—as he himself puts it—so his new film is a departure from *Eat the Document*, as it announces the arrival of a visionary cinematic free spirit.

Conceived over a period of ten years, and edited down by Howard Alk and Dylan from 400 hours of footage, *Renaldo and Clara* was shot during the 1975–76 Rolling Thunder Revue, whose participants make up a cast that includes Bob Dylan (Renaldo), Sara Dylan (Clara), Joan Baez (the Woman in White), Ronnie Hawkins (Bob Dylan), Ronee Blakley (Mrs. Dylan), Jack Elliott (Longheno de Castro), Bob Neuwirth (the Masked Tortilla), Allen Ginsberg (the Father), David Blue (David Blue), and Roger McGuinn (Roger McGuinn).

"Who Are You, Bob Dylan?" was the headline in the French newspaper read by Jean-Pierre Leaud in Jean-Luc Godard's *Masculin-Feminin*. And the mystery of *Renaldo and Clara* is: "Who is Bob Dylan?" "Who is Renaldo?" and "What is the relationship between them?"

I decided to ask Bob Dylan himself.

"There's Renaldo," he told me, "there's a guy in whiteface singing on the stage and then there's Ronnie Hawkins playing Bob Dylan. Bob Dylan is listed in the credits as playing Renaldo, yet Ronnie Hawkins is listed as playing Bob Dylan."

"So Bob Dylan," I surmise, "may or may not be in the film."

"Exactly."

"But Bob Dylan made the film."

"Bob Dylan didn't make it. I made it."

"I is another," wrote Arthur Rimbaud, and this statement is certainly demonstrated by *Renaldo and Clara*, in which characters in masks and hats—often interchangeable—sit in restaurants and talk, disappear, reappear, exchange flowers, argue, visit cemeteries, play music, travel around in trains and vans and, in one exhilarating scene, dance around at the edge of a beautiful bay, where they join hands and begin singing an American Indian/Hindu, Indian-sounding chant to the accompaniment of a bop-shoo-op-doo-wah-ditty chorus—a religion and rock & roll reunion.

To the anagogic eye, however, the film seems to be about just one man—who could pass for the Jack of Hearts—the leading actor of "Lily, Rosemary and the Jack of Hearts," a card among cards, an image among images—and just one woman. Together they find themselves in the grip of a series of romantic encounters that are reenactments of the Great Mystery, culminating in the confrontation of the Woman in White (Joan Baez), Clara (Sara Dylan) and Renaldo (Bob Dylan)—a meeting at the border of myth and reality. Using his physical image and name as the raw material of the film, Bob Dylan—like the Renaissance kings of masque and spectacle—moves daringly and ambiguously between fiction, representation, identification and participation.

Renaldo and Clara, of course, is a film filled with magnificently shot and recorded concert footage of highly charged Dylan performances of songs like "It Ain't Me, Babe," "A Hard Rain's A-Gonna Fall," and "Knockin' on Heaven's Door"—the last of whose delicate and eerie instrumental breaks makes you feel as if you were entering the gates of paradise themselves. Avoiding all of the cinematic clichés of pounding-and-zooming television rock & roll specials, the cameras either subtly choreograph the songs—revealing structures and feelings—or else look at the white faced Dylan and accompanying painted musicians in rapturous and intensely held close-ups.

Around these musical episodes Dylan has woven a series of multilayered and multileveled scenes—unconsciously echoing similar moments in films by Cocteau, Cassavetes and especially Jacques Rivette—each of which lights up and casts light on all the others. Scenes and characters duplicate and mirror each other, are disassociated and recombined—all of them, in the words of the director, "filled with reason but not with logic." Thus, when Clara (Sara Dylan) says to Renaldo: "I am free . . . I can change," it brings back to us the words spoken earlier by the Woman in White (Joan Baez) to Renaldo: "I haven't changed that much. Have you?" To which Renaldo replies: "Maybe."

And then there are the correspondences and the doubled worlds. The scenes in the bordello—with Joan Baez and Sara Dylan playing prostitutes and Allen Ginsberg playing a kind of Buddhist john—become an image of Vajra Hell—the Tantric Buddhist idea of the unbreakable, diamond hell. And a musician blocking someone's way backstage becomes the Guardian at the Gates.

What is most adventurous and mysterious about *Renaldo and Clara*, however, is the way it counterpoints music with action, lyrics with dialogue, songs with other songs. In one scene, for example, Rodeo (Sam Shepard) is trying to win over Clara, and on the soundtrack you hear, almost subliminally, what sounds like the chord progressions of "Oh, Sister," but which you later realize is "One Too Many Mornings"—as if the songs themselves were trying to communicate with each other, as if they were saying goodbye to each other:

> You're right from your side,
> I'm right from mine.
> We're both just one too many mornings
> An' a thousand miles behind.

In another scene, members of the Rolling Thunder Revue join in a reception with members of the Tuscarora Indian tribe, while on the soundtrack we hear Dylan's haunting rehearsal tape version of "People Get Ready." And in finally another scene, Renaldo hurries nervously down a city street—panhandling and making some kind of furtive French connection with the Masked Tortilla (Bob Neuwirth)—to the accompaniment of Dylan's version of "Little Moses," above which we hear powerfully spoken lines from poet Anne Waldman's "Fast Speaking Woman" ("I'm the Druid Woman/I'm the Ibo Woman/I'm the Buddha Woman/I'm the Vibrato Woman").

"Your films make one wonder what's going on in people's minds," says Penelope Gilliatt to Buñuel, to which he responds: "Dreams, and also the most everyday questions: 'What time is it?' 'Do you want to eat?'" "And, in spite of the compression and density of most of the scenes in *Renaldo and*

Clara, there is also a presentational immediacy and clarity that fixes the scenes in one's mind—like a very special dream one wants to remember.

"I expect this will be a very small film," Buñuel said during the shooting of his recent *That Obscure Object of Desire*—which might have served as the title of *Renaldo and Clara*. "One needs just a hole to look out of," Buñuel continued, "like a spider that has spun its web and is remembering what the world outside was like. This hole is the secret of things. An artist can provide an essential margin of alertness."

Renaldo and Clara is a long film, but it is really intimate and evanescent. "Art is the perpetual motion of illusion," says Bob Dylan in the interview that follows—which took place a week before Christmas in L.A. "The highest purpose of art," Dylan continues, "is to inspire. What else can you do? What else can you do for anyone but inspire them?"

If someone asked me what 'Renaldo and Clara' was about, I'd say: art and life, identity and God—with lots of encounters at bars, restaurants, luncheonettes, cabarets and bus stations.

Do you want to see it again? Would it be helpful for you to see it again?

You think I'm too confused about the film?

No, I don't think so at all. It isn't just about bus stations and cabarets and stage music and identity—those are elements of it. But it is mostly about identity—about everybody's identity. More important, it's about Renaldo's identity, so we superimpose our own vision on Renaldo: it's his vision and it's his dream.

You know what the film is about? It begins with music—you see a guy in a mask [Bob Dylan], you can see through the mask he's wearing, and he's singing "When I Paint My Masterpiece." So right away you know there's an involvement with music. Music is confronting you.

So are lines like: "You can almost think that you're seein' double."

Right. Also on a lyrical level. But you still don't really know . . . and then you're getting off that, and there seems to be a tour. You're hearing things and seeing people . . . it's not *quite* like a tour, but there's some kind of energy like being on a tour. There's a struggle, there's a reporter who later appears in the restaurant scenes.

All right, then it goes right to David Blue, who's playing pinball and who seems to be the narrator. He's Renaldo's narrator, he's Renaldo's scribe—he belongs to Renaldo.

Yet David Blue talks not about Renaldo but about Bob Dylan and how he, David Blue, first met Dylan in Greenwich Village in the late Fifties.

They seem to be the same person after a while. It's something you can only feel but never really know. Any more than you can know whether Willie Sutton pulled all those bank jobs. Any more than you can know who killed Kennedy for sure.

And right away, David Blue says: "Well, what happened was that when I first left my parents' house, I bought *The Myth of Sisyphus*." Now, that wasn't really the book, but it was pretty close. It was actually—so he tells us—*Existentialism and Human Emotions*. So that's it: this film is a postexistentialist movie. We're in the postexistentialist period. What is it? That's what it is.

What could be more existentialist than playing pinball? It's the perfect existentialist game.

It is. I've seen rows and rows of pinball players lined up like ducks. It's a great equalizer.

What about the emotions in 'Existentialism and Human Emotions'?

Human emotions are the great dictator—in this movie as in all movies. . . . I'll tell you what I think of the emotions later. But getting back to David Blue: he's left his home, and right away you're in for something like a triple dimension. Just ten minutes into the movie he says: "I got in the bus, I went down to New York, walked around for four hours, got back on the bus and went home." And that is exactly what a lot of people are going to feel when they walk into the movie theater: they got on the bus, walked around for four hours and walked home.

There's another guy, later in the film, who walks out in the night and says to a girl: "This has been a great mistake."

Yeah. You can pick any line in a movie to sum up your feeling about it. But don't forget you don't see that guy anymore after that. . . . He's gone. And that means Renaldo isn't being watched anymore because *he* was watching Renaldo.

Talking about mistakes and seeing double: it's fascinating how crazy it is to mistake people in the film for one another. I mistook you, for instance, for the guy driving the carriage (maybe it was you); for Jack Elliott; and I even mistook you for you.

The Masked Tortilla [Bob Neuwirth] is mistaken for Bob Dylan, Bob Dylan is mistaken for Renaldo. And . . . *Bob Dylan is the one with the hat on.* That's who Bob Dylan is—he's the one with the hat on.

Almost every man in the film has a hat on.

Right.

All those disguises and masks!

The first mask, as I said, is one you can see through. But they're all masks. In the film, the mask is more important than the face.

All the women in the film seem to turn into one person, too, and a lot of them wear hats. It reminds me of "The Ballad of Frankie Lee and Judas Priest":

*He just stood there staring
At that big house as bright as any sun,
With four and twenty windows
And a woman's face in ev'ry one.*

This film was made for you. [*Laughing*] Did you see the Woman in White who becomes a different Woman in White? One's mistaken for the other. At first she's only an idea of herself—you see her in the street, later in the carriage. . . . I think the women in the movie are beautiful. They look like they've stepped out of a painting. They're vulnerable, but they're also strong-willed.

"Breaking just like a little girl."

That's the child in everyone. That's the child in everyone that has to be confronted.

"Just Like a Woman" always seemed to me to be somehow about being born: "I can't stay in here . . . I just can't fit." So by confronting the child in you, saying goodbye to childhood, you're born into something bigger. . . . In a way, it's a frightening song.

It always was a frightening song, but that feeling needs to be eliminated.

I was thinking of what looked like a Yiddish cabaret filled with older women listening intently to Allen Ginsberg reading passages from "Kaddish," his great elegy to his mother.

Those women are strong in the sense that they know their own identity. It's only the layer of what we're going to reveal in the next film, because women are exploited like anyone else. They're victims just like coal miners.

The poet Robert Bly has written about the image of the Great Mother as a union of four force fields, consisting of the nurturing mother, like Isis (though your Isis seems more ambiguous); the Death Mother (like the woman in "It's All Over Now, Baby Blue"); the ecstatic mother (like the girl in "Spanish Harlem Incident"); and the Stone Mother who drives you mad (like the Sweet Melinda who leaves you howling at the moon in "Just like Tom Thumb's Blues"). Traces of these women seem to be in this film as well.

The Death Mother is represented in the film, but I don't know what I should say or can say or shouldn't say about who is who in the movie. I mean *who* is the old woman everyone calls Mamma—the woman who sings, plays guitar and reads palms? She reads Allen's palm, saying: "You've been married twice." And me, later on I'm looking at the grave-stone marked HUSBAND; Ginsberg asks: "Is that going to happen to you?" And I say: "I want an unmarked grave." But of course I'm saying this as Renaldo.

In 'Tarantula' you wrote your own epitaph:

here lies bob dylan
killed by a discarded Oedipus
who turned
around
to investigate a ghost
and discovered that
the ghost too was more than one person.

Yeah, way back then I was thinking of this film. I've had this picture in mind for a long time—years and years. Too many years . . . Renaldo is oppressed. He's oppressed because he's born. We don't really know who Renaldo is. We just know what he isn't. He isn't the Masked Tortilla. Renaldo is the one with the hat, but he's not wearing a hat. I'll tell you what this movie is: it's like life exactly, but not an imitation of it. It transcends life, and it's not like life.

That paradox is toppling me over.

I'll tell you what my film is about: it's about naked alienation of the inner self against the outer self—alienation taken to the extreme. And it's about integrity. My next film is about obsession. The hero is an arsonist . . . but he's not really a hero.

'Renaldo and Clara' seems to me to be about obsession, too.

That's true, but only in the way it applies to integrity.

The idea of integrity comes across in a lot of your songs in lines like: "To live outside the law, you must be honest" and "She doesn't have to say she's faithful, /Yet she's true, like ice, like fire."

We talked about emotions before. You can't be a slave to your emotions. If you're a slave to your emotions you're dependent on your emotions, and you're only dealing with your conscious mind. But the film is about the fact that you have to be faithful to your subconscious, unconscious, superconscious—as well as to your conscious. Integrity is a facet of honesty. It has to do with knowing yourself.

At the end of the film, Renaldo is with two women in a room (the Woman in White played by Joan Baez and Clara played by Sara Dylan), and he says: "Evasiveness is only in the mind—truth is on many levels. . . . Ask me anything and I'll tell you the truth." Clara and the Woman in White both ask him: "Do you love her?" as they point to each other—not: "Do you love me?"

Possessiveness. It was a self-focused kind of question. And earlier, one of the women in the whorehouse talks about the ego-protection cords she wears around her neck. Do you remember that? . . . In the scene you mentioned, did you notice that Renaldo was looking at the newspaper which had an article on Bob Dylan and Joan Baez in it? Joan Baez and Bob Dylan at this point are an illusion. It wasn't planned that way. Joan Baez without Bob Dylan isn't too much of an illusion because she's an independent woman and her independence asserts itself. But Joan Baez with Bob Dylan *is*.

So at the moment you open up that newspaper, art and life really come together.

Exactly.

And what about the moment when Joan Baez, looking at Clara, says: "Who is this woman?" and you cut to your singing "Sara"? Talk about art and life!

It's as far as you can take it—meaning personally and generally. Who is this woman? Obviously, this woman is a figment of the material world. Who is this woman who has no name? Who is this woman, she says . . . who is this woman, as if she's talking about herself. Who this woman is is told to you, earlier on, when you see her coming out of the church carrying a rope. You know she means business, you know she has a purpose.

Another way of putting it is: the singer's character onstage is always becoming Renaldo. By singing "Sara," the singer comes as close to Renaldo as he can get. It brings everything as close as possible without two becoming one.

It was pretty amazing to see you use your personal life and the myth of your life so nakedly in that scene with Renaldo and the two women.

Right, but you're talking to me as a director now.

Still, you do have that scene with Joan Baez and Sara Dylan.

Well, Sara Dylan here is working as Sara Dylan. She has the same last name as Bob Dylan, but we may not be related. If she couldn't have played the role of Clara, she wouldn't have done it.

Is she talking about her real problems or pretending that she's an adventurer?

We can make anybody's problems our problems.

Some people will obviously think that this film either broke up your marriage or is a kind of incantation to make your marriage come back together.

Either one of those statements I can't relate to. It has nothing to do with the breakup of my marriage. My marriage is over. I'm divorced. This film is a film.

Why did you make yourself so vulnerable?

You must be vulnerable to be sensitive to reality. And to me being vulnerable is just another way of saying that one has nothing more to lose. I don't have anything but darkness to lose. I'm way beyond that. The worst thing that could happen is that the film will be accepted and that the next one will be compared unfavorably to this one.

Strangely, the scene where the two women confront Renaldo reminds me of 'King Lear,' in which each of the daughters has to say how much she loves her father.

You're right. Renaldo sees himself as Cordelia.

I've always interpreted some of the 'Basement Tapes' as being concerned with ideas from 'King Lear': "Too much of nothing/Can make a man abuse a king"; "Oh what dear daughter 'neath the sun/ Would treat a father so, /To wait upon him hand and foot/And always tell him, 'No'?"

Exactly. In the later years it changed from "king" to "clown."

King Lear had a fool around him, too, and when the fool leaves, Cordelia comes back. She takes his place, and he takes hers.

The roles are all interchangeable.

As in "Tangled Up in Blue" and as in your movie.

Yes it is.

Were you specifically influenced by 'King Lear' when you wrote songs like "Tears of Rage"?

No, songs like that were based on the concept that one is one.

". . . and all alone and ever more shall be so."

Exactly. What comes is gone forever every time.

But one is difficult to deal with, so Christians gave us the Trinity.

The Christians didn't bring in anything—it was the Greeks.

Jesus is a very strong figure in 'Renaldo and Clara,' I noticed. There's that song by you called "What Will You Do When Jesus Comes?" There's the woman who says to you in the restaurant: "There's nowhere to go. Just stand and place yourself like the cross and I'll receive you." And then there are the shots of the huge cement crucifix in the Catholic Grotto.

Right. Jesus is the most identifiable figure in Western culture, and yet he was exploited, used and exploited. We all have been.

There's also that scene, near the end of the film, where Allen Ginsberg takes you around to see the glassed-in sculptures of the Stations of the Cross—and we see Jesus killed for the second time and then buried under the weight of the cross. On one level, the film is about the Stations of the Cross, isn't it?

Yeah, you're right, like the double vision having to be killed twice. Like why does Jesus really die?

Spiritually or politically?

Realistically. . . . Because he's a healer. Jesus is a healer. So he goes to India, finds out how to be a healer and becomes one. But see, I believe that he overstepped his duties a little bit. He accepted and took on the bad karma of all the people he healed. And he was filled with so much bad karma that the only way out was to burn him up.

In my film, we're looking at masks a lot of the time. And then when the dream becomes so solidified that it has to be taken to the stage of reality, then you'll see stone, you'll see a statue—which is even a further extension of the mask: the statue of Mary in front of the statue of Jesus on the cross in the Crucifix Grotto.

Throughout the film, I also noticed the continual reappearance of the red rose. Every woman has a rose.

It has a great deal to do with what's happening in the movie. Do you remember the woman in the carriage? She's bringing a rose to Renaldo, who gives it back to her.

But then it appears in your hat when you're singing.

By that time it's all fallen apart and shattered, the dream is gone . . . it could be anywhere after that.

Joan Baez carries one when she's with Mamma. And then the violinist Scarlet Rivera gives it to you in your dressing room.

That's right. The rose is a symbol of fertility.

Also of the soul. 'The Romance of the Rose'—the dreamer's vision of the soul.

That's right. . . . The most mysterious figure in the film is the conductor on the train. Do you remember him?

He's the guy who tells the Masked Tortilla—who says he's going to a wedding—that he's only been on the train for four hours (there's that magical four hours again!) and not for the six days that he imagines.

Yeah, he tells him, too, that he's going to possibly the largest city in the East.

I figured it was New York.

No. The largest city in the East!

The Magi!

That's not exactly what he's talking about—it's more like the holy crossroads.

There's another scene like that in which Mick Ronson is blocking Ronnie Hawkins' way to a backstage area. He seemed like some kind of guardian.

He's the Guardian of the Gates. But scenes like these work in terms of feeling. It's like with Tarot cards—you don't have to be confused as to what they mean . . . someone else who knows can read them for you.

"Nothing is revealed," you sing at the end of "The Ballad of Frankie Lee and Judas Priest." Is anything revealed at the end of 'Renaldo and Clara'?

Yeah, I'll tell you what the film reveals: this film reveals that there's a whole lot to reveal beneath the surface of the soul, but it's unthinkable.

[*Silence*]

That's exactly what it reveals. It reveals the depths that there are to reveal. And that's the most you can ask, because things are really very invisible. You can't reveal the invisible. And this film goes as far as we can to reveal that.

Under a statue of Isis in the city of Sais is the following inscription: "I am everything that was, that is, that shall be. . . . Nor has any mortal ever been able to discover what lies under my veil."

That's a fantastic quotation. That's true, exactly. Once you see what's under the veil, what happens to you? You die, don't you, or go blind?

I wanted to tie in two things we've talked about: the idea of integrity and the idea of Jesus. In your song "I Want You," you have the lines:

> *Now all my fathers, they've gone down,*
> *True love they've been without it.*
> *But all their daughters put me down*
> *'Cause I don't think about it.*

These are some of my favorite lines of yours, and to me they suggest that real desire is stronger than frustration or guilt.

I know. It's incredible you find that there. I know it's true. And in *Renaldo and Clara* there's no guilt. But that's why people will take offense at it, if they are offended by it in any way, because of the lack of guilt in the movie. None at all.

This brings us back to Jesus.

Jesus is . . . well, I'm not using Jesus in the film so much as I'm using the *concept* of Jesus—the idea of Jesus as a man, not the virgin birth.

But what about the concept of masochism associated with Jesus?

That's what happened to Jesus. People relate to the masochism, to the spikes in his hand, to the blood coming out, to the fact that he was crucified. What would have happened to him if he hadn't been crucified? That's what draws people to him. There are only signals of that in this film—like a fingernail blade at one point.

What about the line in "Wedding Song": "Your love cuts like a knife."

Well it's bloodletting, it's what heals all disease. Neither aggression nor anger interests me. Violence only does on an interpretive level, only when it's a product of reason.

People are attracted to blood. I'm personally not consumed by the desire to drink the blood. But bloodletting is meaningful in that it can cure disease. But we didn't try to make a film of that nature. This film concerns itself with the dream. There's no blood in the dream, the dream is cold. This film concerns itself only with the depth of the dream—the dream as seen in the mirror.

The next film might have some blood. . . . I'm trying to locate Lois Smith to be in it. She would represent the idea of innocence. Do you know who she is? She was the barmaid in *East of Eden*. I'm trying to line up some people for the film, and I can't find her. . . .

For some reason I've just thought of my favorite singer.

Who is that?

Om Kalsoum—the Egyptian woman who died a few years ago. She was my favorite.

What did you like about her?

It was her heart.

Do you like dervish and Sufi singing, by the way?

Yeah, that's where my singing really comes from . . . except that I sing in America. I've heard too much Leadbelly really to be too much influenced by the whirling dervishes.

Now that we somehow got onto this subject, who else do you like right now? New Wave groups?

No, I'm not interested in them. I think Alice Cooper is an overlooked songwriter. I like Ry Cooder. And I like Dave Mason's version of something which is on the jukebox right now.

I wonder what you think of the guy who ends your movie singing with this fulsome, crooning version of "In the Morning" with those memorable lines: "I'll be yawning into the morning of my life." Why is he there?

The film had to end with him because he represents the fact that Renaldo could be dreaming. And he might be singing for Renaldo—representing him, the darkness representing the light.

He's like what's happened to one sentimental part of rock & roll in the Seventies.

He's not rock & roll.

Rock & roll isn't rock & roll anymore.

You're right, there's no more rock & roll. It's an imitation, we can forget about that. Rock & roll has turned itself inside out. I never did do rock & roll. I'm just doing the same old thing I've always done.

You've never sung a rock & roll song?

No, I never have, only in spirit.

You can't really dance to one of your songs.

I couldn't.

Imagine dancing to "Rainy Day Woman #12 & 35." It's kind of alienating. Everyone thought it was about being stoned, but I always thought it was about being all alone.

So did I. You could write about that for years. . . . Rock & roll ended with Phil Spector. The Beatles weren't rock & roll either. Nor the Rolling Stones. Rock & roll ended with Little Anthony and the Imperials. Pure rock & roll.

With "Goin' Out of My Head"?

The one before that. . . . Rock & roll ended in 1959.

When did it begin for you?

1954.

What is there now?

Programmed music. Quadruple tracking.

What do you think about the Seventies?

The Seventies I see as a period of reconstruction after the Sixties, that's all. That's why people say: well, it's boring, nothing's really happening, and that's because wounds are healing. By the Eighties, anyone who's going to be doing anything will have his or her cards showing. You won't be able to get back in the game in the Eighties.

I came across something you wrote a while back:

Desire. . . never fearful
finally faithful
it will guide me well
across all bridges
inside all tunnels
never failin'.

I even remember where I wrote that. I wrote that in New Hampshire. I think I was all alone.

Here's something else you wrote:

Mine shall be a strong loneliness dissolvin' deep
t' the depths of my freedom
an' that, then, shall
remain my song.

You seem to have stayed true to that feeling.

I haven't had any reason to stray.

In "The Times They Are A-Changin'" you sing: "He that gets hurt/Will be he who has stalled." What has kept you unstalled?

I don't know. Mainly because I don't believe in this life.

The Buddhist tradition talks about illusion, the Jewish tradition about allusion. Which do you feel closer to?

I believe in both, but I probably lean to allusion. I'm not a Buddhist. I believe in life, but not this life.

What life do you believe in?

Real life.

Do you ever experience real life?

I experience it all the time, it's beyond this life.

I wanted to read to you two Hasidic texts that somehow remind me of your work. The first says that in the service of God, one can learn three things from a child and seven from a thief. "From a child you can learn (1) always to be happy; (2) never to sit idle; and (3) to cry for everything one wants. From a thief you should learn: (1) to work at night; (2) if one cannot gain what one wants in one night to try again the next night; (3) to love one's coworkers just as thieves love each other; (4) to be willing to risk one's life even for a little thing; (5) not to attach too much value to things even though one has risked one's life for them—just as a thief will resell a stolen article for a fraction of its real value; (6) to withstand all kinds of beatings and tortures but to remain what you are; and (7) to believe that your work is worthwhile and not be willing to change it."

Who wrote that?

A Hasidic rabbi.

Which one?

Dov Baer, the Mazid of Mezeritch.

That's the most mind-blazing chronicle of human behavior I think I've ever heard. . . . How can I get a copy of that?

I brought it for you actually. I photocopied it from a book called 'The Wisdom of the Jewish Mystics.'

I'll put it on my wall. There's a man I would follow. That's a real hero. A real hero.

Another Hasidic rabbi once said that you can learn something from everything. Even from a train, a telephone and a telegram. From a train, he said, you can learn that in one second one can miss everything. From a telephone you can learn that what you say over here can be heard over there. And from a telegram that all words are counted and charged.

It's a cosmic statement. Where do you get all of these rabbis' sayings? Those guys are really wise. I tell you, I've heard gurus and yogis and philosophers and politicians and doctors and lawyers, teachers of all kinds . . . and these rabbis really had something going.

They're like Sufis, but they speak and teach with more emotion.

As I've said before, I don't believe in emotion. They use their hearts, their hearts don't use them.

In one second missing everything on a train . . . do you think that means that you can miss the train or miss seeing something from the train window?

That's a statement of revelation. I think it means that in one moment you can miss everything because you're not there. You just watch it, and you know you're missing it.

What about the telephone—what you say here is heard over there?

That means you're never that far away from the ultimate God.

And words being counted and charged.

That's very truthful, too. That everything you say and think is all being added up.

How are you coming out?

You know, I'll tell you: lately I've been catching myself. I've been in some scenes, and I say: "Holy shit, I'm not here alone." I've never had that experience before the past few months. I've felt this strange, eerie feeling that I wasn't all alone, and I'd better know it.

Do you watch what you say?

I always try to watch what I say because I try not to say anything I don't mean.

Maybe Renaldo has that problem at the end of your movie?

No, Renaldo's on top of it, he's on top of circumstances. He's not going to say too much 'cause he knows he doesn't know much. Now me, obviously I'm talking and saying things, and I *will* talk and say things, but that's because I think I'm going to mean them . . . or I feel I *mean* them now. I'm not just talking to hear myself. But Renaldo is *not* saying anything just because he knows that *what* he says is being heard and that therefore he doesn't know what to say. No, he says some very incredible and important things when he's confronted with his *allusion*. You know, he does say: "Do I love you like I love her? No." "Do I love her like I love you? No." He can't say any more than that . . . you don't have to know any more about him than that. That's all you have to know about him, that's all you have to know about Bob Dylan.

At that moment in the film, you cut into a performance of your song "Catfish"—"nobody can throw the ball like Catfish can." It's almost jokey after that intense preceding scene.

It's treated more in the way of music, getting back to the idea that music is truthful. And music *is* truthful. Everything's okay, you put on a record, someone's playing an instrument—that changes the vibe. Music attracts the angels in the universe. A group of angels sitting at a table are going to be attracted by that.

So we always get back to the music in the film. We made a point of doing it, as if we had to do it. You're not going to see music in the movies as you do in this film. We don't have any filler. You don't see any doors close or any reverse shots which are just there to take up time until you get to the next one. We didn't want to take time away from other shots.

A lot of hold shots, not enough of them. When the woman is walking down the street with that rope, that's a hold shot. David Blue is on a hold shot for six minutes the first time you see him.

I know this film is too long. It may be four hours too long—I don't care. To me, it's not long enough. I'm not concerned how long something is. I want to see a set shot. I *feel* a set shot. I don't feel all this motion and boom-boom. We can fast cut when we want, but the power comes in the ability to have faith that it is a meaningful shot.

You know who understood this? Andy Warhol. Warhol did a lot for American cinema. He was before his time. But Warhol and Hitchcock and Peckinpah and Tod Browning . . . they were important to me. I figured Godard had the accessibility to make what he made, he broke new ground. I never saw any film like *Breathless*, but once you saw it, you said: "Yeah, man, why didn't I do that, I could have done that." Okay, he did it, but he couldn't have done it in America.

But what about a film like Sam Fuller's 'Forty Guns' or Joseph Lewis' 'Gun Crazy'?

Yeah, I just heard Fuller's name the other day. I think American filmmakers are the best. But I also like Kurosawa, and my favorite director is Buñuel; it doesn't surprise me that he'd say those amazing things you quoted to me before from the *New Yorker*.

I don't know what to tell you. In one way I don't consider myself a filmmaker at all. In another way I do. To me, *Renaldo and Clara* is my first real film. I don't know who will like it. I made it for a specific bunch of people and myself, and that's all. That's how I wrote "Blowin' in the Wind" and "The Times They Are A-Changin'"—they were written for a certain crowd of people and for certain artists, too. Who knew they were going to be big songs?

The film, in a way, is a culmination of a lot of your ideas and obsessions.

That may be true, but I hope it also has meaning for other people who aren't that familiar with my songs, and that other people can see themselves in it, because I don't feel so isolated from what's going on. There are a lot of people who'll look at the film without knowing who anybody is in it. And they'll see it more purely.

Eisenstein talked of montage in terms of attraction—shots attracting other shots—then in terms of shock, and finally in terms of fusion and synthesis, and of overtones. You seem to be really aware of the overtones in your film, do you know what I mean?

I sure do.

Eisenstein once wrote: "The Moscow Art is my deadly enemy. It is the exact antithesis of all I am trying to do. They string their emotions together to give a continuous illusion of reality. I take photographs of reality and then cut them up so as to produce emotions."

What we did was to cut up reality and make it more real. . . . Everyone from the cameraman to the water boy, from the wardrobe people to the sound people was just as important as anyone else in the making of the film. There weren't any roles that well defined. The money was coming in the front door and going out the back door: the Rolling Thunder tour sponsored the movie. And I had faith and trust in the people who helped me do the film, and they had faith and trust in me.

In the movie, there's a man behind a luncheonette counter who talks a lot about truth—he's almost like the Greek chorus of the film.

Yeah, we often sat around and talked about that guy. He *is* the chorus.

That guy at one point talks about the Movement going astray and about how everyone got bought off. How come you didn't sell out and just make a commercial film?

I don't have any cinematic vision to sell out. It's all for me so I can't sell out. I'm not working for anybody. What was there to sell out?

Well, movies like 'Welcome to L.A.' and 'Looking for Mr. Goodbar' are moralistic exploitation films—and many people nowadays think that they're significant statements. You could have sold out to the vision of the times.

Right. I have my point of view and my vision, and nothing tampers with it because it's all that I've got. I don't have anything to sell out.

'Renaldo and Clara' has certain similarities to the recent films of Jacques Rivette. Do you know his work?

I don't. But I wish they'd do it in this country. I'd feel a lot safer. I mean I wouldn't get so much resistance and hostility. I can't believe that people think that four hours is too long for a film. As if people had so much to do. You can see an hour movie that seems like ten hours. I think the vision is strong enough to cut through all of that. But we may be kicked right out of Hollywood after this film is released and have to go back to Bolivia. In India, they show twelve-hour movies. Americans are spoiled, they expect art to be like wallpaper with no effort, just to be there.

I should have asked you this before, but how much of the film is improvised and how much determined beforehand?

About a third is improvised, about a third is determined, and about a third is blind luck.

What about, for instance, the scene in which Ronnie Hawkins tries to get a farm girl to go on tour with him, trying to convince her by saying something like: "God's not just in the country, God's in the city, too . . . God's everywhere, so let's seize the day."

In that scene, Ronnie was given five subjects to hit on. He could say anything he wanted as long as he covered five points. Obviously, God was a subject relevant to the movie. Then he talked about the Father. Now get this: in the film there's the character of the Father played by Allen Ginsberg. But in Ronnie's scene, the farmer's daughter talks about *her* father. That's the same father.

Another half-improvised scene is the one in which Ramone—the dead lover of Mrs. Dylan [played by Ronee Blakley]—appears as a ghost in the bathroom, and they argue in front of the mirror.

How does the audience know that that's "Mrs. Dylan"?

She's so identified later on in the film. It's just like Hitchcock. Hitchcock would lay something down, and an hour later you'd figure it out—but if you want to know, you wait and find out. It's not given to you on a platter.

Hitchcock puts himself into each of his films—once. You put yourself in hundreds of places and times!

Right [*laughing*]. I've tried to learn a lack of fear from Hitchcock.

Did the John Cassavetes movies influence you at all in scenes such as the one in the bathroom?

No, not at all. But I think it all comes from the same place. I'm probably interested in the same things Cassavetes is interested in.

What are those?

Timing, for example, and the struggle to break down complexity into simplicity.

Timing of relationships?

The relationships of human reason. It's all a matter of timing. The movie creates and holds the time. That's what it should do—it should hold that time, breathe in that time and stop time in doing that. It's like if you look at a painting by Cézanne, you get lost in that painting for that period of time. And you breathe—yet time is going by and you wouldn't know it, you're spellbound.

In Cézanne, things that you might take as being decoration actually turn out to be substantial.

That's exactly what happens in *Renaldo and Clara*. Things which appear merely decorative usually, later on, become substantial. It just takes a certain amount of experience with the film to catch on to that. For example, Allen Ginsberg. You first hear his name, just his name. . . .

And then you get a glimpse of him at that weird, monomaniacal poetry reading.

It's not as weird as it should be. Weirdness is exactness.

One quick question about Hurricane Carter, whom you show in the film. Do you think that he was guilty?

I don't personally think he is. I put that sequence in the film because he's a man who's not unlike anyone else in the film. He's a righteous man, a very philosophic man—he's not your typical bank robber or mercy slayer. He deserves better than what he got.

You told me that you plan to make twelve more films, but I gather you're not giving up on songwriting or touring.

I have to get back to playing music because unless I do, I don't really feel alive. I don't feel I can be a filmmaker all the time. I have to play in front of the people in order just to keep going.

In "Wedding Song" you sing: "I love you more than ever/Now that the past is gone." But in "Tangled Up in Blue" you sing: "But all the while I was alone/The past was close behind." Between these two couplets lies an important boundary.

We allow our past to exist. Our credibility is based on our past. But deep in our soul we have no past. I don't think we have a past, any more than we have a name. You can say we have a past if we have a future. Do we have a future? No. So how can our past exist if the future doesn't exist?

So what are the songs on 'Blood on the Tracks' about?

The present.

Why did you say "I love you more than ever/Now that the past is gone"?

That's delusion. That's gone.

And what about "And all the while I was alone/The past was close behind"?

That's more delusion. Delusion is close behind.

When your "Greek chorus" restaurant owner talks about the Movement selling itself out, you next cut to your singing "Tangled Up in Blue" which is, in part, about what has happened in and to the past.

But we're only dealing with the past in terms of being able to be healed by it. We can communicate only because we both agree that this is a glass and this is a bowl and that's a candle and there's a window here and there are lights out in the city. Now I might not agree with that. Turn this glass around and it's something else. Now I'm hiding it in a napkin. Watch it now. Now you don't even know it's there. It's the past. . . . I don't even deal with it. I don't think seriously about the past, the present or the future. I've spent enough time thinking about these things and have gotten nowhere.

But didn't you when you wrote 'Blood on the Tracks'? Why is it so intense?

Because there's physical blood in the soul, and flesh and blood are portraying it to you. Will power. Will power is what makes it an intense album . . . but certainly not anything to do with the past or the future. Will power is telling you that we are agreeing on what is what.

What about "Idiot Wind"?

Will power.

Why have you been able to keep so in touch with your anger throughout the years, as revealed in songs like "Can You Please Crawl Out Your Window?" and "Positively 4th Street"?

Will power. With strength of will you can do anything. With will power you can determine your destiny.

Can you really know where your destiny is leading you?

Yeah, when you're on top of your game. . . . Anger and sentimentality go right next to each other, and they're both superficial. Chagall made a lot of sentimental paintings. And Voltaire wrote a lot of angry books.

What is "Idiot Wind"?

It's a little bit of both because it uses all the textures of strict philosophy, but basically it's a shattered philosophy that doesn't have a title, and it's driven across with will power. Will power is what you're responding to.

In your film you show a bearded poet in Hasidic garb who speaks in an Irish brogue and carries a gun. He tells us that he doesn't care about being fast but about being accurate. Is that how you feel now?

Yeah. Everyone admires the poet, no matter if he's a lumberjack or a football player or a car thief. If he's a poet he'll be admired and respected.

You used to say you were a trapeze artist.

Well, I see the poet in every man and woman.

Rimbaud's grave doesn't even mention the fact that he was a poet, but rather that he was an adventurer.

Exactly. But I don't try to adopt or imitate Rimbaud in my work. I'm not interested in imitation.

I've always associated you with Rimbaud. Illuminations and Fireworks. Do you believe in reincarnation?

I believe in this—if you want to take reincarnation as a subject: let's say a child is conceived inside of a woman's belly, and was planted there by a man. Nine months before that seed is planted, there's nothing. Ten, twelve, thirteen months . . . two years before that seed is planted, maybe there's the germination of that seed. That comes from food intake into the bloodstream. Food can be a side of beef or a carrot on a shelf. But that's what makes it happen.

In another lifetime—you're in a supermarket and there's a package of carrots right there . . . *that* possibly could be *you*. *That* kind of reincarnation. . . . And how did that carrot get there? It got there through the ground. It grew through the ground with the help of a piece of animal shit. It has to do with the creation and destruction of *time*. Which means it's immense. Five million years is nothing—it's a drop in a bucket. I don't think there's enough *time* for reincarnation. It would take thousands or millions of years and light miles for any real kind of reincarnation.

I think one can be conscious of different vibrations in the universe, and these can be picked up. But reincarnation from the twelfth to the twentieth century—I say it's impossible.

So you take reincarnation on a cellular level, and when I say "Rimbaud and you," you take it as an affinity.

Maybe my spirit passed through the same places as his did. We're all wind and dust anyway, and we could have passed through many barriers at different times.

What about your line: "Sweet Goddess/Born of a blinding light and a changing wind" in the song "Tough Mama"?

That's the mother and father, the yin and yang. That's the coming together of destiny and the fulfillment of destiny.

George Harrison once said that your lines:

Look out kid
It's somethin' you did
God knows when
But you're doin' it again

from "Subterranean Homesick Blues" seemed to be a wonderful description of karma.

Karma's not reincarnation. There's no proof of reincarnation and there's no proof of karma, but there's a *feeling* of karma. We don't even have any proof that the universe exists. We don't have any proof that we are even sitting here. We can't prove that we're really alive. How can we prove we're alive by other people saying we're alive?

All I have to do is kick a rock.

Yeah, you're saying you're alive, but the rock isn't going to tell you. The rock don't feel it.

If you take reality to be unreal, than you make unreality real. What's real to you? Art?

Art is the perpetual motion of illusion. The highest purpose of art is to inspire. What else can you do? What else can you do for anyone but inspire them?

What are your new songs like?

My new songs are new for me, and they accomplish what I wanted to accomplish when I started thinking about them. Very seldom do you finish something and then abandon it, and very seldom do you abandon something with the attitude that you've gotten what you started out to get. Usually you think, well, it's too big, you get wasted along the way someplace, and it just trails off . . . and what you've got is what you've got and you just do the best with it. But very seldom do you ever come out with what you put in. And I think I've done that now for the first time since I was writing two songs a day way back when. My experience with film helped me in writing the songs. I probably wouldn't have written any more songs if I hadn't made this film. I would have been bummed out, I wouldn't have been able to do what I knew could be done.

I know I'm being nostalgic, but I loved hearing you sing "Little Moses" in 'Renaldo and Clara'.

I used to play that song when I performed at Gerde's Folk City. It's an old Carter Family song, and it goes something like:

Away by the waters so wide
The ladies were winding their way,
When Pharoah's little daughter
Stepped down in the water
To bathe in the cool of the day.
And before it got dark,
She opened the ark,
And saw the sweet infant so gay.

Then little Moses grows up, slays the Egyptians, leads the Jews—it's a great song. And I thought it fit pretty well into the movie.

Everybody's in this film: the Carter Family, Hank Williams, Woody Guthrie, Beethoven. Who is going to understand this film? Where are the people to understand this film—a film which needs no understanding?

Who understands "Sad-Eyed Lady of the Lowlands"?

I do. . . . It's strange. I finally feel in the position of someone who people want to interview enough that they'll fly you into town, put you up in a hotel, pay all your expenses and give you a tour of the city. I'm finally in that position.

I once went to see the king of the Gypsies in southern France. This guy had twelve wives and 100 children. He was in the antique business and had a junkyard, but he'd had a heart attack before I'd come home to see him. All his wives and children had left. And the gypsy clan had left him with only one wife and a couple of kids and a dog. What happens is that after he dies they'll all come back. They smell death and they leave. That's what happens in life. And I was very affected by seeing that.

Did you feel something like that in the past five years?

You're talking about 1973? I don't even remember 1973. I'm talking about the spring of 1975. There was a lack of targets at that time. But I don't remember what happened last week.

But you probably remember your childhood clearly.

My childhood is so far away . . . it's like I don't even remember being a child. I think it was someone else who was a child. Did you ever think like that? I'm not sure that what happened to me yesterday was true.

But you seem sure of yourself.

I'm sure of my dream self. I live in my dreams, I don't really live in the actual world.

"'I'll let you be in my dreams
if I can be in yours.'
I said that."
BOB DYLAN: 1963

15. Interview with Ron Rosenbaum, *Playboy*

MARCH 1978

It was in March 1966 that *Playboy* published the first full-length interview with Bob Dylan. In the intervening years, he has talked to journalists only rarely, and, shortly before completing his first feature film, he agreed to talk with us. We asked writer Ron Rosenbaum, who grew up listening to Dylan songs, to check in with the elusive artist. His report:

Call it a simple twist of fate, to use a Dylan line, but perhaps psychic twist of fate is more accurate. Because there was something of a turning point in our ten-day series of conversations when we exchanged confidences about psychics. Until that point, things had not been proceeding easily. Dylan has seldom been forthcoming with any answers, particularly in interview situations and has long been notorious for questioning the questions rather than answering them, replying with put-ons and tall tales and surrounding his real feelings with mystery and circumlocution. We would go round in circles, sometimes fascinating metaphysical circles, and I'd got a sense of his intellect but little of his heart. He hadn't given anyone a major interview for many years, but after my initial excitement at being chosen to do this one, I began to wonder whether Dylan really wanted to do it. It's probably unnecessary to explain why getting answers from Bob Dylan has come to mean so much to many people. One has only to recall how Dylan, born Robert Zimmerman in 1941 in Duluth,

Minnesota, burst upon the early sixties folk-music scene with an abrasive voice and an explosive intensity, how he created songs such as "Blowin' in the Wind" and "The Times They Are A-Changin' " that became anthems of the civil rights and antiwar movements. How he and his music raced through the sixties at breakneck speed, leaving his folk followers behind and the politicos mystified with his electrifying, elliptical explorations of uncharted states of mind. How, in songs such as "Mr. Tambourine Man," "Desolation Row," "Like a Rolling Stone" and "Just like a Woman," he created emotional road maps for an entire generation. How, in the midst of increasingly frenzied rock-'n'-roll touring, Dylan continued to surround the details of his personal life with mystery and wise-guy obfuscation, mystery that deepened ominously after his near-fatal motorcycle accident in 1966. And how, after a long period of bucolic retreat devoted to father-hood, family, and country music, he suddenly returned to the stage with big nationwide tours in 1974 and, most recently, in 1976 with the all-star rock-'n'-roll ensemble known as The Rolling Thunder Revue. How his latest songs, particularly on the *Blood on the Tracks* and *Desire* albums, take us into new and often painful investigations of love and lust, and pain and loss, that suggest the emotional predicaments of the seventies in a way few others can approach. The anthologies that chronicle all of that are littered with the bodies of interviewers he's put on, put down, or put off. I was wondering if I were on my way to becoming another statistic when we hit upon the psychic connection. Late one afternoon, Dylan began telling me about Tamara Rand, an L.A. psychic reader he'd been seeing, because when the world falls on your head, he said, "you need someone who can tell you how to crawl out, which way to take." I presumed he was referring obliquely to the collapse of his twelve-year marriage to Sara Dylan. (Since the child-custody battle was in progress as we talked, Dylan's lawyer refused to permit him to address that subject directly.) Dylan seemed concerned that I understand that Tamara was no con artist, that she had genuine psychic abilities. I assured him I could believe it because my sister, in addition to being a talented writer, has some remarkable psychic abilities and is in great demand in New York for her prescient readings. Dylan asked her name (it's Ruth) and when I told him, he looked impressed. "I've heard of her," he said. I think that made the difference, because after that exchange, Dylan became far more forth-coming with me. Some of the early difficulties of the interview might also be explained by the fact that Dylan was physically and mentally drained from an intense three-month sprint to finish editing and dubbing *Renaldo & Clara*, the movie he'd been writing, directing, and coediting for a full two years. He looked pale, smoked a lot of cigarettes and seemed fidgety. The final step in the moviemaking process—the sound mix—was moving slowly, largely because of his own nervous perfectionism. Most of our talks took place in a little shack of a dressing room outside dubbing stage five at the Burbank Studios. Frequently, we'd be interrupted as Dylan would have to run onto the dubbing stage and watch the hundredth run-through of one of the film's two dozen reels to see if his detailed instructions had been carried out. I particularly remember one occasion when I accompanied him onto the dubbing stage. Onscreen, Renaldo, played by Bob Dylan, and Clara, played by Sara Dylan (the movie was shot before the divorce—though not long before), are interrupted in the midst of connubial foolery by a knock at the door. In walks Joan Baez, dressed in white from head to toe, carrying a red rose. She says she's come for Renaldo. When Dylan, as Renaldo, sees who it is, his jaw drops. At the dubbing console, one of the sound men stopped the film at the jaw-drop frame and asked, "You want me to get rid of that footstep noise in the background, Bob?" "What footstep noise?" Dylan asked. "When Joan comes in and we go to Renaldo, there's some kind of footstep noise in the background, maybe from outside the door." "Those aren't footsteps," said Dylan. "That's the beating of Renaldo's heart." "What makes you so sure?" the sound man asked teasingly. "I know him pretty well," Dylan said, "I know him by heart." "You want it kept there, then?" "I want it louder," Dylan said. He turned to me. "You ever read that thing by Poe, 'The Tell-Tale Heart'?" I was surprised at how willing Dylan was to explain the details of his film; he'd never done that with his songs. But he's put two years and more than a piece of his heart into this five-hour epic and it seems clear that he wants to be taken seriously as a filmmaker with serious artistic ambitions. In the "Proverbs of Hell," William Blake (one of Dylan's favorite poets) wrote: "The road of excess leads to the palace of wisdom." Eleven years ago, Dylan's motorcycle skidded off that road and almost killed him. But unlike most Dionysian sixties figures, Dylan survived. He may not have reached the palace of wisdom (and, indeed, the strange palace of marble and stone he has been building at Malibu seems, according to some reports, to be sliding into the sea). But despite his various sorrows, he does seem to be bursting with exhilaration and confidence that he can still create explosive art without having to die in the explosion.

PLAYBOY: *Exactly 12 years ago, we published a long interview with you in this magazine, and there's a lot to catch up on. But we'd like at least to try to start at the beginning. Besides being a singer, a poet, and now a filmmaker, you've also been called a visionary. Do you recall any visionary experiences while you were growing up?*

DYLAN: I had some amazing projections when I was a kid, but not since then. And those visions have been strong enough to keep me going through today.

PLAYBOY: *What were those visions like?*

DYLAN: They were a feeling of wonder. I projected myself toward what I might personally, humanly do in terms of creating any kinds of reality. I was born in, grew up in a place so foreign that you had to be there to picture it.

PLAYBOY: *Are you talking about Hibbing, Minnesota?*

DYLAN: It was all in upper Minnesota.

PLAYBOY: *What was the quality of those visionary experiences?*

DYLAN: Well, in the winter, everything was still, nothing moved. Eight months of that. You can put it together. You can have some amazing hallucinogenic experiences doing nothing but looking out your window. There is also the summer, when it gets hot and sticky and the air is very metallic. There is a lot of Indian spirit. The earth there is unusual, filled with ore. So there is something happening that is hard to define. There is a magnetic attraction there. Maybe thousands and thousands of years ago, some planet bumped into the land there. There is a great spiritual quality throughout the Midwest. Very subtle, very strong, and that is where I grew up. New York was a dream.

PLAYBOY: *Why did you leave Minnesota?*

DYLAN: Well, there comes a time for all things to pass.

PLAYBOY: *More specifically, why the dream of New York?*

DYLAN: It was a dream of the cosmopolitan riches of the mind.

PLAYBOY: *Did you find them there?*

DYLAN: It was a great place for me to learn and to meet others who were on similar journeys.

PLAYBOY: *People like Allen Ginsberg, for instance?*

DYLAN: Not necessarily him. He was pretty established by the time I got there. But it was Ginsberg and Jack Kerouac who inspired me at first—and where I came from, there wasn't the sophisticated transportation you have now. To get to New York, you'd have to go by thumb. Anyway, those were the old days when John Denver used to play sideman. Many people came out of that period of time. Actors, dancers, politicians, a lot of people were involved with that period of time.

PLAYBOY: *What period are you talking about?*

DYLAN: Real early sixties.

PLAYBOY: *What made that time so special?*

DYLAN: I think it was the last go-round for people to gravitate to New York. People had gone to New York since the 1800s, I think. For me, it was pretty fantastic. I mean, it was like, there was a cafe—what was it called?—I forgot the name, but it was Aaron Burr's old livery stable. You know, just being in that area, that part of the world was enlightening.

PLAYBOY: *Why do you say it was the last go-round?*

DYLAN: I don't think it happened after that. I think it finished, New York died after that, late to middle sixties.

PLAYBOY: *What killed it?*

DYLAN: Mass communication killed it. It turned into one big carnival sideshow. That is what I sensed and I got out of there when it was just starting to happen. The atmosphere changed from one of creativity and isolation to one where the attention would be turned more to the show. People were reading about themselves and believing it. I don't know when it happened. Sometime around Peter, Paul, and Mary, when they got pretty big. It happened around the same time. For a long time, I was famous only in certain circles in New York, Philadelphia, and Boston, and that was fine enough for me. I am an eyewitness to that time. I am one of the survivors of that period. You know as well as I do that a lot of people didn't make it. They didn't live to tell about it, anyway.

PLAYBOY: *Why do you think they didn't survive?*

DYLAN: People were still dealing with illusion and delusion at that time. The times really change and they don't change. There were different characters back then and there were things that were undeveloped that are fully developed now. But back then, there was space, space—well, there wasn't any pressure. There was all the time in the world to get it done. There wasn't any pressure, because nobody knew about it. You know, I mean, music people were like a bunch of cotton pickers.

They see you on the side of the road picking cotton, but nobody stops to give a shit. I mean, it wasn't that important. So Washington Square was a place where people you knew or met congregated every Sunday and it was like a world of music. You know the way New York is; I mean, there could be 20 different things happening in the same kitchen or in the same park; there could be 200 bands in one park in New York; there could be 15 jug bands, five bluegrass bands and an old crummy string band, 20 Irish confederate groups, a Southern mountain band, folk singers of all kinds and colors, singing John Henry work songs. There was bodies piled sky-high doing whatever they felt like doing. Bongo drums, conga drums, saxophone players, xylophone players, drummers of all nations and nationalities. Poets who would rant and rave from the statues. You know, those things don't happen anymore. But then that was what was happening. It was all street. Cafes would be open all night. It was a European thing that never really took off. It has never really been a part of this country. That is what New York was like when I got there.

PLAYBOY: *And you think that mass communications, such as 'Time' magazine's putting Joan Baez on the cover—*

DYLAN: Mass communication killed it all. Oversimplification. I don't know whose idea it was to do that, but soon after, the people moved away.

PLAYBOY: *Just to stay on the track, what first turned you on to folk singing? You actually started out in Minnesota playing the electric guitar with a rock group, didn't you?*

DYLAN: Yeah. The first thing that turned me on to folk singing was Odetta. I heard a record of hers in a record store, back when you could listen to records right there in the store. That was in '58 or something like that. Right then and there, I went out and traded my electric guitar and amplifier for an acoustical guitar, a flat-top Gibson.

PLAYBOY: *What was so special to you about that Odetta record?*

DYLAN: Just something vital and personal. I learned all the songs on that record. It was her first and the songs were—"Mule Skinner," "Jack of Diamonds," "Water Boy," " 'Buked and Scorned."

PLAYBOY: *When did you learn to play the guitar?*

DYLAN: I saved the money I had made working on my daddy's truck and bought a Silvertone guitar from Sears Roebuck. I was 12. I just bought a book of chords and began to play.

PLAYBOY: *What was the first song you wrote?*

DYLAN: The first song I wrote was a song to Brigitte Bardot.

PLAYBOY: *Do you remember how it went?*

DYLAN: I don't recall too much of it. It had only one chord. Well, it is all in the heart. Anyway, from Odetta, I went to Harry Belafonte, the Kingston Trio, little by little uncovering more as I went along. Finally, I was doing nothing but Carter Family and Jesse Fuller songs. Then later I got to Woody Guthrie, which opened up a whole new world at the time. I was still only 19 or 20. I was pretty fanatical about what I wanted to do, so after learning about 200 of Woody's songs, I went to see him and I waited for the right moment to visit him in a hospital in Morristown, New Jersey. I took a bus from New York, sat with him and sang his songs. I kept visiting him a lot and got on friendly terms with him. From that point on, it gets a little foggy.

PLAYBOY: *Folk singing was considered pretty weird in those days, wasn't it?*

DYLAN: It definitely was. *Sing Out!* was the only magazine you could read about those people. They were special people and you kept your distance from them.

PLAYBOY: *What do you mean?*

DYLAN: Well, they were the type of people you just observed and learned from, but you would never approach them. I never would, anyway. I remember being too shy. But it took me a long time to realize the New York crowd wasn't that different from the singers I'd seen in my own home town. They were right there, on the backroad circuit, people like the Stanley Brothers, playing for a few nights. If I had known then what I do now, I probably would have taken off when I was 12 and followed Bill Monroe. 'Cause I could have gotten to the same place.

PLAYBOY: *Would you have gotten there sooner?*

DYLAN: Probably would have saved me a lot of time and hassles.

PLAYBOY: *This comes under the category of setting the record straight: By the time you arrived in New York, you'd changed your name from Robert Zimmerman to Bob Dylan. Was it because of Dylan Thomas?*

DYLAN: No. I haven't read that much of Dylan Thomas. It's a common thing to change your name. It isn't that incredible. Many people do it. People change their town, change their country. New appearance, new mannerisms. Some people have many names. I wouldn't pick a name unless I thought I was that person. Sometimes you are held back by your name. Sometimes there are advantages to having a certain name. Names are labels so we can refer to one another. But deep inside us we don't have a name. We have no name. I just chose that name and it stuck.

PLAYBOY: *Do you know what Zimmerman means in German?*

DYLAN: My forebears were Russian. I don't know how they got a German name coming from Russia. Maybe they got their name coming off the boat or something. To make a big deal over somebody's name, you're liable to make a big deal about any little thing. But getting back to Dylan Thomas, it wasn't that I was inspired by reading some of his poetry and going "Aha!" and changing my name to Dylan. If I thought he was that great, I would have sung his poems, and could just as easily have changed my name to Thomas.

PLAYBOY: *Bob Thomas? It would have been a mistake.*

DYLAN: Well, that name changed me. I didn't sit around and think about it too much. That is who I felt I was.

PLAYBOY: *Do you deny being the enfant terrible in those days—do you deny the craziness of it all that has been portrayed?*

DYLAN: No, it's true. That's the way it was. But . . . can't stay in one place forever.

PLAYBOY: *Did the motorcycle accident you had in 1966 have anything to do with cooling you off, getting you to relax?*

DYLAN: Well, now you're jumping way ahead to another period of time. . . . What was I doing? I don't know. It came time. Was it when I had the motorcycle accident? Well, I was straining pretty hard and couldn't have gone on living that way much longer. The fact that I made it through what I did is pretty miraculous. But, you know, sometimes you get too close to something and you got to get away from it to be able to see it. And something like that happened to me at the time.

PLAYBOY: *In a book you published during that period, 'Tarantula,' you wrote an epitaph for yourself that begins: "Here lies Bob Dylan/murdered/ from behind/by trembling flesh. . . ."*

DYLAN: Those were in my wild, unnatural moments. I'm glad those feelings passed.

PLAYBOY: *What were those days like?*

DYLAN: [*Pause*] I don't remember. [*Long pause*]

PLAYBOY: *There was a report in the press recently that you turned the Beatles on to grass for the first time. According to the story, you gave Ringo Starr a toke at J.F.K. Airport and it was the first time for any of them. True?*

DYLAN: I'm surprised if Ringo said that. It don't sound like Ringo. I don't recall meeting him at J.F.K. Airport.

PLAYBOY: *OK. Who turned you on?*

DYLAN: Grass was everywhere in the clubs. It was always there in the jazz clubs and in the folk-music clubs. There was just grass and it was available to musicians in those days. And in coffeehouses way back in Minneapolis. That's where I first came into contact with it, I'm sure. I forget when or where, really.

PLAYBOY: *Why did the musicians like grass so much?*

DYLAN: Being a musician means—depending on how far you go—getting to the depths of where you are at. And most any musician would try anything to get to those depths, because playing music is an immediate thing—as opposed to putting paint on a canvas, which is a calculated thing. Your spirit flies when you are playing music. So, with music, you tend to look deeper and deeper inside yourself to find the music. That's why, I guess, grass was around those clubs. I know the whole scene has changed now; I mean, pot is almost a legal thing. But in the old days, it was just for a few people.

PLAYBOY: *Did psychedelics have a similar effect on you?*

DYLAN: No. Psychedelics never influenced me. I don't know, I think Timothy Leary had a lot to do with driving the last nails into the coffin of that New York scene we were talking about. When psychedelics happened, everything became irrelevant. Because that had nothing to do with making music or writing poems or trying to really find yourself in that day and age.

PLAYBOY: *But people thought they were doing just that—finding themselves.*

DYLAN: People were deluded into thinking they were something that they weren't: birds, airplanes, fire hydrants, whatever. People were walking around thinking they were stars.

PLAYBOY: *As far as your music was concerned, was there a moment when you made a conscious decision to work with an electric band?*

DYLAN: Well, it had to get there. It had to go that way for me. Because that's where I started and eventually it just got back to that. I couldn't go on being the lone folkie out there, you know, strumming "Blowin' in the Wind" for three hours every night. I hear my songs as part of the music, the musical background.

PLAYBOY: *When you hear your songs in your mind, it's not just you strumming alone, you mean?*

DYLAN: Well, no, it is to begin with. But then I always hear other instruments, how they should sound. The closest I ever got to the sound I hear in my mind was on individual bands in the *Blonde on Blonde* album. It's that thin, that wild mercury sound. It's metallic and bright gold, with whatever that conjures up. That's my particular sound. I haven't been able to succeed in getting it all the time. Mostly, I've been driving at a combination of guitar, harmonica, and organ, but now I find myself going into territory that has more percussion in it and [*pause*] rhythms of the soul.

PLAYBOY: *Was that wild mercury sound in "I Want You"?*

DYLAN: Yeah, it was in "I Want You." It was in a lot of that stuff. It was in the album before that, too.

PLAYBOY: *'Highway 61 Revisited'?*

DYLAN: Yeah. Also in *Bringing It All Back Home*. That's the sound I've always heard. Later on, the songs got more defined, but it didn't necessarily bring more power to them. The sound was whatever happened to be available at the time. I have to get back to the sound, to the sound that will bring it all through me.

PLAYBOY: *Can't you just reassemble the same musicians?*

DYLAN: Not really. People change, you know, they scatter in all directions. People's lives get complicated. They tend to have more distractions, so they can't focus on that fine, singular purpose.

PLAYBOY: *You're searching for people?*

DYLAN: No, not searching, the people are there. But I just haven't paid as much attention to it as I should have. I haven't felt comfortable in a studio since I worked with Tom Wilson. The next move for me is to have a permanent band. You know, usually I just record whatever's avail-able at the time. That's my thing, you know, and it's—it's legitimate. I mean, I do it because I have to do it that way. I don't want to keep doing it, because I would like to get my life more in order. But until now, my recording sessions have tended to be last-minute affairs. I don't really use all the technical studio stuff. My songs are done live in the studio; they always have been and they always will be done that way. That's why they're alive. No matter what else you say about them, they are alive. You know, what Paul Simon does or Rod Stewart does or Crosby, Stills and Nash do—a record is not that monumental for me to make. It's just a record of songs.

PLAYBOY: *Getting back to your transition from folk to rock, the period when you came out with 'Highway 61' must have been exciting.*

DYLAN: Those were exciting times. We were doing it before anybody knew we would—or could. We didn't know what it was going to turn out to be. Nobody thought of it as folk-rock at the time. There were some people involved in it like The Byrds, and I remember Sonny and Cher and the Turtles and the early Rascals. It began coming out on the radio. I mean, I had a couple of hits in a row. That was the most I ever had in a row—two. The top ten was filled with that kind of sound—the Beatles, too—and it was exciting, those days were exciting. It was the sound of the streets. It still is. I symbolically hear that sound wherever I am.

PLAYBOY: *You hear the sound of the street?*

DYLAN: That ethereal twilight light, you know. It's the sound of the street with the sunrays, the sun shining down at a particular time, on a particular type of building. A particular type of people walking on a particular type of street. It's an outdoor sound that drifts even into open windows that you can hear. The sound of bells and distant railroad trains and arguments in apartments and the clinking of silverware and knives and forks and beating with leather straps. It's all—it's all there. Just lack of a jackhammer, you know.

PLAYBOY: *You mean if a jackhammer were—*

DYLAN: Yeah, no jackhammer sounds, no airplane sounds. All pretty natural sounds. It's water, you know water trickling down a brook. It's light flowing through the . . .

PLAYBOY: *Late-afternoon light?*

DYLAN: No, usually it's the crack of dawn. Music filters out to me in the crack of dawn.

PLAYBOY: *The "jingle jangle morning"?*

DYLAN: Right.

PLAYBOY: *After being up all night?*

DYLAN: Sometimes. You get a little spacy when you've been up all night, so you don't really have the power to form it. But that's the sound I'm trying to get across. I'm not just up there re-creating old blues tunes or trying to invent some surrealistic rhapsody.

PLAYBOY: *It's the sound that you want.*

DYLAN: Yeah, it's the sound and the words. Words don't interfere with it. They—they—punctuate it. You know, they give it purpose. [*Pause*] And all the ideas for my songs, all the influences, all come out of that. All the influences, all the feelings, all the ideas come from that. I'm not doing it to see how good I can sound, or how perfect the melody can be, or how intricate the details can be woven or how perfectly written something can be. I don't care about those things.

PLAYBOY: *The sound is that compelling to you?*

DYLAN: Mmm-hnh.

PLAYBOY: *When did you first hear it, or feel it?*

DYLAN: I guess it started way back when I was growing up.

PLAYBOY: *Not in New York?*

DYLAN: Well, I took it to New York. I wasn't born in New York. I was given some direction there, but I took it, too. I don't think I could ever have done it in New York. I would have been too beaten down.

PLAYBOY: *It was formed by the sounds back in the ore country of Minnesota?*

DYLAN: Or the lack of sound. In the city, there is nowhere you can go where you don't hear sound. You are never alone. I don't think I could have done it there. Just the struggle of growing up would be immense and would really distort things if you wanted to be an artist. Well . . . maybe not. A lot of really creative people come out of New York. But I don't know anyone like myself. I meet a lot of people from New York that I get along with fine, and share the same ideas, but I got something different in my soul. Like a spirit. It's like being from the Smoky Mountains or the backwoods of Mississippi. It is going to make you a certain type of person if you stay 20 years in a place.

PLAYBOY: *With your love of the country, what made you leave Woodstock in 1969 and go back to the Village?*

DYLAN: It became stale and disillusioning. It got too crowded, with the wrong people throwing orders. And the old people were afraid to come out on the street. The rainbow faded.

PLAYBOY: *But the Village, New York City, wasn't the answer, either.*

DYLAN: The stimulation had vanished. Everybody was in a pretty down mood. It was over.

PLAYBOY: *Do you think that old scene you've talked about might be creeping back into New York?*

DYLAN: Well, I was there last summer. I didn't sense any of it. There are a lot of rock-'n'-roll clubs and jazz clubs and Puerto Rican poetry clubs, but as far as learning something new, learning to teach. . . . New York is full of teachers, that is obvious, but it is pretty depressing now. To make it on the street, you just about have to beg.

PLAYBOY: *So now you're in California. Is there any kind of scene that you can be part of?*

DYLAN: I'm only working out here most, or all, of the time, so I don't know what this town is really like. I like San Francisco. I find it full of tragedy and comedy. But if I want to go to a city in this country, I will still go to New York. There are cities all over the world to go to. I don't know, maybe I am just an old dog, so maybe I feel like I've been around so long I am looking for something new to do and it ain't there. I was looking for some space to create what I want to do. I am only interested in that these days. I don't care so much about hanging out.

PLAYBOY: *Do you feel older than when you sang, "I was so much older then, I'm younger than that now"?*

DYLAN: No, I don't feel old. I don't feel old at all. But I feel like there are certain things that don't attract me anymore that I used to succumb to very easily.

PLAYBOY: *Such as?*

DYLAN: Just the everyday vices.

PLAYBOY: *Do you think that you have managed to resist having to grow up or have you found a way of doing it that is different from conventional growing up?*

DYLAN: I don't really think in terms of growing up or not growing up. I think in terms of being able to fulfill yourself. Don't forget, you see, I've been doing what I've been doing since I was very small, so I have never known anything else. I have never had to quit my job to do this. This is all that I have ever done in my life. So I don't think in terms of economics or status or what people think of me one way or the other.

PLAYBOY: *Would you say you still have a rebellious, or punk, quality toward the rest of the world?*

DYLAN: Punk quality?

PLAYBOY: *Well, you're still wearing dark sunglasses, right?*

DYLAN: Yeah.

PLAYBOY: *Is that so people won't see your eyes?*

DYLAN: Actually, it's just habit-forming after a while, I still do wear dark sunglasses. There is no profound reason for it, I guess. Some kind of insecurity, I don't know: I like dark sunglasses. Have I had these on through every interview session?

PLAYBOY: *Yes. We haven't seen your eyes yet.*

DYLAN: Well, Monday for sure. [The day that *Playboy* photos were to be taken for the opening page.]

PLAYBOY: *Aside from the dark glasses, is it something in the punk quality of Elvis or James Dean that makes you dress a certain way or act a certain way?*

DYLAN: No. It's from the early sixties. Elvis was there. He was there when there wasn't anybody there. He was Elvis and everybody knows about what Elvis did. He did it to me just like he did it to everybody else. Elvis was in that certain age group and I followed him right from Blue Moon in Kentucky. And there were others; I admired Buddy Holly a lot. But Elvis was never really a punk. And neither was James Dean a punk.

PLAYBOY: *What quality did Dean represent?*

DYLAN: He let his heart do the talking. That was his one badge. He was effective for people of that age, but as you grow older, you have different experiences and you tend to identify with artists who had different meanings for you.

PLAYBOY: *Let's talk some more about your influences. What musicians do you listen to today.*

DYLAN: I still listen to the same old black-and-blue blues. Tommy McClennan, Lightnin' Hopkins, the Carter Family, the early Carlyles. I listen to Big Maceo, Robert Johnson. Once in a while, I listen to Woody Guthrie again. Among the more recent people, Fred McDowell, Gary Stewart. I like Memphis Minnie a whole lot. Blind Willie McTell. I like bluegrass music. I listen to foreign music, too. I like Middle Eastern music a whole lot.

PLAYBOY: *Such as?*

DYLAN: Om Kalthoum.

PLAYBOY: *Who is that?*

DYLAN: She was a great Egyptian singer. I first heard of her when I was in Jerusalem.

PLAYBOY: *She was an Egyptian singer who was popular in Jerusalem?*

DYLAN: I think she's popular all over the Middle East. In Israel, too. She does mostly love and prayer-type songs, with violin and drum accompaniment. Her father chanted those prayers and I guess she was so good when she tried singing behind his back that he allowed her to sing professionally, and she's dead now but not forgotten. She's great. She really is. Really great.

PLAYBOY: *Any popular stuff?*

DYLAN: Well, Nana Mouskouri.

PLAYBOY: *How about the Beatles?*

DYLAN: I've always liked the way George Harrison plays guitar—restrained and good. As for Lennon, well, I was encouraged by his book [*In His Own Write*]. Or the publishers were encouraged, because they asked me to write a book and that's how *Tarantula* came about. John has taken poetics pretty far in popular music. A lot of his work is overlooked, but if you examine it, you'll find key expressions that have never been said before to push across his point of view. Things that are symbolic of some inner reality and probably will never be said again.

PLAYBOY: *Do you listen to your own stuff?*

DYLAN: Not so much.

PLAYBOY: *What about your literary influences? You've mentioned Kerouac and Ginsberg. Whom do you read now?*

DYLAN: Rilke. Chekhov. Chekhov is my favorite writer. I like Henry Miller. I think he's the greatest American writer.

PLAYBOY: *Did you meet Miller?*

DYLAN: Yeah, I met him. Years ago. Played Ping-Pong with him.

PLAYBOY: *Did you read 'Catcher in the Rye' as a kid?*

DYLAN: I must have, you know. Yeah, I think so.

PLAYBOY: *Did you identify with Holden Caulfield?*

DYLAN: Uh, what was his story?

PLAYBOY: *He was a lonely kid in prep school who ran away and decided that everyone else was phony and that he was sensitive.*

DYLAN: I must have identified with him.

PLAYBOY: *We've been talking about the arts, and as we've been speaking, you've been in the midst of editing your first film, 'Renaldo & Clara.' What do you feel you can do in films that you can't do in songs?*

DYLAN: I can take songs up to a higher power. The movie to me is more a painting than music. It is a painting. It's a painting coming alive off a wall. That's why we're making it. Painters can contain their artistic turmoil; in another age, moviemakers would most likely be painters.

PLAYBOY: *Although 'Renaldo & Clara' is the first movie you've produced, directed, and acted in, there was a documentary made in 1966 that marked your first appearance in a film — 'Don't Look Back.' What did you think of it?*

DYLAN: *Don't Look Back* was . . . somebody else's movie. It was a deal worked out with a film company, but I didn't really play any part in it. When I saw it in a moviehouse, I was shocked at what had been done. I didn't find out until later that the camera had been on me all the time. That movie was done by a man who took it all out of context. It was documented from his personal point of view. The movie was dishonest, it was a propaganda movie. I don't think it was accurate at all in terms of showing my formative years. It showed only one side. He made it seem

like I wasn't doing anything but living in hotel rooms, playing the typewriter, and holding press conferences for journalists. All that is true, you
know. Throwing some bottles, there's something about it in the movie.
Joan Baez is in it. But it's one-sided. Let's not lean on it too hard. It just
wasn't representative of what was happening in the sixties.

PLAYBOY: *Don't you feel it captured the frenzy of your tour, even though it
focused on you in terms of stardom?*

DYLAN: I wasn't really a star in those days, any more than I'm a star
these days. I was very obviously confused then as to what my purpose
was. It was pretty early, you know. "The Times They Are A-Changin' "
was on the English charts then, so it had to be pretty early.

PLAYBOY: *And you didn't really know what you were doing then?*

DYLAN: Well, look what I did after that. Look what I did after that. I
didn't really start to develop until after that. I mean, I did, but I didn't.
Don't Look Back was a little too premature. I should have been left alone
at that stage.

PLAYBOY: *You were involved in another movie around that period—
1966—that was never released, called 'Eat the Document.' How did that
happen?*

DYLAN: That started as a television special. I wasn't the maker of that
film, either. I was the—I was the victim. They had already shot film,
but at that time, of course, I did—I had a—if I hadn't gotten into that
motorcycle accident, they would have broadcast it, and that would have
been that. But I was sort of—I was taken out of it, you know, and—I
think it was the fall of that year. I had a little more time to, you know,
concentrate on what was happening to me and what had happened.
Anyway, what had happened was that they had made another *Don't Look
Back*, only this time it was for television. I had nothing better to do than
to see the film. All of it, including unused footage. And it was obvious from looking at the film that it was garbage. It was miles and miles
of garbage. That was my introduction to film. My film concept was all
formed in those early days when I was looking at that footage.

PLAYBOY: *From looking at those miles of garbage, you got your concept
of film?*

DYLAN: Yeah, it was mostly rejected footage, which I found beauty
in. Which probably tells you more—that I see beauty where other
people don't.

PLAYBOY: *That reminds us of a poem you wrote for the jacket of an early Joan Baez album, in which you claimed that you always thought something had to be ugly before you found it beautiful. And at some point in the poem, you described listening to Joan sing and suddenly deciding that beauty didn't have to start out by being ugly.*

DYLAN: I was very hung up on Joan at the time. [*Pause*] I think I was just trying to tell myself I wasn't hung up on her.

PLAYBOY: OK. *Would you talk some more about the film concept you got from the rejected footage?*

DYLAN: Well, up until that time, they had been concerned with the linear story line. It was on one plane and in one dimension only. And the more I looked at the film, the more I realized that you could get more onto film than just one train of thought. My mind works that way, anyway. We tend to work on different levels. So I was seeing a lot of those levels in the footage. But technically, I didn't know how to do what my mind was telling me could be done.

PLAYBOY: *What did you feel could be done?*

DYLAN: Well, well, now, film is a series of actions and reactions, you know. And it's trickery. You're playing with illusion. What seems to be a simple affair is actually quite contrived. And the stronger your point of view is, the stronger your film will be.

PLAYBOY: *Would you elaborate?*

DYLAN: You're trying to get a message through. So there are many ways to deliver that message. Let's say you have a message: "White is white." Bergman would say, "White is white" in the space of an hour—or what seems to be an hour. Buñuel might say, "White is black, and black is white, but white is really white." And it's all really the same message.

PLAYBOY: *And how would Dylan say it?*

DYLAN: Dylan would probably not even say it [*laughs*]. He would— he'd assume you'd know that [*laughs*].

PLAYBOY: *You wriggled out of that one.*

DYLAN: I'd say people will always believe in something if they feel it to be true. Just knowing it's true is not enough. If you feel in your gut that it's true, well, then, you can be pretty much assured that it's true.

PLAYBOY: *So that a film made by someone who feels in his guts that white is white will give the feeling to the audience that white is white without having to say it.*

DYLAN: Yes. Exactly.

PLAYBOY: *Let's talk about the message of 'Renaldo & Clara.' It appears to us to be a personal yet fictional film in which you, Joan Baez, and your former wife, Sara, play leading roles. You play Renaldo, Baez plays a "woman in white," and Sara plays Clara. There is also a character in the film called Bob Dylan played by someone else. It is composed of footage from your Rolling Thunder Revue tour and fictional scenes performed by all of you as actors. Would you tell us basically what the movie's about?*

DYLAN: It's about the essence of man being alienated from himself and how, in order to free himself, to be reborn, he has to go outside himself. You can almost say that he dies in order to look at time and by strength of will can return to the same body.

PLAYBOY: *He can return by strength of will to the same body . . . and to Clara?*

DYLAN: Clara represents to Renaldo everything in the material world he's ever wanted. Renaldo's needs are few. He doesn't know it, though, at that particular time.

PLAYBOY: *What are his needs?*

DYLAN: A good guitar and a dark street.

PLAYBOY: *The guitar because he loves music, but why the dark street?*

DYLAN: Mostly because he needs to hide.

PLAYBOY: *From whom?*

DYLAN: From the demon within. [*Pause*] But what we all know is that you can't hide on a dark street from the demon within. And there's our movie.

PLAYBOY: *Renaldo finds that out in the film?*

DYLAN: He tries to escape from the demon within, but he discovers that the demon is, in fact, a mirrored reflection of Renaldo himself.

PLAYBOY: *OK. Given the personalities involved, how do you define the relationship between you, your personal life, and the film?*

DYLAN: No different from Hitchcock making a movie. I am the overseer.

PLAYBOY: *Overseeing various versions of yourself?*

DYLAN: Well, certain truths I know. Not necessarily myself but a certain accumulation of experience that has become real to me and a knowledge that I acquired on the road.

PLAYBOY: *And what are those truths?*

DYLAN: One is that if you try to be anyone but yourself, you will fail; if you are not true to your own heart, you will fail. Then again, there's no success like failure.

PLAYBOY: *And failure's no success at all.*

DYLAN: Oh, well, we're not looking to succeed. Just by our being and acting alive, we succeed. You fail only when you let death creep in and take over a part of your life that should be alive.

PLAYBOY: *How does death creep in?*

DYLAN: Death don't come knocking at the door. It's there in the morning when you wake up.

PLAYBOY: *How is it there?*

DYLAN: Did you ever clip your fingernails, cut your hair? Then you experience death.

PLAYBOY: *Look, in the film, Joan Baez turns to you at one point and says, "You never give any straight answers." Do you?*

DYLAN: She is confronting Renaldo.

PLAYBOY: *Evasiveness isn't only in the mind; it can also come out—in an interview.*

DYLAN: There are no simple answers to these questions. . . .

PLAYBOY: *Aren't you teasing the audience when you have scenes played by Baez and Sara, real people in your life, and then expect the viewers to set aside their preconceptions as to their relationship to you?*

DYLAN: No, no. They shouldn't even think they know anyone in this film. It's all in the context of Renaldo and Clara and there's no reason to get hung up on who's who in the movie.

PLAYBOY: *What about scenes such as the one in which Baez asks you,* "*What if we had gotten married back then?*"

DYLAN: Seems pretty real, don't it?

PLAYBOY: *Yes.*

DYLAN: Seems pretty real. Just like in a Bergman movie, those things seem real. There's a lot of spontaneity that goes on. Usually, the people in his films know each other, so they can interrelate. There's life and breath in every frame because everyone knew each other.

PLAYBOY: *All right, another question: In the movie, Ronnie Hawkins, a 300-pound Canadian rock singer, goes by the name of Bob Dylan. So is there a real Bob Dylan?*

DYLAN: In the movie?

PLAYBOY: *Yes.*

DYLAN: In the movie, no. He doesn't even appear in the movie. His voice is there, his songs are used, but Bob's not in the movie. It would be silly. Did you ever see a Picasso painting with Picasso in the picture? You only see his work. Now, I'm not interested in putting a picture of myself on the screen, because that's not going to do anybody any good, including me.

PLAYBOY: *Then why use the name Bob Dylan at all in the movie?*

DYLAN: In order to legitimize this film. We confronted it head on: The persona of Bob Dylan is in the movie so we could get rid of it. There should no longer be any mystery as to who or what he is—he's there, speaking in all kinds of tongues, and there's even someone else claiming to be him, so he's covered. This movie is obvious, you know. Nobody's hiding anything. It's all right there. The rabbits are falling out of the hat before the movie begins.

PLAYBOY: *Do you really feel it's an accessible movie?*

DYLAN: Oh, perfectly. Very open movie.

PLAYBOY: *Even though Mr. Bob Dylan and Mrs. Bob Dylan are played by different people. . . .*

DYLAN: Oh, yeah.

PLAYBOY: *And you don't know for sure which one he is?*

DYLAN: Sure. We could make a movie and you could be Bob Dylan. It wouldn't matter.

PLAYBOY: *But if there are two Bob Dylans in the film and Renaldo is always changing. . . .*

DYLAN: Well, it could be worse. It could be three or four. Basically, it's a simple movie.

PLAYBOY: *How did you decide to make it?*

DYLAN: As I said, I had the idea for doing my own film back in '66. And I buried it until '76. My lawyer used to tell me there was a future in movies. So I said, "What kind of future?" He said, "Well, if you can come up with a script, an outline, and get money from a big distributor." But I knew I couldn't work that way. I can't betray my vision on a little piece of paper in hopes of getting some money from somebody. In the final analysis, it turned out that I had to make the movie all by myself, with people who would work with me, who trusted me. I went on the road in '76 to make the money for this movie. My last two tours were to raise the money for it.

PLAYBOY: *How much of your money are you risking?*

DYLAN: I'd rather not say. It is quite a bit, but I didn't go into the bank. The budget was like $600,000, but it went over that.

PLAYBOY: *Did you get pleasure out of the project?*

DYLAN: I feel it's a story that means a great deal to me, and I got to do what I always wanted to do—make a movie. When something like that happens, it's like stopping time, and you can make people live into that moment. Not many things can do that in your daily life. You can be distracted by many things. But the main point is to make it meaningful to someone. Take *Shane*, for example. That moved me. *On the Waterfront* moved me. So when I go to see a film, I expect to be moved. I don't want to go see a movie just to kill time, or to have it just show me something I'm not aware of. I want to be moved, because that's what art is supposed to do, according to all the great theologians. Art is supposed to take you out of your chair. It's supposed to move you from one space to another. *Renaldo & Clara* is not meant to put a strain on you. It's a movie to be enjoyed as a movie. I know nothing about film, I'm not a filmmaker. On the other hand, I do consider myself a filmmaker because I made this film: So I don't know. . . . If it doesn't move you, then it's a grand, and was made in the spirit of "All right, if all you people out there want to talk about Dylan breaking up with his wife, about his having an affair with Joan Baez, I'll just put those people into my film and rub people's noses in the gossip, because only I know the truth?"

It's not entirely true, because that's not what the movie is about. I'm not sure how much of Bob Dylan and Joan Baez concern anybody. To me, it isn't important. It's old news to me, so I don't think it's of much interest to anybody. If it is, fine. But I don't think it's a relevant issue. The movie doesn't deal with anything current. This is two years ago. I'm smart enough to know I shouldn't deal with any current subject on an emotional level, because usually it won't last. You need experience to write, or to sing or to act. You don't just wake up and say you're going to do it. This movie is taking experience and turning it into something else. It's not a gossipy movie.

PLAYBOY: *We began this discussion of your movie by comparing filmmakers to painters. Were you as interested in painting as in, say, rock music when you were growing up?*

DYLAN: Yeah, I've always painted. I've always held on to that one way or another.

PLAYBOY: *Do you feel you use colors in the same way you use notes or chords?*

DYLAN: Oh, yeah. There's much information you could get on the meaning of colors. Every color has a certain mood and feeling. For instance, red is a very vital color. There're a lot of reds in this movie, and a lot of blues. A lot of cobalt blue.

PLAYBOY: *Why cobalt blue?*

DYLAN: It's the color of dissension.

PLAYBOY: *Did you study painting?*

DYLAN: A lot of the ideas I have were influenced by an old man who had definite ideas on life and the universe and nature—all that matters.

PLAYBOY: *Who was he?*

DYLAN: Just an old man. His name wouldn't mean anything to you. He came to this country from Russia in the twenties, started out as a boxer and ended up painting portraits of women.

PLAYBOY: *You don't want to mention his name, just to give him a plug?*

DYLAN: His first name was Norman. Every time I mention somebody's name, it's like they get a tremendous amount of distraction and irrelevancy in their lives. For instance, there's this lady in L.A. I respect a lot who reads palms. Her name's Tamara Rand. She's for real, she's not a gypsy fortune-teller. But she's accurate! She'll take a look at your hand and tell you things you feel but don't really understand about where you're heading, what the future looks like. She's a surprisingly hopeful person.

PLAYBOY: *Are you sure you want to know if there's bad news in your future?*

DYLAN: Well, sometimes when the world falls on your head, you know there are ways to get out, but you want to know which way. Usually, there's someone who can tell you how to crawl out, which way to take.

PLAYBOY: *Getting back to colors and chords, are there particular musical keys that have personalities or moods the way colors do for you?*

DYLAN: Yeah. B major and B-flat major.

PLAYBOY: *How would you describe them?*

DYLAN: [*Pause*] Each one is hard to define. Assume the characteristic that is true of both of them and you'll find you're not sure whether you're speaking to them or to their echo.

PLAYBOY: *What does a major key generally conjure up for you?*

DYLAN: I think any major key deals with romance.

PLAYBOY: *And the minor keys?*

DYLAN: The supernatural.

PLAYBOY: *What about other specific keys?*

DYLAN: I find C major to be the key of strength, but also the key of regret. E major is the key of confidence. A-flat major is the key of renunciation.

PLAYBOY: *Since we're back on the subject of music, what new songs have you planned?*

DYLAN: I have new songs now that are unlike anything I've ever written.

PLAYBOY: *Really?*

DYLAN: Yes.

PLAYBOY: *What are they like?*

DYLAN: Well, you'll see. I mean, unlike anything I've ever done. You couldn't even say that *Blood on the Tracks* or *Desire* have led up to this stuff. I mean, it's that far gone, it's that far out there. I'd rather not talk more about them until they're out.

PLAYBOY: *When the character Bob Dylan in your movie speaks the words "Rock 'n' roll is the answer," what does he mean?*

DYLAN: He's speaking of the sound and the rhythm. The drums and the rhythm are the answer. Get into the rhythm of it and you will lose yourself; you will forget about the brutality of it all. Then you will lose your identity. That's what he's saying.

PLAYBOY: *Does that happen to you, to the real Bob Dylan?*

DYLAN: Well, that's easy. When you're playing music and it's going well, you do lose your identity, you become totally subservient to the music you're doing in your very being.

PLAYBOY: *Do you feel possessed?*

DYLAN: It's dangerous, because its effect is that you believe that you can transcend and cope with anything. That it is the real life, that you've struck at the heart of life itself and you are on top of your dream. And there's no down. But later on, backstage, you have a different point of view.

PLAYBOY: *When you're onstage, do you feel the illusion that death can't get you?*

DYLAN: Death can't get you at all. Death's not here to get anybody. It's the appearance of the Devil, and the Devil is a coward, so knowledge will overcome that.

PLAYBOY: *What do you mean?*

DYLAN: The Devil is everything false, the Devil will go as deep as you let the Devil go. You can leave yourself open to that. If you understand what that whole scene is about, you can easily step aside. But if you want the confrontation to begin with, well, there's plenty of it. But then again, if you believe you have a purpose and a mission, and not much time to carry it out, you don't bother about those things.

PLAYBOY: *Do you think you have a purpose and a mission?*

DYLAN: Obviously.

PLAYBOY: *What is it?*

DYLAN: Henry Miller said it: The role of an artist is to inoculate the world with disillusionment.

PLAYBOY: *To create rock music, you used to have to be against the system, a desperado. Is settling down an enemy of rock?*

DYLAN: No. You can be a priest and be in rock 'n' roll. Being a rock-'n'-roll singer is no different from being a house painter. You climb up as high as you want to. You're asking me, is rock, is the lifestyle of rock 'n' roll at odds with the lifestyle of society in general?

PLAYBOY: *Yes. Do you need to be in some way outside society, or in some way an outlaw, some way a . . .*

DYLAN: No. Rock 'n' roll forms its own society. It's a world of its own. The same way the sports world is.

PLAYBOY: *But didn't you feel that it was valuable to bum around and all that sort of thing?*

DYLAN: Yes. But not necessarily, because you can bum around and wind up being a lawyer, you know. There isn't anything definite. Or any blueprint to it.

PLAYBOY: *So future rock stars could just as easily go to law school?*

DYLAN: For some people, it might be fine. But, getting back to that again, you have to have belief. You must have a purpose. You must believe that you can disappear through walls. Without that belief, you're not going to become a very good rock singer, or pop singer, or folk-rock singer, or you're not going to become a very good lawyer. Or a doctor. You must know why you're doing what you're doing.

PLAYBOY: *Why are you doing what you're doing?*

DYLAN: [*Pause*] Because I don't know anything else to do. I'm good at it.

PLAYBOY: *How would you describe "it"?*

DYLAN: I'm an artist. I try to create art.

PLAYBOY: *How do you feel about your songs when you perform them years later? Do you feel your art has endured?*

DYLAN: How many singers feel the same way ten years later that they felt when they wrote their song? Wait till it gets to be 20 years, you know? Now, there's a certain amount of act that you can put on, you know, you can get through on it, but there's got to be something to it that is real—not just for the moment. And a lot of my songs don't work. I wrote a lot of them just by gut—because my gut told me to write them—and they usually don't work so good as the years go on. A lot of them do work. With those, there's some truth about every one of them. And I don't think I'd be singing if I weren't writing, you know. I would have no reason or purpose to be out there singing. I mean, I don't consider myself . . . the life of the party [*laughs*].

PLAYBOY: *You've given new life to some songs in recent performances, such as "I Pity the Poor Immigrant" in the Rolling Thunder tour.*

DYLAN: Oh, yes. I've given new life to a lot of them. Because I believe in them, basically. You know, I believe in them. So I do give them new life. And that can always be done. I rewrote "Lay, Lady, Lay." too. No one ever mentioned that.

PLAYBOY: *You changed it to a much raunchier, less pretty kind of song.*

DYLAN: Exactly. A lot of words to that song have changed. I recorded it originally surrounded by a bunch of other songs on the *Nashville Skyline* album. That was the tone of the session. Once everything was set, that was the way it came out. And it was fine for that time, but I always had a feeling there was more to the song than that.

PLAYBOY: *Is it true that "Lay, Lady, Lay" was originally commissioned for 'Midnight Cowboy'?*

DYLAN: That's right. They wound up using Freddy Neil's tune.

PLAYBOY: *How did it feel doing "Blowin' in the Wind" after all those years during your last couple of tours?*

DYLAN: I think I'll always be able to do that. There are certain songs that I will always be able to do. They will always have just as much meaning, if not more, as time goes on.

PLAYBOY: *What about "Like a Rolling Stone"?*

DYLAN: That was a great tune, yeah. It's the dynamics in the rhythm that make up "Like a Rolling Stone" and all of the lyrics. I tend to base all my songs on the old songs, like the old folk songs, the old blues tunes; they are always good. They always make sense.

PLAYBOY: *Would you talk a little about how specific songs come to you?*

DYLAN: They come to me when I am most isolated in space and time. I reject a lot of inspiring lines.

PLAYBOY: *They're too good?*

DYLAN: I reject a lot. I kind of know myself well enough to know that the line might be good and it is the first line that gives you inspiration and then it's just like riding a bull. That is the rest of it. Either you just stick with it or you don't. And if you believe that what you are doing is important, then you will stick with it no matter what.

PLAYBOY: *There are lines that are like riding wild bulls?*

DYLAN: There are lines like that. A lot of lines that would be better off just staying on a printed page and finishing up as poems. I forget a lot of the lines. During the day, a lot of lines will come to me that I will just say are pretty strange and I don't have anything better to do. I try not to pay too much attention to those wild, obscure lines.

PLAYBOY: *You say you get a single line and then you ride it. Does the melody follow after you write out the whole song?*

DYLAN: I usually know the melody before the song.

PLAYBOY: *And it is there, waiting for that first line?*

DYLAN: Yeah.

PLAYBOY: *Do you hear it easily?*

DYLAN: The melody? Sometimes, and sometimes I have to find it.

PLAYBOY: *Do you work regularly? Do you get up every morning and practice?*

DYLAN: A certain part of every day I have to play.

PLAYBOY: *Has your playing become more complex?*

DYLAN: No. Musically not. I can hear more and my melodies now are more rhythmic than they ever have been, but, really, I am still with those same three chords. But, I mean, I'm not Segovia or Montoya. I don't practice 12 hours a day.

PLAYBOY: *Do you practice using your voice, too?*

DYLAN: Usually, yeah, when I'm rehearsing, especially, or when I'm writing a song, I'll be singing it.

PLAYBOY: *Someone said that when you gave up cigarettes, your voice changed. Now we see you're smoking again. Is your voice getting huskier again?*

DYLAN: No, you know, you can do anything with your voice if you put your mind to it. I mean, you can become a ventriloquist or you can become an imitator of other people's voices. I'm usually just stuck with my own voice. I can do a few other people's voices.

PLAYBOY: *Whose voices can you imitate?*

DYLAN: Richard Widmark. Sydney Greenstreet. Peter Lorre. I like those voices. They really had distinctive voices in the early talkie films. Nowadays, you go to a movie and you can't tell one voice from the other. Jane Fonda sounds like Tatum O'Neal.

PLAYBOY: *Has your attitude toward women changed much in your songs?*

DYLAN: Yeah; in the early period, I was writing more about objection, obsession, or rejection. Superimposing my own reality on that which seemed to have no reality of its own.

PLAYBOY: *How did those opinions change?*

DYLAN: From neglect.

PLAYBOY: *From neglect?*

DYLAN: As you grow, things don't reach you as much as when you're still forming opinions.

PLAYBOY: *You mean you get hurt less easily?*

DYLAN: You get hurt over other matters than when you were 17. The energy of hurt isn't enough to create art.

PLAYBOY: *So if the women in your songs have become more real, if there are fewer goddesses —*

DYLAN: The goddess isn't real. A pretty woman as a goddess is just up there on a pedestal. The flower is what we are really concerned about here. The opening and the closing, the growth, the bafflement. You don't lust after flowers.

PLAYBOY: *Your regard for women, then, has changed?*

DYLAN: People are people to me. I don't single out women as anything to get hung up about.

PLAYBOY: *But in the past?*

DYLAN: In the past, I was guilty of that shameless crime.

PLAYBOY: *You're claiming to be completely rehabilitated?*

DYLAN: In that area, I don't have any serious problems.

PLAYBOY: *There's a line in your film in which someone says to Sara, "I need you because I need your magic to protect me."*

DYLAN: Well, the real magic of women is that throughout the ages, they've had to do all the work and yet they can have a sense of humor.

PLAYBOY: *That's throughout the ages. What about women now?*

DYLAN: Well, here's the new woman, right? Nowadays, you have the concept of a new woman, but the new woman is nothing without a man.

PLAYBOY: *What would the new woman say to that?*

DYLAN: I don't know what the new woman would say, the new woman is the impulsive woman. . . .

PLAYBOY: *There's another line in your movie about "the ultimate woman." What is the ultimate woman?*

DYLAN: A woman without prejudice.

PLAYBOY: *Are there many?*

DYLAN: There are as many as you can see. As many as can touch you.

PLAYBOY: *So you've run into a lot of ultimate women?*

DYLAN: Me, personally? I don't run into that many people. I'm working most of the time. I really don't have time for all that kind of intrigue.

PLAYBOY: *Camus said that chastity is an essential condition for creativity. Do you agree?*

DYLAN: He was speaking there of the disinvolvement with pretense.

PLAYBOY: *Wasn't he speaking of sexual chastity?*

DYLAN: You mean he was saying you have to stay celibate to create?

PLAYBOY: *That's one interpretation.*

DYLAN: Well, he might have been on to something there. It could have worked for him.

PLAYBOY: *When you think about rock and the rhythm of the heartbeat is it tied into love in some way?*

DYLAN: The heartbeat. Have you ever lain with somebody when your hearts were beating in the same rhythm? That's true love. A man and a woman who lie down with their hearts beating together are truly lucky. Then you've truly been in love, m'boy. Yeah, that's true love. You might see that person once a month, once a year, maybe once a lifetime, but you have the guarantee your lives are going to be in rhythm. That's all you need.

PLAYBOY: *Considering that some of your recent songs have been about love and romance, what do you feel about the tendency some people used to have of dividing your work into periods? Did you ever feel it was fair to divide your work, for example, into a political period and a nonpolitical period?*

DYLAN: Those people disregarded the ultimate fact that I am a songwriter. I can't help what other people do with my songs, what they make of them.

PLAYBOY: *But you were more involved politically at one time. You were supposed to have written "Chimes of Freedom" in the backseat of a car while you were visiting some SNCC people in the South.*

DYLAN: That is all we did in those days. Writing in the backseats of cars and writing songs on street corners or on porch swings. Seeking out the explosive areas of life.

PLAYBOY: *One of which was politics?*

DYLAN: Politics was always one because there were people who were trying to change things. They were involved in the political game because that is how they had to change things. But I have always considered politics just part of the illusion. I don't get involved much in politics. I don't know what the system runs on. For instance, there are people who have definite ideas or who studied all the systems of government. A lot of those people with college-educational backgrounds tended to come in and use up everybody for whatever purposes they had in mind. And, of course, they used music, because music was accessible and we would have done that stuff and written those songs and sung them whether there was any politics or not. I never did renounce a role in politics, because I never played one in politics. It would be comical for me to think that I played a role. Gurdjieff thinks it's best to work out your mobility daily.

PLAYBOY: *So you did have a lot of "on the road" experiences?*

DYLAN: I still do.

PLAYBOY: *Driving around?*

DYLAN: I am interested in all aspects of life. Revelations and realizations. Lucid thought that can be translated into songs, analogies, new information. I am better at it now. Not really written yet anything to make me stop writing. Like, I haven't come to the place that Rimbaud came to when he decided to stop writing and run guns in Africa.

PLAYBOY: *Jimmy Carter has said that listening to your songs, he learned to see in a new way the relationship between landlord and tenant, farmer and sharecropper, and things like that. He also said that you were his friend. What do you think of all that?*

DYLAN: I am his friend.

PLAYBOY: *A personal friend?*

DYLAN: I know him personally.

PLAYBOY: *Do you like him?*

DYLAN: Yeah, I think his heart's in the right place.

PLAYBOY: *How would you describe that place?*

DYLAN: The place of destiny. You know, I hope the magazine won't take all this stuff and edit—like, Carter's heart's in the right place of destiny, because it's going to really sound . . .

PLAYBOY: *No, it would lose the sense of conversation. The magazine's pretty good about that.*

DYLAN: Carter has his heart in the right place. He has a sense of who he is. That's what I felt, anyway, when I met him.

PLAYBOY: *Have you met him many times?*

DYLAN: Only once.

PLAYBOY: *Stayed at his house?*

DYLAN: No. But anybody who's a governor or a Senate leader or in a position of authority who finds time to invite a folk-rock singer and his band out to his place has got to have . . . a sense of humor . . . and a feeling of the pulse of the people. Why does he have to do it? Most people in those kinds of positions can't relate at all to people in the music field unless it's for some selfish purpose.

PLAYBOY: *Did you talk about music or politics?*

DYLAN: Music. Very little politics. The conversation was kept in pretty general areas.

PLAYBOY: *Does he have any favorite Dylan songs?*

DYLAN: I didn't ask him if he had any favorite Dylan songs. He didn't say that he did. I think he liked "Ballad of a Thin Man," really.

PLAYBOY: *Did you think that Carter might have been using you by inviting you there?*

DYLAN: No, I believe that he was a decent, untainted man and he just wanted to check me out. Actually, as presidents go, I liked Truman.

PLAYBOY: *Why?*

DYLAN: I just liked the way he acted and things he said and who he said them to. He had a common sense about him, which is rare for a president. Maybe in the old days it wasn't so rare, but nowadays it's rare. He had a common quality. You felt like you could talk to him.

PLAYBOY: *You obviously feel you can talk to President Carter.*

DYLAN: You do feel like you can talk to him, but the guy is so busy and overworked you feel more like, well, maybe you'd just leave him alone, you know. And he's dealing with such complicated matters and issues that people are a little divided and we weren't divided in Truman's time.

PLAYBOY: *Is there anything you're angry about? Is there anything that would make you go up to Carter and say, "Look, you fucker, do this!"?*

DYLAN: Right. [*Pause*] He's probably caught up in the system like everybody else.

PLAYBOY: *Including you?*

DYLAN: I'm a part of the system. I have to deal with the system. The minute you pay taxes, you're part of the system.

PLAYBOY: *Are there any heroes or saints these days?*

DYLAN: A saint is a person who gives of himself totally and freely, without strings. He is neither deaf nor blind. And yet he's both. He's the master of his own reality, the voice of simplicity. The trick is to stay away from mirror images. The only true mirrors are puddles of water.

PLAYBOY: *How are mirrors different from puddles?*

DYLAN: The image you see in a puddle of water is consumed by depth: An image you see when you look into a piece of glass has no depth or life-flutter movement. Of course, you might want to check your tie. And, of course, you might want to see if the makeup is on straight. That's all the way. Vanity sells a lot of things.

PLAYBOY: *How so?*

DYLAN: Well, products on the market. Everything from new tires to bars of soap. Need is—need is totally overlooked. Nobody seems to care about people's needs. They're all for one purpose. A shallow grave.

PLAYBOY: *Do you want your grave unmarked?*

DYLAN: Isn't that a line in my film?

PLAYBOY: *Yes.*

DYLAN: Well, there are many things they can do with your bones, you know. [*Pause*] They make neckpieces out of them, bury them. Burn them up.

PLAYBOY: *What's your latest preference?*

DYLAN: Ah—put them in a nutshell.

PLAYBOY: *You were talking about vanity and real needs. What needs? What are we missing?*

DYLAN: There isn't anything missing. There is just a lot of scarcity.

PLAYBOY: *Scarcity of what?*

DYLAN: Inspirational abundance.

PLAYBOY: *So it's not an energy crisis but an imagination crisis?*

DYLAN: I think it's a spiritual crisis.

PLAYBOY: *How so?*

DYLAN: Well, you know, people step on each other's feet too much. They get on each other's case. They rattle easily. But I don't particularly stress that. I'm not on a soapbox about it, you know. That is the way life is.

PLAYBOY: *We asked about heroes and saints and began talking about saints. How about heroes?*

DYLAN: A hero is anyone who walks to his own drummer.

PLAYBOY: *Shouldn't people look to others to be heroes?*

DYLAN: No; when people look to others for heroism, they're looking for heroism in an imaginary character.

PLAYBOY: *Maybe that in part explains why many seized upon you as that imaginary character.*

DYLAN: I'm not an imaginary character, though.

PLAYBOY: *You must realize that people get into a whole thing about you.*

DYLAN: I know they used to.

PLAYBOY: *Don't you think they still do?*

DYLAN: Well, I'm not aware of it anymore.

PLAYBOY: *What about the 1974 tour? Or the Rolling Thunder tour of 1976?*

DYLAN: Well, yeah, you know, when I play, people show up. I'm aware they haven't forgotten about me.

PLAYBOY: *Still, people always think you have answers, don't they?*

DYLAN: No, listen: If I wasn't Bob Dylan, I'd probably think that Bob Dylan has a lot of answers myself.

PLAYBOY: *Would you be right?*

DYLAN: I don't think so. Maybe he'd have a lot of answers for him, but for me? Maybe not. Maybe yes, maybe no. Bob Dylan isn't a cat, he doesn't have nine lives, so he can only do what he can do. You know: not break under the strain. If you need someone who raises someone else to a level that is unrealistic, then it's that other person's problem. He is just confronting his superficial self somewhere down the line. They'll realize it, I'm sure.

PLAYBOY: *But didn't you have to go through a period when people were claiming you had let them down?*

DYLAN: Yeah, but I don't pay much attention to that. What can you say? Oh, I let you down, big deal, OK. That's all. Find somebody else, OK? That's all.

PLAYBOY: *You talked about a spiritual crisis. Do you think Christ is an answer?*

DYLAN: What is it that attracts people to Christ? The fact that it was such a tragedy, is what. Who does Christ become when he lives inside a certain person? Many people say that Christ lives inside them: Well, what does that mean? I've talked to many people whom Christ lives inside; I haven't met one who would want to trade places with Christ. Not one of his people put himself on the line when it came down to the final hour. What would Christ be in this day and age if he came back? What would he be? What would he be to fulfill his function and purpose? He would have to be a leader, I suppose.

PLAYBOY: *Did you grow up thinking about the fact that you were Jewish?*

DYLAN: No, I didn't. I've never felt Jewish. I don't really consider myself Jewish or non-Jewish. I don't have much of a Jewish background. I'm not a patriot to any creed. I believe in all of them and none of them. A devout Christian or Moslem can be just as effective as a devout Jew.

PLAYBOY: *You say you don't feel Jewish. But what about your sense of God?*

DYLAN: I feel a heartfelt God. I don't particularly think that God wants me thinking about Him all the time. I think that would be a tremendous burden on Him, you know. He's got enough people asking Him for favors. He's got enough people asking Him to pull strings. I'll pull my own strings, you know. I remember seeing a *Time* magazine on an airplane a few years back and it had a big cover headline, "IS GOD DEAD?" I mean, that was—would you think that was a responsible thing to do? What does God think of that? I mean, if you were God, how would you like to see that written about yourself? You know, I think the country's gone downhill since that day.

PLAYBOY: *Really?*

DYLAN: Uh-huh.

PLAYBOY: *Since that particular question was asked?*

DYLAN: Yeah; I think at that point, some very irresponsible people got hold of too much power to put such an irrelevant thing like that on a magazine when they could be talking about real issues. Since that day, you've had to kind of make your own way.

PLAYBOY: *How are we doing, making our own way?*

DYLAN: The truth is that we're born and we die. We're concerned here in this life with the journey from point A to point Z, or from what we think is point A to point Z. But it's pretty self-deluding if you think that's all there is.

PLAYBOY: *What do you think is beyond Z?*

DYLAN: You mean, what do I think is in the great unknown? [*Pause*] Sounds, echoes of laughter.

PLAYBOY: *Do you feel there's some sense of karmic balance in the universe, that you suffer for acts of bad faith?*

DYLAN: Of course. I think everybody knows that's true. After you've lived long enough, you realize that's the case. You can get away with anything for a while. But it's like Poe's "The Tell-Tale Heart" or Dostoyevsky's *Crime and Punishment*: Somewhere along the line, sooner or later, you're going to have to pay.

PLAYBOY: *Do you feel you've paid for what you got away with earlier?*

DYLAN: Right now, I'm about even.

PLAYBOY: *Isn't that what you said after your motorcycle accident— "Something had to be evened up"?*

DYLAN: Yes.

PLAYBOY: *And you meant . . . ?*

DYLAN: I meant my back wheel had to be aligned [*laughter*].

PLAYBOY: *Let's take one last dip back into the material world. What about an artist's relationship to money?*

DYLAN: The myth of the starving artist is a myth. The big bankers and prominent young ladies who buy art started it. They just want to keep the artist under their thumb. Who says an artist can't have any money? Look at Picasso. The starving artist is usually starving for those around him to starve. You don't have to starve to be a good artist. You just have to have love, insight, and a strong point of view. And you have to fight off depravity. Uncompromising, that's what makes a good artist. It doesn't matter if he has money or not. Look at Matisse; he was a banker. Anyway, there are other things that constitute wealth and poverty besides money.

PLAYBOY: *What we were touching on was the subject of the expensive house you live in, for example.*

DYLAN: What about it? Nothing earthshaking or final about where I live. There is no vision behind the house. It is just a bunch of trees and sheds.

PLAYBOY: *We read in the papers about an enormous copper dome you had built.*

DYLAN: I don't know what you read in the papers. It's just a place to live for now. The copper dome is just so I can recognize it when I come home.

PLAYBOY: *OK, back to less worldly concerns. You don't believe in astrology, do you?*

DYLAN: I don't think so.

PLAYBOY: *You were quoted recently as having said something about having a Gemini nature.*

DYLAN: Well, maybe there are certain characteristics of people who are born under certain signs. But I don't know, I'm not sure how relevant it is.

PLAYBOY: *Could it be there's an undiscovered twin or a double to Bob Dylan?*

DYLAN: Someplace on the planet, there's a double of me walking around. Could very possibly be.

PLAYBOY: *Any messages for your double?*

DYLAN: Love will conquer everything—I suppose.

16. Interview with Karen Hughes, *Rock Express*

APRIL 1, 1978

Sometimes when you speak, it's as though words are energy and too many words are wasted energy which could be better put into your songs. Is that how you feel?

Absolutely, yeah. I seldom talk. I seldom like to talk to anybody also because it's false, because when you talk and you speak, that's all you're doing. And it has to be direct. I can't do it in any other way unless it's direct. And most people don't want to be direct . . . you find yourself drifting.

Into social conventions of communication?

Yeah, into opinions and ideas. I don't care about those things . . . [*pause*] . . . I do and I don't.

Or do you care about them if they have feelings to back them up?

Well, feelings, yeah, and experience. If they have experience to back them up alright. It's like somebody telling you about Australia is one thing, but you being there and seeing it for yourself is another. I don't like to be told things.

Do you think that you've got to be selfish and shut everything off in order to write?

I think so, don't you?

Yeah, but don't you find that paradoxical?

To what?

Communication.

Well, you need something to communicate to so . . . no I don't think so at all.

What kind of outlet does touring provide for you?

It's hard to explain to someone who doesn't do it. Since I was just a kid, just a little kid, I used to watch touring bands come through my hometown. It always seemed like that was where to go. And the only escape out of it was to get down to the bus . . .

What about now then?

It's the same thing.

Ray Davies once said about touring, "When I tour I realize that I have to communicate with the outside. If I don't have an audience and I just write, my mind meanders round and round the subject, but when I know I have to communicate it to people, it goes straight to the subject. So I like to tour." Would you agree with that?

I would agree to that. I like to sing to the people. I just don't like to sing into microphones in a studio.

Many people who come to your concerts here regard it as a kind of pilgrimage. Most would like to meet you. What do you feel you have to offer your fans on this kind of individual level?

In India they have men that live in the Himalayas and people make long journeys to sit at their feet. And what happens when they sit at their feet? Nothing. Nothing happens, they're usually given a big dose of silence.

That's an answer of a kind, throwing it back at the questioner?

I don't know whether that's an answer. Sometimes it's better to be quiet than to make a lot of noise; because when you're quiet, you're usually more in tune with the birds and the bees and the phantoms of life.

Do you meditate?

Oh, I know a little bit about these things, but I don't follow any daily ritual.

You can't see any parallel between your fans seeking a private audience with you and the time long ago when you went to visit Woody Guthrie in a New Jersey hospital?

No, when I went to see him there wasn't many people seeing him. He was sick. No one had heard of him in those days, except just a few people who played folk music. So I went to see him, and it wasn't like seeing the king you know.

What kind of feeling have you been getting get back from the audiences in Australia?

[*Long pause*] That they understand without having to be told what it's all about, what the music's all about. Why I'm different from all the rest of the groups of people playing around. I mean, I mean I've been at this now a long time. What usually happens is that you are at it until someone else comes along, and I'm still at it. And I'm still going to be at it until someone else comes along.

But surely no one else ever comes along that's the same?

Well, that's true, but usually the way things go is that someone else comes out, out of the crowd, of considerable ability who can cover what you're doing and take it another step . . . [*pause*] . . . When the fire's burned out, I'll just be doing this until the fire's burned out. Muddy Waters is still playing, he's sixty-five, sixty-six.

Do you think you can stand it that long, the touring?

If those people can do it, I don't see why I can't do it.

Yeah, it doesn't take a lot out of you, physically?

Well, it takes more out of you when you're young because you don't know yourself that well. If you're dealing in the whole and not just fragments I don't see why you can't last as long as you want to last. It's not uncommon to be sixty-five to seventy. Muddy Waters, I keep coming back to Muddy Waters because . . . Lightnin' Hopkins was very old. I don't know how old he is 'cause he doesn't really say, but he's gotta be beyond fifty. Bill Monroe is still going and he's in his fifties.

How does the audience reaction here in Australia compare with Japan, New Zealand and the United States?

The States I can't tell you, I haven't been in the States with this show, I've been in the States many times. In Japan they were very reserved, as if something was destroyed. I don't know what. Well, you know what, I know what. Everybody knows what it was. Yeah, they were very reserved, but maybe there was a language barrier. There probably was, I don't see how there couldn't be really. But they were great, they got better and better with every show.

What about New Zealand?

New Zealand was an outdoor show. We played an outdoor show in New Zealand and the audience was very supportive.

Do you like New Zealand as a country?

Well, I was only in Auckland, but the sky was deep and . . .

They have mountains and sea together.

Yeah, the flowers are strange and the birds were interesting. I have never seen those kind before.

Do you find that touring gives you a more direct communication and therefore speeds up the creative process?

One feeds the other.

You were saying touring was a way of getting out of where you lived in Minnesota.

Well, it was an escape, it was like sitting all day . . . like when the train rolled through town you always looked at those faces that were peering out of the windows.

Yeah, like when you sit in the airports and see all those people going.

Yeah, it was like that, that was it.

How do you feel about Minnesota now, do you feel some kind of attraction?

Yeah, I still go back now and then.

Because you've got some land there haven't you?

Yeah, I still know some people there, I go back every now and then.

Do you still go to class reunions?

No, I don't do that.

You did once?

I went to one in er . . . I did go to one, I went to the tenth one.

When was that, in '63?

Nineteen sixty-nine, I just poked in, poked my face in.

Do you draw much these days?

No.

Why not?

Time.

Would you like to?

Yeah.

What kind of satisfaction do you get out of it?

One time I was doing it all day for a couple of months in New York. This was a couple of years back, it was '74, '75. I did it every day from eight till four with a break or something, and it locked me into the present time more than anything else I ever did. More than any experiences I've ever had, any enlightenment I've ever had. Because I was constantly being intermingled with myself and all the different selves that were in there, until this one left, then that one left, and finally I got down to the one that I was familiar with.

Who are your friends these days?

I just have the same old friends that I've always had. People who are akin to me. None of my friends look at me in awe, there's no one hanging around me that thinks I'm the leader. It's hard to explain who they are; they're just people; people like you and me.

You're working very hard at the moment, what are you working on?

Trying to get another album organized.

Can you tell me something about the songs and ideas involved?

They're hard to define. Some ballads, some narrative ballads, and some which aren't. I don't really write about anything. I don't know where these come from. Sometimes I'm thinking in some other age that I lived through. I must have had the experience of all these songs because sometimes I don't know what I'm writing about until years later it becomes clearer to me.

Do you find that as a composer, you're more like a medium, tuning into something greater happening?

I think that every composer does that. No one in his right mind would think that it was coming from him, that he has invented it. It's just coming through him.

What kind of force compels you to write?

Well, any departure, like from my traditional self, will kick it off.

How do you go about composing these songs, working them out?

Well, I usually get a melody. A melody just happens to appear as I'm playing and after that the words come in and out. Sometimes the words come first.

Does it come quickly or do you have to work on it?

Well sometimes it doesn't come quickly and other times it does come very quickly. I've written songs in five minutes complete, other songs I've had laying around for months.

Does it relate to anything going on outside of you?

No, just when I have the time to finish it or the inspiration or whatever it needs to finish it.

Previously when you recorded you just used to go into the studio and do it once—put down each track completely with no overdubbing.

I still do that. [*Dylan at this point noticed my copy of Brian Vesey-Fitzgerald's 'Gypsies of Britain' lying on the coffee table, which he picked up, became quickly absorbed, flipping through the pages, taking in the contents with astounding speed. Occasionally he stopped at significant points, while still continuing with the interview, for closer scrutiny and comment.*] Yeah in the Gypsy way of life, death is a very happy thing.

It's nice. Lots of nomadic cultures are like that.

Yeah, I can see that point of view.

Didn't you once visit a Gypsy king in the south of France?

Yeah, he was an old man at this time and the person I went to see him with knew him when he was young, not young but ten years earlier, when he was still vital and active. And at that time he had maybe sixteen to twenty wives and over 100 children. At the time we saw him, he'd had a heart attack so the smell was around and most of his family abandoned him. Fifteen or sixteen of his wives had left him and gone, and he only had about two or three children there, so he was pretty much alone. But he still had his scene going; he was into dealing in antiques and junk-metal junk.

Getting back to the album, is there anything else you can tell me about it?

Is this your book? You didn't bring it for me, did you?

No, but you can have it, would you like it?

Sure, I'd appreciate it.

What kind of arrangements will you be using?

Well, they're all new songs, very simple arrangements.

Similar to what you've done in the past?

Yeah, the arrangements are . . .

You're not going to change drastically like Joan Baez has on her last album, more towards funk?

I didn't think it was all that funky. Oh, maybe it was for her . . . [*pause*] . . . Funk is not something that you capture on record, funk is a way of life. It's a way you feel, you can't just make a funky sounding record. But I know what you mean. Funk has to do with throwing coins into the coffin, that kind of thing.

Throwing coins into the coffin?

Yeah, funk has to do with different beliefs.

Do you think there's still a lot to say about people that hasn't yet been said?

Individual people, yeah, but not people in general. Yeah, you can go on and on about individual people because of the really different characteristics and different attitudes of many people. And then of course once you get two people together there's some different types of relationship between different types of people. There are many different levels of how people can relate to one another. Some are casual, some are business, some are adventurous, and some are romantic, some are . . .

So what do you choose to be involved in?

Well, I'm just aware of the different areas of relationships.

Do you think that films are an ideal medium to explore that?

I do, yeah.

What's the significance of the title 'Renaldo and Clara'?

Well, people keep asking me that. There isn't any more significance to that than what's the significance to Queen Jane, why she had that name. Tolstoy wrote a book called *Anna Karenina* and what was the significance of that name? Renaldo is a fox and Clara is supposedly the clear understanding of the future which doesn't exist.

What kind of relationship do you have with women?

What kind of relationship?

How do you view women, what do you get out of relationships with women, do you think that they're equal or . . .

Well, I do think that everybody's equal, but I get past the attraction kinds rather quickly. I don't have time for that anymore.

And then what?

How many relationships can you really have in your life and what kind are they?

Why I brought that up was because the other night you were saying how difficult you found it to have girlfriends because they always had to fit into YOUR life. And I was wondering if, given your belief in equality, you should expect that?

No, but anyone who is in my life at all respects that. That I don't come home every night.

You seem in your songs to have a capacity to love many women. Would you like to have many wives, like the Gypsy king?

Well yeah, I'd like to have a wife for every degree.

Do you have a home?

A home? I don't have all my possessions in any one place. My clothes are all over the place, but I thrive in different places. I'd love to have a home somewhere ideally.

It can be a person or a feeling or a . . .

You know that old corny saying "a home is where the heart is"?

It's true?

[Nods]

You once said that after visiting Rubin Carter in prison that you left knowing that "this man's philosophy and my philosophy were running on the same road, and you don't meet too many people like that." Well, how do you feel about your fans who buy your records? Surely there's some kind of empathy there?

I'm not sure if they think like me. They might feel as I do, but thinking like me? I don't think we can talk about thought, we just have to talk about feeling. I'm only dealing in the feeling aspect. I'm only dealing with feelings that seem to be unbreakable and the people that follow me and feel that way, feel that. And that is what I think combines everything.

Do you think that in any way the public and the press have made you into something you're not?

Uh, no, I don't think that the public are that gullible. If I wasn't doing what it is that they think I'm doing, I'm sure that no amount of press would be skillful enough to say that I was. What do you think of this shirt?

I like the penguins, where did you get it?

Off the street.

Here?

Yeah.

Are you going to wear it on stage tonight?

This shirt with the penguins? No, I don't wear my street clothes on the stage anymore.

Do you have a designer?

Somebody made up all these clothes. I just got too depressed having to go on in my street clothes all the time.

What's the name of your designer?

A guy in L.A. named Billy, he designed these clothes.

I was wondering if you exercise a lot? Is your body in good shape?

I hope so . . . I'm running around so much you know that I guess . . . I don't know, I can't remember . . .

In the songs that you've been writing, have you written anything about your experiences in Australia?

No, not as a traveler. I haven't had that much time to experience too much.

Have you managed to hear any live bands or artists while you've been here?

No, just on television. But a couple of the guys went to see this guy, Dave Warner, and somebody managed to get a taped cassette and it sounded pretty good.

Have you heard Richard Clapton at all?

Yeah, I heard Richard Clapton in Auckland. I liked him very much. In fact I tried to get him on the bill for Australia, because you know what the law says that you have to have an Australian support act.

He always cites you as an influence.

I thought he was real good, no pretense.

You met him too?

No I didn't, I just heard his records. I like the harp . . .

What do you think characterizes the Australian that you know?

Well, in Brisbane, I noticed that everybody has a great ability to laugh.

What about elsewhere?

Elsewhere I find it . . . it's very . . . [*pause*] . . . I don't think it's a land for explorers.

You mean you don't consider it a land for explorers because there isn't much to discover?

No, I find you have to have permission for everything.

Creatively?

No, just a general feeling in the air, I can't explain it. It's like a feeling when all the windows are closed and you can't open them. And I can't explain it but it seems to be very large too. I've seen a lot more and I've got a lot better feeling for it this time than the last time when I was here and I probably will come back again.

When do you think you will come back?

Well, the next go around.

You have no idea when that will be?

No, whenever resembles the right time. I like Australia, I like all the towns that we've played in and I liked all the people that we've played to.

Do you think that feeling of having to ask permission for something is linked with the inferiority complex that Australians are reputed to have? Like "No, you can't do that, because this is Australia"—going back to the convict days?

Yeah, because we have some friends. I have a good friend who wanted to come to a concert, who wanted to see this show and he couldn't get a visa—he was coming from Singapore. He couldn't get a visa and it was outrageous of them and he said, well they didn't understand why he just wanted to come for a few days.

If you could think of one image to sum up how you see yourself, what would it be?

During the last 100 years or the next 100 years?

Both.

I don't know. Basically I just have common qualities. I feel primitive in a lot of ways and in a lot of ways I feel advanced and neither one of these feelings really matter to me. I can imagine every situation in life as if I've done it, no matter what it might be: whether it be self-punishment or marrying my half sister, I mean, I can imagine, I can feel all these things for some reason. I don't know why.

You once wrote in "Idiot Wind," "What's good is bad, what's bad is good, you'll find out when you've reached the top, you're on the bottom." Does that sum up how you feel about the cyclic way of things?

Yeah, everything that goes out comes around. I feel that way, don't you? I mean, I don't feel that I have to be quarantined for thinking that,

that's just a very common way to think. And it isn't all that irregular either, it happens to be true. The simple things which are true usually astound people. "What's good is bad, what's bad is good." Sounds very simple really.

Yeah, it struck me as being very true, that's why I noted it.

Right, it's a piece of raw meat.

Frank Zappa once said he thought the universe was based on a Möbius vortex.

Oh, yeah. Well, I can see that. I also find it very uncertain. I had a great flash into what the universe was all about when I saw a man burning a fiddle on a roof, but I can't explain to you what it was that I felt.

What other artists around at the moment do you find exciting musically?

You mean contemporary?

Yeah, around at the moment, doing things now.

Well, everybody can be exciting on a certain night.

But for you?

For me? Usually the old people every time are the only people exciting musically. Of my crowd, Eric Clapton's always pretty exciting musically, but I usually listen to older records.

You mentioned liking Joan Armatrading?

I like her, yeah. I only have heard her records. I haven't seen her in person. I liked her.

What about Roy Harper? Have you heard him?

Isn't he an English . . . er . . . Yeah, years ago, I heard his records and I liked them.

Ray Davies?

I think he's a genius. Nobody ever asks me about him. I've always been a fan of Ray Davies ever since way back when. I've always liked him and his brother and that group.

What do you admire about the Kinks?

Well, whenever you come up with something it's like being a chemist. Whenever you come up with something new you've created something new so I have to admire anyone that can do that. And that song—like I say I don't know what he's doing these days, but he did those songs, "You Really Got Me" and the one after that, that was new, that was different—it was new and it had never been done before. So I admire that when I hear that and I appreciate that . . . [*pause*] . . . Yeah, I was going to try to contact him next time I go over there, to see what he was doing.

Do you find people working in other areas interesting, like scientists for example?

Well, I don't recognize too many of those people so . . . yeah, people who are working on cancer research, I'm not gonna put that down.

How self-sufficient are you?

In what way?

Mentally I suppose.

Well, I'm not under any narcotics.

That's not really what I meant.

How do you mean it then?

How much can you exist in isolation without needing other people?

Without drinking any hemlock?

Yeah.

I don't know. I really don't know. I mean I have to go out and see people, but I still need to pull the night shades down too.

With each successive step do you feel that you're coming closer to working out your own destiny?

Yeah, 99 percent of the time I do.

Do you believe in reincarnation?

In a casual but not astonishing way.

Can you recall other lives?

No, personally, I can't.

Not even flashes?

Um, the flash without the desire to . . . once in a while . . . no, I can't say as I do. I don't pretend that I have been living in some other time although I admit that it's possible.

Do you find that most things come from within?

Most things come from taking chances.

And you're always taking a lot?

Yeah.

17. Interview with Jonathan Cott, ROLLING STONE

NOVEMBER 16, 1978

On the evening of September 15th, the Boston Red Sox were in New York City trying to get back into first place. In New Orleans, just before Muhammad Ali made his comeback, TV commentator Howard Cosell introduced the fighter by quoting from the song "Forever Young": "May your hands always be busy,/May your feet always be swift,/May you have a strong foundation/When the winds of changes shift." And in Augusta, Maine, the composer of that song was inaugurating a three-month tour of the United States and Canada that will include sixty-five concerts in sixty-two cities.

According to an Associated Press review of the opening night, Bob Dylan "drove a packed-house audience of 7,200 into shrieks of ecstasy. The thirty-seven-year-old folk-rock singer mixed old songs and new. His audience in the Augusta Civic Center was a mixture of people who first knew Dylan as an angry young poet in the early Sixties and high-school students more accustomed to punk rock. Dylan satisfied both, although his veteran fans seemed the happiest."

After a highly successful series of concerts in Japan, Australia, New Zealand and western Europe earlier this year, it might seem peculiar to think of Dylan's latest American tour as a kind of comeback. But, at least in this country, Dylan recently has been the recipient of some especially negative reviews, both for his film, *Renaldo and Clara* (which, incidentally, was warmly greeted at this year's Cannes Film Festival), and his latest album, *Street-Legal*. This billingsgate, moreover, has come from a number of Dylan's "veteran fans." In the *Village Voice*, seven reviewers—a kind of firing squad—administered justice to the film with a fusillade of abuse. And ROLLING STONE, in its two August issues, featured a column and review that pilloried the album.

Yet *Street-Legal* seems to me one of Dylan's most passionate, questing and questioning records. It presents two songs of ironic and bittersweet explanations and resolutions ("True Love Tends to Forget" and "We Better Talk This Over"); a song of waiting and searching ("Señor"); a song of black magic ("New Pony"); a song of need ("Is Your Love in Vain?"); a song of pleading ("Baby Stop Crying"); a song of the stripping bare of personality ("No Time to Think"); a song of loss and encounters ("Where Are You Tonight?"); and a song that combines medieval romance, Tarot dreams and a Palace of Mirrors in which each image is seen as if on a different floor ("Changing of the Guards"). *Street-Legal* reflects the night and day sides of Dylan's art and personality—the last three songs mentioned being among the singer's most complex lunar landscapes (illumined with imagination, intuition and magic), the first two radiating with the solar attributes of intellection and objectivity—while the other songs hover around like mysterious satellites.

Dylan recorded this album in a week, and much as I like its rough, deglamorized sound, the LP hardly gives an idea of the brilliance, dexterity and inventiveness of his new band—which he has taken on all his recent tours and which includes lead guitarist Billy Cross; rhythm guitarist Steve Soles; bassist Jerry Scheff; keyboardist Alan Pasqua; drummer Ian Wallace; David Mansfield on steel guitar, violin and mandolin; Bobbye Hall on percussion; Steve Douglas on woodwinds; and backup singers Carolyn Dennis, Jo Ann Harris and Helena Springs.

I caught up with Dylan and his group at their second concert, on September 16th at the Portland Civic Center. It began with the band—dressed in black and white velvet and satin—performing a lilting, gossamerlike instrumental version of "My Back Pages." As that concluded, Dylan—wearing white sneakers, black jeans decorated with diamond stars, a black leather jacket and a purple scarf—appeared and led the band in a sultry reworking of Muddy Waters' "I'm Ready," which featured the lines, "I'm ready as I can be/I'm ready for you/I hope you're ready for me." (Quite a different opening from "Most Likely You Go Your Way and I'll Go Mine," which introduced his 1974 tour with the Band.)

Next came an eerily high-pitched and intense rendition of "Is Your Love in Vain?" that combined the vocal inflections of James Brown and Little Anthony with the Dylan voice of *Highway 61 Revisited*. He furnished "Shelter from the Storm" with a new, romantic, rootless-sounding melodic line, full of unresolved cadences and sang it in a kind of incantatory style reminiscent of Kurt Weill.

After a calypso-flavored version of "Love Minus Zero"—which featured his first harmonica solo of the evening—Dylan gave a soulful, torch-ballad rendition of "Tangled Up in Blue," singing it to the accompaniment of tenor sax and Yamaha synthesizer as if he were on the stage of a Parisian music hall. "Ballad in Plain D," "Maggie's Farm" and "I Don't Believe You" followed—the first delivered in an ironically showbiz manner, the second featuring a driving Stax-Volt riff, and the third insinuating itself in a sly, feline way. In "Like a Rolling Stone," Dylan gave an entranced recitation of the words against a pulsating wall of sound, after which he switched gears and sang "I Shall Be Released" with the vocal timbre he once used on *Nashville Skyline*. He ended the first half of the set with an occasionally newly worded version of "Going, Going, Gone."

He began the second half with a sardonic, taunting version of "I Threw It All Away." Then, after the band withdrew, the audience started cheering as Dylan performed his one acoustic number of the night, an unadorned version of "It Ain't Me Babe." In the light of Dylan's continually changing presence and sound, this moment betokened both cultural nostalgia and artistic vulnerability.

The band returned to accompany Dylan on one of his recent R&B songs, "You Treat Me Like a Stepchild," which was followed by a Bo Diddley–propelled version of "One More Cup of Coffee" and a beautiful, slow, gospel-haunted "Blowin' in the Wind." As with "Tangled Up in Blue," Dylan sang "I Want You" as a torch ballad—you could almost imagine Edith Piaf performing it in the same spirit. After a powerful rendition of "Señor" ("I wrote this song on a train from Monterey to San Diego," he announced), Dylan sang "Masters of War" as a kind of reggae war chant that concluded with an almost psychedelic blaze. Then came "Just Like a Woman"—and it took your breath away: a grave waltz, surrendering, rejecting and erotic, with tenor sax and harmonica solos at the end.

An impassioned version of "Baby Stop Crying" led into "All Along the Watchtower," a rhythmic, satanic march that ended with a demonic, tour-de-force violin solo by David Mansfield. A hand-clapping, foot-stomping version of "All I Really Want to Do" was followed by an almost orchestral-sounding rendition of "It's Alright Ma." "You all have a safe trip home and see you next time, y'hear?" he told the audience, and concluded the set with a down-home version of "Forever Young." The encore was a light, brisk performance of "Changing of the Guards."

Dylan and the band have seventy songs in their repertoire. Moreover, they have been rehearsing some brand-new tunes, five of which—spare, intense love songs—I heard during a sound check before the concert in New Haven, Connecticut. At a subsequent New York City concert, Dylan sang one of these, "I Love You Too Much," but basically the Portland concert is the model for the program audiences will be hearing on this tour.

I ran into Dylan in the hallway of his Portland motel at noon on September 17th—an hour before the entourage was to take off for New Haven. He was heading to breakfast and wasn't looking forward to it. "I ran into a girl last night," he told me as we walked to the dining room, "whom I knew in the Village in 1964. She figured the food wouldn't be too good up here, so she said she'd bring some with her this morning. But I haven't seen her."

"Maybe her love's in vain," I joked.

"Maybe," Dylan laughed.

But just after we had sat down and were told that breakfast wasn't being served any longer, a lovely woman appeared next to us with the promised feast in a basket. We ate, saved the muffins to give to the band later on, and went out to catch the Scenicruiser bus that was to drive us to the local airport for the flight—on a chartered Bac III Jet—to New Haven, where the group was to perform that night at the Veterans' Memorial Coliseum.

Dylan and I sat at the back of the bus. The musicians and tour organizers—the most organized and sweet-tempered people I've met in years—listened to a cassette recording of Ray Charles and the Raelettes. As the bus started, I foolhardily tried to interest Dylan in a theory I had about "Changing of the Guards"—namely, that the song could be seen to have a coded subtext revealed by the characters of various Tarot cards: the Moon, the Sun, the High Priestess, the Tower and, obviously, the King and Queen of Swords—the two cards Dylan specifically mentions. My idea was that the attributes associated with these images make up the "plot" of the song.

"I'm not really too acquainted with that, you know," he warded me off. (What was that Tarot card doing on the back of the jacket of *Desire*? I wondered.) Undaunted, I mentioned that it had been said that Tarot diviners discover the future by intuition, with "prophetic images drawn from the vaults of the subconscious." Didn't Dylan think that a song like "Changing of the Guards" wakens in us the images of our subconscious? Certainly, I continued, songs such as that and "No Time to Think" suggested the idea of spirits manifesting their destiny as the dramatis personae of our dreams.

Dylan wasn't too happy with the drift of the discussion and fell silent. "I guess," I said, "there's no point in asking a magician how he does his tricks."

"Exactly!" Dylan responded cheerfully.

"Okay," I said, "we have to start someplace. What about the first line of 'Changing of the Guards.' Does 'sixteen years' have anything to do with the number of years you've been on the road?"

"No," Dylan replied, "sixteen is two short of eighteen years. Eighteen years is a magical number of years to put in time. I've found that threes and sevens . . . well, things come up in sevens. . . . What am I saying? I mean, what am I saying?"

I started rambling on about the possible mystical significance of numbers (sixteen equals one plus six, which equals seven, love minus zero, etc.), but by this time I realized that only the bus was going anywhere. It was time to get the interview rolling.

THE BUS

When I tell ROLLING STONE what we've been talking about, they won't believe it.

They had the nerve to run the reviews they did on *Street-Legal*—why should I give them an interview anyway?

Are you going to kick me off the bus?

No, it's your interview. It's okay. But if you were doing it for another magazine, it'd be okay, too.

Think I should go somewhere else with it?

Yeah—*Business Week.*

[The tape of Ray Charles and the Raelettes that has been counterpointing our banter has now given way to Joe Cocker's 'Mad Dogs and Englishmen.'] It's strange, but I noticed in your last two performances that your phrasing and the timbre of your voice at certain points resemble those of Little Anthony, Smokey Robinson and Gene Chandler. Are you aware of this?

No. When your environment changes, you change. You've got to go on, and you find new friends. Turn around one day and you're on a different stage, with a new set of characters.

In your new song, "No Time to Think," you list a series of qualities and concepts like loneliness, humility, nobility, patriotism, etc.

Is pregnancy in there?

It wasn't in there the last time I heard it. But I was thinking that it's these kinds of concepts that both free and imprison a person. What do you think?

I never have any time to think.

I should have known you'd say something like that. Maybe someone else should be up here doing this interview—a different character.

Someone who's not so knowledgeable. You're too knowledgeable.

I had the idea of just asking you the questions from "A Hard Rain's A-Gonna Fall": Where have you been? What did you see? What did you hear? Whom did you meet? What'll you do now?

[*Laughing*] I'd be here the rest of my life talking to you. . . . Just look outside the window at the picket fences and the pine trees. New England falls are so beautiful, aren't they? Look at those two kids playing by the train tracks. They remind me of myself. Both of them.

Did you ever lie down on the tracks?

Not personally. I once knew someone who did.

What happened?

I lost track of him. . . . You should describe in your interview this village we're passing through, Jonathan. It's real special. Go ahead, describe it.

There's a little pond at the edge of the road . . .

. . . and here's the Stroudwater Baptist Church. We just turned the corner and are heading on down . . . I'll tell you in a minute. What do you call this kind of architecture? . . . Look at the ducks over there . . .

. . . and that little waterfall.

This is Garrison Street, we've just passed Garrison Street—probably never will again.

You're never coming back?

Oh, I bet we come back.

Clothes on the line behind that house.

Yeah, clothes on the line. Someone's frying chicken—didn't Kristof-ferson say something like that? You don't see this in New York City . . . well, maybe at McDonald's. [*The bus pulls into the airport.*] This may be our last chance to talk, Jonathan. I hope we've got it down right this time.

THE PLANE

Let's find something to talk about.

Maybe I should ask a question that Jann Wenner, the editor of ROLLING STONE, *wanted to ask you.*

Ask me one of his.

Okay, why are you doing this tour?

Well, why did I do the last one? I'm doing this one for the same reason I did the last one.

And what reason was that?

It was for the same reason that I did the one before that. I'm doing this tour for one reason or another, but I can't remember what the reason is anymore. Articles about the tour always mention that you're doing it for the money. They always say that. There are more important things in the world than money. It means that to the people who write these articles, the most important thing in the world is money. They could be saying I'm doing the tour to meet girls or to see the world. Actually, it's all I know how to do. Ask Muhammad Ali why he fights one more fight. Go ask Marlon Brando why he makes one more movie. Ask Mick Jagger why he goes on the road. See what kind of answers you come up with. Is it so surprising I'm on the road? What else would I be doing in this life—meditating on the mountain? Whatever someone finds fulfilling, whatever his or her purpose is—that's all it is.

You recently said that you do new versions of your older songs because you believe in them—as if to believe in something is to make it real.

They *are* real, and that's why I keep doing them. As I said before, the reason for the new versions is that I've changed. You meet new people in your life, you're involved on different levels with people. Love is a force, so when a force comes in your life—and there's love surrounding you—you can do anything.

Is that what's happening to you now?

Something similar to that, yeah.

When you introduce the singers onstage as your childhood sweethearts, your present girlfriend, your former girlfriend—is that literal?

Oh, of course.

May I list the themes I found on 'Street-Legal'?

Yeah.

Survival, homelessness, trust, betrayal, sacrifice, exile, tyranny and victimization.

All right, those themes go through all of my songs because I feel those things. And those feelings touch me, so naturally they're going to appear in the songs.

I've got twenty-two or twenty-three albums out on Columbia alone and about seventy-five bootleg records floating around, so it gets to a point where it doesn't matter anymore. You want each new record to be your best, but you know you're going to write more songs and make another album anyway. People who get hit with the new album for the first time . . . it surprises them, it's coming at them from someplace and maybe they haven't thought about things that way. But that's not for me to say. That's my life, and if they can find identity in that, okay—and if they can't, that's okay, too.

A song like "No Time to Think" sounds like it comes from a very deep dream.

Maybe, because we're all dreaming, and these songs come close to getting inside that dream. It's all a dream anyway.

As in a dream, lines from one song seem to connect with lines from another. For example: "I couldn't tell her what my private thoughts were/But she had some way of finding them out" in "Where Are You Tonight?" and "The captain waits above the celebration/Sending his thoughts to a beloved maid" in "Changing of the Guards."

I'm the first person who'll put it to you and the last person who'll explain it to you. Those questions can be answered dozens of different ways, and I'm sure they're all legitimate. Everybody sees in the mirror what he sees—no two people see the same thing.

Usually you don't specify things or people in your songs. We don't know who Marcel and St. John are in "Where Are You Tonight?" or who the "partner in crime" is in that same song.

Who *isn't* your partner in crime?

But in a song like "Sara" you seem fairly literal.

I've heard it said that Dylan was never as truthful as when he wrote *Blood on the Tracks*, but that wasn't necessarily *truth*, it was just *perceptive*. Or when people say "Sara" was written for "his wife Sara"—it doesn't necessarily have to be about her just because my wife's name happened to be Sara. Anyway, was it the real Sara or the Sara in the dream? I still don't know.

Is "Is Your Love in Vain?" to be taken literally? You've been accused of being chauvinistic in that song, especially in the line, "Can you cook and sew, make flowers grow?"

That criticism comes from people who think that women should be karate instructors or airplane pilots. I'm not knocking that—everyone should achieve what she wants to achieve—but when a man's looking for a woman, he ain't looking for a woman who's an airplane pilot. He's looking for a woman to help him out and support him, to hold up one end while he holds up another.

Is that the kind of woman you're looking for?

What makes you think I'm looking for any woman?

You could say that the song isn't necessarily about you, yet some people think that you're singing about yourself and your needs.

Yeah, well, I'm everybody anyway.

There's a lot of talk about magic in 'Street-Legal': "I wish I was a magician/I would wave a wand and tie back the bond/That we've both gone beyond" in "We Better Talk This Over"; "But the magician is quicker and his game/Is much thicker than blood" in "No Time to Think."

These are things I'm really interested in, and it's taken me a while to get back to it. Right through the time of *Blonde on Blonde* I was doing it unconsciously. Then one day I was half-stepping, and the lights went out. And since that point, I more or less had amnesia. Now, you can take that statement as literally or metaphysically as you need to, but that's what happened to me. It took me a long time to get to do consciously what I used to be able to do unconsciously.

It happens to everybody. Think about the periods when people don't do anything, or they lose it and have to regain it, or lose it and gain something else. So it's taken me all this time, and the records I made along the way were like openers—trying to figure out whether it was this way or that way, just what *is* it, what's the simplest way I can tell the story and make this feeling real.

So now I'm connected back, and I don't know how long I'll be there because I don't know how long I'm going to live. But what comes now is for real and from a place that's . . . I don't know, I don't care who else cares about it.

John Wesley Harding was a fearful album—just dealing with fear [*laughing*], but dealing with the devil in a fearful way, almost. All I wanted to do was to get the words right. It was courageous to do it because I could have not done it, too. Anyway, on *Nashville Skyline* you had to read between the lines. I was trying to grasp something that would lead me on to where I thought I should be, and it didn't go nowhere—it just went down, down, down. I couldn't be anybody but myself, and at that point I didn't know it or want to know it.

I was convinced I wasn't going to do anything else, and I had the good fortune to meet a man in New York City who taught me how to see. He put my mind and my hand and my eye together in a way that allowed me to do consciously what I unconsciously felt. And I didn't know how to pull it off. I wasn't sure it could be done in songs because I'd never written a song like that. But when I started doing it, the first album I made was *Blood on the Tracks*. Everybody agrees that that was pretty different, and what's different about it is that there's a code in the lyrics and also there's no sense of time. There's no respect for it: you've got yesterday, today and tomorrow all in the same room, and there's very little that you can't imagine not happening.

In 'Tarantula' you write about a woman named Justine who tells you that "only God can be everywhere at the same Time and Space."

That's right, but that was unconscious. And that drilled me down—doing it unconsciously was doing it like a primitive, and it took everything out of me. Everything was gone, I was drained. I found out later that it was much wiser to do it consciously, and it could let things be much stronger, too. Actually, you might even live longer, but I'm not sure about that.

From that point I went on to *Desire*, which I wrote with Jacques Levy. And I don't remember who wrote what. And then I disappeared for a while. Went on the Rolling Thunder tour, made *Renaldo and Clara*—in which I also used that quality of no-time. And I believe that that concept of creation is more real and true than that which does have time.

When you feel in your gut what you are and then dynamically pursue it—don't back down and don't give up—then you're going to mystify a lot of folks. Some people say, "I don't like him anymore." But other people do, and my crowd gets bigger and bigger. But who cares, really [*laughing*]? If you fall down and you're hurting, you care about that immediate situation—if you have the energy to care. Who *really* cares? It's like that line—how does it go?—"Propaganda, who really cares? . . ."

I wanted to ask you about love.

Go ahead, but I'm not too qualified on that subject. Love comes from the Lord—it keeps all of us going. If you want it, you got it.

In "Love Is Just a Four-Letter Word," you wrote:

> After waking enough times to think I see
> The Holy Kiss that's supposed to last eternity
> Blow up in smoke, its destiny
> Falls on strangers, travels free
> Yes, I know now, traps are only set by me
> And I do not really need to be
> Assured that love is just a four-letter word.

You've described and communicated the idea of two aspects of love—the love that longs for commitment and the love that longs to be free. Which is the most real to you?

All of it. It's all love that needs to be love.

You often sing about having a twin, a sister/wife, a dream/lover for one's life.

Everyone feels these feelings. People don't like to admit that that's the way things are because it's too confusing.

A famous short poem by William Blake goes: "He who binds to himself a joy/Doth the winged life destroy/But he who kisses the joy as it flies/Lives in Eternity's sun rise."

Allen Ginsberg quoted that to me all the time. Blake's been a big influence on Kristofferson, too.

What about soul mates?

What about them?

Do they exist?

Sure they do, but sometimes you never meet them. A soul mate . . . what do they mean by soul mate? There's a male and a female in everyone, don't they say that? So I guess the soul mate would be the physical mate of the soul. But that would mean we're supposed to be with just one other person. Is a soul mate a romantic notion or is there real truth in that, señor?

That's what I was asking you.

How would I know?

Well, a lot of your songs are concerned with that. . . . Someone once said that one's real feelings come out when one's separated from somebody one loves.

Who said that?

Nietzsche.

Well, I guess he's right. Your real feelings come out when you're free to be alone. Most people draw a line that they don't want you to cross—that's what happens in most petty relationships.

In a song such as "Like a Rolling Stone," and now "Where Are You Tonight?" and "No Time to Think," you seem to tear away and remove the layers of social identity—burn away the "rinds" of received reality—and bring us back to the zero state.

That's right. "Stripped of all virtue as you crawl through the dirt/You can give but you cannot receive." Well, I said it.

[At this point the pilot announces that we'll be landing in five minutes.] Just a few quick questions before we land. Coming back to "Changing of the Guards" . . .

It means something different every time I sing it.

The lines, "She's smelling sweet like the meadows where she was born,/On midsummer's eve, near the tower," are so quiet and pure.

Oh, yeah?

Those lines seem to go back a thousand years into the past.

They do. "Changing of the Guards" is a thousand years old. Woody Guthrie said he just picked songs out of the air. That meant that they were already there and that he was tuned into them. "Changing of the Guards" might be a song that might have been there for thousands of years, sailing around in the mist, and one day I just tuned into it. Just like "Tupelo Honey" was floating around and Van Morrison came by.

It's been said that the Stones' song "Some Girls" hints at being about you a bit.

I've never lived at Zuma Beach.

Jagger imitates your phrasing, though.

He always does. . . . He imitates Otis Redding, too, and Riley Puckett and Slim Harpo.

In "One More Cup of Coffee" you sing about a sister who sees the future, and in "Changing of the Guards" you sing about "treacherous young witches."

I meet witchy women. Somehow I attract them. I wish they'd leave me alone.

Well, there are some good witches, too, though that voodoo girl in "New Pony" was giving you some trouble.

That's right. By the way, the Miss X in that song is Miss X, not ex-.

In "We Better Talk This Over," is the line, "I'm exiled, you can't convert me," in some way about being Jewish?

Listen, I don't know how Jewish I am, because I've got blue eyes. My grandparents were from Russia, and going back that far, which one of those women didn't get raped by the Cossacks? So there's plenty of Russian in me, I'm sure. Otherwise, I wouldn't be the way I am.

Do you agree with Octavio Paz' idea that "all of us are alone, because all of us are two"?

I can't disagree, but I've got to think there's more than two. Didn't Leonard Cohen sing something like, "I'm the one who goes from nothing to two"? I don't remember.

We're back to numbers.

Leonard Cohen was really interested in numbers: "I'm the one who goes from nothing to one."

You're a Gemini, and the Gemini twins have been seen by one writer, Marius Schneider, as symbols of the "harmonious ambiguity of paradise and inferno, love and hate, peace and war, birth and death, praise and insult, clarity and obscurity, scorching rocks and swamps surrounding the fountains and waters of salvation." That sounds like a good description of some of your new songs.

Right, but you can't choose the month of the year you're born in.

"Sacrifice is the code of the road" is what you sing in "Where Are You Tonight?" To die before dying, shedding your skin, making new songs out of old ones.

That's my mission in life. . . . "He not busy being born is busy dying." Did you bring your parachute?

The interview was that bad, huh?

[*Talking to a friend*] Bring a parachute for Jonathan.

I'd prefer the pathway that leads up to the stars.

THE DRESSING ROOM

[*I ran into Dylan backstage half an hour before a sound check at the Veterans' Memorial Coliseum in New Haven. He invited me into his room, where we concluded our talk.*]

When I was waiting to pick up my ticket for your Portland concert last night, I happened to ask the woman behind the desk where all these kids were coming from. And she said: "For Bobby Dylan, from heaven—for Black Sabbath, who knows?"

Well, I believe it, don't you? Where else could my particular audience come from?

I've already met two angelic types—one in your dressing room here in New Haven, the other the girl whom you knew fifteen years ago who brought you a breakfast in Portland.

They're all angels. . . . But I wanted to ask you about something Paul

Wasserman [who's in charge of Dylan's publicity] said that you said to him, and that is: "A genius can't be a genius on instinct alone."

I said that? Maybe, but really late at night.

Well, I disagree. I believe that instinct is what makes a genius a genius.

What do you think of all the criticisms of 'Street-Legal'?

I read some of them. In fact, I didn't understand them. I don't think these people have had the experiences I've had to write those songs. The reviews didn't strike me as being particularly interesting one way or another, or as compelling to my particular scene. I don't know who these people are. They don't travel in the same crowd, anyway. So it would be like me criticizing Pancho Villa.

The reviews in this country of 'Renaldo and Clara' weren't good, either. The writers went out of their way to call you presumptuous, pretentious and egocentric.

These people probably don't like to eat what I like to eat, they probably don't like the same things I like, or the same people. Look, just one time I'd like to see any one of those assholes try and do what I do. Just once let one of them write a song to show how they feel and sing it in front of ten, let alone 10,000 or 100,000 people. I'd like to see them just try that one time.

Some of these critics have suggested that you need more sophisticated record production.

I probably do. The truth of it is that I can hear the same sounds that other people like to hear, too. But I don't like to spend the time trying to get those sounds in the studio.

So you're really not a producer-type?

I'm not. Some musicians like to spend a lot of time in the studio. But a lot of people try to make something out of nothing. If you don't have a good song, you can go into the studio and make it appear to be good, but that stuff don't last.

You've had producers — Tom Wilson, Bob Johnson, Don DeVito . . .

But that wasn't all that sophisticated. I mean, John Hammond produced my first record, and it was a matter of singing into a microphone. He'd say, "It sounded good to me," and you'd go on to the next song. That's still the way I do it.

Nowadays, you start out with anything *but* the song—the drum track, for instance—and you take a week getting the instruments all sounding the way they should. They put down the rhythm track or whatever sound they want to hear in the ghost tracks. If you have a good song, it doesn't matter how well or badly it's produced. Okay, my records aren't produced that well, I admit it.

Personally, I love the "primitive" sound of Buddy Holly demo tapes or the original Chuck Berry discs.

But in those days they recorded on different equipment and the records were thicker. If you buy one of my early records—and you can't today—they weren't like Saran Wrap, as they are now. There was quality to them . . . and the machinery was different and the boards were different. The Beach Boys did stuff on two-track in the garage.

But you do need a producer now?

I think so. You see, in the recent past my method, when I had the songs, was to go in, record them and put them out. Now I'm writing songs on the run again—they're dear to me, the songs I'm doing now—and I can't perfect them. So if I can just block time out, here and there, I can work on an album the way the Eagles do. I've got so many records out that it doesn't matter when I put out a new one. I could release one a year from now—start working on it in January and have it produced right.

What's the longest it's taken you to record a song?

About six or seven hours. It took us a week to make *Street-Legal*—we mixed it the following week and put it out the week after. If we hadn't done it that fast we wouldn't have made an album at all, because we were ready to go back on the road.

You've got a bigger sound now—on record and onstage—than you've ever had before.

I do—and I might hire two more girls and an elephant—but it doesn't matter how big the sound gets as long as it's behind me emphasizing the song. It's still pretty simple. There's nothing like it in Vegas—no matter what you've heard—and it's anything but disco. It's not rock & roll—my roots go back to the Thirties, not the Fifties.

On this tour, you've again been changing some of the radically new versions of songs that I heard you perform in Europe this past summer.

Yeah, we've changed them around some—it's a different tour and a different show. The band has to relearn the songs, but they're fast and the best at that.

Do you write songs now with them in mind?

I've had this sound ever since I was a kid—what grabs my heart. I had to play alone for a long time, and that was good because by playing alone I had to write songs. That's what I didn't do when I first started out, just playing available songs with a three-piece honky-tonk band in my hometown. But when I was first living in New York City—do you remember the old Madison Square Garden? Well, they used to have gospel shows there every Sunday, and you could see everyone from the Five Blind Boys, the Soul Stirrers and the Swan Silvertones to Clara Ward and the Mighty Clouds of Joy. I went up there every Sunday. I'd listen to that and Big Bill Broonzy. Then I heard the Clancy Brothers and hung out with them—all of their drinking songs, their revolutionary and damsel-in-distress songs. And I listened to Jean Ritchie, Woody Guthrie, Leadbelly.

What about the doo-wop groups?

They played at shows, and those artists didn't have to be onstage for more than twenty minutes. They just got on and got off, and that was never what I wanted to do. I used to go to the Brooklyn Fox a lot, but the band I liked the best at that time was Bobby Blue Bland's, and I heard them at the Apollo. But the people whose floors I was sleeping on were all into the Country Gentlemen, Uncle Dave Macon, the Stanley Brothers, Bill Monroe. So I heard all that, too.

You seem to like music that's real and uncorrupted, no matter what its tradition. But some of your folk-music followers didn't care much for your own musical changes.

But don't forget that when I played "Maggie's Farm" electric at Newport, that was something I would have done years before. They thought I didn't know what I was doing and that I'd slipped over the edge, but the truth is . . . Kooper and Michael Bloomfield remember that scene very well. And what the newspapers say happened didn't actually happen that way. There wasn't a whole lot of resistance in the crowd.

Don't forget they weren't equipped for what we were doing with the sound. But I had a legitimate right to do that.

The Beatles and the Rolling Stones were already popular in this country at that time, though.

I remember hanging out with Brian Jones in 1964. Brian could play the blues. He was an excellent guitar player—he seemed afraid to sing for some reason—but he could play note for note what Robert Johnson or Son House played.

In songs like "Buckets of Rain" or "New Pony," you seem just to go in and out of musical traditions, pick up what you want and need, and transform them as you please.

That's basically what I do, but so do the Stones. Mick and Keith know all that music. America's filled with all kinds of different music.

When you sang "Baby Stop Crying" the other night in Portland, I remember thinking that your voice sounded as if it combined the following qualities: tenderness, sarcasm, outraged innocence, indignation, insouciant malice and wariness.

The man in that song has his hand out and is not afraid of getting it bit.

He sounds stronger than the woman he's singing to and about.

Not necessarily. The roles could be reversed at any time—don't you remember "To Ramona"? "And someday maybe, who knows baby, I'll come and be cryin' to you."

In the song "Baby Stop Crying," it sounds as if the singer is getting rejected—that the woman's in love with someone else.

She probably is.

There's also a "bad man" in the song. It's almost as if three or four different movies were taking place in one song, all held together by the chorus. And the same thing seems to be happening in "Changing of the Guards" and some of your other new songs. What's that all about?

Lord knows.

How come you write in that way?

I wouldn't be doing it unless some power higher than myself were guiding me on. I wouldn't be here this long. Let me put it another way. . . . What was the question?

There are all these different levels in many of your recent songs.

That's right, and that's because my mind and my heart work on all those levels. Shit, I don't want to be chained down to the same old level all the time.

I've seen you tell people who don't know you that some other person standing nearby is you.

Well sure, if some old fluff ball comes wandering in looking for the real Bob Dylan, I'll direct him down the line, but I can't be held accountable for that.

A poet and critic named Elizabeth Sewell once wrote, "Discovery, in science and poetry, is a mythological situation in which the mind unites with a figure of its own devising as a means toward understanding the world." And it seems as if you have created a figure named Bob Dylan . . .

I didn't create Bob Dylan. Bob Dylan has always been here . . . always was. When I was a child there was Bob Dylan. And before I was born, there was Bob Dylan.

Why did you have to play that role?

I'm not sure. Maybe I was best equipped to do it.

The composer Arnold Schönberg once said the same thing: someone had to be Arnold Schönberg.

Sometimes your parents don't even know who you are. No one knows but you. Lord, if your own parents don't know who you are, who else in the world is there who would know except you?

Then why do children keep on wanting things from their parents they can't give them?

Misunderstanding.

In contradistinction to the idea of being true to oneself, there's an idea of personality—suggested by Yeats—which states that "man is nothing till he is united to an image." You seem to have your foot in both camps.

I don't know about that. Sometimes I think I'm a ghost. Don't you have to have some poetic sense to be involved in what we're talking about? It's like what you were saying about people putting my record down. I couldn't care less if they're doing that but, I mean, who are these people, what qualifications do they have? Are they poets, are they musicians? You find me some musician or poet, and then maybe we'll talk. Maybe that person will know something I don't know and I'll see it that way. That could happen. I'm not almighty. But my feelings come from the gut, and I'm not too concerned with someone whose feelings come from his head. That don't bother me none.

This criticism has been going on for a long time. It's like a lover: you like somebody and then you don't want to like them anymore because you're afraid to admit to yourself that you like them so much. . . . I don't know, you've just got to try, try to do some good for somebody. The world is full of nonsupporters and backbiters—people who chew on wet rags. But it's also filled with people who love you.

There are lines in your new songs about the one you love being so hard to recognize, or about feeling displaced and in exile. It seems as if the tyranny of love makes people unhappy.

That's the tyranny of man-woman love. That ain't too much love.

What's your idea of love?

[*Pause*] Love like a driving wheel. That's my idea of love.

What about Cupid with his bow and arrow aimed toward your heart?

Naw, Cupid comes in a beard and a mustache, you know. Cupid has dark hair.

18. Radio interview with Bruce Heiman, KMEX (Tucson, Arizona)

DECEMBER 7, 1979

OK, my name is Bruce Heiman. I'm with KMEX radio here in Tucson. We got a press release from the Tucson chapter of the American Atheists and they said in response to your recent embrace of the born-again Christian movement they plan to leaflet your upcoming concert. They say they recognize the need to inform those in the audience that the new Dylan cause-celebre is a repressive and reactionary ideology and that members intend to draw attention to the contradictions between the previous content of your art form and the message which your songs now expound.

Uh-huh. I still don't quite grasp what you're saying or who's saying it or . . .

OK. It's the American Atheists in Tucson.

Is this a group?

Yeah. Actually the American Atheists is a worldwide group headed by Madalyn Murray O'Hair, and they have a chapter here in Tucson, and I think basically what they are talking about is your stand in the past and the type of music you played and the message you tried to get across and the music you're playing today and the different message you're trying to get across.

Yeah, well, whatever the old message was, the Bible says, "All things become new, old things are passed away." I guess this group doesn't believe that. What is it exactly that they're protesting?

I think what they're against . . . there's another statement, that they make. It says . . .

Are they against the doctrine of Jesus Christ, or that he died on the cross or that man is born into sin? Just what exactly is it they're protesting?

Well the Atheists are against any sort of religion, be it Christianity . . .

Well, Christ is no religion. We're not talking about religion . . . Jesus Christ is the Way, the Truth, and the Life.

There's another statement they made that maybe you could shed some light on. They said they would like to remind Dylan fans and audiences that one's right to say something does not per se lend any validity to the statement. So in essence what they're saying is that you have followers who are going to be at the concert and are going to listen to the message of your music.

Right. I follow God, so if my followers are following me, indirectly they're gonna be following God too, because I don't sing any song which hasn't been given to me by the Lord to sing.

OK. They believe that all religion is repressive.

Well, religion is repressive to a certain degree. Religion is another form of bondage which man invents to get himself to God. But that's why Christ came. Christ didn't preach religion. He preached the Truth, the Way and the Life. He said He'd come to give life and life more abundantly. He talked about life, not necessarily religion . . .

They say that your songs now expound passive acceptance of one's fate. Do you agree with that? I'm not exactly sure what they mean by that.

I'm not exactly sure what they mean by that either. But I don't feel that that's true. But I'm not sure what that means—"passive acceptance to man's fate." What is man's fate?

I don't know. These aren't my ideologies. They are just a group of atheists.

Well, this ideology isn't my ideology either. My ideology now would be coming out of the Scripture. You see, I didn't invent these things— these things have just been shown to me. I'll stand on that faith—that they are true. I believe they're true. I *know* they're true.

Do you feel that the message of your music has changed over the years from music which talked about war to music that talks about Christianity?

No. There's gonna be war. There's always war and rumors of war. And the Bible talks about a war coming up which will be a war to end all wars. The spirit of the atheist will not prevail, I can tell you that much. It's a deceiving spirit.

Why do you maintain that it will not prevail?

Is it anti-God? Is an atheist anti-God?

Yes, I'm trying to think . . . I interviewed Madalyn Murray O'Hair a couple of weeks ago and she said it's anti-religion, anti-God. I think that she was saying that anybody who believes in a Supreme Being is—to use her word—stupid. So they are against anything to do with religion.

Uh-huh.

Sometimes it's hard for me to grasp what they're saying.

Well, a religion which says you have to do certain things to get to God—they're probably talking about that kind of religion, which is a religion which is by works: you can enter into the Kingdom by what you do, what you wear, what you say, how many times a day you pray, how many good deeds you may do. If that's what they mean by religion, that type of religion will not get you into the Kingdom, that's true. However there is a Master Creator, a Supreme Being in the Universe.

Alright. In another one of their statements they say that: "For years Dylan cried out against the Masters of War and the power elite. The new Dylan now proclaims that we must serve a new master, a master whose nebulous origins were ignorance, foolishness, stupidity, and blind faith. The Dylan who inspired us to look beyond banal textbooks and accepted ideologies now implores us to turn inwards to the pages of the Holy Bible, a book filled with contradictions, inaccuracies, outrages and absurdities." Now this is what they're saying.

Well, the Bible says: "The Fool has said in heart, There's no God . . ."

OK. They're saying the movement is a fraud and evasive . . .

Well, I don't know what movement. What movement are they talking about. The American Atheists?

No, the Jesus Movement.

Well, it isn't a fraud. There's nothing fraudulent about it. It's all true. It's always been true. It is true and will be true.

They're calling upon your admirers, the people who support you, who will attend your concert, to go on and appreciate your art form but to avoid the psychological and social pitfalls — this is their words — or being victimized by your newfound religious fantasy.

Well, they can't do that. You can't separate the words from the music. I know people try to do that. But they can't do that. It's like separating the foot from the knee.

You're saying it's all one.

It is all one.

OK, Bob, I appreciate your time, I really do.

19. Interview with Karen Hughes, *The Dominion* (Wellington, New Zealand)

MAY 21, 1980

Bob Dylan stretched out his hand and reached for a cigarette from a half-empty pack on the table. "It would have been easier," he sighed, "if I had become a Buddhist or a Scientologist or if I had gone to Sing Sing."

I asked him if many of his friends had forsaken him.

"My REAL friends?" Dylan responded tellingly, blowing cigarette smoke away from my face, in the tiny hotel room in Dayton, Ohio, where we talked as his tour was cutting across America's Bible Belt and winding its way back to Los Angeles, Dylan's home of nine years.

"At every point in my life I've had to make decisions for what I believed in. Sometimes I've ended up hurting people that I've loved. Other times I've ended up loving people that I never thought I would.

"You ask me about myself," Dylan said at the end of an intensive session of questioning, "but I'm becoming less and less defined as Christ becomes more and more defined.

"Christianity," he explained, "is not Christ and Christ is not Christianity. Christianity is making Christ the Lord of your life. You're talking about your life now, you're not talking about just part of it, you're not talking about a certain hour every day. You're talking about making Christ the Lord and the Master of your life, the King of your life. And you're also talking about Christ, the resurrected Christ who is Lord of your life. We're talking about that type of Christianity."

"It's HIM through YOU. 'He's alive,' Paul said, 'I've been crucified with Christ, nevertheless I live. Yet not I but Christ who liveth in me.' See, Christ is not some kind of figure down the road. We serve the living God, not dead monuments, dead ideas, dead philosophies. If he had been a dead God, you'd be carrying around a corpse inside you."

Dylan speaks of having constant dialogue with Christ, of surrendering his life to God's will much in the same way as Joan of Arc or St. Francis of Assisi would have done. It is, he says, the only thing that matters. When you ask about his band, he replies, "I think Jim Keltner and Tim Drummond are the best rhythm section that God ever invented."

His view on American politics is, "God will stay with America as long as America stays with God. A lot of people, maybe even the president, maybe a lot of senators, you hear them speak and they'll speak of the attributes of God. But none of them are speaking about being a disciple of Christ.

"There's a difference between knowing who Christ is and being a disciple of Christ and recognizing Christ as a personality and being of God. I'm more aware of that than anything and it dictates my very being. So I wouldn't have much to offer anybody who wants to know about politics or history or art or any of that. I've always been pretty extreme in all them areas anyway."

Whether on or off the road Dylan worships whenever he can at the Assembly of God, a fundamentalist, Pentecostal, evangelical denomination that believes in the literal Bible and speaking in tongues. He came to Christ through a revelation, a personal experience with Jesus.

"Jesus put his hand on me. It was a physical thing. I felt it. I felt it all over me. I felt my whole body tremble. The glory of the Lord knocked me down and picked me up.

"Being born again is a hard thing. You ever seen a mother give birth to a child? Well it's painful. We don't like to lose those old attitudes and hang-ups.

"Conversion takes times because you have to learn to crawl before you can walk. You have to learn to drink milk before you can eat meat. You're reborn, but like a baby. A baby doesn't know anything about this world and that's what it's like when you're reborn. You're a stranger. You have to learn all over again. God will show you what you need to know.

"I guess He's always been calling me," Dylan said gently. "Of course, how would I have ever known that? That it was Jesus calling me. I always thought it was some voice that would be more identifiable. But

Christ is calling everybody; we just turn him off. We just don't want to hear. We think he's gonna make our lives miserable, you know what I mean. We think he's gonna make us do things we don't want to do. Or keep us from doing things we want to do.

"But God's got his own purpose and time for everything. He knew when I would respond to His call."

20. Interview with Robert Hilburn, *The Los Angeles Times*

NOVEMBER 23, 1980

Bob Dylan has finally confirmed in an interview what he's been saying in his music for 18 months: He's a born-again Christian.

Dylan said he accepted Jesus Christ in his heart in 1978 after a "vision and feeling" during which the room moved: "There was a presence in the room that couldn't have been anybody but Jesus."

He was initially reluctant to tell his friends or put his feelings into songs but he was so committed to his gospel music by late 1979 that he didn't perform any of his old songs during a tour. He said he feared that they might be "anti-God."

Believing now that the old and new songs are compatible, Dylan sings such stinging rockers as "Like a Rolling Stone" alongside such born-again treatises as "Gotta Serve Somebody" on a tour that includes a stop Wednesday at San Diego's Golden Hall.

Sitting in a hotel room here before a concert, Dylan, whose family is Jewish, sat on a couch and smoked a cigarette as he discussed his religious experience for the first time in an interview.

"The funny thing is a lot of people think that Jesus comes into a person's life only when they are either down and out or are miserable or just old and withering away. That's not the way it was for me.

"I was doing fine. I had come a long way in just the year we were on the road [in 1978]. I was relatively content, but a very close friend of mine mentioned a couple of things to me and one of them was Jesus.

"Well, the whole idea of Jesus was foreign to me. I said to myself, 'I can't deal with that. Maybe later.' But later it occurred to me that I trusted this person and I had nothing to do for the next couple of days so I called the person back and said I was willing to listen about Jesus."

Through a friend, Dylan met two young pastors.

"I was kind of skeptical, but I was also open. I certainly wasn't cynical. I asked lots of questions, questions like, 'What's the son of God, what's all that mean?' and 'What does it mean—dying for my sins?'"

Slowly, Dylan began to accept that "Jesus is real and I wanted that. . . . I knew that He wasn't going to come into my life and make it miserable, so one thing led to another . . . until I had this feeling, this vision and feeling."

Dylan, the most acclaimed songwriter of the rock era, had been unwilling to grant interviews since the release last year of the gospel-dominated *Slow Train Coming* album, suggesting that anyone who wanted to know what he felt could simply listen to that work.

Though the album became one of Dylan's biggest sellers, many of his own fans felt confused, even betrayed. The man who once urged his audience to question was suddenly embracing what some felt was the most simplistic of religious sentiments. Furthermore, some critics argued, Dylan's attitudes were smug. Surely, many insisted, this was just another peculiar turn in Dylan's ever-shifting persona.

Even when he returned last spring with another gospel album, the less commercially successful *Saved*, rumors abounded that he had abandoned his born-again beliefs. But his shows in San Francisco on this tour refuted that speculation. Ten of his seventeen songs on opening night were from the last two albums.

In the interview, too, Dylan stressed that his beliefs are deeply rooted: "It's in my system."

At the same time, Dylan showed that he hasn't lost his questioning spirit.

Asked about the political activism of fundamentalist Christian groups like the Moral Majority, he replied, "I think people have to be careful about all that. . . . It's real dangerous. You can find anything you want in the Bible. You can twist it around any way you want and a lot of people do that. I just don't think you can legislate morality. . . . The basic thing, I feel, is to get in touch with Christ yourself. He will lead you. Any preacher who is a real preacher will tell you that: 'Don't follow me, follow Christ.'"

Dylan still seemed uncertain about discussing his religious views when he began the current tour at the Warfield on November 9th, side-stepping questions on the topic at a mini-press conference backstage after the opening show. But once he touched on the subject in the hotel interview, he spoke freely.

The interview centers on his new direction in music because that was the topic I wanted to pursue in the time he had before the show, but it'd be wrong to infer that Dylan has become a "Jesus freak" stereotype, interested in only discussing that subject. During the interview and during other, more informal chats, he spoke with equal zest about various matters, including the decision to do his old material again.

Some people would love you to go on stage and just sing the old songs like a living "Beatlemania." Isn't there a danger in doing that? That's what Elvis Presley ended up doing.

Elvis changed. The show that people always talk about Elvis was that 1969 TV show, but it's not quite the same as when he did those songs in the beginning. When he did "That's Alright Mama" in 1955, it was sensitivity and power. In 1969, it was just full-out power. There was nothing other than just force behind that. I've fallen into that trap, too. Take the 1974 tour.

It's a very fine line you have to walk to stay in touch with something once you've created it. . . . Either it holds up for you or it doesn't. A lot of artists say, "I can't sing those old songs anymore," and I can understand it because you're no longer the same person who wrote those songs.

However, you really are still that person some place deep down. You don't really get that out of your system. So, you can still sing them if you can get in touch with the person you were when you wrote the songs. I don't think I could sit down now and write "It's Alright Ma" again. I wouldn't even know where to begin, but I can still sing it and I'm glad I've written it.

Why didn't you do any of the old songs on the 1979 tour?

I truly had a born-again experience. If you want to call it that. It's an over-used term, but it's something that people can relate to. It happened in 1978. I always knew there was a God or a creator of the universe and a creator of the mountains and the seas and all that kind of thing, but I wasn't conscious of Jesus and what that had to do with the supreme creator.

After you had the vision, I understand you attended a three-month Bible course at a church in Reseda.

At first, I said, "There's no way I can devote three months to this. I've got to be back on the road soon." But I was sleeping one day and I just sat up in bed at seven in the morning and I was compelled to get dressed and drive over to the Bible school. I couldn't believe I was there.

But you had already accepted Jesus in your heart?

Yeah, but I hadn't told anybody about it because I felt they would say, "Aw, come on." Most of the people I know don't believe that Jesus was resurrected, that He is alive. It's like He was just another prophet or something, one of many good people. That's not the way it was any longer for me. I had always read the Bible, but only looked at it as literature. I was never really instructed in it in a way that was meaningful to me.

I had assumed that these feelings came to you at a crisis point in your life, a time when you were desperately needing something else to believe in.

No. I had gone so far that I didn't even think there was anything left. I thought, "Well, everybody has got their own truth." What works for one man is fine as long as it works for him. I had given up looking and searching for it.

But didn't you go to Israel? You seemed to be searching for some religious . . .

Not really. If I was searching, it was just to . . . get down to the root reality of the way things really are, to pull the mask off. My thing was always to pull the mask off of whatever was going on. It's like war. People don't look at war as a business. They look at it as an emotional thing.

When you get right down to it, however, war—unless one people need another people's land—is a business. If you look at it that way, you can come to terms with it. There are certain people who make a lot of money off of war the same way people make money off blue jeans. To say it was something else always irritated me.

Did you start telling friends about it when you went to Bible classes?

No, I didn't want to set myself up. I didn't want to reflect on the Lord at all because if I told people and then I didn't keep going, they'd say, "Oh well, I guess it was just another one of those things that didn't work out." I didn't know myself if I could go for three months. But I did begin telling a few people after a couple of months and a lot of them got angry at me.

Did you have any second thoughts when that happened?

No. By that time, I was into it. When I believe in something, I don't care what anybody else thinks.

Did you have any fear that what you're saying now may come back to haunt you in five years—that you aren't really committed?

I don't think so. If I would have felt anything like that, I think I would have come up to the surface by now.

But we've seen so many rock stars get involved with gurus and maharishis and then move on.

Well, this is no maharishi trip with me. Jesus is definitely not that to me.

When did you start writing the songs for 'Slow Train Coming'?

After about two months. I didn't even want to sing them. I was going to give them to Carolyn Dennis [a singer on the current tour] and have her sing them. I thought maybe I could produce her record.

Why didn't you want to sing them?

I didn't want to step out there yet.

What did you think about some of the hostile reviews to 'Slow Train Coming'?

You can't look at reviews.

Do you see how people could think some of the messages in the album were heavy-handed?

I didn't mean to deliver a hammer blow. It might come out that way, but I'm not trying to kill anybody. You can't put down people who don't believe. Anybody can have the answer I have. I mean, it's free.

What about the decision in 1979 to do only new songs?

I wasn't in touch with those old songs then.

But you're singing them again now.

It's like I said, this show evolved out of that last tour. It's like the songs aren't . . . how can I put it? Those songs weren't anti-God at all. I wasn't sure about that for a while.

Are the early songs still meaningful to you or do you just do them because people want to hear them?

I love those songs, they're still part of me.

Is there any way you can talk about the changes in your life, how the religious experiences make you feel or act differently?

It's in my system. I don't really have enough time to talk about it. If someone really wants to know, I can explain it to them, but there are other people who can do it just as well. I don't feel compelled to do it. I was doing a bit of that last year on the stage. I was saying stuff I figured people needed to know. I thought I was giving people an idea of what was behind the songs. I don't think it's necessary anymore.

When I walk around some of the towns we go to, however, I'm totally convinced people need Jesus. Look at the junkies and the winos and the troubled people. It's all a sickness which can be healed in an instant. The powers that be won't let that happen. The powers that be say it has to be healed politically.

What about some of the new songs? Some seem only remotely religious.

They've evolved. I've made my statement and I don't think I could make it any better than in some of those songs. Once I've said what I need to say in a song, that's it. I don't want to repeat myself.

So you can work from a larger canvas again?

Yeah, but that doesn't mean that I won't keep singing these songs.

Is music still important to you?

Music has given me a purpose. As a kid, there was rock. Later on, there was folk-blues music. It's not something that I just listen to as a passive person. It has always been in my blood and it has never failed me. Because of that, I'm disconnected from a lot of the pressures of life. It disconnects you from what people think about you. Attitudes don't really make too much difference when you can get on stage and play the guitar and sing songs. It's natural for me. I don't know why I was chosen to do it. I'm almost 40 now and I'm not tired of it yet.

21. Interview with Kurt Loder, ROLLING STONE

JUNE 21, 1984

On a typically soggy March mess of a day in Manhattan, Bob Dylan, wearing black jeans, biker boots and a white sport coat over a white T-shirt, sat slouched on a stool at the far end of a small downtown studio. The crowd of cameramen, lighting technicians, makeup people and producers had withdrawn for a bit to consult their equipment, leaving Dylan to strum and hum on his own. As his long nails raked the strings of his Martin guitar, he began huffing softly into the harmonica racked around his neck, and soon a familiar melody filled the air. Could it be? I moved closer to cock an ear as Dylan cranked up the chorus. Yes, no doubt about it—Bob Dylan was running down the first-ever folkie arrangement of "Karma Chameleon," the Culture Club hit.

Soon, however, he was surrounded by tech people again. The audio crew punched up the tape of "Jokerman," a song off Dylan's latest album, *Infidels*, and as the video cameras rolled, the star obediently lip-synced along. Dylan had been doing take after take of the number all morning and most of the afternoon without complaint. "Jokerman" would be the second video for *Infidels*, and he knew it had to be good. The first, for the lovely ballad "Sweetheart Like You," had been a flat and lifeless embarrassment. So two of Dylan's most trusted friends—Larry "Ratso" Sloman, author of a book about Bob's 1975 Rolling Thunder Revue tour, and

George Lois, a brilliant New York adman who met Dylan during the ill-fated legal-defense concerts for fighter Rubin "Hurricane" Carter a decade ago—were called in to assist.

It was Lois who came up with an agreeable video format for the stiff, camera-shy Dylan. Bob's face would only be seen onscreen during the song's choruses; the verses would be illustrated by classic art prints from Lois' own library: paintings by Michelangelo, Dürer, Munch—and, in a wry touch, a Hieronymus Bosch painting titled *The Musicians' Hell*. Lois' most innovative concept, however, was to superimpose the song's apocalyptic lyrics over the images throughout the video—a technique Lois laughingly dubbed "poetry right in your fuckin' face." The result, as it later turned out, makes most run-of-the-mill rock videos look like the glorified cola commercials they generally are.

But can a single thought-provoking video make Bob Dylan once again relevant to youthful record buyers? The man has been many things over the years: the voice of youth in the Sixties, the voice of aging youth in the Seventies and, now, in the Eighties—what?

Certainly, he remains a completely unpredictable character, as I discovered when we met a few hours later at a Greek café on Third Avenue. Smoking steadily from a pack of Benson & Hedges ("Nothing can affect my voice, it's so bad") and downing cup after cup of coffee with cream, he proved both guarded and gracious, sweet and sometimes acerbic. Not at all the arrogant young superstar who verbally demolished a *Time* magazine reporter in the 1966 documentary *Don't Look Back*, but still no dummy either.

There was, of course, much to talk about. The man who had transformed the folk world with his raw, exciting acoustic debut LP in 1962, and who later alienated many folkies altogether when he appeared at the 1965 Newport Folk Festival backed by an electric rock band, was still, in 1984, as capable as ever of stirring controversy. Thirteen years ago, to the surprise of virtually everyone, he turned up in Jerusalem at the Wailing Wall, wearing a yarmulke and reportedly searching for his "Jewish identity." Subsequently, he studied at the Vineyard Christian Fellowship, a Bible school in California, and shocked many fans by releasing three albums of fundamentalist, gospel-swathed rock. (The first, 1979's *Slow Train Coming*, went platinum, but the next two, *Saved* and *Shot of Love*, didn't even go gold.) Next, he became associated with an ultra-Orthodox Jewish sect, the Lubavitcher Hasidim, and last year returned to Jerusalem to celebrate his son Jesse's bar mitzvah. Then came *Infidels*. Although it continued the Biblical bent of Dylan's three previous albums (with an added overlay of what some critics took to be cranky political conservatism), *Infidels* was also one of his best-produced records ever—thanks to Dire Straits guitarist Mark Knopfler's ministrations at the recording console. With precious little promotional push from Dylan himself, the LP had already sold nearly three-quarters of a million copies, and now he had not only wrapped up an excellent video, but had also made a rare TV appearance on the *Late Night with David Letterman* show—a rickety but riveting event in which Dylan, backed by a barely prepared, young three-piece band, whomped his way through two *Infidels* tracks and the old Sonny Boy Williamson tune "Don't Start Me to Talking." (It could have been even more curious. At rehearsals, he'd tried out a version of the Roy Head rock nugget "Treat Her Right.") Bob Dylan was once again on the scene. And with concert promoter Bill Graham already booking dates, he was preparing to embark on a major European tour with Santana on May 28th, four days after his forty-third birthday.

So here he is once more—but *who* is he? A divorced father of five (one is his ex-wife Sara's daughter, whom he adopted), Dylan divides his time among California, where he owns a sprawling, eccentric heap of a house; Minnesota, where he maintains a farm; and the Caribbean, where he island-hops on a quarter-million-dollar boat. While in New York—a city to which he soon hopes to relocate again—he caught a gig by his former keyboardist Al Kooper, dropped in on a recording session for ex–J. Geils Band singer Peter Wolf and hung out with old pals Keith Richards and Ronnie Wood of the Rolling Stones. Despite his spiritual preoccupations, he insists that he's no prude ("I think I had a beer recently") and that his religious odyssey has been misrepresented in the press. Although he contends he doesn't own any of his song-publishing rights prior to 1974's *Blood on the Tracks* ("That's Keith's favorite"), he is probably quite well-off—"Some years are better than others" is all he'll say on the subject—and is known to be extraordinarily generous to good friends in need. He apparently does not envision any future retirement from music. When I asked if he thought he'd painted his masterpiece yet, he said, "I hope I never do." His love life—he's been linked in the past with singer Clydie King, among others—remains a closed book.

As we spoke, a drunken youth approached our table for an autograph, which Dylan provided. A few minutes later, a toothless old woman wearing hot pants appeared at our side, accompanied by a black wino. "You're Bob Dylan!" she croaked. "And you're Barbra Streisand, right?" said Dylan, not unpleasantly. "I only wondered," said the crone, "because there's a guy out front selling your autograph." "Yeah?" said Dylan. "Well, how much is he askin'?"

A good question, I thought. How much might such a souvenir still command in these waning End Days?

People have put various labels on you over the past several years: "He's a born-again Christian"; "he's an ultra-Orthodox Jew." Are any of those labels accurate?

Not really. People call you this or they call you that. But I can't respond to that, because then it seems like I'm defensive, and, you know, what does it matter, really?

But weren't three of your albums — 'Slow Train Coming,' 'Saved' and 'Shot of Love' — inspired by some sort of born-again religious experience?

I would never call it that. I've never said I'm born again. That's just a media term. I don't think I've been an agnostic. I've always thought there's a superior power, that this is not the real world and that there's a world to come. That no soul has died, every soul is alive, either in holiness or in flames. And there's probably a lot of middle ground.

What is your spiritual stance, then?

Well, I don't think that *this is it*, you know—this life ain't nothin'. There's no way you're gonna convince me this is all there is to it. I never, ever believed that. I believe in the Book of Revelation. The leaders of this world are eventually going to play God, if they're not *already* playing God, and eventually a man will come that everybody will think *is* God. He'll do things, and they'll say, "Well, only God can do those things. It must be him."

You're a literal believer of the Bible?

Yeah. Sure, yeah. I am.

Are the Old and New Testaments equally valid?

To me.

Do you belong to any church or synagogue?

Not really. Uh, the Church of the Poison Mind [*laughs*].

Do you actually believe the end is at hand?

I don't think it's *at hand*. I think we'll have *at least* 200 years. And the new kingdom that comes in, I mean, people can't even imagine what it's gonna be like. There's a lot of people walkin' around who think the new kingdom's comin' next year and that they're gonna be right in there among the top guard. And they're wrong. I think when it comes in there *are* people who'll be prepared for it, but if the new kingdom happened tomorrow and you were sitting there and I was sitting here you wouldn't even *remember* me.

Can you converse and find agreement with Orthodox Jews?

Yeah, yeah.

And with Christians?

Oh, yeah. Yeah, with anybody.

Sounds like a new synthesis.

Well no. If I thought the world needed a new religion I would start one. But there are a lot of other religions, too. There's those Indian religions, Eastern religions, Buddhism, you know? They're happening, too.

When you meet up with Orthodox people, can you sit down with them and say, "Well, you should really check out Christianity"?

Well, yeah, if somebody asks me, I'll tell 'em. But you know, I'm not gonna just offer my opinion. I'm more about playing music, you know?

Your views apparently seemed clear to many record buyers. Were you frustrated by the commercial resistance—both on record and on the road—to your fundamentalist-influenced music?

Well after the '78 gospel tour, I wanted to keep touring in '79. But I knew that we'd gone everywhere in '78, so how you gonna play in '79? Go back to the same places? So, at that point I figured, "Well I don't care if I draw no crowds no more." And a lotta places we played on the last tour, we filled maybe half the hall.

And you don't think that was because of the material you were doing?

I don't think so. I don't think it had to do with *anything*. I think when your time is your time it don't matter what you're doin'. It's either your time, or it's not your time. And I didn't feel the last few years was really my time. But that's no reason for me to make any kinda judgment call on what it is I'm gonna be. The people who reacted to the gospel stuff would've reacted that way if I hadn't done, you know, "Song to Woody."

You think so?

Yeah, I know it. I can usually anticipate that stuff—what's going on, what's the mood. There's a lotta young performers around. And they look good and they move good and they're sayin' stuff that is, uh, *excitable*, you know? Face it, a lotta that stuff is just made and geared for twelve-year-old kids. It's like baby food.

Your latest album, 'Infidels,' is hardly subteen fodder. Some critics have even detected a new note of conservatism in some of the songs—even outright jingoism in "Neighborhood Bully," in which the metaphorical subject is said to be "just one man" whose "enemies say he's on their land." That's clearly a strong Zionist political statement, is it not?

You'd have to point that out to me, you know, what line is in it that spells that out. I'm not a political songwriter. Joe Hill was a political songwriter; uh, Merle Travis wrote some political songs. "Which Side Are You On?" is a political song. And "Neighborhood Bully," to me, is not a political song, because if it were, it would fall into a certain political party. If you're talkin' about it as an Israeli political song—in Israel alone, there's maybe twenty political parties. I don't know where that would fall, what party.

Well, would it be fair to call that song a heartfelt statement of belief?

Maybe it is, yeah. But just because somebody feels a certain way, you can't come around and stick some political-party slogan on it. If you listen closely, it really could be about other things. It's simple and easy to define it, so you got it pegged, and you can deal with it in that certain kinda way. However, I wouldn't *do* that. 'Cause I don't know what the politics of Israel is. I just don't know.

So you haven't resolved for yourself, for instance, the Palestinian question?

Not really, because I live *here*.

Would you ever live in Israel?

I don't know. It's hard to speculate what tomorrow may bring. I kinda live where I find myself.

At another point in the song, you say, "He got no allies to really speak of," and while "he buys obsolete weapons and he won't be denied, . . . no one sends flesh and blood to fight by his side." Do you feel that America should send troops over there?

No. The song doesn't say that. Who should, who shouldn't—who am I to say?

Well, do you think Israel should get more help from the American Jewish community? I don't want to push this so far, but it just seems so . . .

Well, you're not pushing it too far, you're just making it *specific*. And you're making it specific to what's going on today. But what's going on today isn't gonna last, you know? The battle of Armageddon is specifically spelled out: where it will be fought, and if you wanna get technical, *when* it will be fought. And the battle of Armageddon definitely will be fought in the Middle East.

Do you follow the political scene, or have any sort of fix on what the politicians are talking about this election year?

I think politics is an instrument of the Devil. Just that clear. I think politics is what kills; it doesn't bring anything alive. Politics is corrupt; I mean, anybody knows that.

So you don't care who is president? It doesn't make any difference?

I don't think so. I mean, how long is Reagan gonna be president? I've seen like four or five of 'em myself, you know? And I've seen two of 'em die in office. How can you deal with Reagan and get so serious about that, when the man isn't even gonna *be* there when you get your thing together?

So you don't think there's any difference between, say, a Kennedy and a Nixon? It doesn't matter at all?

I don't know. Who was a better president? Well, you got *me*. I don't know what people's errors are; nobody's perfect, for sure. But I thought Kennedy—both Kennedys—I just liked them. And I liked Martin . . . Martin Luther King. I thought those were people who were blessed and touched, you know? The fact that they all went out with bullets doesn't change nothin', because the good they do gets planted. And those seeds live on longer than that.

Do you still hope for peace?

There is not going to *be* any peace.

You don't think it's worth working for?

No. It's just gonna be a false peace. You can reload your rifle, and that moment you're reloading it, that's peace. It may last for a few years.

Isn't it worth fighting for that?

Nah, none of that matters. I heard somebody on the radio talkin' about what's happenin' in Haiti, you know? "We must be concerned about what's happening in Haiti. We're *global people* now." And they're gettin' everybody in that frame of mind—like, we're not just the United States anymore, we're *global*. We're thinkin' in terms of the whole world because communications come right into your house. Well, that's what the Book of Revelation is all *about*. And you can just about *know* that anybody who comes out for peace is *not* for peace.

But what if someone genuinely is for peace?

Well, you can't be for peace and be *global*. It's just like that song "Man of Peace." But none of this matters, if you believe in another world. If you believe in *this* world, you're stuck; you really don't have a chance. You'll go *mad*, 'cause you won't see the end of it. You may wanna stick around, but you won't be able to. On another level, though, you *will* be able to see this world. You'll look back and say, "Ah, that's what it was all about all the time. Wow, why didn't I *get* that?"

That's a very fatalistic view, isn't it?

I think it's *realistic*. If it is fatalistic, it's only fatalistic on this level, and this level dies anyway, so what's the difference? So you're fatalistic, so what?

There's a lyric in "License to Kill": "Man has invented his doom/First step was touching the moon." Do you really believe that?

Yeah, I do. I have no idea why I wrote that line, but on some level, it's like just a door into the unknown.

Isn't man supposed to progress, to forge ahead?

Well . . . but not there. I mean, what's the purpose of going to the moon? To *me*, it doesn't make any sense. Now they're gonna put a space station up there, and it's gonna cost, what—$600 billion, $700 billion? And who's gonna benefit from it? Drug companies who are gonna be able to make better drugs. Does that make sense? Is that supposed to be something that a person is supposed to get excited about? Is that progress? I don't think they're gonna get better drugs. I think they're gonna get more *expensive* drugs.

Everything is computerized now, it's all computers. I see that as the beginning of the end. You can see everything going global. There's no nationality anymore, no I'm this or I'm that: "We're all the same, all workin' for one peaceful world, blah, blah, blah."

Somebody's gonna have to come along and figure out what's happening with the United States. Is this just an island that's going to be blown out of the ocean, or does it really figure into things? I really don't know. At this point right now, it seems that it figures into things. But later on, it will have to be a country that's self-sufficient, that can make it by itself without that many imports.

Right now, it seems like in the States, and most other countries, too, there's a big push on to make a big *global* country—*one big country*—where you can get all the materials from one place and assemble them someplace else and sell 'em in another place, and the whole world is just all one, controlled by the same people, you know? And if it's not there already, that's the point it's tryin' to get to.

In "Union Sundown," the Chevrolet you drive is "put together down in Argentina by a guy makin' thirty cents a day." Are you saying he'd be better off without that thirty cents a day?

What's thirty cents a day? He don't need the thirty cents a day. I mean, people survived for 6,000 years without having to work for slave wages for a person who comes down and . . . well, actually, it's just colonization. But see, I saw that stuff firsthand, because where I come from, they *really* got that deal good, with the ore.

In Minnesota, in the Iron Range, where you grew up?

Yeah. *Everybody* was workin' here at one time. In fact, ninety percent of the iron for the Second World War came out of those mines, up where I'm from. And eventually, they said, "Listen, this is costing too much money to get this out. We must be able to get it someplace else." Now the same thing is happening, I guess, with other products.

What was it like growing up in Hibbing, Minnesota, in the Fifties?

You're pretty much ruled by nature up there. You have to sort of fall into line with that, regardless of how you're feeling that day or what you might want to do with your life or what you think about. And it still is like that, I think.

Were you aware of any anti-Semitism there when you were a kid?

No. Nothing really mattered to me except learning another song or a new chord or finding a new place to play, you know? Years later, when

I'd recorded a few albums, *then* I started seeing in places: "Bob Dylan's a Jew," stuff like that. I said, "Jesus, I never knew that." But they kept harping on it; it seemed like it was *important* for people to *say* that—like they'd say "the one-legged street singer" or something. So after a period of time, I thought, "Well, gee, maybe I'll look into that."

I don't know. I never noticed it occurring with any other artists; I mean, I've never seen it about Barbra Streisand or Neil Diamond. But it *has* occurred with me. As a kid, though, I never felt anything, like, I had to fight my way through schoolyard crowds, you know? As long as I had a guitar, I was happy.

Was Hibbing an oppressive place? Did it just make you want to get out?

Not really. I didn't really know anything else except, uh, Hank Williams. I remember hearin' Hank Williams one or two years before he died. And that sort of introduced me to the guitar. And once I had the guitar, it was never a problem. Nothing else was ever a problem.

Did you get to see any of the original rock & roll guys, like Little Richard, Buddy Holly?

Yeah, sure. I saw Buddy Holly two or three nights before he died. I saw him in Duluth at the armory. He played there with Link Wray. I don't remember the Big Bopper. Maybe he'd gone off by the time I came in. But I saw Ritchie Valens. And Buddy Holly, yeah. He was great. He was incredible. I mean, I'll never forget the image of seeing Buddy Holly up on the bandstand. And he died—it must have been a week after that. It was unbelievable.

Late at night, I used to listen to Muddy Waters, John Lee Hooker, Jimmy Reed and Howlin' Wolf blastin' in from Shreveport. It was a radio show that lasted all night. I used to stay up till two, three o'clock in the morning. Listened to all those songs, then tried to figure them out. I started playing myself.

How did you take to the guitar?

First, I bought a Nick Manoloff book. I don't think I could get past the first one. And I had a Silvertone guitar from Sears. In those days, they cost thirty or forty dollars, and you only had to pay five dollars down to get it. So I had my first electric guitar.

I had a couple of bands in high school, maybe three or four of 'em. Lead singers would always come in and take my bands, because they would have connections, like maybe their fathers would know somebody,

so they could get a job in the neighboring town at the pavilion
for a Sunday picnic or something. And I'd lose my band. I'd see it all
the time.

That must have made you a little bitter.

Yeah, it did actually. And then I had another band with my cousin
from Duluth. I played, you know, rock & roll, rhythm & blues. And then
that died out pretty much, in my last year of high school.

And after that, I remember I heard a record—I think maybe it was
the Kingston Trio or Odetta or someone like that—and I sorta got into
folk music. Rock & roll was pretty much finished. And I traded my stuff
for a Martin that they don't sell anymore, an 0018, maybe, and it was
brown. The first acoustic guitar I had. A *great* guitar. And then, either
in Minneapolis or St. Paul, I heard Woody Guthrie. And when I heard
Woody Guthrie, that was it, it was all over.

What struck you about him?

Well, I heard them old records, where he sings with Cisco Houston
and Sonny [Terry] and Brownie [McGhee] and stuff like that, and then
his own songs. And he really struck me as an independent character. But
no one ever talked about him. So I went through all his records I could
find and picked all that up by any means I could. And when I arrived in
New York, I was mostly singing his songs and folk songs. At that time, I
was runnin' into people who were playing the same kind of thing, but I
was kinda combining elements of Southern mountain music with bluegrass stuff, English-ballad stuff. I could hear a song once and know it. So
when I came to New York, I could do a lot of different stuff. But I never
thought I'd see rock & roll again when I arrived here.

Did you miss it?

Not really, because I *liked* the folk scene. It was a whole community,
a whole world that was all hooked up to different towns in the United
States. You could go from here to California and always have a place to
stay, and always play somewhere, and meet people. Nowadays, you go to
see a folk singer—what's the folk singer doin'? He's singin' all his own
songs. *That* ain't no folk singer. Folk singers sing those old folk songs,
ballads.

I met a lot of folk singers in New York, and there were a lot of 'em
in the Twin Cities. But I ran into some people in England who *really*
knew those songs. Martin Carthy, another guy named Nigel Davenport.

Martin Carthy's incredible. I learned a lot of stuff from Martin. "Girl from the North Country" is based on a song I heard *him* sing—that "Scarborough Fair" song, which Paul Simon, I guess, just took the whole thing.

Could folk ever become big again?

Well, yeah, it could become big again. But people gotta go back and find the songs. They don't do it no more. I was tellin' somebody that thing about when you go to see a folk singer now, you hear somebody singin' his own songs. And the person says, "Yeah, well, *you* started that." And in a sense, it's true. But I never would have written a song if I didn't play all them old folk songs first. I never would have thought to write a song, you know? There's no *dedication* to folk music now, no *appreciation* of the art form.

Do you notice that you've influenced a lot of singers over the years?

It's phrasing. I think I've phrased everything in a way that it's never been phrased before. I'm not tryin' to brag or anything—or maybe I am [*laughs*]. But yeah, I hear stuff on the radio, doesn't matter what kinda stuff it is, and I *know* if you go back far enough, you'll find somebody listened to Bob Dylan somewhere, because of the phrasing. Even the content of the tunes. Up until I started doin' that stuff, nobody was talkin' about that sort of thing. For music to succeed on any level . . . Well, you're always gonna have your pop-radio stuff, but the only people who are gonna succeed, really, are the people who are sayin' somethin' that is given to them to say. I mean, you can only carry "Tutti Frutti" so far.

Like the current rockabilly revival?

The rockabilly revival was just about spirit and attitude.

Were you aware of punk rock when it happened—the Sex Pistols, the Clash?

Yeah. I didn't listen to it all the time, but it seemed like a logical step, and it still does. I think it's been hurt in a lotta ways by the fashion industry.

You've seen the Clash, I understand?

Yeah. I met them way back in 1977, 1978. In England. I think they're great. In fact, I think they're greater now than they were.

You mean since Mick Jones left?

Yeah. It's interesting. It took two guitar players to replace Mick.

How about Prince—have you ever run into him in Minneapolis?

No, I never have.

Have you met Michael Jackson yet?

No, I don't think so. I met Martha and the Vandellas.

Do your kids tell you about new groups: "You gotta check out Boy George"?

Well, they used to, a few years ago. I kind of like everything.

Are your kids musical?

Yeah, they all play.

Would you encourage them to go into the music business?

I would never push 'em or encourage 'em to. I mean, I never went into it as a *business*. I went into it as a matter of *survival*. So I wouldn't tell anybody to go into it as a business. It's a pretty cutthroat business, from what I've seen.

What do you tell your kids about things like sex and drugs?

Well, they don't really ask me too much about that stuff. I think they probably learn enough just by hangin' around me, you know?

You had a drug period at one time, didn't you?

I never got hooked on any drug—not like you'd say, uh, "Eric Clapton: His drug period."

Ever take LSD?

I don't wanna say anything to encourage anybody, but, uh, who knows? Who knows what people stick in your drinks or what kinda cigarettes you're smokin'?

When people like Jimi Hendrix and Janis Joplin started dropping away, did you look upon that as a waste?

Jimi, I thought, was a big waste. I saw Jimi . . . oh, man, that was sad when I saw him. He was in the back seat of a limousine on Bleecker Street, just . . . I couldn't even tell then whether he was dead or alive.

Do your old songs still mean the same to you as when you wrote them?

Yeah. Sittin' here, it's hard to imagine it, but yeah. Once you look into that stuff, it's like it was just written yesterday. When I'm singin' the stuff, sometimes I say, "Wow! Where'd these lyrics *come* from?" It's *amazing*.

Do you still look back on some of it as protest material? Or did you ever see it as protest material?

I think all my stuff is protest material in some kinda way. I always felt like my position and my place came after that first wave, or maybe second wave, of rock & roll. And I felt like I would never have done the things I did if I just had to listen to popular radio.

At one point, didn't you disassociate yourself from the protest form?

Well, you see, I never called it protest. Protest is anything that goes against the ordinary and the established. And who's the founder of protest? Martin Luther.

Is it true that "Like a Rolling Stone" was done in one take?

Yeah, one take. It's amazing. It sounds like it's so together. That was back in the days when we used to do . . . oh, man, six, eight, ten tunes a session. We used to just go in and come out the next day.

Wasn't 'Another Side of Bob Dylan' the result of an all-night session, too?

Well, that was pretty quick, too. But that was easier to do, it was just me. But we used to do the same thing when there was a band in there. I don't think a song like "Rolling Stone" could have been done any other way. What are you gonna do, chart it out?

How do you maintain a balance between the requirements of the modern recording studio and the fact that a lot of your best stuff in the past has been done very quickly?

Right now, I'm changing my views on that. But I plan to do a little bit more acoustic stuff in the future. I think my next album is probably just gonna be me and my guitar and harmonica. I'm not saying all of it will be that way, but I'm sure a few songs will be. I *know* they will be.

What's your latest stuff like?

I just write 'em as they come, you know? They're not about anything different than what I've ever written about, but they're probably put together in a way that other ones aren't put together. So it might seem like somethin' new. I don't think I've found any new chords or new progressions, or any new words that haven't been said before. I think they're pretty much all the same old thing, just kinda reworked.

I heard an outtake from the 'Infidels' sessions called "Blind Willie McTell." Is that ever going to come out? It's a great song.

I didn't think I recorded it right. But I don't know why that stuff gets out on me. I mean, it never seems to get out on other people.

There's a lot of interest out there. You could put all your unreleased stuff out in, like, a twenty-volume set or something.

Yeah, like *The Basement Tapes*. But it doesn't occur to me to put it out. If I wrote a song three years ago, I seldom go back and get that. I just leave 'em alone.

I never really liked The Basement Tapes. I mean, they were just songs we had done for the publishing company, as I remember. They were used only for other artists to record those songs. I wouldn't have put 'em out, But, you know, Columbia wanted to put 'em out, so what can you do?

You don't think that album has a great feeling to it? That material really has an aura.

I can't even remember it. People have told me they think it's very Americana and all that. I don't know what they're talkin' about.

So, then, it wouldn't occur to you to put out, say, the 1966 tapes of the Royal Albert Hall concert in London, another great bootleg?

No. Uh-uh. I wouldn't put 'em out because I didn't think they were quality.

That stuff's great. I'm amazed you wouldn't want to see it done legitimately and really do the tapes right.

Well, but you see, Columbia's never offered to do that. They have done that with *The Basement Tapes* and the *Budokan* album. But they've never offered to put that out as a historical album or whatever. And believe me, if they wanted to do it, they could.

Speaking of the 'Budokan' album . . .

The *Budokan* album was only supposed to be for Japan. They twisted my arm to do a live album for Japan. It was the same band I used on

Street-Legal, and we just started findin' our way into things on that tour when they recorded it. I never meant for it to be any type of representation of my stuff or my band or my live show.

That was when the critics started saying you were going Las Vegas, wasn't it?

Well, I think the only people who would have said somethin' like that were people who've never been to Las Vegas.

I think it was the clothes you wore at the time. They said it made you look like Neil Diamond.

Well, it just goes to show you how times have changed since 1978, if you could be criticized for what you were *wearing*. I mean, *now* you can wear anything. You see a guy wearing a dress onstage now, it's like, "Oh, yeah, right." You expect it.

I've seen a lot of stuff written about me. People must be crazy. I mean *responsible* people. Especially on that *Street-Legal* tour. That band we assembled then, I don't think that will ever be duplicated. It was a big ensemble. And what did people say? I mean, responsible people who *know* better. All I saw was "Bruce Springsteen" because there was a *saxophone* player. And it was "disco"—well, there wasn't any *disco* in it.

It always seemed to me that you were sort of infallible in your career up until 'Self Portrait,' in 1970. What's the story behind that album?

At the time, I was in Woodstock, and I was getting a great degree of notoriety for doing *nothing*. Then I had that motorcycle accident, which put me outta commission. Then, when I woke up and caught my senses, I realized I was just workin' for all these *leeches*. And I didn't wanna do that. Plus, I had a family, and I just wanted to see my *kids*.

I'd also seen that I was representing all these things that I didn't know anything *about*. Like I was supposed to be on acid. It was all storm-the-embassy kind of stuff—Abbie Hoffman in the streets—and they sorta figured me as the kingpin of all that. I said, "Wait a minute, I'm just a *musician*. So my songs are about this and that. So *what?*" But people need a leader. People need a leader more than a leader needs people, really. I mean, anybody can step up and be a leader, if he's got the people there that want one. I didn't want that, though.

But then came the big news about Woodstock, about musicians goin' up there, and it was like a wave of insanity breakin' loose around the house day and night. You'd come in the house and find people there, people comin' through the *woods*, at all hours of the day and night, knockin' on your door. It was really dark and depressing. And there was no way to *respond* to all this, you know? It was as if they were suckin' your very *blood* out. I said, "Now, wait, these people can't be my *fans*. They just *can't* be." And they kept comin'. We *had* to get out of there!

This was just about the time of that Woodstock Festival, which was the sum total of all this bullshit. And it seemed to have something to do with *me*, this Woodstock Nation, and everything it represented. So we couldn't *breathe*. I couldn't get any space for myself and my family, and there was no help, nowhere. I got very resentful about the whole thing, and we got outta there.

We moved to New York. Lookin' back, it really was a stupid thing to do. But there was a house available on MacDougal Street, and I always remembered that as a nice place. So I just bought this house, sight unseen. But it wasn't the same when we got back. The Woodstock Nation had overtaken MacDougal Street also. There'd be crowds outside my house. And I said, "Well, fuck it. I wish these people would just *forget* about me. I wanna do something they *can't* possibly like, they *can't* relate to. They'll see it, and they'll listen, and they'll say, 'Well, let's go on to the next person. He ain't sayin' it no more. He ain't givin' us what we want,' you know? They'll go on to somebody else." But the whole idea backfired. Because the album went out there, and the people said, "*This* ain't what we want," and they got *more* resentful. And then I did this portrait for the cover. I mean, there was no title for that album. I knew somebody who had some paints and a square canvas, and I did the cover up in about five minutes. And I said, "Well, I'm gonna call this album *Self Portrait*."

Which was duly interpreted by the press as "This is what he is . . ."

Yeah, *exactly*. And to me, it was a *joke*.

But why did you make it a double-album joke?

Well, it wouldn't have held up as a single album—then it *really* would've been bad, you know. I mean, if you're gonna put a lot of crap on it, you might as well *load it up!*

In the Sixties, there was feeling that this society really was changing. Looking back, do you feel it changed that much?

I think it did. A lot of times people forget. These modern days that we know now, where you can get on an airplane and fly anywhere you want nonstop, direct, and be there—that's recent. That's since what,

1940? Not even that—after the war, it was. And telephones? *Forget it.* I mean, when I was growin' up, I remember we had a phone in the house, but you had to dial it; and I also remember there was a party line of maybe six other people. And no matter when you got on the phone, you know, there might be somebody else on it. And I never grew up with television. When television first came in, it came on at like four in the afternoon, and it was off the air by seven at night. So you had more time to . . . I guess to think. It can never go back to the way it was, but it was all changing in the Fifties and Sixties.

My kids, they know television, they know telephones. They don't think about that stuff, you know? Even airplanes: I never rode on an airplane until 1964 or somethin'. Up till that time, if you wanted to go across the country, you took a train or a Greyhound bus, or you hitchhiked. I don't know. I don't think of myself as that *old,* or having seen that much, but . . .

Do you have MTV at home?

No, I don't get that. I have to go to the city to see MTV. And then, once I do find a set that has it, I'll just watch it for, you know, as long as my eyes can stay open. Until they pop out, I'll just watch it.

What do you make of video? Do you think it's all that important?

Uh, to sell records, yeah—but videos have always been around. David Bowie's been makin' 'em since he started. There was one thing I saw on a video, and I thought it was great. Then I heard the record on the radio, and it was *nothin'*, you know? But video does give you something to hook onto.

I was just talkin' to Ronnie Wood the other night. He went to the Duran Duran show at the Garden, and he said it was really funny, because they had a great big screen up over the stage with huge close-ups of the band members. And every time they showed a close-up of somebody in the band, the audience would just go crazy—they'd go *mad,* you know? So while they were showing a close-up of somebody in the band, the guitar player'd be playing a lick. So *he'd* think they were all doing it for *him.* Then he'd play the same lick again to get the same response—and get *nothing.*

I remember you were trying to get together with Ronnie and Keith [Richards] the other night. How'd it go?

It was pretty subdued, actually. But I always like to see Keith or

Woody or Eric or . . . There's a few people I like to see whenever I can. People who play like that. It has to do with a style of music, you know?

Do you ever collaborate?

Yeah, but usually it never happens. It's, "Okay, that's great, we'll pick that up later and finish it." But nothin' ever really gets finished.

Are your best friends mostly musicians?

My best friends? Jeez, let me try to think of one [*laughs*].

There must be a few.

Best friends? Jesus, I mean, that's . . .

You've got to have a best friend.

Whew! Boy, there's a question that'll really make you think. Best friend? Jesus, I think I'd go into a deep, dark depression if I were to think about who's my best friend.

There have to be one or two, don't there?

Well, there *has* to be . . . there *must* be . . . there's *gotta* be. But hey, you know, a best friend is someone who's gonna die for you. I mean, that's your best friend, really. Yeah, I'd be miserable trying to think who my best friend is.

What do you do with your year, aside from doing an album and maybe a tour?

Well, I'm happy doin' nothin' [*laughs*].

Do you spend a lot of time in Minnesota?

I get back there when I can, yeah. I got some property outside of St. Paul back in '74, a sort of farm.

Do you actually farm on this farm?

Well, it grows potatoes and corn, but I don't sit on the *tractor*, if that's what you mean. I'm usually either here or on the West Coast or down in the Caribbean.

Me and another guy have a boat down there. "Jokerman" kinda came to me in the islands. It's very mystical. The shapes there, and shadows, seem to be so ancient. The song was sorta inspired by these spirits they call *jumbis*.

Do you still have that house in California, that big, strange-looking place?

That's a story—you could write a baroque novel offa that. I had five kids, and I just couldn't find a house that was suitable. I liked this area because there was a public school in the neighborhood, and the kids could ride their bikes to it. So I bought this house on about an acre of land, past Malibu. And my wife looked at it and said, "Well, it's okay, but it needs another bedroom." So I got somebody to design another bedroom. You had to file plans, and they had to be passed—that's the way the red tape is out there. So we had architects come in, and right away they said, "Oh, yeah, Bob Dylan, right. We'll really make somethin' spectacular here." Anyway, it took six months to get the plans passed. Just to put on another room. I mean, *one room*. Jesus! So I went out there one day to see how the room was progressing, and they'd knocked down the house. *They'd knocked down the house!* I asked the guys who were workin', "Where's the house?" And they said they had to knock it down to restructure it for this bedroom upstairs.

Sounds like somebody was making a lot of money off you.

Ain't that the truth? I mean, has it ever been otherwise? So, one thing led to another, and I said as long as they're knockin' this place down, we're just gonna add more rooms on to it. And any time some craftsman passed by—hitchhiking to Oregon or coming back down to Baja—we'd say, "Hey, you wanna do some work on this place?" And they'd do woodwork, tile work, all that kinda thing. And eventually, it was built. But then they closed the school out there, and the kids moved away, and Sara moved away, and, uh . . . So I was stuck with this place. As a matter of fact, I've never even put anything on the living-room floor. It's just cement.

Since you've spent a lot of time in the Caribbean, you must be familiar with Rastafarianism.

Not really. I know a lot of Rastas. I know they're Bible-believing people, and it's very easy for me to relate to any Bible-believing person.

Well, what if someone is born in a place where there are no Bibles—the Tibetan mountains, say. Could they still be saved?

I don't know. I really don't. Allen Ginsberg is a Tibetan—a Buddhist, or something like that. I'm just not familiar enough with that to say anything about it.

Speaking of Allen Ginsberg, doesn't the Bible say that homosexuality is an abomination?

Yeah, it does. It says that.

And yet Ginsberg's a good guy, right?

Yeah, well, but that's no reason for *me* to condemn somebody, because they drink or they're corrupt in orthodox ways or they wear their shirt inside out. I mean, that's *their* scene. It certainly doesn't matter to *me*. I've got no ax to grind with any of that.

Were you up in Minnesota when they tried to pass that antiporn law in Minneapolis? The contention was that pornography is a violation of women's civil rights. What do you think?

Well, pornography is pretty deeply embedded. I mean, it's into everything, isn't it? You see commercials on TV that millions of dollars have been put into, and they look pretty sexy to me. They look like they're pushin' sex in some kinda way.

In a way, that's the real pornography, because the point isn't to get you off sexually, it's to sell you something.

Yeah, it's to stick the idea in your brain. But it's too far gone. I mean, if you start makin' laws against porno magazines and that kinda stuff, well, then where do you draw the line? You gotta stop the prime-time television shows also.

Any thoughts on abortion?

Abortion? I personally don't think abortion is that important. I think it's just an issue to evade whatever issues *are* makin' people think about abortion.

Well, I mean, when abortion's used as a form of birth control . . .

Well, I think birth control is another hoax that women shouldn't have bought, but they did buy. I mean, if a man don't wanna knock up a woman, that's *his* problem, you know what I mean? It's interesting: They arrest prostitutes, but they never arrest the guys *with* the prostitutes. It's all very one-sided. And the same with birth control. Why do they make women take all them pills and fuck themselves up like that? People have used contraceptives for years and years and years. So all of a sudden some scientist invents a *pill*, and it's a billion-dollar industry. So we're talkin' about *money*. How to *make money* off of a sexual idea. "Yeah, you can go out and fuck anybody you want now; just take this pill." You know? And it puts that in a person's mind: "Yeah, if I take a pill . . ." But who *knows* what those pills do to a person? I think they're gonna be passé. But they've caused a lot of damage, a lot of damage.

So it's the man's responsibility? Vasectomy's the best way?

I think so. A man don't wanna get a woman pregnant, then *he's* gotta take care of it. Otherwise, that's just ultimate *abuse*, you know?

But the problem is not abortion. The problem is the whole concept behind abortion. Abortion is the end result of going out and screwing somebody to begin with. Casual sex.

But the abortion question is, Is it taking a life? Is it a woman's decision?

Well, if the woman wants to take that upon herself, I figure that's her business. I mean, who's gonna take care of the baby that arrives—these people that are callin' for no abortion?

In regard to these feminist sympathies . . .

I think women rule the world, and that no man has ever done anything that a woman either hasn't allowed him to do or encouraged him to do.

In that regard, there's a song on 'Infidels' called "Sweetheart Like You," in which you say, "A woman like you should be at home . . . takin' care of somebody nice."

Actually, that line didn't come out exactly the way I wanted it to. But, uh . . . I could easily have changed that line to make it not so overly, uh, *tender*, you know? But I think the concept still woulda been the same. You see a fine-lookin' woman walking down the street, you start goin', "Well, what are you doin' on the street? You're so fine, what do you need all this for?"

A lot of women might say they're on the street because they're on the way to their jobs.

Well, I wasn't talkin' to that type of woman. I'm not talkin' to Margaret Thatcher or anything.

Are you in love at the moment?

I'm *always* in love.

Would you ever marry again? Do you believe in the institution?

Yeah, I do. I don't believe in *divorce*. But I'm a strong believer in marriage.

One last question. I think a lot of people take you for a pretty gloomy character these days, just judging by your photos. Why reinforce that image by calling this latest album 'Infidels'?

Well, there were other titles for it. I wanted to call it *Surviving in a Ruthless World*. But someone pointed out to me that the last bunch of albums I'd made all started with the letter *s*. So I said, "Well, I don't wanna get bogged down in the letter *s*." And then *Infidels* came into my head one day. I don't know what it *means*, or anything.

Don't you think when people see that title, with that sort of dour picture on the front, they'll wonder, "Does he mean us?"

I don't know. I could've called the album *Animals*, and people would've said the same thing. I mean, what would be a term that people would *like* to hear about themselves?

How about 'Sweethearts'?

Sweethearts. You *could* call an album that. *Sweethearts*.

With a big smiling picture?

Yeah.

22. Radio interview with Bert Kleinman and Artie Mogull, Westwood One Radio

NOVEMBER 17, 1984

B.K.: *Is it true that you taught yourself guitar and harmonica?*

Well, nobody really teaches themselves guitar and harmonica, you know, when you don't know anything first of all you get yourself a book or something. What I remember is learning a couple of chords from some books and then going out to watch people, you know, to see how they're doing it. You don't go so much to hear 'em . . . you just go to see how they do what they do, get as close as you can, see what their fingers are doing. In those early stages it's more like a learning thing, and that can sometimes take . . . years, many years. But to me I kind of picked it up fairly quickly, I didn't really play with that much technique. And people really didn't take to me because of that, because I didn't go out of my way to learn as much technique as other people . . . I mean I know people who spent their whole lives learning John Lee Hooker chords, just hammering on, you know, on the E string, and that was all. But they could play it in such a beautiful way it looked like a ballet dancer. Everybody had a different style, they had styles and techniques, especially in folk music, you know there was your Southern mountain banjo, then flat picking, then your finger-picking techniques, and just all of these different runs you know, different styles of ballads. Folk-music was a world that was very split-up . . . and there was a purist side to it. Folk people didn't want to hear it if you couldn't play the song exactly the way that . . . Aunt Molly Jackson played it. And I just kind of blazed my way through all that stuff [*laughs*]. I would hear somebody do something and it would get to a certain point that you'd say, what do you want from that, you'd want to see what style they were playing . . . I don't know, I just stayed up day and night just barnstorming my way though all that stuff. And then I heard Woody Guthrie, and then it all came together for me . . .

B.K.: *Do you remember the first Woody Guthrie record you heard?*

Yeah, I think the first Woody Guthrie song I heard was "Pastures of Plenty." And "Pretty Boy Floyd" and another song . . . he used to write a lot of his songs from existing melodies, you know, "Grand Coulee Dam." They just impressed me.

B.K.: *Got to you?*

Oh, yeah. Because they were original, they just had a mark of originality on them, well the lyrics did. I just heard all those songs and I learned them all off the records. All the songs of Woody Guthrie that I could find, anybody that had a Woody Guthrie record or that knew a Woody Guthrie song. And in St. Paul at the time, where I was, there were some people around who not only had his records but who knew his songs. So I just learned them all. Some of the best records that I heard him make were these records that he made on the Stinson label, with Cisco Houston and Sonny Terry. I don't know if Leadbelly was on there too, I learned a bunch of Leadbelly's stuff too and learned how to play like that. But one of the biggest thrills I ever actually had was when I reached New York, whenever it was, and I got to play with Cisco Houston, I think I got to play with him at a party someplace. But I used to watch him, he used to play at Folk City. He was an amazing looking guy, he looked like Clark Gable, like a movie star.

A.M.: *He reminded me a little of Tennessee Ernie actually.*

Yeah.

A.M.: *Also very unheralded.*

Oh, completely. He was one of the great unsung heroes. One of the great American figures of all time, and no one . . . you know you can ask people about him and nobody knows anything about him.

B.K.: *When do you think you started to develop something that was uniquely yours? You were talking about playing Woody Guthrie . . .*

Well, when I came to New York that's all I played—Woody Guthrie songs. Then about six months after that I'd stopped playing all Woody Guthrie songs. I used to play in a place called Cafe Wha?, and it always used to open at noon, and closed at six in the morning. It was just a nonstop flow of people, usually they were tourists who were looking for beatniks in the Village. There'd be maybe five groups that played there. I used to play with a guy called Fred Neil, who wrote the song "Everybody's Talking" that was in the film *Midnight Cowboy*. Fred was from Florida I think, from Coconut Grove, Florida, and he used to make that scene, from Coconut Grove to Nashville to New York. And he had a strong powerful voice, almost a bass voice. And a powerful sense of rhythm . . . And he used to play mostly these types of songs that Josh White might sing. I would play harmonica for him, and then once in a while get to sing a song. You know, when he was taking a break or something. It was his show, he would be on for about half an hour, then a conga group would get on, called Los Congueros, with twenty conga drummers and bongos and steel drums. And they would sing and play maybe half an hour. And then this girl, I think she was called Judy Rainey, used to play sweet Southern Mountain Appalachian ballads, with electric guitar and small amplifier. And then another guy named Hal Waters used to sing, he used to be a sort of crooner. Then there'd be a comedian, then an impersonator, and that'd be the whole show, and this whole unit would go around nonstop. And you get fed there, which was actually the best thing about the place.

A.M.: *How long a set would you do?*

I'd do . . . oh, about half an hour. If they didn't like you back then you couldn't play, you'd get hooted off. If they liked you, you played more, if they didn't like you, you didn't play at all. You'd play one or two songs and people would just boo or hiss . . .

B.K.: *This wasn't your own stuff you were singing there?*

No, I didn't start playing my own stuff until . . . much later.

B.K.: *Well, when did you start to perform your own stuff?*

Well, I just drifted into it you know, I just started writing. Well I'd always kinda written my own songs but I never played them. Nobody played their own songs then. The only person that did that was Woody

Guthrie. And then one day I just wrote a song, and the first song I ever wrote that I performed in public was the song I wrote to Woody Guthrie. And I just felt like playing it one night—and so I played it.

B.K.: *Was writing something that'd you'd always wanted to do?*

No, not really. It wasn't a thing I wanted to do ever. I wanted just a song to sing, and there came a certain point where I couldn't sing anything. So I had to write what I wanted to sing 'cause nobody else was writing what I wanted to sing. I couldn't find it anywhere. If I could, I probably would have never started writing.

B.K.: *Was the writing something that came easy to you? Because it is a craft that you do very well and you talk about it so casually.*

Well, yeah, it does come easy. But then . . . after so many records sometimes you just don't know anymore whether . . . am I doing this because I want to do it or because you think it's expected of you. Do you know what I mean? So you'd start saying, well, it's time to write a song—I'll write a song. And you'll try to do something but sometimes it just won't come out right. At those kind of times it's best just to go sing somebody's songs.

B.K.: *Was it a lot of work writing? Was it a labor?*

No. It was just something I'd kinda do. You'd just sit up all night and write a song, or . . . in those days I used to write a lot of songs in cafés. Or at somebody's house with the typewriter. "A Hard Rain's A-Gonna Fall" . . . I wrote that in the basement of the Village Gate. All of it, at Chip Monck's, he used to have a place down there in the boiler room, an apartment that he slept in . . . next to the Greenwich Hotel. And I wrote "A Hard Rain's A-Gonna Fall" down there. I'd write songs in people's houses, people's apartments, wherever I was.

B.K.: *Were you much of a polisher, I mean did you write it and then pore over it?*

Pretty much I'd just leave them the way they were . . .

[*break*]

Well, I don't know why I walked off that show [*Ed Sullivan*, 1963]. I could have done something else but we'd rehearsed the song so many times and everybody had heard it. They'd run through the show, you know, and they'd put you on and you'd run through your number, and it always got a good response, and I was looking forward to singing it. Even Ed Sullivan seemed to really like it. I don't know who objected to it, but just before I was going to sing it they came in, and this was show time you know. They came in, there was this big huddle, I could see people talking about something. I was just getting ready to play you know . . . and then someone stepped up and said I couldn't sing that song. They wanted me to sing a Clancy Brothers song, and it just didn't make sense to me to sing a Clancy Brothers song on nationwide TV at that time. So . . . I just left.

A.M.: *Do you remember that time you were down in San Juan, Puerto Rico, at the CBS convention? And . . . it was being held at the San Juan Hilton I guess . . . this huge record convention, and it was just as Bob was beginning to hit. And the President of CBS at the time was a fabulous man named Goddard Lieberson. And . . . they wouldn't let Bob in the hotel, because he was not wearing a tie or a jacket . . .*

Yeah, or a shirt.

A.M.: *And Lieberson, to his credit, told the hotel manager either he comes in the hotel or I'm pulling the whole convention out of here. Have I told the story right?*

Yeah, he was a big supporter of mine. Goddard Lieberson, as was John Hammond. Without those people like that I don't think anything would have happened for me. If I was to come along now, in this day, with the kind of people that are running record companies now, they would . . . you know . . . bar the doors I think. But you had people back then who were more entrenched in individuality.

A.M.: *And also not as insecure in their jobs.*

No, they ran things, you know, they made decisions and it stuck. Now, I mean, it seems like everybody chats with somebody else, it's like well, I'll tell you tomorrow, call me back later, yeah we almost got a deal, stuff like that.

B.K.: *Did you get along with Lieberson okay . . . ?*

Oh, yeah, he was great . . . he even used to come to some sessions of mine. He'd stop in and say hello you know . . .

B.K.: *Was there ever any pressure on you? I mean some people considered your music almost subversive. Although I always considered it very American.*

I guess they did . . . I don't know. But, like I said, they seemed to run things. You know other people may have been talking under their breath or something, behind their back, and things like that. But at this time their big acts were Mitch Miller, Andy Williams, Johnny Matthis. I didn't really begin to sell many records until the second record . . . and the "Subterranean Homesick Blues" that made the charts.

B.K.: *That was an amazing single when you think of what the singles were like at the time.*

They made some good records then, that you know were good pop records. Not on Columbia though. Phil Spector was doing a lot of stuff at the time, and Jerry Leiber and Mike Stoller . . .

B.K.: *Were you listening to a lot of pop stuff at the time?*

Yeah, I listened to a lot of pop stuff, but it never influenced what I was doing. At least to any great degree. It had earlier, like the really earlier stuff, when rock & roll came in after Elvis, Carl Perkins, Buddy Holly, those people. Chuck Berry, Little Richard, that stuff influenced me . . . You know, nostalgia to me isn't really rock & roll. Because when I was a youngster the music I heard was Frankie Laine, Rosemary Clooney, Dennis . . . what's his name? Dennis Day? And you know, Dorothy Collins . . . the Mills Brothers, all that stuff. When I hear stuff like that it always strikes a different chord than all the rock & roll stuff. The rock & roll stuff I had a conscious mind at that time, but ten years before that it was like "Mule Train" and . . . Johnnie Ray knocked me out. Johnnie Ray was the first person to actually really knock me out.

B.K.: *What was it? What do you think it was about Johnnie Ray?*

Well, he was just so emotional, wasn't he? I ran into him in an elevator in Australia . . . he was like one of my idols you know. I mean I was speechless, there I was in an elevator with Johnnie Ray! I mean what do you say?

B.K.: *When you started to move from the pure folk style into a more electric style, was that a tough one?*

We're getting into a touchy subject [*laughter*].

B.K.: *Well, I mean today you go on stage and both of those things coexist. Nobody thinks twice.*

Yeah, they always did coexist . . .

B.K.: *I'm not talking so much about that, but at least what it seemed like from the outside was that people were trying to tell you how to make your music.*

Oh . . . there's always people trying to tell you how to do everything in your life. If you really don't know what to do and you don't care what to do—then just ask somebody's opinion. You'll get a million different opinions. If you don't want to do something, ask someone's opinion and they'll just verify it for you. The easiest way to do something is to just not ask anybody's opinion. I mean if you really believe in what you're doing . . . I've just asked people's opinion and it's been a great mistake, in different areas. In my personal life, I've asked people what do you think about doing this and they've said . . . Oh wow! . . . You know, and you end up not using it or else using it wrong.

A.M.: *As a matter of fact I think the artist has to make the innate decision about their . . .*

Yeah, you know what's right. When those things come you know what's right. A lot of times you might be farming around and not knowing what's right and you might do something dumb, but that's only because you don't know what to do in the first place. But if you know what's right and it strikes you at a certain time then you can usually believe that instinct. And if you act on it, then you'll be successful at it. Whatever it is.

B.K.: *Recording is a whole other thing from being on stage. And you, from what I've read, try and record as spontaneously as possible . . . ?*

I have, yeah, I have, but I don't do that so often anymore. I used to do that . . . because recording a song bores me, you know, it's like working in a coal mine. Well I mean it's not really as serious as that, you're not completely that far underground! Maybe not in a literal sense, but . . . you could be indoors for months. And then what you think is real just, is just not anymore, you're just listening to sounds and your whole world is just working with tapes and things. I'm not . . . I've never liked that side of things. Plus I've never gotten into it on that level, when I first recorded I just went in and recorded the songs I had. That's the way people recorded then. But people don't record that way now, and I shouldn't record that way either because they can't even get it down that way anymore. To do what I used to do, or to do what anybody used to do you have to stay in the studio a longer time to get that right. Because you know technology has messed everything up so much.

B.K.: *It's messed it up?*

Yeah, it's messed it up. Technology is giving a false picture. Like if you listen to any of the records that are done now they're all done in a technology sort of way. Which is a conniving kind of way, you can dream up what you want to do and just go in and dream it up! But you go see some of that stuff live and you're gonna be very disappointed, because . . . er . . . I mean if you want to see some of it live. You may not want to, you know. Well, I think it's messed it up, but that's progress, you know. You can't go back the way it used to be. For a lot of people it's messed things up, but then for a lot of other people it's a great advantage. In other words you can get something right now, it doesn't have to be right but you can get it right. You know, it can be totally wrong but you can get it right! And it can be done just with sound and . . . We were just recording something the other night and we were gonna put some hand-claps on it. And the guy sitting behind the board, he was saying, "Well do you guys wanna go out there and actually clap . . . ? I got a machine right here that can do that." And the name of this thing was Roland or something [*laughs*]. So we went out and clapped instead. It wasn't any big deal, we could have had some machine do it . . . But that's just a small example of how everything is just machine oriented, you know.

B.K.: *You talk almost like . . . I don't really know how to put it . . . like the world's gone here and you're old-fashioned.*

Well, I feel I'm old-fashioned, but I don't believe I'm old-fashioned in the way that I'm not modern fashioned. You know on a certain level there is no old-fashioned and there's no new fashioned . . . really nothing has changed. I don't think I'm old-fashioned in the kind of way that I feel I'm a passé person that's sitting somewhere . . . you know out in Montana . . . just watching it snow. But even if I was, I'm sure that would be okay.

A.M.: *Yeah, Bob, but you can't go to a concert like Wembley and get that kind of . . .*

Yeah, okay . . . but life is like that, you don't get that many years to live, right? So how long can you manage to keep up with things . . . ? And when you're keeping up with things what are you keeping up with? Who buys most of the records nowadays? Twelve-year-old kids? Who buys Michael Jackson's records? Twelve-year-olds. Fourteen-year-olds. Sixteen, twenty . . . I don't know who buys 50 million records of somebody. You know you can't compete with a market that's geared for a market for twelve-year-olds. You know you have rock & roll critics that are forty years old writing about records that are geared for people that are ten years old! And making an intellectual philosophy out of it.

B.K.: *But you don't listen to that stuff?*

No, I don't listen to that stuff, and I don't listen to those critics. I've come up with a lot of people who should know a whole lot better, who have made a career about writing about rock & roll. Writing about rock & roll . . . ! I mean . . . you know, how indecent can you be? Well, I'm not saying that it's all bad, people have to express themselves. So rock & roll gives them a thrill, or did give them a thrill. Well most of the people that I can think of as rock & roll authorities are people who have documented down what I remember growing up with as it started . . . right? So everybody knows where the roots of rock & roll are. Everybody knows who does what, but to make such an intellectual game out of it is beside the point, you know it's not really going to add anything to the history of popular music. It's just going to feed a lot of cynical people and self-righteous people who think they've got a claim on a rock & roll goldmine . . . or whatever. So I find that very distasteful.

B.K.: *Do you have . . . I'm going to ask you which ones . . . but are there any things that you look back on and say, "Jesus, that was a good one . . . ?"*

Oh, yeah. Some of the songs you're talking about, you know I can't write those songs today. No way. But I look at those songs, 'cause I sing 'em all the time, I wonder where they came from and how they came . . . how it's constructed. Even the simpler songs, I look at them that way. I couldn't do them now, and I don't even try, I'd be a fool to try. I think there are a lot of good songwriters though, what I've done I've done all alone, but there's a lot of other good songwriters . . . of my era.

A.M.: *Like who, Bob?*

Randy Newman writes good songs, Paul Simon's written some good songs, I think "America" is a good song, I think "The Boxer" is a good song. I think "Bridge Over Troubled Water" is a good song. I mean he's written a lot of bad songs too, but everybody's done that. Let's see . . . some of the Nashville writers . . . Shel Silverstein writes great songs. Really. Like he's one of my favorite songwriters. You know, whatever you're expressing it out of the amount of knowledge and light and inspiration you're giving on it. If you're just given an inch, you know . . . well you've just got to make of that as much as you can.

B.K.: *Have you ever tried your hand at any of the other arts?*

Yeah, painting.

B.K.: *Really, do you do much of it?*

Yeah, well not so much in recent years, but it's something that I would like to do if I could . . . you've got to be in the right place to do it, you have to commit a lot of time . . . because one thing leads to another and you tend to discover new things as you go along. So it takes time to develop it, but I know how to do it fundamentally so once I get into the rhythm of it, and if I can hang with it long enough . . .

B.K.: *Do you take time for yourself?*

Oh, yeah, I take time for myself. I don't have any public time. People think I do but that's my time.

B.K.: *That's a great place to be.*

Well, that's the place you were at when you were born. That's the place you should be. I mean what's there to make you not be in that place? Do you have to be part of the machine . . . so what if you're not part of the machine?

[*break*]

I don't know if I've ever been happy if we're talking straight. I don't know . . . I mean . . . happy? I don't consider myself happy and I don't consider myself unhappy, I've just never thought of life in terms of happiness and unhappiness. It just never occurred to me.

B.K.: *Do you think of it in terms of growth?*

No! I never think in terms of growth. I tell you what I do think though, that you never stop anywhere, there's no place to stop in. You know them places at the side of the road that you can stop, they're just an illusion.

B.K.: *The road goes on . . .*

Yeah, you've got to get back on the road. And you may want to stop but you can't stay there.

B.K.: *When you talk about getting back on the road, isn't that in a sense growth . . . or at least it's movement. From point A to point B.*

Yeah, that's growth. But what's growth? I mean everything grows, that's just the way life is, life just grows. You know, it grows and it dies, it lives and it dies. Whenever you get to a plateau, that's not it, you got to go on to the next one. You can't stay nowhere, there's no place to stay, there's no place that will keep you.

B.K.: *Because of boredom or because that's the way it is?*

No, because that's just the nature of things . . .

B.K.: *So you see yourself just moving onward?*

I see everybody like that, I see the whole world that way. That which doesn't do that is stuff that's . . . that's just dead.

B.K.: *Ha . . . what's that line? Those that are not busy being born are . . .*

. . . busy dying? What a line!

B.K.: *Didn't somebody write that?*

Classic line that . . . You know people say, well isn't it great to be able to do what you do? Well it is to a degree but they forget that an artist . . . a touring artist, anybody that is out touring . . . playing live from town to town night after night. They think that's easy. It's not easy. People think you're having a ball, they say, "Howya doin'?" I say, "I'm in Schenectady!" [*Laughs*] And they say, oh well you're having a great time and I'm stuck here in Orlando. But it's not . . . you know you just have to get up and then you just have to do what you're supposed to do. I know that when I get off the road, oh man! For the first two or three weeks . . . I mean you can get up any time you want! You don't have to go to sleep at this hour and get up at that hour, and get yourself lined up to do this, and be there at that certain place, and go through this and go through that, and get back and get the proper amount of sleep. You know, eat right . . . in case you're afraid you'll get sick, or afraid you're gonna hurt yourself somewhere along the line. All those things . . . they just disappear on the last show, then you can do anything you want. It's a high feeling.

B.K.: *You go sailing?*

[*long pause*]

B.K.: *Yeah?*

Yeah.

B.K.: *I mean do you want to talk about anything you like to do other than . . .*

I like to do a lot of things but I don't want to talk about the things I like to do . . .

B.K.: *Okay.*

I'll talk about things I don't like to do!

B.K.: *You said that you consider yourself a pretty regular kind of a guy, would you say you're just like anybody else?*

Well, sure, you know I breathe the same air as everybody else does. I have to do the same things most people do.

B.K.: *Well . . . in a lot of the earlier songs there's a sense of separation . . .*

Oh, well . . . there's always a sense of separation, I mean even in the later songs. There wouldn't be any point to it if there wasn't a sense of separation. I mean if I didn't have anything different to say to people then what would be the point of it? I mean . . . I could do a Ronettes album!

A.M.: *I think the most interesting thing you've said so far, Bob . . .*

Have I said anything interesting?

A.M.: *One thing that was exceedingly interesting to me was when you started writing because nobody was writing the songs you wanted to sing.*

Yeah, that's when I started writing . . . and that's why I'm still writing . . . I wish someone would come along and give me some songs that I could do. I mean it would be such a burden taken off my shoulder, I mean it's heavy, man! [*Laughs*]

B.K.: *There's still a lot of expectation. Have you been able to get beyond that, to stop worrying about what people expect from you?*

Who expects what? I mean anybody that expects anything from me is just a borderline case. Nobody with any kind of reality is going to expect anything from me. I've already given them enough you know, what do they want from me. You can't keep on depending on one person to give you everything.

What I usually do is say, okay, I'm gonna write a song, whether it's a lyric or a rhythm . . . but for me, I have to go out and play, and er . . . I'm not an admirer of stuff like videos. I mean I don't mind making videos, but it's nothing for me to try and attempt to do . . . because it's fake, you know . . . it's all about how good it looks . . . anybody can make a video.

Anybody. As long as you have a camera, what kind of camera do you want? 16mm, video camera, anybody can do it. And anybody can make a good one, and . . . er . . . people will like it. Everything is done in a technological kind of way . . . you can dress it up in so many different kind of ways. So people don't know what to think. Nobody's gonna sit there and say oh this is bullshit, or this is awful . . . this don't make any sense at all . . . it's been a long time since I've even seen one of those things, but the last time I saw one, I mean I was appalled. And then when you go see some of these groups, and I've seen some of them, they aren't anything, you know they're just nothing. That's because they go for the faking thing so much, and you know . . . in the other arena, you have to do it live or you just don't do it. I've always played live since I started out, and that's where it's always counted for me. It don't count on a video or a movie, I don't care about being a movie star or a video star or any of that stuff you know.

[break]

I'm usually in a numb state of mind before my shows, and I have to kick in at some place along the line, usually it takes me one or two songs, or sometimes now it takes much longer. Sometimes it takes me up to the encore! [Laughs]

B.K.: *The band I would imagine has an effect on that.*

Oh, absolutely. I've played with some bands that have gotten in my way so much that it's just been a struggle to get through the show. Oh yeah . . . at certain times it gets ridiculous you know.

B.K.: *I'd imagine the flip side too, have there been bands that turn you on?*

Yeah, this last band . . . I thought they were pretty good.

B.K.: *Rolling Thunder was an interesting tour, it wasn't just the performing but the whole idea of the thing. There was a spontaneity of a kind to it.*

Yeah . . . there was definitely a lot of spontaneity to that.

B.K.: *Was it scary or exciting?*

A little of both. We were doing double shows on the Rolling Thunder shows. We'd be in a hall say for . . . fourteen hours. You know Rolling Thunder shows were six hours long!

B.K.: *That had to be people loving making music.*

Well . . . [*laughs*] . . . there were so many people . . . you know the people in the audience came and went . . . people would bring their lunch or dinner or something.

A.M.: *Like a Grateful Dead concert?*

Yeah, yeah.

B.K.: *Was that your idea, did it come from you?*

No, it just happened. We started out with a small show and it just evolved into the . . .

B.K.: *That's an amazing thing to me, that you're able to maintain that . . . a lot of people when they get to a certain place in the business . . .*

I thought the Rolling Thunder shows were great, I think someday somebody should make a movie out of them!

B.K.: *And call it . . .*

Rolling Thunder!

B.K.: *[Laughs] You've been smiling a lot and laughing a lot here, but you don't do that much on stage. But you say you really enjoy yourself . . . you look so serious.*

Well, those songs take you through different trips you see. I mean what's there to smile about in singing "A Hard Rain's A-Gonna Fall" or "Tangled Up in Blue" or "With God on Our Side" . . . or "Mr. Tambourine Man" or "Like a Rolling Stone" or "License to Kill" or "Shot of Love" or "Poisoned Love" . . . any of that. How can you sing that with a smile on your face? I mean it'd be kind of hypocritical.

You'll do things on certain nights, which you know are just great, you'll know they're great, and you'll get no response. And then you'll go someplace else and it'll be . . . you just don't have it that night, you just don't have it, for a variety of reasons. You don't have it and you're just trying to get through it . . . but it's really always got to be consistent, you've got to get it to a place where it's consistent. Then it stays on that level . . . it can get great, which is really, you know, triple consistent . . . You know I've done things where I might have had a temperature of 104, or you know, I might have been kicked in the side that day and couldn't hardly stand up. I have done shows where I could hardly stand up, you know, where it's been painful to stand there. And that's kind of humiliating in a way, because you know there's no way that you can be as good as you wanna be. Before it even starts you know you're not gonna be as good, not even as you wanna be, as you can be. There's only been one time when I've wanted to replay one show, that was in Montreal. We played a show in Montreal in 1978, I had a temperature of 104, couldn't even stand up . . . but the promoter said, "Well, you gotta play the show . . ." And we played the show and I didn't have nothing, nothing! And the response . . . you'd think the Pope was there! [*Laughs*] And I've played other shows where I've had everything happening, I mean I just rewrote the book, nothing—no response.

When I do whatever it is I'm doing there is rhythm involved and there is phrasing involved. And that's where it all balances out, in the rhythm of it and the phrasing of it. It's not in the lyrics, people think it's in the lyrics, maybe on the records it's in the lyrics, but in a live show it's not all in the lyrics, it's in the phrasing and the dynamics and the rhythm. It's got nothing whatsoever to do with the lyrics, I mean it does—the lyrics have to be there, sure they do. But . . . you know there was this Egyptian singer Om Khalsoum, have you ever heard of her? She was one of my favorite singers of all time—and I don't understand a word she sings! She'd sing one song—it might last for 40 minutes, same song, and she'll sing the same phrase over and over and over again. But in a different way every time. I don't think there's any U.S. or Western singer that's in that kind of category . . . except possibly me! [*Laughs*] But on another level, do you know what I mean?

[*break*]

To me it's not a business, and to the people who have survived along with me—it's not a business. It just isn't. It's never been a business and never will be a business. It is just a way of surviving, you know, it's just what you do, you know. It's just like somebody who's trained to be a carpenter, that's what they do, it's what they do best. And that's how they make a living I guess.

B.K.: *Were you ever going to be anything else . . . were you ever going to be an insurance salesman?*

I was never gonna be anything else, never. I was playing when I was twelve years old, and that was all I wanted to do—play my guitar. I was always going to these parties where all these biggest guys were . . . you know . . . and it was a way of getting attention and whatever . . . It starts out that way but I never really knew where it was going to lead. Now that it's led me here—I still don't know where it is.

B.K.: *You sound like . . . well obviously you're older than you were in the sixties, but also you seem to have a degree of self-knowledge and certainty of where you're going as a person . . .*

I don't know where I'm going as a person . . .

A.M.: *I hear contentment . . .*

Well, in certain areas—yeah, I hope so. I don't know what's gonna happen when I'm not around to sing anymore. I hope somebody else comes along who could pick up on what I'm doing and learn exactly what it is . . . that makes it quite different. I keep looking for that somebody . . . not necessarily to cover me, but to take it a step further. I've already taken it as far as I can take it, maybe I won't see that person—I don't know. But somebody, sometime will come along and take it that step further. But I haven't seen anyone . . . now I don't want to say that in a bragging sort of way, it just hasn't gone any further.

B.K.: *But there is something . . . that's why you go back to the stage.*

Yeah, well I'm just thankful I can play on stage and people will come and see me. Because I couldn't make it otherwise, I mean if I went out to play and nobody showed up, that would be the end of me. I wouldn't be making records I'll tell you that. I only make records because people see me live. So as long as they're coming along to see me live I'll just make some more records.

23. Interview with Toby Creswell, ROLLING STONE (Australia)

JANUARY 16, 1986

It doesn't really matter now whether Bob Dylan is a fundamentalist Christian, any more than it mattered whether he was going to the synagogue when he recorded *Blood on the Tracks* ten years ago. Amongst all the crucial lines that Dylan has sung, one sticks out—"He not busy being born is busy dying." Dylan, of all the great creators of his generation, has been busy being born over a series of almost thirty albums, each of which has added to all that had come before.

However, there have been some constants. There has always been a sense of engagement with the external world. When Dylan gave up writing specific protest songs in 1964, he began writing songs about hypocrisy, prejudice, injustice, malice, exploitation and cruelty. Those concerns are still the subject of his songs. At the same time he was writing love songs like "Love Minus Zero/No Limit," which is a tender and complete statement of affection that is also a religious statement. Dylan has sung of both sacred and profane love throughout his career, sometimes concentrating on one, sometimes on the other. Then there was the electric bite of pure rock & roll as portrayed on "Subterranean Homesick Blues," a song that Dylan notes, on the five-album *Biograph* retrospective, was recorded in one take.

All these are still elements of Dylan's current work. His choice of Tom Petty and the Heartbreakers as a backing band suggests that he's still after that fire in his rock & roll. Moreover, the news that he is working with Dave Stewart of the Eurythmics suggests that he still sees himself as contemporary.

Given all of that and the quality of the last album, *Empire Burlesque*, the presence of the Heartbreakers on Dylan's Australian tour promises us an extraordinary series of concerts.

CBS has just issued the *Biograph* box set: ten sides of Dylan from *Bob Dylan* to *Shot of Love*. It is an awesome body of work, unequaled in rock & roll, even the outtakes and the unfinished songs like "Jet Pilot," which later became "Tombstone Blues."

As somebody who has listened to Bob Dylan for twenty years, I jumped at the chance of an interview. But what do you say over the telephone to someone whom you have grown up with? My friend Danny said you usually talk about how the family is doing. What do you ask Bob Dylan, though?

This tour you'll be playing with the Heartbreakers, the first time you've played with a band since the Band tour a decade ago. It must be good to get back to that format.

We don't really know what the format is going to be yet. It's a lot easier, though, because as band members they sort of think as one person. When you put people together who've never played together before, there's so many different people; it takes years for people to play together like the Tom Petty band. We were all raised on the same sort of music.

You played with the Heartbreakers for Farm Aid. You seem to have been doing rather a lot of those shows lately.

These things pop up every once in a while. I don't think it'll become a regular thing. This year there seem to have been a couple of those kind of shows.

It seems that these shows have become such huge events that they tend to overshadow the issues.

I know what you mean. That can happen. The atmosphere is like a carnival. But by raising that kind of money, they must be getting these problems into the minds of a lot of people who wouldn't have had it on their minds before, and that's a good thing.

You have said in the past that the function of art is to lead you to God. There were the three gospel albums: 'Slow Train Coming,' 'Saved' and 'Shot of Love,' but your last two records have taken a different slant.

Well, it all depends where you come at it from. I come at things from different sides to get a different perspective on what it is I'm trying to focus in on. Maybe all my songs are focusing on the same thing. I don't know; maybe I'm just coming in from all sides.

The difference between the gospel records and the recent stuff seems to be that earlier you were laying down the law.

Every so often you have to have the law laid down so that you know what the law is. Then you can do whatever you please with it. I haven't heard those albums in quite a while; you're probably right.

You have said recently that you didn't think rock & roll still existed in its pure form, that it was no longer viable. Would you put yourself in with that?

I don't think I put myself in that category. I'm not coming up anymore, you know what I mean? I probably was speaking about the industry itself. I listen to it but mostly I don't pay much attention to modern music. It's everywhere, in places that maybe it shouldn't be. There comes a time to shut off the radio, there's a time to turn off the tube, but the way it's projected into society there's not much of a chance that you can get to do that. There are very few people I know who play the real old-style music. When it first appeared, as I remember it, it was an escape from everything that was going on, which was mainly lies, so when music came it was a direction to pull you in that was out of this myth. But now nobody wants to get pulled out of the myth because they don't recognize it as being a myth. That's what it's like here anyway. They like where they're at, they like what's going on, and music is just an extension of that, so they like it, too. It's nothing different, it doesn't pull you anywhere.

So what's the solution?

Turn it off. It's a decision people have to make. That's what the sixties and the fifties were all about. There are other ways to operate, to survive. There's got to be some type of light, some type of brightness outside of everything that you're given on a mass consumer level. What I can see is the mass monster. I don't know what it's like in Australia, but in America it's everywhere. It's invaded your home, your bed, it's in your closet. It's come real close to kicking over life itself. Unless you're able to go into the woods, the back country, and even there it reaches you. It seems to want to make everybody the same. People who are different are looked at as being a little bit crazy or a little bit odd. It's hard to stand outside of all that and remain sane. Even outrageousness gets to be in fashion. Anything you can think of to do, someone is going to come along and market it. I think it's going to change. I don't think it can stay like this forever, that's for sure. I think it's going to change but for the moment it's hard to find anything that's really hot.

'Empire Burlesque' seems a very straightforward record by comparison with some of your earlier work. Is simplicity something you are striving for?

I strive for something that feels right to me. It could be a lot of different kinds of moods and phrasings, or lines that might not seem to be too connected at the time with the music. They're all connected. A lot of times people will take the music out of my lyrics and just read them as lyrics. That's not really fair because the music and the lyrics I've always felt are pretty closely wrapped up. You can't separate one from the other that simply. A lot of time the meaning is more in the way a line is sung, and not just in the line.

These last few years have been very prolific for you.

Yeah, I've been trying to find different things that are offshoots of the things I would normally do. I feel like something might open up in the next couple of months in different areas. There's a bunch of songs I want to write that I haven't been able to get close to. I almost know what they are but the information that I need is not really available to me so I have to go out and get it and I haven't done that. I expected to have a little more of that on *Empire Burlesque* but I just didn't do it. They are the true story type things, real things that have happened that I would like to comment on. I need to talk to the people involved but I haven't followed through yet. I hope to have some of that stuff on the next album I do.

Were you pleased with the way 'Empire Burlesque' turned out?

Yes, for what it was I thought it was really good. I think the next record is going to sound even better. I'm not too experienced at having records sound good. I don't know how to go about doing that, though I thought I got pretty close last time with Arthur Baker. I think next time, working with Dave Stewart here, the stuff we're doing has been happening a lot easier, quicker, so I think it's going to sound a lot more together than the last record.

You recorded that album yourself and gave it to Arthur Baker to mix?

Pretty much so. I just went out and recorded a bunch of stuff all over the place and then when it was time to put this record together I brought it all to him and he made it sound like a record. Usually I stay out of that side of the finished record.

Why?

I'm not good at it. There are guys that don't mind sitting in the control booth for days and days. I'm just not like that; I'm a one-mix man. I can't tell the difference after that.

Your music often seems to get ignored as compared with the emphasis that's placed on the lyrics, but there have been some really nice instrumental passages like "Pat Garrett and Billy the Kid," for example.

Yes, I just did a bunch of tracks with Dave Stewart that have no lyrics, and you don't even miss the lyrics, really. They're just different chord patterns that make up a melody. My records usually don't have a lot of guitar solos or anything like that on them. The vocals mean a lot and the rhythm means a lot, that's about it.

Your voice seems to have changed a lot over the years.

Maybe it has, I don't know.

It sounded different to me, particularly after 'Street-Legal' when you started using girl singers.

I'm not aware of any significant difference, really. I've always heard that sound [female backing] with my music. I just hear it in there, it's just like another way of putting horns in. That sound has always been one of my favorites, just that vocal part, because I don't do anything with solo-type work—it's all part of the overall effect, it's more just playing the song and getting the structure of it right. The vocal parts are like another instrument but not a solo instrument. Apart from that, I just like the gospel sound.

Seeing the latest videos and the "We Are the World" video, you seem to have less of the legend around your neck, you seem freed of the burden of being Bob Dylan.

I don't think I ever carried that around except for 1974, when I did that tour with the Band. That was pretty much of a heavy tour because of the notoriety and the legendary quality of the people involved. I had to step into Bob Dylan's shoes for that tour. Since that time, I never thought about it. I wouldn't do half the things I do if I was thinking about having to live up to a Bob Dylan myth.

Do you feel that you've been guided to where you are?

You're always guided to where you are, but you have the choice to mess it up. Sooner or later everything that goes around comes around. So, yeah, I feel like I've been guided to wherever it is I'm at right now, but I don't know whatever it is I'm supposed to be doing. I might have something else to do. I can't figure out what it would be, though, because I like doing what I do. Who's to say? There's a lot of luck involved, a lot of circumstance. You can't do anything alone, though. You've always got to have somebody supporting you or nobody would get anywhere.

Do you think that with time comes wisdom?

With experience. Things don't really change, just attitudes.

You've been doing videos with Dave Stewart. What do you think of the video age?

I don't think much about it at all. It's not going to go away. Everyplace you look, you're drowning in it. You can't turn on your TV without seeing music videos. It's like the unions. Unions in the early thirties were all communist organizations and now they're big business.

It's got to the point where everybody seems to be using rock & roll for their own ends. In America, you have politicians associating themselves with rock & roll songs.

Absurd, isn't it? The rock & roll songs they're quoting from don't deserve to be quoted from like that. You couldn't do that with the early stuff, Little Richard and Chuck Berry—what politician is going to quote Chuck Berry? Who's going to quote Carl Perkins or Gene Vincent or any of those guys? It was outside then.

Today it's image rather than content. People hold up an image of a star and hope to attach themselves to that image.

That's absolutely correct. It's destroying the fabric of our minds and all we can do is complain about it, so we just have to shut it out. You just have to cut it off and not let it get into your framework, because that's the only way you're going to escape it. You can't meet it head on. You've probably got a little more space to breathe over there, but here it's heavy.

There's not many places you can go where you're not reminded of the current cultural ambitions of people who are on their way to be stars.

When you started out you must have wanted to be a star in some way?

I wanted to be a star in my own mind, I wanted to be my own star. I didn't want to be a star for people I didn't really identify with. For me, what I did was a way of life, it wasn't an occupation.

Has it been all it was cracked up to be?

Yes and no. I'm still doing it, you know. It seems to be what I've done more years than I haven't done it, but I'm just going to keep on doing it till it runs out. Yes, it was all it was cracked up to be, because I never strayed from it. Maybe I would've gone down if I'd gone into being a movie star or if I'd started believing what other people said of me or if I'd started to think I was this person that everybody was talking about. I know there are a lot of people that did go down. They started believing what the newspapers said about them. I never believed it one way or another, so for me, I don't really feel much of a change. I feel very little change between now and ten years ago, twenty years ago. I don't feel like I've traveled that far or done that much.

You mentioned the unions earlier and I was thinking of the song "Union Sundown," on 'Infidels,' which is a very specific commentary. Do you still feel a need to make that type of comment?

Oh, yes, that comes with the territory.

There seems to be two types of songs you've written, those which are here and now, and a lot that seem to focus on the eternals.

Well, that's the important thing, if you lose that, you start getting into stuff that is mindless and meaningless. Usually there's a voice that goes on, there's some kind of warning point if that ever happens, but mostly what this kind of music is about is your ability to feel things. There's a lot of stuff going on that you hear that you know nobody felt nothing about; you can hear it in the spirit. So much stuff gets thrown at you with no feeling behind it because nobody feels anything anymore. But there are a lot of good things going on that I don't understand. A lot of music that's coming out is way beyond me. There are some people who are really gifted musicians, I mean in a classical sense, and they're coming out with a lot of different stuff that is being thought out and preplanned.

There does seem to be an attempt by people, like Miami Steve on the "Sun City" record, to say things about apartheid and about what is happening in America today.

Yes, he's highly committed to that.

It seems like a very difficult struggle.

Well, it is a very difficult struggle, because most people don't want to hear that.

There's a lot of red-baiting going on again.

That's been going on since the fifties.

The cold war seems to be coming back.

I don't think it ever went away, you know. It just lays low for a while. People need something to hate, you've got to hate something. As soon as you're old enough, people try to make you hate something or somebody. Blacks are a little easier, communists you can't really see. The early Christians were like communists. The Roman Empire treated the early Christians the same way as the Western world treats the communists.

So it doesn't really change?

No, things don't, it's just got a different name on it. There's always someone you're told you've got to step on so you can rise up a little higher.

Your kids are grown up now. What's the perspective like as a father?

It gives you a perspective on what kids are doing. I don't think kids are any different from what they ever were, really. It's like my daddy once said, when he was twelve years old he asked his dad something and he didn't think his dad knew too much about what he was talking about. When he got to twenty-five, he asked him the same question and he got the same answer and he was amazed how his father got to be so smart.

24. Interview with Mikal Gilmore, ROLLING STONE

JULY 17, 1986

"Subterranean," declares Bob Dylan, smiling with delight. It is just past midnight, and Dylan is standing in the middle of a crowded, smoke-laden recording studio tucked deep into the remote reaches of Topanga Canyon. He is wearing brown-tinted sunglasses, a sleeveless white T-shirt, black vest, black jeans, frayed black motorcycle boots and fingerless black motorcycle gloves, and he puffs hard at a Kool while bobbing his head rhythmically to the colossal blues shuffle that is thundering from the speakers above his head. Sitting on a sofa a few feet away, also nodding their heads in rapt pleasure, are T-Bone Burnett and Al Kooper—old friends and occasional sidemen of Dylan. Several other musicians—including Los Lobos guitarist Cesar Rosas, R&B saxophonist Steve Douglas and bassist James Jamerson Jr., the son of the legendary Motown bass player—fill out the edges of the room. Like everyone else, they are smiling at this music: romping, bawdy, jolting rock & roll—the sort of indomitable music a man might conjure if he were about to lay claim to something big.

The guitars crackle, the horns honk and wail, the drums and bass rumble and clamor wildly, and then the room returns to silence. T-Bone Burnett, turning to Kooper, seems to voice a collective sentiment. "Man," he says, "that *gets* it."

"Yeah," says Kooper. "So *dirty*."

Everyone watches Dylan expectantly. For a moment he appears to be in some distant, private place. "Subterranean," is all he says, still smiling. "Posi*tiv*ely subterranean," he adds, running his hand through his mazy brown hair, chuckling. Then he walks into an adjoining room, straps on his weatherworn Fender guitar, tears off a quick, bristling blues lick and says, "Okay, who wants to play lead on this? I broke a string."

Dylan has been like this all week, turning out spur-of-the-moment, blues-infused rock & roll with a startling force and imagination, piling up instrumental tracks so fast that the dazed, bleary-eyed engineers who are monitoring the sessions are having trouble cataloging all the various takes—so far, well over twenty songs, including gritty R&B, Chicago-steeped blues, rambunctious gospel and raw-toned hillbilly forms. In part, Dylan is working fast merely as a practical matter: rehearsals for his American tour with Tom Petty and the Heartbreakers start in only a couple of weeks, and though it hardly seems possible in this overmeticulous, high-tech recording era, he figures he can write, record, mix and package a new studio LP in that allotted term. "You see, I spend too much time working out the *sound* of my records these days," he had told me earlier. "And if the records I'm making only sell a certain amount anyway, then why should I take so long putting them together? . . . I've got a lot of different records inside me, and it's time just to start getting them *out*."

Apparently this is not idle talk. Dylan has started perusing songs for a possible collection of new and standard folk songs and has also begun work on a set of Tin Pan Alley covers—which, it seems safe to predict, will be something to hear. At the moment, though, as Dylan leads the assembled band through yet another roadhouse-style blues number, a different ambition seems to possess him. This is Bob Dylan the rock & roller, and despite all the vagaries of his career, it is still an impressive thing to witness. He leans lustily into the song's momentum at the same instant that he invents its structure, pumping his rhythm guitar with tough, unexpected accents, much like Chuck Berry or Keith Richards, and in the process, prodding his other guitarists, Kooper and Rosas, to tangle and burn, like good-natured rivals. It isn't until moments later, as everybody gathers back into the booth to listen to the playback, that it's clear that this music sounds surprisingly like the riotous, dense music of *Highway 61 Revisited*—music that seems as menacing as it does joyful, and that, in any event, seems to erupt from an ungovernable imagination. Subterranean, indeed.

—

It was with rock & roll remarkably like this that, more than twenty years ago, Bob Dylan permanently and sweepingly altered the possibilities of both folk music and the pop-song form. In that epoch, the reach of his influence seemed so pervasive, his stance so powerful and mysterious, that he was virtually changing the language and aspirations of popular culture with his every work and gesture. But Dylan barely got started in rock & roll before he got stopped. In the spring of 1966, he was recording *Blonde on Blonde* and playing fiery, controversial electric concerts with his backing band, the Hawks (later renamed the Band); a few months later, he was nearly killed in a motorcycle accident and withdrew from recording and performing for nearly a year and a half.

For many, his music never seemed quite the same after that, and although much of it proved bold and lovely, for about twenty years now Bob Dylan hasn't produced much music that transfigures either pop style or youth culture. To some former fans, that lapse has seemed almost unforgivable. Consequently, Dylan has found himself in a dilemma shared by no other rock figure of his era: he has been sidestepped by the pop world he helped transform, at a time when contemporaries like the Rolling Stones attract a more enthusiastic audience than ever before. This must hurt an artist as scrupulous as Dylan, who, for whatever his lapses, has remained pretty true to both his moral and musical ideals.

In the last couple of years, though, there have been signs that some kind of reclamation might be in the offing. For one thing, there's been his participation in the pop world's recent spate of social and political activism, including his involvement in the USA for Africa and Artists United Against Apartheid projects and his appearance at the Live Aid and Farm Aid programs (the latter, an event inspired by an off-the-cuff remark Dylan had made at Live Aid). More important, there were intriguing indications in 1983's *Infidels* and 1985's *Empire Burlesque* that the singer seemed interested in working his way back into the concerns of the real-life modern world—in fact, that he may even be interested in fashioning music that once more engages a pop-wise audience. And, as demonstrated by the strong response to his recent tour of Australia and Japan, as well as to his summer tour of America, there is still an audience willing to be engaged.

Of course, Dylan has his own views about all this talk of decline and renewal. A little later in the evening at the Topanga studio, while various musicians are working on overdubs, he sits in a quiet office, fiddling with one of his ever-present cigarettes and taking occasional sips from a plastic cup filled with white wine. We are discussing a column that appeared in the April issue of *Artforum*, by critic Greil Marcus. Marcus has covered Dylan frequently over the years (he penned the liner notes for the 1975 release of *The Basement Tapes*), but he has been less than compelled by the artist's recent output. Commenting on Dylan's career, and about the recent five-LP retrospective of Dylan's music, *Biograph*, Marcus wrote: "Dylan actually did something between 1963 and 1968, and . . . what he did then created a standard against which everything he has putatively done since can be measured. . . . The fact that the 1964 'It Ain't Me, Babe' can be placed on an album next to the 1974 'You Angel You' is a denial of everyone's best hopes."

Dylan seems intrigued by Marcus's comments, but also amused. "Well, he's right and he's wrong," he says. "I did that accidentally. That was all accidental, as every age is. You're doing something, you don't know what it is, you're just doing it. And later on you'll look at it and . . ." His words trail off, then he begins again. "To me, I don't have a 'career.' . . . A career is something you can look back on, and I'm not ready to look back. Time doesn't really exist for me in those kinds of terms. I don't really remember in any monumental way 'what I have done.' This isn't my career, this is my life, and it's still vital to me."

He removes his sunglasses and rubs at his eyes. "I feel like I really don't want to prove any points," he continues. "I just want to do whatever it is I do. These lyrical things that come off in a unique or a desolate sort of way, I don't know. I don't feel I have to put that out anymore to please anybody. Besides, anything you want to do for posterity's sake, you can just sing into a tape recorder and give it to your mother, you know?"

Dylan laughs at his last remark. "See," he says, "somebody once told me—and I don't remember who it was or even where it was—but they said, 'Never give a hundred percent.' My thing has always been just getting by on whatever I've been getting by on. That applies to that time, too, that time in the Sixties. It never really occurred to me that I had to do it for any kind of motive except that I just felt like I wanted to do it. As things worked, I mean, I could never have predicted it."

I tell him it's hard to believe he wasn't giving a hundred percent on *Highway 61 Revisited* or *Blonde on Blonde*.

He flashes a sly grin and shrugs. "Well, maybe I was. But there's something at the back of your mind that says, 'I'm not giving you a hundred percent. I'm not giving *anybody* a hundred percent. I'm gonna give you this much, and this much is gonna have to do. I'm good at what I do. I can afford to give you this much and still be as good as, if not better than, the guy over across the street.' I'm not gonna give it all—I'm not Judy Garland, who's gonna die onstage in front of a thousand clowns. If we've learned anything, we should have learned that."

A moment later an engineer is standing in the doorway, telling Dylan the overdubs are done. "This is all gonna pass," Dylan says before getting up to go back into the studio. "All these people who say whatever it is I'm supposed to be doing—that's all gonna pass, because, obviously, I'm not gonna be around forever. That day's gonna come when there aren't gonna be any more records, and then people won't be able to say, 'Well *this* one's not as good as the last one.' They're gonna have to look at it all. And I don't know what the picture will be, what people's judgment will be at that time. I can't help you in that area."

"Everyone's always saying to me, 'What's Bob Dylan *like?*' " says Tom Petty a few nights later, seated in the tiny lounge area of a Van Nuys recording studio. Petty and his band, the Heartbreakers, have gathered here to work out material for a forthcoming album and also to help supervise the sound mix for *Bob Dylan in Concert*, the HBO special documenting their recent tour of Australia with Dylan. "It's funny," Petty continues, "but people still attach a lot of mystery to Bob. . . . I think they figure that, since we've spent time around him, we can *explain* him, as if he's somebody who needs to be explained."

Petty shakes his head. "I mean, Dylan's just a guy like anybody else—except he's a guy who has something to say. And he has a personality that makes it his own. There's not many people that can walk into a room of 20,000, stare at them and get their attention. That's not an easy trick."

Petty may be a little too modest to admit it, but Dylan also has something else going for him these days. A good part of the excitement over Dylan's current U.S. tour owes to the singer's alliance with a band as rousing as the Heartbreakers—a band more given to propulsive rock & roll than any group Dylan has worked with in over a decade. Judging from the HBO special, the Heartbreakers can render the *Highway 61* sound—that unmistakable mix of fiery keyboards and stray-cat guitars—with a convincing flair. Yet rather than simply replicate the sound, the group reinvigorates it and applies it evenly to a broad range of Dylan's music, helping bring a new coherence to his sprawling body of styles. As a result, many of Dylan's more recent songs—such as "When the Night Comes Falling from the Sky" and "Lenny Bruce"—come across in concert with an uncommon force and conviction, perhaps even a bit more force than some of the older songs.

But Dylan isn't the only one whose music has benefited from this association. Ever since the end of the Australasian tour, Petty and the Heartbreakers seem to be on an inspired streak, cranking out blues-tempered rock and pop songs in the same impromptu fashion that Dylan so often employs. It isn't so much that the group's new music resembles Dylan's (actually, it suggests nothing so much as the reckless blues of *Exile on Main Street*), but rather that it seems born of the same freewheeling intensity and instinctive ferocity that has marked Dylan's most ambitious efforts.

But there is something more to it—something that belongs only to Petty and the Heartbreakers. I have seen this band on numerous occasions, both in the studio and onstage, and though they've always seemed adept and exciting, they've never struck me as particularly inspired improvisers, in the way, say, that the Rolling Stones or the E Street Band can seem. Now, here they are, jamming with unqualified verve, playing not only head to head but also heart to heart and, in the process, creating what is probably their most inspiring music to date.

"We've never done anything like this before," says Petty, fishing a pack of cigarettes from his shirt pocket. "It's not like we're even thinking we're making a record. . . . Yet here we are with enough for a double album."

Petty plants a cigarette between his lips, lights it and settles back into the sofa. "Tonight was a good night," he continues. "In fact, this has been a good time for us in general. I think we feel pretty glad to be together."

Though nobody likes to admit it, following the 1982 release of *Long After Dark*, the Heartbreakers more or less dissolved. Petty withdrew into his home, where he was building a state-of-the-art studio and anticipating a solo project; drummer Stan Lynch joined T-Bone Burnett's band for a brief tour; keyboardist Benmont Tench played onstage and in the studio with Lone Justice; guitarist Mike Campbell began experimenting with some new aural textures on a twenty-four-track machine in his basement, where he would eventually compose "The Boys of Summer" for Don Henley; and bassist Howie Epstein did some session work and began assembling material for a possible record of his own.

"It was reaching a point," says Campbell, "where everybody was getting a bit stale with each other, inspirationwise. We just weren't committed as a band." Adds Stan Lynch, "It's like we all faced this ultimate question: If I'm not doing what I do now, what would I do? That's a horrible thing, but we all faced it and realized we wouldn't roll over and die if we lost this gig."

Then, in 1984, inspired by some conversations with Robbie Robertson, Petty came up with an idea that couldn't be realized without the band's contribution. He wanted to make an album about the modern American South—the common homeland that most of the group's members had emerged from but had never quite forgotten. "I'd seen these people I'd grown up around struggling with that experience," Petty had said in an earlier conversation, "with all the things about that legacy they couldn't shake free of, and I think that was tearing at me." The result was *Southern Accents*—a work that examined the conflict between old ways and new ideals and that also aimed to broaden and update the band's musical scope. Though some band members now feel that the record was a bit overworked, they all credit it as a reconciliatory experience. "They've been real supportive of me through this record," Petty says. "I think in the last album we were in a lot of different camps. . . . Now they laugh about *Southern Accents* and its sitars. They had to let me get this out of my system."

Then along came Bob Dylan. He had already employed Tench on *Shot of Love*, and Tench, Campbell and Epstein on *Empire Burlesque*, and was now looking for an electric band to support him at Farm Aid. When Neil Young, one of the event's organizers, mentioned that Petty and the Heartbreakers had also committed themselves to the show, Dylan decided to ask the group to accompany him. "He called me," says Petty, "and I said, 'Yeah, come over,' and shit, we had a great time. We rehearsed about a week, playing maybe a million different songs. That was one of the best times I ever had. We were blazing. So we went off to Farm Aid and had a great night: the Heartbreakers had a good set and Bob had a good set. But it was over too quick."

Well, not quite. Dylan had been considering offers for a possible Australian tour, but was reluctant to assemble a makeshift band. Plus, the Heartbreakers had just finished their own tour and were firming up their schedules for February. "The next thing I knew," says Petty, "we were doing the Australian tour, and we *wanted* to do it."

According to some reviews, the tour got off to a shaky start in New Zealand, where the opening-night audiences responded more fervently to Petty's set than Dylan's. But within a few shows, Dylan was storming into such songs as "Clean Cut Kid," "Positively 4th Street," "Rainy Day Women" and "Like a Rolling Stone," often facing off with Campbell and Petty in fierce three-way guitar exchanges and launching suddenly into songs that nobody had rehearsed, and that some band members hardly knew. "One night," recalls Tench, "Dylan turns around and goes, ' "Just Like Tom Thumb's Blues." ' We'd never played it. . . . At times that tour sounded like some bizarre mix of the Stooges and Van Morrison."

"There's nothing tentative about Dylan onstage," adds Lynch. "I've seen gigs where the songs have ended in all the wrong places, where it's fallen apart, and it's almost as if, in some perverse way, he gets energy from that chaos."

Dylan can also seem daunting in other ways. "He has more presence than anyone I've ever met," says Mike Campbell. "But when you're working together, you sort of forget about that. Then all of a sudden it will hit you. I mean, I can remember when I was in junior high school: I was in a diner eating a hamburger, and 'Like a Rolling Stone' came on. I got so excited by the song and the lyric, I thought, 'There's somebody singing and writing for me.' I went out and got a guitar. I'd forgotten about that until one night in Australia, and I realized, 'This is the first song I ever learned on the guitar, and here I am *playing* it with the person who wrote it.' "

Dylan was also the object of much intense feeling in Australia. "I pretty much saw it all," says Lynch. "I saw the girl who slept in the elevator claiming to be his sister from Minnesota; I saw the one who claimed to be his *masseuse* who flew in from Perth and was riding up and down the elevator trying to figure out what floor he was on. I also saw the people that were genuinely moved, who felt they had to make some connection with him, that this was an important thing in their life. They wanted to be near him and tell him they're all right, because they probably feel that Bob was telling them that it was going to be all right when they *weren't* all right, as if Bob *knew* they weren't doing so well at the time.

"They forget one important thing: Bob doesn't know them; they just know him. But that's all right. That's not shortsightedness on their part. That's just the essence of what people do when you talk to them at a vulnerable time in their lives. It doesn't matter that he was talking to them by way of a record; he was still talking to them."

Two weeks later, Bob Dylan sits on a dogeared sofa in the Van Nuys studio where Petty is working, sipping at a plastic cup full of whiskey and water. He blows a curt puff of smoke and broods over it. His weary air reminds me of something he'd said earlier: "Man, sometimes it seems I've spent half my life in a recording studio. . . . It's like living in a coal mine."

Dylan and Petty have been holed up in this room the better part of the night, working on a track called "Got My Mind Made Up," which they have co-written for Dylan's album. By all appearances, it's been a productive session: the tune is a walloping, Bo Diddley–like raveup with Delta blues–style slide guitar, and Dylan has been hurling himself into the vocal with a genuinely staggering force. Yet there's also a note of tension about the evening. The pressure of completing the album has reportedly been wearing on Dylan, and his mood is said to have been rather dour and unpredictable these last several days. In fact, somewhere along the line he has decided to put aside most of the rock & roll tracks he had been working on in Topanga, and is apparently now assembling the album from various sessions that have accrued over the last year. "It's all sorts of stuff," he says. "It doesn't really have a theme or a purpose."

While waiting for his backup singers to arrive, Dylan tries to warm up to the task of the evening's interview. But in contrast to his manner in our earlier conversation, he seems somewhat distracted, almost edgy, and many questions don't seem to engender much response. After a bit, I ask him if he can tell me something about the lyrical tenor of the songs. "Got My Mind Made Up," for example, includes a reference to Libya. Will this be a record that has something to say about our national mood?

He considers the subject. "The kinds of stuff I write now come out over all the years I've lived," he says, "so I can't say anything is really that current. . . . But you have to go on. You can't keep doing the same old thing all the time."

I try a couple more questions about political matters—about whether he feels any kinship with the new activism in pop music—but he looks exhausted at the possibility of seriously discussing the topic. "I'm opposed to whatever oppresses people's intelligence," he says. "We all have to be against that sort of thing, or else we have nowhere to go. But that's not a fight for one man, that's everybody's fight."

Over the course of our interviews, I've learned you can't budge him on a subject if he's not in the mood, so I move on. We chat a while, but nothing much seems to engage him until I ask if he's pleased by the way the American public is responding to the upcoming tour. Demand has been so intense that the itinerary has been increased from twenty-six to forty shows, with more dates likely. In the end, it's estimated that he'll play to a million people.

"People forget it," he says, "but since 1974, I've never stopped working. I've been out on tours where there hasn't been *any* publicity. So for me, I'm not getting caught up in all this excitement of a big tour. I've played big tours and I've played small tours. I mean, what's such a big deal about this one?"

Well, it *is* his first cross-country tour of America in eight years.

"Yeah, but to me, an audience is an audience, no matter where they are. I'm not particularly into this *American* thing, this Bruce Springsteen–John Cougar–'America first' thing. I feel just as strongly about the American principles as those guys do, but I personally feel that what's important is more eternal things. This American pride thing, that don't mean nothing to me. I'm more locked into what's real forever."

Quickly, Dylan seems animated. He douses one cigarette, lights another and begins speaking at a faster clip. "Listen," he says, "I'm not saying anything bad about these guys, because I think Bruce has done a tremendous amount for real gutbucket rock & roll—and folk music, in his own way. And John Cougar's great, though the best thing on his record, I thought, was his grandmother singing. That knocked me out. But that ain't what music's about. Subjects like 'How come we don't have our jobs?' Then you're getting political. And if you want to get political, you ought to go as far out as you can."

But certainly he understands that Springsteen and Mellencamp aren't exactly trying to fan the flames of American pride. Instead, they're trying to say that if the nation loses sight of certain principles, it also forfeits its claim to greatness.

"Yeah? What are those principles? Are they Biblical principles? The only principles you can find are the principles in the Bible. I mean, Proverbs has got them all."

They are such principles, I say, as justice and equality.

"Yeah, but . . ." Dylan pauses. As we've been talking, others—including Petty, Mike Campbell, the sound engineers and the backup singers—have entered the room. Dylan stands up and starts pacing back and forth, smiling. It's hard to tell whether he is truly irked or merely spouting provocatively for the fun of it. After a moment, he continues. "To me, America means the Indians. They were here and this is their country and *all* the white men are just trespassing. We've devastated the natural resources of this country, for no particular reason except to make money and buy houses and send our kids to college and shit like that. To me, America is the Indians, period. I just don't go for nothing more, Unions, movies, Greta Garbo, Wall Street, Tin Pan Alley or Dodgers baseball games." He laughs. "It don't mean shit. What we did to the Indians is disgraceful. I think America, to get right, has got to start there first."

I reply that a more realistic way of getting right might be to follow the warning of one of his own songs, "Clean Cut Kid," and not send our young people off to fight another wasteful war.

"Who sends the young people out to war?" says Dylan. "Their parents do."

But it isn't the parents who suited them up and put them on planes and sent them off to die in Vietnam.

"Look, the parents could have said, 'Hey, we'll talk about it.' But parents aren't into that. They don't know how to deal with what they should do or shouldn't do. So they leave it to the government."

Suddenly, loudly, music blares up in the room. Perhaps somebody—maybe Petty—figures the conversation is getting a little too tense. Dylan smiles and shrugs, then pats me on the shoulder. "We can talk a little more later," he says.

For the next couple of hours, Dylan and Petty attend to detail work on the track—getting the right accent on a ride cymbal and overdubbing the gospel-derived harmonies of the four female singers who have just arrived. As always, it is fascinating to observe how acutely musical Dylan is. In one particularly inspired off-hand moment, he leads the four singers—Queen Esther Morrow, Elisecia Wright, Madelyn Quebec and Carol Dennis—through a lovely a cappella version of "White Christmas," then moves into a haunting reading of an old gospel standard, "Evening Sun." Petty and the rest of us just stare, stunned. "Man," says Petty frantically, "we've *got* to get this on tape."

Afterward, Dylan leads me out into the lounge area to talk some more. He leans on top of a pinball machine, a cigarette nipped between his teeth. He seems calmer, happy with the night's work. He also seems willing to finish the conversation we were having earlier, so we pick up where we left off. What would he do, I ask, if his own sons were drafted?

Dylan looks almost sad as he considers the question. After several moments, he says, "They could do what their conscience tells them to do, and I would support them. But it also depends on what the government wants your children to do. I mean, if the government wants your children to go down and raid Central American countries, there would be no moral value in that. I also don't think we should have bombed those people in Libya." Then he flashes one of those utterly guileless, disarming smiles of his as our talk winds down. "But what I want to know," he says, "is, what's all this got to do with folk music and rock & roll?"

Quite a bit, since he, more than any other artist, raised the possibility that folk music and rock & roll could have political impact. "Right," said Dylan, "and I'm proud of that."

And the reason questions like these keep coming up is because many of us aren't so sure where he stands these days—in fact, some critics have charged that, with songs like "Slow Train" and "Union Sundown," he's even moved a bit to the right.

Dylan muses over the remark in silence for a moment. "Well, for me," he begins, "there is no right and there is no left. There's truth and there's untruth, y'know? There's honesty and there's hypocrisy. Look in the Bible, you don't see nothing about right or left. Other people might have other ideas about things, but I don't, because I'm not that smart. I hate to keep beating people over the head with the Bible, but that's the only instrument I know, the only thing that stays true."

Does it disturb him that there seem to be so many preachers these days who claim that to be a good Christian one must also be a political conservative?

"Conservative? Well, don't forget, Jesus said that it's harder for a rich man to enter the kingdom of heaven than it is for a camel to enter the eye of a needle. I mean is *that* conservative? I don't know, I've heard a lot of preachers say how God wants everybody to be wealthy and healthy. Well, it doesn't say that in the Bible. You can twist anybody's words, but that's only for fools and people who follow fools. If you're entangled in the snares of this world, which everybody is . . ."

Petty comes into the room and asks Dylan to come hear the final overdubs. Dylan likes what he hears, then decides to take one more pass at the lead vocal. This time, apparently, he nails it. "Don't ever try to change me/I been in this thing too long/There's nothing you can say or do/To make me think I'm wrong," he snarls at the song's outset, and while it is hardly the most inviting line one has ever heard him sing, tonight he seems to render it with a fitting passion.

It is midnight in Hollywood, and Bob Dylan, Tom Petty and the Heartbreakers are clustered in a cavernous room at the old Zoetrope Studios, working out a harmonica part to "License to Kill," when Dylan suddenly begins playing a different, oddly haunting piece of music. Gradually, the random tones he is blowing begin to take a familiar shape and it becomes evident that he's playing a plaintive, bluesy variation of "I Dreamed I Saw St. Augustine." Benmont Tench is the first to recognize the melody, and quickly embellishes it with a graceful piano part; Petty catches the drift and underscores Dylan's harmonica with some strong, sharp chord strokes. Soon, the entire band, which tonight includes guitarist Al Kooper, is seizing Dylan's urge and transforming the song into a full and passionate performance. Dylan never sings the lyrics himself but instead signals a backup singer to take the lead and immediately "I Dreamed I Saw St. Augustine" becomes a full-fledged, driving spiritual.

Five minutes later, the moment has passed. According to Petty and Tench, Dylan's rehearsals are often like this: inventive versions of wondrous songs come and go and are never heard again, except in those rare times when they may be conjured onstage. In a way, an instance like this leaves one wishing that every show in the current True Confessions Tour were simply another rehearsal: Dylan's impulses are so sure-handed and imaginative, they're practically matchless.

Trying to get Dylan to talk about where such moments come from—or trying to persuade him to take them to the stage—is, as one might expect, not that easy. "I'm not sure if people really want to hear that sort of thing from me," he says, smiling ingenuously. Then he perches himself on an equipment case and puts his hands into his pockets, looking momentarily uncomfortable. Quickly, his face brightens. "Hey," he says, pulling a tape from his pocket, "wanna hear the best album of the year?" He holds a cassette of *AKA Grafitti Man*, an album by poet John Trudell and guitarist Jesse Ed Davis. "Only people like Lou Reed and John Doe can dream about work like this. Most don't have enough talent."

Dylan has his sound engineer cue the tape to a song about Elvis Presley. It is a long, stirring track about the threat that so many originally perceived in Presley's manner and the promise so many others discovered in his music. "We heard Elvis's song for the first time/Then we made up our own mind," recites Trudell at one point, followed by a lovely, blue guitar solo from Davis that quotes "Love Me Tender." Dylan grins at the line, then shakes his head with delight. "Man," he says, "that's about all anybody ever needs to say about Elvis Presley."

I wonder if Dylan realizes that the line could also have been written about him—that millions of us heard his songs, and that those songs not only inspired our own but, in some deep-felt place, almost seemed to *be* our own. But before there is even time to raise the question, Dylan has put on his coat and is on his way across the room.

"I'm thinking about calling this album *Knocked Out Loaded*," Bob Dylan says. He repeats the phrase once, then chuckles over it. "Is that any good, you think, *Knocked Out Loaded?*"

Dylan and a recording engineer are seated at a mixing board at the Topanga recording studio, poring over a list of song titles and talking about possible sequences. Dylan seems downright affable, more relaxed than earlier in the week. Apparently, the album has fallen into place with sudden ease. In the last few days, he has narrowed the record's selections down to a possible nine or ten songs, and tonight he is polishing two of those tracks and attempting a final mix on a couple of others.

So far, it all sounds pretty good—not exactly the back-snapping rock & roll I'd heard a few weeks earlier but, in a way, something no less bold. Then Dylan plays one more track, "Brownsville Girl," a piece he wrote last year with playwright Sam Shepard. A long, storylike song, it begins with a half-drawled, half-sung remembrance about a fateful scene from a western the singer had once seen, then opens up from there into two or three intersecting, dreamlike tales about pursued love and forsaken love, about fading heroes and forfeited ideals—about hope and death. It's hard to tell where Dylan ends and Shepard begins in the lyrics, but it is quite easy to hear whom the song really belongs to. In fact, I've only known of one man who could put across a performance as exhilarating as this one, and he is sitting there right in front of me, concentrating hard on the tale, as if he too were hearing its wondrous involutions for the first time. If this is the way Bob Dylan is going to age as a songwriter, I decide, I'm happy to age with him.

Twelve minutes later, the song closes with a glorious, explosive chorus. I don't know exactly what to say, so Dylan picks up the slack. He lights a cigarette, moves over to the sofa, takes off his glasses and smiles a shy smile. "You know," he says, "sometimes I think about people like T-Bone Walker, John Lee Hooker, Muddy Waters—these people who played into their sixties. If I'm here at eighty, I'll be doing the same thing. This is all I want to do—it's all I *can* do. I mean, you don't have to be a nineteen- or twenty-year-old to play this stuff. That's the vanity of that youth-culture ideal. To me that's never been the thing. I've never really aimed myself at any so-called youth culture. I directed it at people who I imagined, maybe falsely so, had the same experiences that I've had, who have kind of been through what I'd been through. But I guess a lot of people just haven't."

He falls silent for a moment, taking a drag off his cigarette. "See," he says, "I've always been just about being an individual, with an individual point of view. If I've been anything, it's probably that, and to let some people know that it's possible to do the impossible."

Dylan leans forward and snuffs out his cigarette. "And that's really all. If I've ever had anything to tell anybody, it's that: You can do the impossible. *Anything* is possible. And that's it. No more."

25. A Short Life of Trouble by Sam Shepard, Esquire

1987

Scene: In the dark, a Jimmy Yancey piano solo is heard very softly, floating in the background. Soft, blue, foggy light creeps in, extreme upstage, revealing a large, weathered brick patio bordered by shaggy grass upstage and opening out to a distant view of the Pacific Ocean. The distant rhythmic splashing of waves is heard underneath the piano music and continues throughout the play, always in the background. The only set piece onstage is a round red wood table with a big yellow umbrella stuck in the middle of it and two redwood benches set across from each other at the table. The table and benches are set down left (from the actors' point of view).

As the light keeps rising, a short, skinny guy named Bob is seen center stage dressed in nothing but a pair of light-green boxer shorts. His arms are clasped across his chest with each hand gripping the opposite shoulder, as though warding off the cold. He turns in a slow circle to his right and then repeats the circle to the left, looking out to the ocean as his gaze passes it. He stops, facing audience, covers his face with both hands, then rubs his eyes and draws his hands slowly down his cheeks to his chin. His mouth drops open and his head slowly drops back on his shoulders to stare at the sky. He holds that position. Piano music stops abruptly. Sam, a tall, skinny guy dressed in jeans and a T-shirt, carrying a tape recorder, several notebooks, a six-pack of beer, enters from right. He stops. Bob drops his hands and stares at Sam. Pause. Sound of distant waves continues.

SAM: Ready?

BOB: Yeah, I just gotta make a couple of phone calls first.

[*Bob moves toward stage right, then stops.*]

BOB: Oh, you know where I just was?

SAM: Where?

BOB: Paso Robles. You know, on that highway where James Dean got killed?

SAM: Oh yeah?

BOB: I was there at the spot. On the spot. A windy kinda place.

SAM: They've got a statue or monument to him in that town, don't they?

BOB: Yeah, but I was on the curve where he had the accident. Outsida town. And this place is incredible. I mean the place where he died is as powerful as the place he lived.

SAM: Nebraska?

BOB: Where'd he live?

SAM: He came from the farm, didn't he? Somewhere.

BOB: Yea, Iowa or Indiana. I forget. But this place up there has this kind of aura about it. It's on this kind of broad expanse of land. It's like that place made James Dean who he is. If he hadn't've died there he wouldn't've been James Dean.

SAM: Hm.

[*Bob moves as though to exit stage right again, but stops again.*]

BOB: You know what Elvis said? He said that if James Dean had sang he'd've been Ricky Nelson.

SAM: Is that right?

BOB: Yeah. [*pause*] You need anything?

SAM: Nope.

BOB: You brought some beer?

SAM: Yeah.

BOB: I just gotta make a couple phone calls.

SAM: Good.

[*Bob exits stage right as Sam moves down left toward table. Just as Bob exits, the sound of screeching tires and a loud car crash comes from off right. Sam pays no attention, but goes about setting tape recorder, beer, and notebooks on table. Bob reenters from right but with no reaction to car crash sounds.*]

BOB: Who was playin' that music before?

SAM: What music?

BOB: That piano music.

SAM: I dunno.

BOB: Hm.

SAM: "If James Dean sang he'd've been Ricky Nelson"? Elvis said that?

BOB: Yeah. Poor ol' Ricky. I wish he was here with us today. I wonder if anyone ever told him, when he was alive, how great he was. I mean like the rock-and-roll critics.

SAM: You got me.

BOB: You know, Emilio Fernandez used to shoot the critics that didn't like his movies. At parties.

[*Bob exits stage right. Sam sits on bench facing stage right, pulls out a cassette tape and sticks it in recorder, punches a button, and the same Jimmy Yancey tune is heard coming from the machine itself. Only a snatch is heard before Bob's voice comes from offstage right, speaking on the phone. As soon as Bob's voice is heard, Sam shuts the recorder off and starts leafing through his notebooks, scribbling in them now and then.*]

BOB'S VOICE [*off right*]: Maria? Listen, what's the thing gonna be like tonight? [*pause*] Yeah. There gonna be a lotta people there? [*pause*] Well, that's what I'm tryin' to figure out. [*pause*] Yeah. I don't know. How many people you think there'll be? [*pause*] Okay, well look, I got somebody here so. [*pause*] Yeah, I know. Yeah, well, I seen their act before. Yeah, I seen it. I seen it in St. Louis. Yeah. [*pause*] I dunno—'59 or '60, somethin' like that. [*laughs, pause*] I was around. I been around a long time. I can't count anymore. Okay, look, I'll talk to you later and see what's goin' on. [*pause*] Okay. Bye.

[*Bob hangs up offstage. Sam looks in that direction, then returns to his notebooks, cracks open a can of beer, and drinks.*]

BOB'S VOICE [*off right*]: Sam, what's this thing supposed to be about anyway?

SAM: I dunno.

BOB'S VOICE [*off*]: Are we supposed to have a theme?

SAM: I got a buncha questions here.

BOB'S VOICE [*off*]: You brought questions?

SAM: Yeah.

BOB'S VOICE [*off*]: How many questions?

SAM: Couple.

BOB'S VOICE: What if I don't have the answers?

SAM: Make it up.

BOB'S VOICE: Okay, so ask me a question.

SAM: [*quickly putting a cassette in recorder*] Okay, wait a second. I gotta see if this thing is working.

BOB'S VOICE: You got a tape?

SAM: [*punching* RECORD *button*] Yeah. Okay. All right. It's rolling.

BOB'S VOICE: Ask me somethin'.

SAM: Right. [*Referring to notebook*] Let's see—okay—let's see now—okay—here we go—Do you have any ideas about angels? Do you ever think about angels?

BOB'S VOICE: That's the first question?

SAM: You want me to start with something else?

BOB'S VOICE [still off]: No, that's okay. Angels. Yeah, now, angels now—what is it? [pause] Oh—the pope says this about angels—he says they exist.

SAM: Yeah? The pope?

BOB'S VOICE: Yeah. And they're spiritual beings. That's what he says.

SAM: Do you believe it?

BOB'S VOICE: Yeah.

SAM: Have you had any direct experience with angels?

BOB'S VOICE [off]: Yeah. Yeah, I have. I just gotta make one more phone call, all right?

SAM: Yeah. [*shuts tape off*]

BOB'S VOICE: You need anything?

SAM: Naw, I'm fine.

[*Sam drinks more beer, scribbles more notes. Pause. Bob's voice is heard again offstage right on phone. Sound of waves continue.*]

BOB'S VOICE [off right]: Maria? Hi, it's me again. [pause, laughs] Yeah, I just like the sound of your voice. Listen, what's the area code for Tulsa, do you know? [pause] Tulsa, yeah. [pause] All right. Good. [pause] Yeah, that's okay. I don't need it right away. [pause]. Oh, ya did? [pause] Yeah? [pause] So, it's just a few people then? What's a few? [pause] That's more than a few. [laughs] Yeah, but, that's not what you'd call a few. [pause] Aw, I dunno. Look, I'll just have to think about it—see how the day goes—then I'll get back to you. [pause] Yeah, okay. Bye. [hangs up]

SAM: [*after pause*] You want me to come back? I could go out and come back if you want. Have some lunch.

BOB'S VOICE [off]: Naw, you're here. Stay. I'm just gettin' some clothes on. I'll be right there. Ask me another question.

SAM: *Oh, okay*—[*punching recorder on*] uh—let's see— [*referring to notebooks*] okay—What was the first music you can remember listening to? Way back.

BOB'S VOICE [off]: First music. First music?

SAM: Yeah.

BOB'S VOICE [*off*]: Live, ya mean? Live?

SAM: Yeah. Live.

BOB'S VOICE [*off*]: First music ever?

SAM: Yeah.

[*pause*]

BOB'S VOICE [*off*]: Polka music.

SAM: Really?

[*Bob enters from right wearing a sleeveless T-shirt, black jeans, and motorcycle boots with brass buckles. He carries a beat-up old acoustic guitar strung around his neck with an old piece of rope. He continually fingers the neck of the guitar and keeps picking out little repetitive melody lines, short blues progressions, gospel chords—whatever comes into his mind. He keeps this up through all the dialogue, even when he's talking, rarely resting into complete silence.*]

BOB [*onstage now*]: Yeah, polka.

SAM [*drinking beer*]: Where? Up in Hibbing?

BOB: Yeah, Hibbing.

SAM: Hibbing's near Duluth, right?

BOB: Right.

SAM: I love Duluth.

BOB: Great town.

SAM: That lake.

BOB: Superior?

SAM: Yeah. Tough town, too.

BOB: [always moving, picking guitar] Especially when it freezes over. Indians come out. Fur trappers.

SAM: Beaver.

BOB: Yeah, beaver too. Loons.

SAM: So you heard this polka music in what—dance halls or something?

BOB: Yeah—no—taverns. Beer joints. They played it in all the taverns. You just walk down the street and hear that all the time. People'd come flyin' out into the street doin' the polka. Accordions would come flyin' out.

SAM: Were they fighting or dancing?

BOB: Both, I guess. Mostly just having a good time. People from the old country.

SAM: Polish?

BOB: Some, I guess.

SAM: Were they singing in Polish?

BOB: They were singin' in somethin'. Swedish maybe. Some language. But you know how you don't need to know the language when it's music. You understand the music no matter what language it's in. Like when I went down and heard that Tex-Mex border music— that sounded like the same music to me even though the language was different. It all sounds the same to me.

SAM: Three-quarter time.

BOB: Yeah—waltz. I love to waltz.

SAM: How old were you then?

BOB: Aw. I dunno. Nine—ten.

SAM: Did you feel like you were cut off back then?

BOB: How d'ya mean?

SAM: I mean being up in the Far North like that. In the boondocks.

BOB: Nah, 'cause I didn't know anything else was goin' on. Why, did you?

SAM: Yeah. I still do [*laughs*].

BOB: [*sings a snatch and plays*]
Down in the boondocks / Down in the boondocks / Lord have mercy on a boy / From down in the boondocks.

SAM: So you didn't have any big burning desire to get to New York or anything?

BOB: Naw. The only reason I wanted to go to New York is 'cause James Dean had been there.

SAM: So you really liked James Dean?

BOB: Oh, yeah. Always did.

SAM: How come?

BOB: Same reason you liked anybody, I guess. You see somethin' of yourself in them.

SAM: Did you dream about music back than?

BOB: I had lotsa dreams. Used to dream about things like Ava Gardner and Wild Bill Hickok. They were playin' cards, chasin' each other, and gettin' around. Sometimes I'd even be there in the dreams myself. Radio-station dreams. You know how, when you're a kid, you stay up late in bed, listening to the radio, and you sort of dream off the radio into sleep. That's how you used to fall asleep. That's when disc jockeys played whatever they felt like.

SAM: I used to fall asleep listening to baseball.

BOB: Yeah. Same thing. Just sorta dream off into the radio. Like you were inside the radio kinda.

SAM: Yeah—I could see the diamond with the lights lit up and the green lawn of the outfield and the pitcher's eyes looking for the catcher's signals.

BOB: But I don't know if you ever dream about music. How do you dream about music?

SAM: Well, I mean, for instance, a song like "Pledging My Love."

BOB: Forever my darling.

SAM: Yeah.

BOB: What about it?

SAM: Well, I used to dream myself into that kind of a song.

BOB: Really? I didn't think you were that romantic.

SAM: Oh yeah, I'm very romantic.

BOB: So, you mean you kinda put yourself into the song when you were listening to it?

SAM: Yeah. Put myself in the place of the singer.

BOB: I see what you mean. [pause, still moving and picking] Yeah, I guess I used to dream about music then. You have all different kinda dreams with music, though. I mean, sometimes I'd hear a guy sing a tune and I'd imagine the guy himself. What's the guy himself like? You know? Like Hank Williams or Buddy Holly or John Lee Hooker. You'd hear a line like black snake moan or Mississippi Flood—you could see yourself waist-high in muddy water.

SAM: Or maybe an image would come up from a line—like, I remember always seeing this image of my algebra teacher's scalp when I heard that Chuck Berry line, *The teacher is teachin' the golden rule*, from "School Day."

BOB: His scalp?

SAM: Yeah, he had one of those Marine-style crew cuts where the scalp shows through on the top. I still see his scalp when I hear that line.

BOB: You don't hear that line much these days.

SAM: Nope. [*pause*] So, you'd mainly imagine the singer when you heard the song?

BOB: Yeah. A faceless singer. I'd fill in the face.

SAM: Is that the reason you went to see Woody Guthrie when he was sick? You'd heard his music?

BOB: Yeah. I heard his songs.

SAM: Is there anybody in your life you wished you'd met and didn't?

BOB: [quick, still playing] Yeah, Bob Marley.

SAM: Really.

BOB: Yeah. We were playin' in Waco, Texas, one time. And I missed him.

SAM: That was pretty close to miss each other.

BOB: Yeah. I wish I'd met him.

[*rest*]

SAM: So you went to see Guthrie in the hospital.

BOB: Uh-huh.

SAM: And you were there at his death bed?

BOB: Close.

SAM: Were you with him up to where he passed?

[*Long pause. Bob starts playing and thinks hard.*]

BOB: No.

[*Bob immediately jumps back into playing and moving.*]

SAM: You spent a lotta time with him in the hospital?

BOB: Yeah.

SAM: Was he coherent?

BOB: Yeah—no—he was coherent but he had no control over his reflexes. So he'd be . . .

[*pause*]

SAM: What'd you talk about?

BOB: Not too much. I never really did speak too much to him. He would call out the name of a song. A song that he wrote that he wanted to hear, and I knew all his songs.

SAM: So you played 'em to him?

BOB: Yeah.

SAM: Did you ask him anything?

BOB: No, I mean there was nothin' to ask him. What're you gonna ask him? He wasn't the kinda guy you asked questions to.

[*pause*]

SAM: So you just kinda sat with him for days.

BOB: Yeah—I'd go out there. You had to leave at 5:00. It was in Greystone—Greypark or Greystone—it's in New Jersey. Out somewhere there. Bus went there. Greyhound bus. From the Forty-second Street terminal. You'd go there and you'd get off and you walked up the hill to the gates. Actually it was a pretty foreboding place.

SAM: How old were you?

[*Bob stops still. Stops picking. Thinks.*]

BOB: How old was I? [*pause*] I don't know. Nineteen, I guess.

SAM: Nineteen. And what kinda stuff were you listening to back then?

BOB: Oh, Bill Monroe, New Lost City Ramblers, Big Mama Thornton. People like that. Peggy Seeger. Jean Ritchie.

SAM: Hank Snow?

BOB: I'd always listened to Hank Snow. "Golden Rocket."

SAM: At the time were you fishin' around for a form?

BOB: Well you can't catch a fish 'les you trow de line, mon.

SAM: This is true.

BOB: Naw, I've always been real content with old forms. I know my place by now.

SAM: So you feel like you know who you are?

BOB: Well, you always know who you are. I just don't know who I'm gonna become.

[*Pause. Bob keeps moving and picking.*]

BOB: Did we ever see each other back then?

SAM: When?

BOB: When we were nineteen.

SAM: I saw you one time on the corner of Sixth Avenue and Houston Street.

BOB: What year?

SAM: Musta been '66, '67. Somethin' like that. You were wearin' a navy-blue pea jacket and tennis shoes.

BOB: Yeah, that musta been me. Naw, this was earlier than that. I was listenin' to all them records on Stinson label and Folkways.

SAM: Stinson?

BOB: Yeah, Sonny Terry, Brownie McGhee, Almanac Singers.

SAM: Almanac Singers?

BOB: Yeah.

SAM: What about gospel?

BOB: I always listened to gospel music. Dixie Hummingbirds, Highway QC's, Five Blind Boys, and, of course, the Staple Singers.

SAM: What about Skip James or Joseph Spence?

BOB: Yeah. Bahama mama. [*pause*] Skip James. Once there was a Skip James. Elmore James.

SAM: *Rather be buried in some old cypress grove.*

BOB: *So my evil spirit can grab that Greyhound bus and ride.*

SAM: *I'd rather sleep in some old hollow log than have a bad woman you can't control.*

BOB: Now, what was it he died of?

SAM: Skip James?

BOB: Yeah.

SAM: Cancer of the balls.

BOB: What?!

SAM: Yeah. Cancer of the balls. He refused to go to any white doctors 'cause he was afraid they'd cut his nuts off.

BOB: Don't blame him one bit.

[*Phone rings off right. Bob exits off right, leaving Sam alone. Sam turns off tape then rewinds it a short ways and plays it back. Again, the Jimmy Yancey piano music comes from recorder. No voices. As Bob's voice is heard off right on phone, Sam keeps rewinding tape, playing it back in short snatches, trying to find their voices, but all that comes out is the piano music.*]

BOB'S VOICE [*off right*]: Four oh five? Four oh five. You're sure? [*pause*] I dunno. Four oh five sounds like Oklahoma City. I can't remember. [*pause*] All right. [*pause*] Yeah. Four oh five. [*pause*] Naw, I think I'm gonna pass. [*pause*] I dunno. Sounds like too many record producers. [*pause*] Yeah. I'll just hang around here probably. [*pause*] Okay. All right. [*pause*] Yeah.

[*Bob enters again, with guitar, carrying a glass of whiskey on ice. He crosses to table, sets glass down after taking a sip, then starts picking the guitar again. Sam is still trying to find their voices on the tape but gets only the piano music.*]

SAM: [*fooling with tape*] This is incredible.

BOB: What.

SAM: There's nothin' on here but piano music.

BOB: [*laughs, keeps picking*] You mean our voices aren't on there?

SAM: Listen.

[*He lets tape play. Jimmy Yancey rolls out.*]

BOB: [*listens*] That's the same music I was askin' you about.

SAM: When?

BOB: Before. When you first came. That's the music.

SAM: Well, our voices ain't on here.

BOB: Don't matter.

SAM: Well, I can't remember all this stuff. How am I gonna remember all this stuff?

BOB: Make it up.

SAM: Well, there's certain things you can't make up.

BOB: Like what?

SAM: Certain turns of phrase.

BOB: Try it again. It's gotta be on there. You had it on RECORD, right?

SAM: Yeah.

BOB: So it must be on there somewhere. You just gotta fool around with it.

[*Sam rewinds, then plays tape. Their voices are heard this time, coming out of recorder.*]

BOB'S VOICE [*from tape*]: "Golden Rocket."

SAM'S VOICE [*from tape*]: At that time were you fishin' around for a form?

BOB'S VOICE [*from tape*]: Well, you can't catch fish 'les you trow de line, mon.

[*Sam shuts tape off.*]

BOB: There. See. It was just hidin' out. [*laughs*]

SAM: This is amazing. Where'd that music come from?

BOB: Must have been on there already. Is it an old tape?

SAM: No, I just bought it this morning.

[*Bob takes a sip of whiskey, sets glass down.*]

BOB: Angels.

[*Sam punches RECORD button. They continue. Bob keeps moving and playing guitar.*]

SAM: Weird.

BOB: Is it on now?

SAM: Yeah. I guess.

BOB: Okay. Fire away.

SAM: Okay. Let's see. [*referring to notebook*] Do you think it's possible to have a pact with someone?

BOB: A pact? Yeah. I know that's possible. I mean you should have a pact with someone. That presents a small problem for me, though—for instance, how many people can you have a pact with? And how many at the same time?

SAM: Not too many. How about women?

BOB: Nah, I don't know anything about women.

SAM: How 'bout waitresses?

BOB: Well, it seems to me that waitresses are gettin' younger and younger these days. Some of 'em look like babies.

SAM: So, you don't have much hope for women?

BOB: On the contrary. Women are the *only* hope. I think they're a lot more stable than men. Only trouble with women is they let things go on too long.

SAM: What things?

BOB: The whole Western sense of reality. Sometimes women have a tendency to be too lenient. Like a kid can go down and bust some old man in the head, rob a buncha old ladies, burglarize his brother's joint, and blow up a city block, and his momma will still come down and cry over him.

SAM: Yeah, but that's just nature, isn't it? The nature of being a mother.

BOB: Yeah, I guess so. Nature.

SAM: Have you ever felt like a couple?

BOB: A couple? You mean two? Yeah. All the time. Sometimes I feel like ten couples.

SAM: I mean like you're a part of another person. Like you belong. That other person carries something of you around and visee-versee.

BOB: Visee-versee?

SAM: Yeah.

BOB: Yeah. Sure. A couple. Sure. I've felt like that. Absolutely. Look—

listen to this: [*sings and plays*] *You must learn to leave the table when love is no longer being served! Just show them all that you are able! Just get up and leave without saying a word.*

SAM: Who wrote that?

BOB: You got me. Roy Orbison or somebody, dunno.

SAM: Roy Orbison?

BOB: Naw, I dunno. Good lyric.

SAM: Yeah. [*writing a note*] *You must learn to leave the table* . . .

BOB: I mean you gravitate toward people who've got somethin' to give you and maybe you've got somethin' that they need.

SAM: Yeah, right.

BOB: And then maybe one day you wake up and see that they're not givin' it to you anymore. Maybe that's the way it is.

SAM: But maybe you're not, either.

BOB: Yeah. Maybe you haven't been givin' it to 'em for years. Maybe the rhythm's off.

SAM: You know, I've heard this theory that women are rhythmically different from men. By nature.

BOB: Oh yeah? I'll drink to that.

SAM: Yeah. That the female rhythm is a side-to-side, horizontal movement and the male rhythm is vertical—up and down.

BOB: You mean sorta like a flying horse?

SAM: Yeah. Sorta.

BOB: But then the two come together, don't they?

SAM: Right.

BOB: So they become one rhythm then.

SAM: Yeah.

BOB: So there's no such thing as "sides" in the long run. It's all the same.

SAM: It's just a theory.

BOB: Yeah. Well, you can make a theory outta anything, I suppose.

SAM: Do you feel those two different kinds of rhythms in you?

BOB: Yeah, sure. We all do. There's that slinky side-to-side thing and the jerky, up-and-down one. But they're a part of each other. One can't do without the other. Like God and the Devil.

SAM: Did you always feel those two parts?

BOB: Yeah. Always. Like you feel the lie and the truth. At the same time, sometimes. Both, together. Like remember in *Giant*—

SAM: The movie?

BOB: Yeah. That last scene in *Giant*. You know that scene where Jett Rink stumbles all over himself across the table.

SAM: Yeah.

BOB: Well, I never did like that scene. Always felt like there was somethin' phony about it. Didn't quite ring true. Always bothered me. Like there was a lie hiding in there somewhere, but I couldn't quite put my finger on it.

SAM: Yeah, I never did either. You mean where he's drunk and alone in the convention hall or whatever it was?

BOB: Yeah. You know why that was? Why it felt phony?

SAM: The makeup. All that gray in his hair?

BOB: No, no. I wish it was the makeup. Turns out Nick Adams, an actor at that time, who was a friend of James Dean's, he overdubbed that speech because James Dean had died by that time.

SAM: Is that right?

BOB: Yeah. And that makes perfect sense because that don't ring true. The end of that movie. But that's what I mean—the lie and the truth, like that.

[*pause*]

SAM: Well, what happened to his voice?

BOB: Whaddya mean?

SAM: I mean what happened to James Dean's original voice on the track? They must've had his voice track if they had the film on him.

BOB: I dunno. Maybe it was messed up or something.

SAM: Maybe it disappeared.

BOB: Maybe. Just vanished. I dunno.

[*Again, the sound of screeching brakes and car crash off right. Neither of the characters pay any attention. Long pause as Bob moves and picks guitar. Sam makes notes.*]

BOB: Sometimes I wonder why James Dean was great. Because—was he great or was everybody around him great?

SAM: No, he was great.

BOB: You think so?

SAM: Yeah. I mean, remember the scene in *Rebel Without a Cause* with Sal Mineo on the steps of the courthouse? Where he gets shot.

BOB: Plato.

SAM: Yeah, and he's holding Plato in his arms, and in the other hand he's got the bullets.

BOB: Yeah.

SAM: What was it he says? "They're not real bullets" or—no—what was it?

BOB: "I've got the bullets!"

SAM: Right. [*suddenly screaming with his arm outstretched in imitation of James Dean*] "I've got the bullets!" [*back to normal voice*] I mean, that's spectacular acting. Where do you see that kind of acting these days?

BOB: Nowhere. He didn't come up overnight either. I mean he really studied whatever it was he was about.

SAM: I guess.

BOB: Well, why do you suppose—I mean what was it that he did that was so different? For instance, in that scene with the bullets. What made that scene so incredible?

SAM: It was this pure kind of expression.

BOB: Of what?

SAM: Of an emotion. But it went beyond the emotion into another territory. Like most actors in that scene would express nothing but self-pity, but he put across a true remorse.

BOB: Remorse?

SAM: Yeah. For mankind. A pity for us all. This wasted life. This dumb death of an innocent kid. The death of the innocent.

BOB: So he actually did have a cause then?

SAM: I don't know.

BOB: "Rebel *with* a Cause." See, that's the devil's work.

SAM: What?

BOB: Words have lost their meaning. Like "rebel." Like "cause." Like "love." They mean a million different things.

SAM: Like "Hank Williams"?

BOB: Naw, you can never change the meaning of Hank Williams. That's here to stay. Nobody'll ever change that.

SAM: Did you used to listen to him a lot?

BOB: Overload. Who can you listen to if you can't listen to Hank?

SAM: Did he mean the same thing to you as James Dean?

BOB: Yeah, but in different ways. They both told the truth.

SAM: They both died in cars.

BOB: Yeah.

SAM: A Cadillac and a Porsche.

BOB: He was on his way to Ohio, I think. Some gig in Ohio.

SAM: I saw the car he died in. Cadillac coupe, convertible. I looked in the backseat of that car and this overwhelming sense of loneliness seized me by the throat. It was almost unbearable. I couldn't look very long. I had to turn away.

BOB: Maybe you shouldn'ta looked at all.

SAM: Maybe. [*pause*] Are you superstitious?

BOB: Naw.

SAM: You had a crash, right? A motorcycle.

BOB: Oh, yeah. Way back. Triumph 500.

SAM: What happened?

BOB: I couldn't handle it. I was dumbstruck.

SAM: How do you mean?

BOB: I just wasn't ready for it. It was real early in the morning on top of a hill near Woodstock. I can't even remember exactly how it happened. I was blinded by the sun for a second. This big orange sun was comin' up. I was driving right straight into the sun, and I looked up into it even though I remember someone telling me a long time ago when I was a kid never to look straight at the sun 'cause you'll get blinded. I forget who told me that. My dad or an uncle or somebody. Somebody in the family. I always believed that must be true or else why would an adult tell you something like that. And I never did look directly at the sun when I was a kid, but this time, for some reason, I just happened to look up right smack into the sun with both eyes and, sure enough, I went blind for a second and I kind of panicked or something, I stomped down on the brake and the rear wheel locked up on me and I went flyin'.

SAM: Were you out?

BOB: Yeah. Out cold.

SAM: Who found you?

BOB: Sarah. She was followin' me in a car. She picked me up. Spent a week in the hospital, then they moved me to this doctor's house in town. In his attic. Had a bed up there in the attic with a window lookin' out. Sarah stayed there with me. I just remember how bad I wanted to see my kids. I started thinkin' about the short life of trouble. How short life is. I'd just lay there listenin' to birds chirping. Kids playing in the neighbor's yard or rain falling by the window. I realized how much I'd missed. Then I'd hear the fire engine roar, and I could feel the steady thrust of death that had been constantly looking over its shoulder at me. [*pause*] Then I'd just go back to sleep.

[*Phone rings off right. Bob turns and looks in that direction but doesn't move toward it. He stops playing guitar. Phone keeps ringing. He just stares off right. Lights begin to fade very slowly. Bob stays still, staring off right. Sam stops recorder, then rewinds and punches* PLAY *button. The Jimmy Yancey music fills the room, joining the sound of waves. Lights keep dimming to black. The phone keeps ringing. The waves keep crashing. Jimmy Yancey keeps playing in the dark.*]

26. Interview with Paul Zollo, *SongTalk*

1991

> *"I've made shoes for everyone, even you,*
> *while I still go barefoot"*
>
> —from "I and I" by Bob Dylan

"Songwriting? What do I know about songwriting?" Bob Dylan asked, and then broke into laughter. He was wearing blue jeans and a white tank-top T-shirt, and drinking coffee out of a glass. "It tastes better out of a glass," he said grinning. His blonde acoustic guitar was leaning on a couch near where we sat. Bob Dylan's guitar. His influence is so vast that everything that surrounds him takes on enlarged significance: Bob Dylan's moccasins. Bob Dylan's coat.

Pete Seeger said, "All songwriters are links in a chain," yet there are few artists in this evolutionary arc whose influence is as profound as that of Bob Dylan. It's hard to imagine the art of songwriting as we know it without him. Though he insists in this interview that "somebody else would have done it," he was the instigator, the one who knew that songs could do more, that they could take on more. He knew that songs could contain a lyrical richness and meaning far beyond the scope of all previous pop songs, that they could possess as much beauty and power as the greatest poetry, and that by being written in rhythm and rhyme and merged with music, they could speak to our souls.

Starting with the models made by his predecessors, such as the talking blues, Dylan quickly discarded old forms and began to fashion new ones. He broke all the rules of songwriting without abandoning the craft and care that holds songs together. He brought the linguistic beauty of Shakespeare, Byron, and Dylan Thomas, and the expansiveness and beat experimentation of Ginsberg, Kerouac, and Ferlinghetti, to the folk poetry of Woody Guthrie and Hank Williams. And when the world was still in the midst of accepting this new form, he brought music to a new place again, fusing it with the electricity of rock & roll.

"Basically, he showed that anything goes," Robbie Robertson said. John Lennon said that it was hearing Dylan that allowed him to make the leap from writing empty pop songs to expressing the actuality of his life and the depths of his own soul. "Help" was a real call for help, he said, and prior to hearing Dylan it didn't occur to him that songs could contain such direct meaning. When he asked Paul Simon how he made the leap in his writing from fifties rock & roll songs like "Hey Schoolgirl" to writing "The Sounds of Silence" he said, "I really can't imagine it could have been anyone else besides Bob Dylan."

There's an unmistakable elegance in Dylan's words, an almost biblical beauty that he has sustained in his songs throughout the years. He refers to it as a "gallantry" in the following, and pointed to it as the single thing that sets his songs apart from others. Though he's maybe more famous for the freedom and expansiveness of his lyrics, all of his songs possess this exquisite care and love for the language. As Shakespeare and Byron did in their times, Dylan has taken English, perhaps the world's plainest language, and instilled it with a timeless, mythic grace.

As much as he has stretched, expanded, and redefined the rules of songwriting, Dylan is a tremendously meticulous craftsman. A brutal critic of his own work, he works and reworks the words of his songs in the studio and even continues to rewrite certain ones even after they've been recorded and released. "They're not written in stone," he said. With such a wondrous wealth of language at his fingertips, he discards imagery and lines other songwriters would sell their souls to discover.

He was born Robert Allen Zimmerman on May 24, 1941, in Duluth, Minnesota. Inspired by the writing and music of Woody Guthrie, he moved to New York in 1961 ostensibly to meet Woody, who was suffering in a New Jersey hospital from the illness that eventually took his life, Huntington's disease. Marjorie Guthrie, Woody's wife, told me that Dylan was a nice enough kid, and quite respectful of Woody, but she didn't like his singing, and suggested he try to better enunciate the words to his songs.

More impressed than Mrs. Guthrie was the producer John Hammond, who heard Dylan sing at Gerde's in Greenwich Village, and signed him to a record deal with Columbia. Though his debut album contained only two original songs, including his tribute to Guthrie, "Song to Woody," by the second album he'd already written classics such as "Blowin' in the Wind" and "Masters of War," manifesting the new potential inherent in popular songs.

He went on to change the world and bend our minds with successive masterpieces, including such classics as *The Freewheelin' Bob Dylan, Blonde on Blonde, Nashville Skyline, The Basement Tapes* [made with the Band], *John Wesley Harding, Blood on the Tracks, Desire, Oh Mercy,* and much more.

"It's too much and not enough," he said, in reference to the extended nature of many of his songs. The same could be said of any attempt to express the full impact of his greatness in words. Such an attempt would take volumes and still be lacking, as the countless books on the subject attest. Suffice it to say that, like the writing of Shakespeare, the full significance of Dylan's work may not be understood for centuries, at which time scholars might very well look back in wonder that one man could have produced such an immense and amazing body of work.

"Yes, well, what can you know about anybody?" Dylan asked, and it's a good question. He's been a mystery for years, "kind of impenetrable, really," said Paul Simon, and that mystery is not penetrated by this interview or any interview. Dylan's answers were often more enigmatic than my questions, and like his songs, they offer a lot to think about while not necessarily revealing much about the man.

In person, as others have noted, he is Chaplinesque. His body is smaller and his head bigger than one might expect, giving the effect of a kid wearing a Bob Dylan mask. He possesses one of the world's most striking faces; while certain stars might seem surprisingly normal and unimpressive in the flesh, Dylan is perhaps even more startling to confront than one might expect. Seeing those eyes, and that nose, it's clear it could be no one else than he, and to sit at a table with him and face those iconic features is no less impressive than suddenly finding yourself sitting face to face with William Shakespeare. It's a face we associate with an enormous, timeless body of work, work that has changed the world. But it's not really the kind of face one expects to encounter in everyday life.

Though Van Morrison called him the world's greatest poet, he doesn't think of himself as a poet. "Poets drown in lakes," he said. Yet he's written some of the most beautiful poetry the world has known, poetry of love and outrage, of abstraction and clarity, of timelessness and relativity. Though he is faced with the evidence of a catalog of songs that could contain the whole careers of a dozen fine songwriters, Dylan told me that he doesn't consider himself to be a professional songwriter. "For me it's always been more con-fessional than pro-fessional," he said in distinctive Dylan cadence. "My songs aren't written on a schedule."

Well, how are they written, I asked? This is the question at the heart of this interview, the main one that comes to mind when looking over all the albums, or witnessing the amazing array of moods, masks, styles and forms he's presented over the years. How has he done it? It was the first question asked, and though he deflected it at first with his customary humor, it's a question I tried to return to a few times.

"Start me off somewhere," he said smiling, as if he might be left alone to divulge the secrets of his songwriting, and our talk began.

Arlo Guthrie recently said, "Songwriting is like fishing in a stream; you put in your line and hope you catch something. And I don't think anyone downstream from Bob Dylan ever caught anything."

[*Much laughter*]

Any idea how you've been able to catch so many?

[*Laughs*] It's probably the bait. [*More laughter*]

What kind of bait do you use?

[*Pause*] Bait. You've got to use some bait. Otherwise you sit around and expect songs to come to you. Forcing it is using bait.

Does that work for you?

Well, no. Throwing yourself into a situation that would demand a response is like using bait. People who write about stuff that hasn't really happened to them are inclined to do that.

When you write songs, do you try to consciously guide the meaning or do you try to follow subconscious directions?

Well, you know, motivation is something you never know behind any song, really. Anybody's song, you never know what the motivation was.

It's nice to be able to put yourself in an environment where you can completely accept all the unconscious stuff that comes to you from your inner workings of your mind. And block yourself off to where you can control it all, take it down . . .

Edgar Allan Poe must have done that. People who are dedicated writers, of which there are some, but mostly people get their information today over a television set or some kind of a way that's hitting them on all their senses. It's not just a great novel anymore.

You have to be able to get the thoughts out of your mind.

How do you do that?

Well, first of all, there's two kinds of thoughts in your mind: there's good thoughts and evil thoughts. Both come through your mind. Some people are more loaded down with one than another. Nevertheless, they come through. And you have to be able to sort them out, if you want to be a songwriter, if you want to be a song singer. You must get rid of all that baggage. You ought to be able to sort out those thoughts, because they don't mean anything, they're just pulling you around, too. It's important to get rid of all them thoughts.

Then you can do something from some kind of surveillance of the situation. You have some kind of place where you can see it but it can't affect you. Where you can bring something to the matter, besides just take, take, take, take, take. As so many situations in life are today. Take, take, take, that's all that it is. What's in it for me? That syndrome which started in the Me Decade, whenever that was. We're still in that. It's still happening.

Is songwriting for you more a sense of taking something from someplace else?

Well, someplace else is always a heartbeat away. There's no rhyme or reason to it. There's no rule. That's what makes it so attractive. There isn't any rule. You can still have your wits about you and do something that gets you off in a multitude of ways. As you very well know, or else you yourself wouldn't be doing it.

Your songs often bring us back to other times, and are filled with mythic, magical images. A song like "Changing of the Guard" seems to take place centuries ago, with lines like "They shaved her head/she was torn between Jupiter and Apollo/a messenger arrived with a black nightingale. . . ." How do you connect with a song like that?

[*Pause*] A song like that, there's no way of knowing, after the fact, unless somebody's there to take it down in chronological order, what the motivation was behind it. [*Pause*] But on one level, of course, it's no different from anything else of mine. It's the same amount of metric verses like a poem. To me, like a poem.

The melodies in my mind are very simple, they're very simple, they're just based on music we've all heard growing up. And that and music which went beyond that, which went back further, Elizabethan ballads and whatnot . . .

To me, it's old [*laughs*]. It's old. It's not something, with my minimal amount of talent, if you could call it that, minimum amount . . . To me somebody coming along now would definitely read what's out there if they're seriously concerned with being an artist who's going to still be an artist when they get to be Picasso's age. You're better off learning some music theory. You're just better off, yeah, if you want to write songs. Rather than just take a hillbilly twang, you know, and try to base it all on that. Even country music is more orchestrated than it used to be. You're better off having some feel for music that you don't have to carry in your head, that you can write down.

To me those are the people who . . . are serious about this craft. People who go about it that way. Not people who just want to pour out their insides and they got to get a big idea out and they want to tell the world about this, sure, you can do it through a song, you always could. You can use a song for anything, you know.

The world don't need any more songs.

You don't think so?

No. They've got enough. They've got way too many. As a matter of fact, if nobody wrote any songs from this day on, the world ain't gonna suffer for it. Nobody cares. There's enough songs for people to listen to, if they want to listen to songs. For every man, woman, and child on earth, they could be sent, probably, each of them, a hundred records, and never be repeated. There's enough songs. Unless someone's gonna come along with a pure heart and has something to say. That's a different story. But as far as songwriting, any idiot could do it. If you see me do it, any idiot could do it [*laughs*]. It's just not that difficult of a thing. Everybody writes a song just like everybody's got that one great novel in them.

There aren't a lot of people like me. You just had your interview with Neil [Young], John Mellencamp . . . Of course, most of my ilk that came along write their own songs and play them. It wouldn't matter if anybody ever made another record. They've got enough songs.

To me, someone who writes really good songs is Randy Newman. There's a lot of people who write good songs. As songs. Now Randy might not go out on stage and knock you out, or knock your socks off. And he's not going to get people thrilled in the front row. He ain't gonna do that. But he's gonna write a better song than most people who can do it.

You know, he's got that down to an art. Now Randy knows music. He knows music. But it doesn't get any better than "Louisiana" or "Cross Charleston Bay" ["Sail Away"]. It doesn't get any better than that. It's like a classically heroic anthem theme. He did it. There's quite a few people who did it. Not that many people in Randy's class.

Brian Wilson. He can write melodies that will beat the band. Three people could combine on a song and make it a great song. If one person would have written the same song, maybe you would have never heard it. It might get buried on some . . . rap record [*laughs*].

Still, when you've come out with some of your new albums of songs, those songs fit that specific time better than any songs that had already been written. Your new songs have always shown us new possibilities.

It's not a good idea and it's bad luck to look for life's guidance to popular entertainers. It's bad luck to do that. No one should do that. Popular entertainers are fine, there's nothing the matter with that but as long as you know where you're standing and what ground you're on. Many of them, they don't know what they're doing either.

But your songs are more than pop entertainment . . .

Some people say so. Not to me.

No?

Pop entertainment means nothing to me. Nothing. You know, Madonna's good. Madonna's good, she's talented, she puts all kinds of stuff together, she's learned her thing . . . But it's the kind of thing which takes years and years out of your life to be able to do. You've got to sacrifice a whole lot to do that. Sacrifice. If you want to make it big, you've got to sacrifice a whole lot. It's all the same, it's all the same [*laughs*].

Van Morrison said that you are our greatest living poet. Do you think of yourself in those terms?

[*Pause*] Sometimes. It's within me. It's within me to put myself up and be a poet. But it's a dedication. [*Softly*] It's a big dedication.

[*Pause*] Poets don't drive cars [*laughs*]. Poets don't go to the supermarket. Poets don't empty the garbage. Poets aren't on the PTA. Poets, you know, they don't go picket the Better Housing Bureau, or whatever. Poets don't . . . Poets don't even speak on the telephone. Poets don't even talk to anybody. Poets do a lot of listening and . . . and usually they know why they're poets! [*Laughs*]

Yeah, there are . . . what can you say? The world don't need any more poems, it's got Shakespeare. There's enough of everything. You name it, there's enough of it. There was too much of it with electricity, maybe, some people said that. Some people said the lightbulb was going too far.

Poets live on the land. They behave in a gentlemanly way. And live by their own gentlemanly code. [*Pause*] And die broke. Or drown in lakes. Poets usually have very unhappy endings. Look at Keats' life. Look at Jim Morrison, if you want to call him a poet. Look at him. Although some people say that he is really in the Andes.

Do you think so?

Well, it never crossed my mind to think one way or the other about it, but you do hear that talk. Piggyback in the Andes. Riding a donkey.

People have a hard time believing that Shakespeare really wrote all of his work because there is so much of it. Do you have a hard time accepting that?

People have a hard time accepting anything that overwhelms them.

Might they think that of you, years from now, that no one man could have produced so much incredible work?

They could. They could look back and think nobody produced it. [*Softly*] It's not to anybody's best interest to think about how they will be perceived tomorrow. It hurts you in the long run.

But aren't there songs of your own that you know will always be around?

Who's gonna sing them? My songs really aren't meant to be covered. No, not really. Can you think of . . . Well, they do get covered, but it's covered. They're not intentionally written to be covered, but okay, they do.

Your songs are much more enjoyable to sing and play than most songs . . .

Do you play them on piano or guitar?

Both.

Acoustic guitar?

Mostly.

Do you play jazz? It never hurts to learn as many chords as you can. All kinds. Sometimes it will change the inflection of a whole song, a straight chord, or, say, an augmented seventh chord.

Do you have favorite keys to work in?

On the piano, my favorite keys are the black keys. And they sound better on guitar, too. Sometimes when a song's in a flat key, say B flat, bring it to the guitar, you might want to put it in A. But . . . that's an interesting thing you just said. It changes the reflection. Mainly in mine the songs sound different. They sound . . . when you take a black key song and put it on the guitar, which means you're playing in A flat, not too many people like to play in those keys. To me it doesn't matter [*laughs*]. It doesn't matter because my fingering is the same anyway. So there are songs that, even without the piano, which is the dominant sound if you're playing in the black keys—why else would you play in that key except to have that dominant piano sound?—the songs that go into those keys right from the piano, they sound different. They sound deeper. Yeah. They sound deeper. Everything sounds deeper in those black keys. They're not guitar keys, though. Guitar bands don't usually like to play in those keys, which kind of gives me an idea, actually, of a couple of songs that could actually sound better in black keys.

Do keys have different colors for you?

Sure. Sure. [*Softly*] Sure.

You've written some great A minor songs. I think of "One More Cup of Coffee" . . .

Right. B minor might sound even better.

Why?

Well, it might sound better because you're playing a lot of open chords if you're playing in A minor. If you play in B minor, it will force you to play higher. And the chords . . . you're bound, someplace along the line, because there are so many chords in that song, or seem to be anyway, you're bound someplace along the line to come down to an open chord on the bottom. From B. You would hit E someplace along the line.

Try it in B minor [laughs]. Maybe it will be a hit for you.

A hit is a number one song, isn't it? Yeah.

When you sit down to write a song, do you pick a key first that will fit a song? Or do you change keys while you're writing?

Yeah. Yeah. Maybe like in the middle of the thing.

There are ways you can get out of whatever you've gotten into. You want to get out of it. It's bad enough getting into it. But the thing to do as soon as you get into it is realize you must get out of it. And unless you get out of it quickly and effortlessly, there's no use staying in it. It will just drag you down. You could be spending years writing the same song, telling the same story, doing the same thing.

So once you involve yourself in it, once you accidentally have slipped into it, the thing is to get out. So your primary impulse is going to take you so far. But then you might think, well, you know, is this one of these things where it's all just going to come? And then all of a sudden you start thinking. And when my mind starts thinking, "What's happening now? Oh, there's a story here," and my mind starts to get into it, that's trouble right away. That's usually big trouble. And as far as never seeing this thing again.

There's a bunch of ways you can get out of that. You can make yourself get out of it by changing key. That's one way. Just take the whole thing and change key, keeping the same melody. And see if that brings you any place. More times than not, that will take you down the road. You don't want to be on a collision course. But that will take you down the road. Somewhere.

And then if that fails, and that will run out, too, then you can always go back to where you were to start. It won't work twice, it only works once. Then you go back to where you started. Yeah, because anything you do in A, it's going to be a different song in G. While you're writing it, anyway. There's too many wide passing notes in G [on the guitar] not to influence your writing, unless you're playing barre chords.

Do you ever switch instruments, like from guitar to piano, while writing?

Not so much that way. Although when it's time to record something, for me, sometimes a song that has been written on piano with just lyrics here in my hand, it'll be time to play it now on guitar. So it will come out differently. But it wouldn't have influenced the writing of the song at all.

Changing keys influences the writing of the song. Changing keys on the same instrument. For me, that works. I think for somebody else, the other thing works. Everything is different.

I interviewed Pete Seeger recently—

He's a great man, Pete Seeger.

I agree. He said, "All songwriters are links in a chain." Without your link in that chain, all of songwriting would have evolved much differently. You said how you brought folk music to rock music. Do you think that would have happened without you?

Somebody else would have done it in some other kind of way. But, hey, so what? So what? You can lead people astray awfully easily.

Would people have been better off? Sure. They would have found somebody else. Maybe different people would have found different people, and would have been influenced by different people.

You brought the song to a new place. Is there still a new place to bring songs? Will they continue to evolve?

[*Pause*] The evolution of song is like a snake with its tail in its mouth. That's evolution. That's what it is. As soon as you're there, you find your tail.

Would it be okay with you if I mentioned some lines from your songs out of context to see what response you might have to them?

Sure. You can name anything you want to name, man.

"I stand here looking at your yellow railroad/in the ruins of your balcony . . ." [from "Absolutely Sweet Marie"]

[*Pause*] Okay. That's an old song. No, let's say not even old. How old? Too old. It's matured well. It's like old wine. Now, you know, look, that's as complete as you can be. Every single letter in that line. It's all true. On a literal and on an escapist level.

And is it that truth that adds so much resonance to it?

Oh yeah, exactly. See, you can pull it apart and it's like, "Yellow railroad?" Well, yeah. Yeah, yeah. All of it.

"I was lying down in the reeds without any oxygen/I saw you in the wilderness among the men/I saw you drift into infinity and come back again . . ." [from "True Love Tends to Forget"]

Those are probably lyrics left over from my songwriting days with Jacques Levy. To me, that's what they sound like.

Getting back to the yellow railroad, that could be from looking someplace. Being a performer you travel the world. You're not just looking off the same window every day. You're not just walking down the same old street. So you must make yourself observe whatever. But most of the time it hits you. You don't have to observe. It hits you. Like "yellow railroad" could have been a blinding day when the sun was bright on a railroad someplace and it stayed on my mind. These aren't contrived images. These are images which are just in there and have got to come out. You know, if it's in there it's got to come out.

"And the chains of the sea will be busted in the night . . ." [*from "When the Ship Comes In"*]

To me, that song says a whole lot. Patti LaBelle should do that. You know?

You know, there again, that comes from hanging out at a lot of poetry gatherings. Those kind of images are very romantic. They're very gothic and romantic at the same time. And they have a sweetness to it, also. So it's a combination of a lot of different elements at the time. That's not a contrived line. That's not sitting down and writing a song. Those kind of songs, they just come out. They're in you so they've got to come out.

"Standing on the water casting your bread/while the eyes of the idol with the iron head are glowing . . ." [*from "Jokerman"*]

[*Blows small Peruvian flute*] Which one is that again?

That's from "Jokerman."

That's a song that got away from me. Lots of songs on that album [*Infidels*] got away from me. They just did.

You mean in the writing?

Yeah. They hung around too long. They were better before they were tampered with. Of course, it was me tampering with them [*laughs*]. Yeah. That could have been a good song. It could've been.

I think it's tremendous.

Oh, you do? It probably didn't hold up for me because in my mind it had been written and rewritten and written again. One of those kinds of things.

"But the enemy I see wears a cloak of decency . . ." [*from "Slow Train"*]

Now don't tell me . . . wait . . . Is that "When You Gonna Wake Up"?

No, that's from "Slow Train."

Oh, wow. Oh, yeah. Wow. There again. That's a song that you could write a song to every line in the song. You could.

Many of your songs are like that.

Well, you know, that's not good either. Not really. In the long run, it could have stood up better by maybe doing just that, maybe taking every line and making a song out of it. If somebody had the willpower.

But that line, there again, is an intellectual line. It's a line, "Well, the enemy I see wears a cloak of decency," that could be a lie. It just could be. Whereas "Standing under your yellow railroad," that's not a lie.

To Woody Guthrie, see, the airwaves were sacred. And when he'd hear something false, it was on airwaves that were sacred to him. His songs weren't false. Now we know the airwaves aren't sacred but to him they were.

So that influenced a lot of people with me coming up. Like, "You know, all those songs on the Hit Parade are just a bunch of shit, anyway." It influenced me in the beginning when nobody had heard that. Nobody had heard that. You know, "If I give my heart to you, will you handle it with care?" Or "I'm getting sentimental over you." Who gives a shit! It could be said in a grand way, and the performer could put the song across, but come on, that's because he's a great performer not because it's a great song. Woody was also a performer and songwriter. So a lot of us got caught up in that. There ain't anything good on the radio. It doesn't happen.

Then, of course, the Beatles came along and kind of grabbed everybody by the throat. You were for them or against them. You were for them or you joined them, or whatever. Then everybody said, Oh, popular song ain't so bad, and then everyone wanted to get on the radio [*laughs*]. Before that it didn't matter. My first records were never played on the radio. It was unheard of! Folk records weren't played on the radio. You never heard them on the radio and nobody cared if they were on the radio.

Going on into it further, after the Beatles came out and everybody from England, rock and roll still is an American thing. Folk music is not. Rock and roll is an American thing, it's just all kind of twisted. But the English kind of threw it back, didn't they? And they made everybody respect it once more. So everybody wanted to get on the radio.

Now nobody even knows what radio is anymore. Nobody likes it that you talk to. Nobody listens to it. But, then again, it's bigger than it ever was. But nobody knows how to really respond to it. Nobody can shut it off [*laughs*]. You know? And people really aren't sure whether they want to be on the radio or whether they don't want to be on the radio. They might want to sell a lot of records, but people always did that. But being a folk performer, having hits, it wasn't important. Whatever that has to do with anything . . . [laughs]

Your songs, like Woody's, always have defied being pop entertainment. In your songs, like his, we know a real person is talking, with lines like "You've got a lot of nerve to say you are my friend."

That's another way of writing a song, of course. Just talking to somebody that ain't there. That's the best way. That's the truest way. Then it just becomes a question of how heroic your speech is. To me, it's something to strive after.

Until you record a song, no matter how heroic it is, it doesn't really exist. Do you ever feel that?

No. If it's there, it exists.

You once said that you only write about what's true, what's been proven to you, that you write about dreams but not fantasies.

My songs really aren't dreams. They're more of a responsive nature. Waking up from a dream is . . . when you write a dream, it's something you try to recollect and you're never quite sure if you're getting it right or not.

You said your songs are responsive. Does life have to be in turmoil for songs to come?

Well, to me, when you need them, they appear. Your life doesn't have to be in turmoil to write a song like that but you need to be outside of it. That's why a lot of people, me myself included, write songs when one form or another of society has rejected you. So that you can truly write about it from the outside. Someone who's never been out there can only imagine it as anything, really.

Outside of life itself?

No. Outside of the situation you find yourself in. There are different types of songs and they're all called songs. But there are different types of songs just like there are different types of people, you know? There's an infinite amount of different kinds, stemming from a common folk ballad verse to people who have classical training. And with classical training, of course, then you can just apply lyrics to classical training and get things going on in positions where you've never been in before.

Modern twentieth-century ears are the first ears to hear these kind of Broadway songs. There wasn't anything like this. These are musical songs. These are done by people who know music first. And then lyrics.

To me, Hank Williams is still the best songwriter.

Hank? Better than Woody Guthrie?

That's a good question. Hank Williams never wrote "This Land Is Your Land." But it's not that shocking for me to think of Hank Williams singing "Pastures of Plenty" or Woody Guthrie singing "Cheatin' Heart." So in a lot of ways those two writers are similar. As writers. But you mustn't forget that both of these people were performers, too. And that's another thing which separates a person who just writes a song . . .

People who don't perform but who are so locked into other people who do that, they can sort of feel what that other person would like to say in a song and be able to write those lyrics. Which is a different thing from a performer who needs a song to play on stage year after year.

And you always wrote your songs for yourself to sing—

My songs were written with me in mind. In those situations, several people might say, "Do you have a song laying around?" The best songs to me—my best songs—are songs which were written very quickly. Yeah, very, very quickly. Just about as much time as it takes to write it down is about as long as it takes to write it. Other than that, there have been a lot of ones that haven't made it. They haven't survived. They could need to be dragged out, you know, and looked at again, maybe.

You said once that the saddest thing about songwriting is trying to recon-nect with an idea you started before, and how hard that is to do.

To me it can't be done. To me, unless I have another writer around who might want to finish it . . . outside of writing with the Traveling Wilburys, my shared experience writing a song with other songwriters is not that great. Of course, unless you find the right person to write with as a partner . . . [*laughs*] . . . you're awfully lucky if you do, but if you don't, it's really more trouble than it's worth, trying to write something with somebody.

Your collaborations with Jacques Levy came out pretty great.

We both were pretty much lyricists. Yeah, very panoramic songs because, you know, after one of my lines, one of his lines would come out. Writing with Jacques wasn't difficult. It was trying to just get it down. It just didn't stop. Lyrically. Of course, my melodies are very simple anyway so they're very easy to remember.

With a song like "Isis" that the two of you wrote together, did you plot that story out prior to writing the verses?

That was a story that [*laughs*] meant something to him. Yeah. It just seemed to take on a life of its own [*laughs*], as another view of history [*laughs*]. Which there are so many views that don't get told. Of history, anyway. That wasn't one of them. Ancient history but history nonetheless.

Was that a story you had in mind before the song was written?

No. With this "Isis" thing, it was "Isis" . . . you know, the name sort of rang a bell but not in any kind of vigorous way. So therefore, it was name-that-tune time. It was anything. The name was familiar. Most people would think they knew it from somewhere. But it seemed like just about any way it wanted to go would have been okay, just as long as it didn't get too close [*laughs*].

Too close to what?

[*Laughs*] Too close to me or him.

People have an idea of your songs freely flowing out from you, but that song and many others of yours are so well-crafted; it has an ABAB rhyme scheme which is like something Byron would do, interlocking every line—

Oh, yeah. Oh, yeah. Oh, sure. If you've heard a lot of free verse, if you've been raised on free verse, William Carlos Williams, e.e. cummings, those kind of people who wrote free verse, your ear is not going to be trained for things to sound that way. Of course, for me it's no secret that all my stuff is rhythmically oriented that way.

Like a Byron line would be something as simple as "What is it you buy so dear/With your pain and with your fear?" Now that's a Byron line, but that could have been one of my lines.

Up until a certain time, maybe in the twenties, that's the way poetry was. It was that way. It was . . . simple and easy to remember. And always in rhythm. It had a rhythm whether the music was there or not.

Is rhyming fun for you?

Well, it can be, but, you know, it's a game. You know, you sit around . . . you know, it's more like it's mentally . . . mentally . . . it gives you a thrill. It gives you a thrill to rhyme something you might think, "Well, that's never been rhymed before." But then again, people have taken rhyming now, it doesn't have to be exact anymore. Nobody's going to care if you rhyme "represent" with "ferment," you know. Nobody's gonna care.

That was a result of a lot of people of your generation for whom the craft elements of songwriting didn't seem to matter as much. But in your songs the craft is always there, along with the poetry and the energy—

My sense of rhyme used to be more involved in my songwriting than it is . . . Still staying in the unconscious frame of mind, you can pull yourself out and throw up two rhymes first and work it back. You get the rhymes first and work it back and then see if you can make it make sense in another kind of way. You can still stay in the unconscious frame of mind to pull it off, which is the state of mind you have to be in anyway.

So sometimes you will work backwards, like that?

Oh, yeah. Yeah, a lot of times. That's the only way you're going to finish something. That's not uncommon, though.

Do you finish songs even when you feel that maybe they're not keepers?

Keepers or not keepers . . . you keep songs if you think they're any good, and if you don't . . . you can always give them to somebody else. If you've got songs that you're not going to do and you just don't like them . . . show them to other people, if you want.

Then again, it all gets back to the motivation. Why you're doing what you're doing. That's what it is [*laughs*]. It's confrontation with that . . . goddess of the self.

God of the self or goddess of the self? Somebody told me it was goddess of the self. Somebody told me that the goddess rules over the self. Gods don't concern themselves with such earthly matters. Only goddesses . . . would stoop so low. Or bend down so low.

You mentioned that when you were writing "Every Grain of Sand" that you felt you were in an area where no one had ever been before—

Yeah. In that area where Keats is. Yeah. That's a good poem set to music.

A beautiful melody.

It's a beautiful melody, too, isn't it? It's a folk derivative melody. It's nothing you can put your finger on, but, you know, yeah, those melodies are great. There ain't enough of them, really.

Even a song like that, the simplicity of it can be . . . deceiving. As far as . . . a song like that just may have been written in great turmoil, although you would never sense that. Written but not delivered. Some songs are better written in peace and quiet and delivered in turmoil. Others are best written in turmoil and delivered in a peaceful, quiet way.

It's a magical thing, popular song. Trying to press it down into everyday numbers doesn't quite work. It's not a puzzle. There aren't pieces that fit. It doesn't make a complete picture that's ever been seen.

But, you know, as they say, thank God for songwriters.

Randy Newman said that he writes his songs by going to it every day, like a job—

Tom Paxton told me the same thing. He goes back with me, way back. He told me the same thing. Every day he gets up and he writes a song. Well, that's great, you know, you write the song and then take your kids to school? Come home, have some lunch with the wife, you know, maybe go write another song. Then Tom said for recreation, to get himself loose, he rode his horse. And then pick up his child from school, and then go to bed with the wife.

Now to me that sounds like the ideal way to write songs. To me, it couldn't be any better than that.

How do you do it?

Well, my songs aren't written on a schedule like that. In my mind it's never really been seriously a profession . . . It's been more confessional than professional. Then again, everybody's in it for a different reason.

Do you ever sit down with the intention of writing a song, or do you wait for songs to come to you?

Either or. Both ways. It can come . . . some people are . . . It's possible now for a songwriter to have a recording studio in his house and record a song and make a demo and do a thing. It's like the roles have changed on all that stuff.

Now for me, the environment to write the song is extremely important. The environment has to bring something out in me that wants to be brought out. It's a contemplative, reflective thing. Feelings really aren't my thing. See, I don't write lies.

It's a proven fact: Most people who say I love you don't mean it. Doctors have proved that. So love generates a lot of songs. Probably more so than a lot. Now it's not my intention to have love influence my songs. Any more than it influenced Chuck Berry's songs or Woody Guthrie's or Hank Williams'. Hank Williams', they're not love songs. You're degrading them songs calling them love songs. Those are songs from the Tree of Life. There's no love on the Tree of Life. Love is on the Tree of Knowledge, the Tree of Good and Evil. So we have a lot of songs in popular music about love. Who needs them? Not you, not me.

You can use love in a lot of ways in which it will come back to hurt you. Love is a democratic principle. It's a Greek thing.

A college professor told me that if you read about Greece in the history books, you'll know all about America. Nothing that happens will puzzle you ever again. You read the history of Ancient Greece and when the Romans came in, and nothing will ever bother you about America again. You'll see what America is.

Now, maybe, but there are a lot of other countries in the world besides America . . . [*laughs*]. Two. You can't forget about them [*laughs*].

Have you found there are better places in the world than others to write songs?

It's not necessary to take a trip to write a song. What a long, strange trip it's been, however. But that part of it's true, too.

Environment is very important. People need peaceful, invigorating environments. Stimulating environments.

In America there's a lot of repression. A lot of people who are repressed. They'd like to get out of town, they just don't know how to do it. And so, it holds back creativity. It's like you go somewhere and you can't help but feel it. Or people even tell it to you, you know?

What got me into the whole thing in the beginning wasn't songwriting. That's not what got me into it. When "Hound Dog" came across the radio, there was nothing in my mind that said, "Wow, what a great song, I wonder who wrote that?" It didn't really concern me who wrote it. It didn't matter who wrote it. It was just . . . it was just there.

Same way with me now. You hear a good song. Now you think to yourself, maybe, "Who wrote it?" Why? Because the performer's not as good as the song, maybe. The performer's got to transcend that song. At least come up to it. A good performer can always make a bad song sound good. Record albums are filled with good performers singing filler stuff.

Everybody can say they've done that. Whether you wrote it or whether somebody else wrote it, it doesn't matter.

What interested me was being a musician. The singer was important and so was the song. But being a musician was always first and foremost in the back of my mind. That's why, while other people were learning . . . whatever they were learning. What were they learning way back then?

"Ride, Sally, Ride"?

Something like that. Or "Run, Rudolph, Run." When the others were doing "Run, Rudolph, Run," my interests were going more to Leadbelly kind of stuff, when he was playing a Stella 12-string guitar. Like, how does the guy do that? Where can one of these be found, a 12-string guitar? They didn't have any in my town.

My intellect always fell that way. Of the music. Like Paul Whiteman. Paul Whiteman creates a mood. Bing Crosby's early records. They created a mood, like that Cab Calloway, kind of spooky horn kind of stuff. Violins, when big bands had a sound to them, without the Broadway glitz. Once that Broadway trip got into it, it became all sparkly and Las Vegas, really. But it wasn't always so.

Music created an environment. It doesn't happen anymore. Why? Maybe technology has just booted it out and there's no need for it. Because we have a screen which supposedly is three-dimensional. Or comes across as three-dimensional. It would like you to believe it's three-dimensional. Well, you know, like old movies and stuff like that that's influenced so many of us who grew up on that stuff.

[*Picks up Peruvian flute*] Like this old thing, here, it's nothing, it's some kind of, what is it? . . . Listen: [*Plays a slow tune on the flute*]. Here, listen to this song. [*Plays more*] Okay. That's a song. It don't have any words. Why do songs need words? They don't. Songs don't need words. They don't.

Do you feel satisfied with your body of work?

Most everything, yeah.

Do you spend a lot of time writing songs?

Well, did you hear that record that Columbia released last year, *Down in the Groove?* Those songs, they came in pretty easy.

I'd like to mention some of your songs, and see what response you have to them.

Okay.

"One More Cup of Coffee."

[*Pause*] Was that for a coffee commercial? No . . .

It's a gypsy song. That song was written during a gypsy festival in the south of France one summer. Somebody took me there to the gypsy high holy days which coincide with my own particular birthday. So somebody took me to a birthday party there once, and hanging out there for a week probably influenced the writing of that song.

But the "valley below" probably came from someplace else.

My feeling about the song was that the verses came from someplace else. It wasn't about anything, so this "valley below" thing became the fixture to hang it on. But "valley below" could mean anything.

"Precious Angel." [from 'Slow Train Comin' ']

Yeah. That's another one, it could go on forever. There's too many verses and there's not enough. You know? When people ask me, "How come you don't sing that song anymore?" It's like it's another one of those songs: it's just too much and not enough. A lot of my songs strike me that way. That's the natural thing about them to me.

It's too hard to wonder why about them. To me, they're not worthy of wondering why about them. They're songs. They're not written in stone. They're on plastic.

To us, though, they are written in stone, because Bob Dylan wrote them. I've been amazed by the way you've changed some of your great songs —

Right. Somebody told me that Tennyson often wanted to rewrite his poems when he saw them in print.

"I and I." [from 'Infidels']

[*Pause*] That was one of them Caribbean songs. One year a bunch of songs just came to me hanging around down in the islands, and that was one of them.

"Joey." [from 'Desire']

To me, that's a great song. Yeah. And it never loses its appeal.

And it has one of the greatest visual endings of any song.

That's a tremendous song. And you'd only know that singing it night after night. You know who got me singing that song? [Jerry] Garcia. Yeah. He got me singing that song again. He said that's one of the best songs ever written. Coming from him, it was hard to know which way to take that [*laughs*]. He got me singing that song again with them [the Grateful Dead].

It was amazing how it would, right from the gate go, it had a life of its own, it just ran out of the gate and it just kept on getting better and better and better and better and it keeps on getting better. It's in its infant stages, as a performance thing. Of course, it's a long song. But, to me, not to blow my own horn, but to me the song is like a Homer ballad. Much more so than "A Hard Rain," which is a long song, too. But, to me, "Joey" has a Homeric quality to it that you don't hear every day. Especially in popular music.

"Ring Them Bells." [from 'Oh Mercy']

It stands up when you hear it played by me. But if another performer did it, you might find that it probably wouldn't have as much to do with bells as what the title proclaims.

Somebody once came and sang it in my dressing room. To me [*laughs*]. To try to influence me to sing it that night [*laughs*]. It could have gone either way, you know.

Which way did it go?

It went right out the door [*laughs*]. It went out the door and didn't come back. Listening to this song that was on my record, sung by someone who wanted me to sing it . . . There was no way he was going to get me to sing it like that. A great performer, too.

"Idiot Wind."

"Idiot Wind." Yeah, you know, obviously, if you've heard both versions you realize, of course, that there could be a myriad of verses for the thing. It doesn't stop. It wouldn't stop. Where do you end? You could still be writing it, really. It's something that could be a work continually in progress.

Although, on saying that, let me say that my lyrics, to my way of thinking, are better for my songs than anybody else's. People have felt about my songs sometimes the same way as me. And they say to me, your songs are so opaque that, people tell me, they have feelings they'd like to express within the same framework. My response, always, is go ahead, do it, if you feel like it. But it never comes off. They're not as good as my lyrics.

There's just something about my lyrics that just have a gallantry to them. And that might be all they have going for them [*laughs*]. However, it's no small thing.

27. Interview with Jon Pareles,
The New York Times

September 28, 1997

Bob Dylan can barely sit still. He pulls at his curly hair, fidgets with his black T-shirt, constantly shifts position on a comfortable couch. Sitting in his publicist's oceanside hotel suite for a rare interview, the songwriter who transformed rock is in a jovial mood. He's wearing two-tone patent-leather shoes, there's a twinkle in his blue eyes, and he smiles easily and often.

Dylan is proud of his new album, *Time Out of Mind*, and rightfully so. The album, to be released on Tuesday, is far and away his best sustained work since the mid-1970s; it reaches the exalted level of *Blood on the Tracks*. His new songs—his first set of them since 1990—are embittered, heartsick and weary: "When you think that you've lost everything, you find out you can always lose a little more," he sings in a rasping voice whose familiar cracks have become potholes. It's the voice of a 56-year-old man who's not hiding any of his bruises. Yet the character who runs through all the songs on the album seems nothing like the relaxed, buoyant songwriter who's talking about them. Asked who the woman was who broke his heart in song after song, he laughs and asks, "Which one? Which song?"

"That's just the nature of my personality," he says. "I can be jubilant one moment and pensive the next, and a cloud could go by and make that happen. I'm inconsistent, even to myself."

During a recording career that now spans 35 years, Dylan has been a cornucopia of inconsistency. Visionary and crank, innovator and conservator, irritant and stimulant, skeptic and proselytizer, rebel and sellout, pathfinder and lost patrol: Dylan has been all of those things, and many more. He may well be the most restless figure in rock history, constitutionally incapable of doing the same thing twice. Apparently he meant it when he sang, in 1965, that artists "don't look back." *Time Out of Mind* is a typical Dylan album only because it eludes expectations.

In the 1960s, Dylan taught folk singers how to transcend the topical, then taught rock songwriters how to think about something more than the next romance. Casually, he created whole genres: folk rock, country rock and what's now called Americana. Every facet of his 1960s music has been imitated, lately by his son Jakob's band, the Wallflowers. Through the 1970s and 1980s, Dylan followed more wayward, less reliable inspirations. He created the rock-and-roll caravan called Rolling Thunder. He embraced born-again Christianity and then returned to Judaism. He toured with the Grateful Dead and Tom Petty's Heartbreakers, and he sold his anthem "The Times They Are A-Changin' " so it could be used in an accounting firm's commercial.

At first deliberately, and even after he repudiated the role, he became a voice for the baby-boomer generation by singing what was on his mind. Just ahead of many of his listeners, he moved from political fervor and apocalyptic visions to marriage and divorce, from searching for faith to grumbling at the nightly news. Since his bitter divorce from the former Sara Lowndes in the late 1970s, which left her with custody of her five children, including the four they had had together, he has had a home in Malibu, Calif., and kept his private life private. But his reactions to people, ideas and the world have resounded in his songs.

Year in and year out, almost constantly since 1988, Dylan has hit the road. He has become an itinerant musician like the bluesmen and hillbilly troubadours who were his musical education, although his endless tour includes dates like the 1993 inaugural celebration for Bill Clinton and a scheduled show yesterday in Bologna, Italy, before the Pope. "Night or day, it doesn't matter where I go anymore, I just go," he sings in "Can't Wait."

"A lot of people don't like the road," he says, "but it's as natural to me as breathing. I do it because I'm driven to do it, and I either hate it or love it. I'm mortified to be on the stage, but then again, it's the only place where I'm happy. It's the only place you can be who you want to be. You can't be who you want to be in daily life. I don't care who you are, you're going to be disappointed in daily life. But the cure-all for all that is to get on the stage, and that's why performers do it. But in saying that, I don't want to put on the mask of celebrity. I'd rather just do my work and see it as a trade."

During the 1990s, touring with his best group since he was backed by the Band, Dylan has garnered a new audience. His shows a decade ago, often yelled or sung in a monotone, exasperated even longtime fans. But at Dylan concerts lately, collegiate types in the tie-dyed shirts of Dead-heads have joined balding baby-boomer loyalists. Audiences respond to the blues and country roots of his band and to Dylan's mercurial, improvisatory side, knowing he sings his songs differently at every show.

"I like those people who come to see me now," Dylan says. "They're not aware of my early days, but I'm glad of that. It lifts that burden of responsibility, of having to play everything exactly like it was on some certain record. I can't do that. Which way the wind is blowing, they're going to come out different every time, but the intent is going to be the same.

"I've got to know that I'm singing something with truth to it. My songs are different than anybody else's songs. Other artists can get by on their voices and their style, but my songs speak volumes, and all I have to do is lay them down correctly, lyrically, and they'll do what they need to do."

Dylan has not lacked for recognition in the 90s. He has collected a lifetime achievement Grammy Award, was named a Commandeur dans l'Ordre des Arts et des Lettres in France and will collect a Kennedy Center Honors award in December. Until the 90s, there was one thing that Dylan had not been: silent. Songs had always poured out of him: great, good, indifferent and awful songs, but in a steady stream. That changed after his mediocre 1990 album, *Under the Red Sky*. He went on performing older songs while releasing two albums of traditional folk and blues material, *Good As I Been to You* and *World Gone Wrong*, played solo like an early-1960s Greenwich Village folkie. *Dignity*, the one new song he released after *Red Sky*, was an outtake from the 1989 album *Oh Mercy*.

What made him quit recording new songs? "Disillusion," he says. "Disillusion with the whole process of it. I started out when you could go in the studio and record your songs and leave. I don't remember when that changed. But I found myself spending more and more time in the studio doing less and less. There wasn't any gratification in it, really. I was writing the songs, because that's what I do anyway. And then I had my stage band, so I figured, well, I'll write them and I'll play them when I play them. It's not like we lack any songs to play on a stage."

Longtime fans fretted that Dylan wasn't introducing new songs in concert. The reason, he says, was simple: "I don't like to bring out new material because of the bootleg situation." Yet backstage and at sound checks, extraordinary new songs were taking shape.

Time Out of Mind (Columbia) is bleak and riveting. Its 11 songs are about the loneliness, anger and desolation of lost love, and about looming mortality. (The album was recorded before Dylan was hospitalized over the summer with a life-threatening heart infection.)

"I've been walking through the middle of nowhere, trying to get to heaven before they close the door," Dylan sings. He has rarely sounded optimistic; spite and self-righteous contempt animate many of his best songs. But *Time Out of Mind* provides fewer comforts than ever.

"Environment affects me a great deal," Dylan says. "A lot of the songs were written after the sun went down. And I like storms, I like to stay up during a storm. I get very meditative sometimes, and this one phrase was going through my head: 'Work while the day lasts, because the night of death cometh when no man can work.' I don't recall where I heard it. I like preaching, I hear a lot of preaching, and I probably just heard it somewhere. Maybe it's in Psalms, it beats me. But it wouldn't let me go. I was, like, what does that phrase mean? But it was at the forefront of my mind, for a long period of time, and I think a lot of that is instilled into this record."

Many of the songs echo the chord structures of 1960s classics like "Ballad of a Thin Man" and "Just Like a Woman," but with the youthful cockiness of those sessions turned inside out. The producer Daniel Lanois (who has also worked with U2, Peter Gabriel and Emmylou Harris) makes the band sound as if it is coalescing on the spot. Instruments enter one by one, feeling their way into the tunes as if they're sneaking into a speakeasy jam session.

Yet the impromptu, unsettled sound is a very deliberate choice. "I wasn't interested in making a record that took the songs and made them into a contemporary setting," Dylan says. "My music, my songs, they have very little to do with technology. They either work or they don't work. Daniel and I made that record *Oh Mercy* a while back, and that was pretty good at the time. But these songs, I felt, were more all-encompassing. They were more filled with the dread realities of life.

"Many of my records are more or less blueprints for the songs. This time, I didn't want blueprints, I wanted the real thing. When the songs are done right they're done right, and that's it. They're written in stone when they're done right."

Instead of constructing the music layer by layer, Dylan worked through the songs with his musicians, including the Tex-Mex electric-organ legend Augie Meyers, the guitarist Duke Robillard and the linchpin of Dylan's touring band, Tony Garnier on bass. Nearly everything on the album, including vocals, was recorded live in the studio.

"We all know what the thing should sound like. We're just getting further and further away from it," Dylan says. "I wanted something that goes through the technology and comes out the other end before the technology knows what it's doing."

The purposely unpolished music—clattering rockabilly drums and ricocheting guitars in "Cold Irons Bound," loping blues with raw guitar jabs in " 'Til I Fell in Love With You," slinky electric piano over a reggae backbeat in "Love Sick," tentative gospel in "Tryin' to Get to Heaven"—has a haunted, precarious tone that connects it to the most harrowing depths of the blues.

The blues has always been a Dylan touchstone, for both words and music. In many ways, his groundbreaking 1960s songs were transmuted blues, from the surreal juxtapositions of the lyrics to the rough-hewn vocals to the blues bands he hired when he plugged in.

Throughout *Time Out of Mind*, Dylan quotes hoary blues lines like "Going down the road feeling bad." And in his maturity, he is closer than ever to the clear-eyed fatalism of classic blues. In song after song, the singer walks down dark, empty roads, muttering accusations at a woman who left him; he's still wishing she would come back and wondering, in one song, whether he would kiss her or kill her if she did.

When he's not brooding over shattered romance, he's feeling his age and contemplating death. In the 17-minute "Highlands," he watches young people drinking and dancing, and his voice grows hollow with sadness: "I'd trade places with any of 'em in a minute if I could."

"I can't help those feelings," he says. "I'm not going to try to make a fake Pollyanna view. Why would I even want to? And I'm not going to deny them just because they might be a little dismal to look at. I try to let it speak for itself, but I'm not emotionally involved in it. I can deliver the message. I learned a while ago not to get personally involved, because if you're personally involved you're going to go over the top."

Watching his son Jakob turn into a multimillion-selling hit maker, Dylan tempers his pride with caution. "He's had an amazing amount of success in a short time," Dylan says. "I just don't want to see his heart get broken in this business, that's all."

For Dylan, the songs he grew up on continue to provide the models, and the yardstick, for his own music; *Good As I Been to You* and *World Gone Wrong* only strengthened the connection. "My songs come out of folk music," he says. "I love that whole pantheon. To me there's no difference between Muddy Waters and Bill Monroe."

Going through the tracks on *Time Out of Mind*, he points out what he borrowed: among other things, a jug-band guitar line in "Not Dark Yet," an inverted rockabilly lick in "Dirt Road Blues," and a riff and a country-blues lilt from Charley Patton in "Highlands."

"There's a lot of clever people around who write songs," Dylan says. "My songs, what makes them different is that there's a foundation to them. That's why they're still around, that's why my songs are still being performed. It's not because they're such great songs. They don't fall into the commercial category. They're not written to be performed by other people. But they're standing on a strong foundation, and subliminally that's what people are hearing.

"Those old songs are my lexicon and my prayer book," he adds. "All my beliefs come out of those old songs, literally, anything from 'Let Me Rest on That Peaceful Mountain' to 'Keep on the Sunny Side.' You can find all my philosophy in those old songs. I believe in a God of time and space, but if people ask me about that, my impulse is to point them back toward those songs. I believe in Hank Williams singing 'I Saw the Light.' I've seen the light, too." Dylan says he now subscribes to no organized religion.

While Dylan idolized the likes of Mississippi John Hurt and Jimmie Rodgers in the 1960s, he has now achieved their kind of gravity himself. If anything, he sounds more woeful. The voice of a generation has become a voice of experience, telling us that experience hasn't taught him anything he needs. Explicitly or not, the blues and folk masters offered their own survival as reassurance.

But on *Time Out of Mind*, Dylan refuses listeners that solace; he often sounds as if he would welcome death. "It's not dark yet, but it's getting there," he sings, unguarded and matter-of-fact.

"I've written some songs that I look at, and they just give me a sense of awe," Dylan says. "Stuff like 'It's Alright, Ma,' just the alliteration in that blows me away. And I can also look back and know where I was tricky and where I was really saying something that just happened to have a spark of poetry to it.

"But when you get beyond a certain year, after you go on for a certain number of years, you realize, hey, life is kind of short anyway. And you might as well say the way you feel."

28. Interview with Robert Hilburn, *The Los Angeles Times*

DECEMBER 14, 1997

In *Time Out of Mind*, Bob Dylan's most acclaimed album in 20 years, there are moments that sound like the reflections of a man who is nearing the last rites.

"When you think that you've lost everything you find out that you could always lose a little more," Dylan sings in one song that summarizes the soul of the album, which, in contrast to the youthful optimism of his landmark '60s works, focuses on love and life at a time when options and expectations have been greatly lowered.

So it's surprising to see the classic songwriter in an upbeat, even playful mood as he sits this evening on a couch in a private room just off the lower lobby of a Santa Monica hotel.

Dylan, 56, has disliked interviews for years because he's always asked to reveal something about his personal life or to interpret his lyrics, whether from one of his socially conscious folk anthems like "Blowin' in the Wind" or a snarling, self-affirming rock anthem such as "Like a Rolling Stone."

Even now, he quickly deflects questions about how much his songs, some of which express bitterness over relationships, are from his own experience.

Yet a smile accompanies his rejoinder, rather than the icy defiance that he once might have shown. "They are songs meant to be sung," he says when pressed on the autobiographical aspect. "I don't know if they are meant to be discussed around the coffee table."

It's easy to see why Dylan is in good spirits. *Time Out of Mind*, his first collection of new songs in seven years, was not only hailed by critics, but the album, which entered pop charts at No. 10 in October, has already been declared gold (sales of 500,000). It's his first gold studio collection since 1983's *Infidels*. The album (his 40th, including retrospectives) brings his total U.S. sales to nearly 31 million.

Dylan, whose songwriting in the '60s revolutionized rock by bringing commentary and literary ambition to a musical form that had chiefly relied simply on attitude and energy, also received the prestigious Kennedy Center Honor last Sunday in Washington, D.C. About Dylan, President Clinton said, "He probably had more impact on people of my generation than any other artist."

But it becomes clear during the interview that there is a deeper reason for Dylan's sense of satisfaction—one that grows out of what he describes as the rediscovery in recent years of the self-identity as performer that he lost during the acclaim and hoopla of his '70s and '80s arena and stadium tours.

"I remember playing shows [with Tom Petty and the Heartbreakers in the '80s] and looking out [thinking] I didn't have that many fans coming to see me," he says. "They were coming to see Tom Petty and the Heartbreakers."

About that period, he adds, "I was going on my name for a long time, name and reputation, which was about all I had. I had sort of fallen into an amnesia spell. . . . I didn't feel I knew who I was on stage. . . ."

But Dylan says he regained his sense of identity and purpose in the hundreds of concerts he has done in the '90s, an ambitious series of mostly theater dates that has been dubbed by the media the Never-Ending Tour. That invigorating experience apparently contributed to the creative outburst in the new album.

On the eve of a sold-out, five-night stand at the El Rey Theatre, Dylan—who says he feels fine after being hospitalized in May for treatment of pericarditis—speaks about the new album, the "missing" years and, gingerly, about the success of his son Jakob's band, the Wallflowers.

You seem to be in good spirits. Do you think the word "happy" might even apply?

I think that it's hard to find happiness as a whole in anything [*laughs*]. The days of tender youth are gone. I think you can be delirious in your youth, but as you get older, things happen. We take our instruction from the media. The media just gloats over tragedy and sin and shame, so why are people supposed to feel any different?

Some of the words used by critics to describe the songs in the album are . . . brooding, gloomy, misery, wary. Do you see the album that way?

I don't know . . . It's certainly not an album of felicity . . . I try to live within that line between despondency and hope. I'm suited to walk that line, right between the fire . . . I see [the album] right straight down the middle of the line, really.

Why were your two albums before this one simply acoustic songs by other writers? Did it take this long to write these songs?

I had written these songs, but . . . I forgot about recording for a while. I didn't feel like I wanted to put forth the effort to record anything. The acoustic albums were easy enough. I was pretty content to let it be that.

What was different about this album?

Part of the—I don't know what you want to call it—maybe the effectiveness of these songs is the fact that they weren't just written and taken into the studio the way so many of my songs have been, where you are stuck with the arrangement, stuck with who's playing on them, stuck with the lyrics. So many of my records were made that way. So many that people elevate on such a high level were in some sense only first drafts of songs . . . and they have changed over the years. I had lived with these songs long enough to know what I wanted.

The 16-minute "Highlands" is the highlight of the album. How did that song come about?

I had the guitar run off an old Charley Patton record [in his head] for years and always wanted to do something with that. I was sitting around, maybe in the dark Delta or maybe in some unthinkable trench somewhere, with that sound in my mind and the dichotomy of the highlands with that seemed to be a path worth pursuing.

What about writing the song? Is it something you do in one sitting or is it something you piece together over time?

It starts off as a stream of consciousness thing and you add things to it. I take things from all parts of life and then I see if there is a connection, and if there's a connection I connect them. The riff was just going repeatedly, hypnotically in my head, then the words eventually come along. Probably every song on the album came that way.

There are a dozen lines in that song alone that it'd be interesting to have you talk about, but how about the one with Neil Young? "I'm listening to Neil Young / I gotta turn up the sound / Someone's always yelling, / 'Turn it down.'" Is that a tip of the hat or . . . ?

It's anything you want it to be [*smiles*]. I don't give too much thought to individual lines. If I thought about them in any kind of deep way, maybe I wouldn't use them because I'd always be second-guessing myself. I learned a long time ago to trust my intuition.

How do you feel when one album is praised much more than another one? Do you understand why people respond differently to albums or do you think a lot of it seems arbitrary?

I never listen to my albums, once they are completed. I don't want to be reminded. To me, I've done them. I find it like looking into a lifeless mirror. I do, however, listen to this album quite a bit.

If you were so pleased with these songs, why didn't you do them in concert before you recorded them if you had them for so long?

That's the funny thing. People don't think they can respond to a song that they haven't heard on a record. It didn't used to be that way, but I think we are living in an age where we are so bombarded—everything from satellite news to biological weapons—and people want to be familiar with something before they are ready to accept it.

Even your fans? Aren't they a pretty adventurous bunch?

I don't know. I don't think I have the same fans I had earlier. In fact, I know they aren't the same people. Those fans left me years ago. If I was a fan of me back then, I wouldn't [still] be either.

What do you mean?

I wasn't giving anybody anything that they felt comfortable with, and I understood that, but I understood it much later than it was happening. I don't have any one kind of fan or follower of this kind of music, like say, U2, or Bruce [Springsteen] or any of these young groups today who consistently keep their followers because what they are doing is variations of the same things. My situation is peculiar. I didn't come out of the same environment. My tradition is older than all that. I came out of the environment of folk music.

Is there any way to describe your goals when you were starting out?

I knew growing up that I wanted to do something different than anybody else. I wanted to do something that no one else did or could do, and I wanted to do it better than anyone else had. I didn't know where that was going to lead me, but where it did lead me was to folk music at a time when it was totally off the radar screen. Maybe there were 12 people in all of America who even heard of Woody Guthrie, Roscoe Holcomb, the Carter Family, Leadbelly—at least 12 people my age. They were free spirits who took chances, and I never wished to annul any of that spirit.

You've never seemed comfortable with your success and acclaim. Is that true?

I'm still not. I still don't consider myself in the same realm as someone like James Taylor or Randy Newman, someone who, in my book, is a "songwriter for the times." I feel my stuff is very hard-edged and not everybody's cup of tea.

You've been touring for more than 20 years now. Do you see a time when you might stop? Or do you think you'll be doing it until your final breath?

I could stop any time . . . I can see an end to everything, really.

You did once stop playing for eight years, during the late '60s. Why were you off the road for so long?

I didn't want to go on the road. I didn't feel it was as important to me as personal matters. I had a family. It wouldn't work for me if I was on the road. So I stayed off. Then we came to California . . . and I forgot what I did [on stage] . . . totally . . . when I got back [on tour in 1974], I was looked upon as a songwriter of a generation or mouthpiece of a generation. That was the slogan put on me at the time. I had to meet that head on.

Was that uncomfortable?

402 • *Dylan on Dylan*

Sure, because when I went back [to touring], nothing was working right for me. . . . I had lost my raison d'être. . . . I didn't know what I was doing out there, people throwing flowers and whatever. I didn't know who they expected me to be. It was a crazy time.

So, what turned it around for you?

At a certain point [on the Petty tour], I had a revelation about a bunch of things, which is hard to explain [briefly]. . . . I realized that it was necessary to go out and turn things around.

How did you do that?

On some night when lightning strikes, this gift was given back to me and I knew it. . . . The essence was back.

So you learned to enjoy yourself again on stage in recent years?

Yes, it took a long time to develop back into what it would have been if I hadn't taken the time off. It's a strange story, I'll admit it.

Speaking of joy, what about Jakob's success with the Wallflowers?

It's sensational what has happened to the Wallflowers. It's like one in a million or something.

When you heard he was going to start a band, did you worry about him? Did you advise him at all?

It was inconsequential what I thought.

As a father, though, were you worried about all he would have to go through, like the pain of being dropped by his label after the first album?

I was concerned after the label dropped him and they still were involved in trying to get another record deal, but he made it on his own. If anything, his name would have held him back. I think that held him back on his first records, to tell you the truth. I think that first record would have been accepted if he wasn't who he was.

What about honors, such as the Kennedy honors? Do you appreciate them?

It's always nice to be appreciated, especially while you are still alive.

29. Interview with Murray Engleheart, *Guitar World* and *Uncut*

MARCH 1999

Greil Marcus once said something to the effect that Skip James' records always sound best at night. 'Time Out of Mind' seems like that too. Do you feel that?

It sounds like Skip James?

In a sense, but Marcus was saying that it's always like night when his albums are playing and . . .

Oh yeah, yeah. That would be a tremendous compliment to me to hear that it would have any kind of an appeal like Skip James would have. I've never seen that before. But if anything it would probably radiate the same kind of intensity that Skip James would do. I would hope that it would be in that kind of a realm anyway.

The album has got an immediacy to it but also a sense that a lot of hard work went into it as well . . .

A lot of hard work did go into it. In the emergence of that particular sound the producer and the engineer worked very hard to make the atmosphere hospitable enough to make it happen that way. The record for me—I didn't want it to be a stopping place. We talked about that before we started. It really needed to be something where the music was interjected onto the disc in a permanent way.

It's almost like there's ghosts running through it in terms of mood and ambience. Are those ghosts of or for anybody in particular?

Uh, no. I'm not versed in the psychological part of it. I don't know. The ghosts you're probably talking about are just probably instruments that are more in the background as opposed to being in the front and in the side and just different echoes which emanate from just the complete sound of the record, something which will protrude but in any case make themselves noticed.

Jim Dickinson had a lot to do with the record . . .

He did.

He said something years ago which I thought was fascinating. He said that a lot of people don't realize that the recording process is about freeze framing the soul. You seem to have achieved that with 'Time Out of Mind' . . .

Yeah. The recording process is very difficult for me. I lose my inspiration in the studio real easy and it's very difficult for me to think that I'm going to eclipse anything that I've ever done. I get bored easy and my mission, which starts out wide, becomes very dim after a few failed takes and this and that. So it's very difficult for me these days to record.

Getting back to the Skip James thing again: There are elements of country blues and Sun Records on the album that are often overlooked in your work . . .

Well it's always there. It always has been there. But in the past when my records were made, which disillusioned me actually from making the records in the past, producers or whoever's in charge of my sessions, they feel it's enough just to have me singing an original song so the orchestration of these songs really never gets fully developed. *Time Out of Mind* is more illuminated in something which is completely articulate rather than just a song and just the singing of that song. Arrangements or structures can be really thought about and entangled into it.

The Grammys experience. Did that protester scar the moment for you?

He was part of the show . . . Yeah.

You looked like you were going to break up laughing at one point . . .

Yeah, exactly. He was supposed to, he was part of . . . [*starts to laugh*] . . . He did good, don't you think?

'Time Out of Mind' was recorded just before you fell ill . . .

That's right.

Would it have been a good final chapter for you on reflection?

No, I don't think so. I think we were just starting with getting my identifiable sound onto the disc. I think we just started. I think there's plenty more to do. We just opened up that door at that particular time and in the passage of time we'll go back in and extend that. But I didn't feel like it was an ending to anything. I thought it was more the beginning.

Back on the Grammys, you mentioned Buddy Holly. What was it his spirit brought to the record?

Buddy Holly. You know, it's hard to take myself back there. You know, I don't really recall exactly what I said about Buddy Holly. But while we were recording down in Florida where we made that record every place I turned there was Buddy Holly. You know what I mean? It was one of those things. Every place you turned. You walked down a hallway and you heard Buddy Holly records. Then you'd get in the car to go over to the studio and "Rave On" is playing. Then you walk into this studio and someone's playing a cassette of "That'll Be the Day" or "It's So Easy." And this would happen day after day after day. Phrases of Buddy Holly songs would just come out of nowhere. It was spooky [*laughs suddenly after a brief pause*]. But after we recorded and left, you know, it stayed in our minds. Well, Buddy Holly's spirit must have been some-place hastening this record in a kind of way.

You mentioned opening new doors. B.B. King benefited from touring with U2 in terms of his audience base, and Neil Young has a godfatherly-like connection with what was grunge. Have you found a shift in your audience as well?

Ah, no I haven't found any shift but I've found a different audience. If you'd asked me now what does my audience look like as compared to ten years ago, I would say there's a great shift. But if you're asking me year after year, it's difficult to tell because we play for so many different types of people all over the world. What one crowd looks like one night looks like a different crowd of people another night. You could play like a charity event where people are all in tuxedos and black ties. Then you can play an event where people are kind of like all in some kind of an open field in the middle of the day. We play to all kinds of people. It's hard to say just what the difference in the crowd would be. But over a ten-year period I would say that my audience has changed. I'm not good at reading how old people are but they're lively people and the difference between now and maybe ten years ago when I was playing is that these people who see me now—they can react immediately. They don't come with a lot of preconceived ideas about who they would like me to be or who they think I am. They're there just across all kinds of generational gaps. But these people seem to be there and to be able to react quickly. Whereas a few years ago they couldn't react quickly. They had to get through too much . . .

Baggage?

Mental, yeah, mental psychic stuff so [*sighs*] I was still kind of bogged down with a certain crowd of people. It has taken a long time to bust through that crowd. Even the last time I played Australia. When I was playing there with Tom Petty we were kind of facing that same old crowd. But the last time we were there . . . I still get letters from all those places. I still get letters from Brisbane, you know, Sydney and Melbourne and, you know, Perth. I get a lot of letters from up around there and those people really don't know the Petty shows. They know us from the last time we were there. I think it was in '93 or something where we played theaters and that show has remained in people's minds. Those are the people I assume I'm going to play for when I get back there. Those people. Not the people who might know me as some kind of figurehead from another age or a symbol or a generational thing. But I don't really have to deal with that anymore. If I ever did.

You mentioned tuxedos.

Yeah.

You did the Kennedy Center Honors night with Gregory Peck.

Yeah [*seems to laugh quietly*].

That must have been weird.

Well, listen, everything's weird. You tell me something that's not weird.

Wasn't Charlton Heston there and Springsteen did "Blowin' in the Wind"?

You know, everything's surreal. I've just gotten comfortable with that [*laughs*]. I don't know what's weird and what's not weird.

Do you find that song selection for your sets gets harder or easier as the years go on?

I have so many songs that having the songs is the least of my prob-lems. I've got songs that I've never even sung yet live. I've got 500, 600, 700 songs. I don't have a problem with the backlog of songs. Some fade away and diminish in time but others take their place.

With the reinterpretation of your work does it get to a point where chang-ing the phrasing or altering the timing changes the thrust of the song or do you enjoy that ambiguity?

Well, it's not ambiguous. There's no ambiguity in it. There's also, speaking now in musicological terms? There really isn't any spontaneity.

Really?

No. There isn't any improvisation. There isn't any changing the inflection of the lyrics. Oh well, there might be because you sing the same song every night so it might come out different. But it doesn't begin and end there. It begins with the structure of all the songs. If you're going to ask me what's the difference between now and what the difference was earlier when I used to play in the seventies, eighties and even back in the sixties, there wasn't any structure to the songs. The structure is the architecture of the song. And that's why the performances are effective because measure for measure they don't stray from the actual structure of the song. It's difficult to explain, but it's a mental thing. It doesn't have anything to do with energy or doesn't have anything to do with how I might feel a certain night. It's more all mechanics. Mechanical. But it's an endless . . . once you set the archi-tecture up then a song can be done in an endless amount of ways. That's what keeps my live shows . . . they're non-adulterated because they're not diluted or they're not jumbled up, they're not scrambled, they're not just a bunch of screaming, a conglomerated sound mix. What I'm saying might sound confused and unclassified in a way but it just matters mostly how to take it all apart and then adhesively put it back together, where it makes sense on a structural level musically. That's why you can't quite put a finger on what it is that I'm doing [*laughs*]. I've never seen anybody, I've never seen it in print anywhere, I've never seen anybody . . . it's like you mentioned Skip James. Well, I don't know. Did you know that Skip James was the guy that said I don't want to entertain? What I want to do is impress with skill and deaden the minds of my listeners? If you listen to his records, his old records, you know he can do that. But if you listen to the records he made in the sixties when they rediscovered him, you find that there's something missing. And what's missing is that interconnecting thread of the structure of the songs which, let's face it, might be . . . it's not an idea that most people would, they wouldn't want to come up with this idea because basically people wouldn't really have to do it. But I need to do it because I have to play sometimes every night of the week. I don't know if this is making sense. If you were a musician you would understand probably what I'm saying a whole lot more.

Your heart attack did that . . .

Well, let me say first of all it was not a heart attack. It was an infection that went into my heart area. It was something called histoplasmosis that came from just accidentally inhaling a bunch of stuff that was out on one of the rivers here. It was probably like being probably where you are maybe. Being like up on the Peel River or something? In a stormy kind of season? Maybe one month or one or two days out of the year when that stuff is all in the air like after it rains? And then there's a tornado? Then the banks around the river get all mucky and then the wind blows and it's all a bunch of swirling mess in the air and I happened to inhale a bunch of that. That's what made me sick. It went into the heart area. But it wasn't anything really attacking my heart.

You were pretty seriously ill though, right?

Oh, I was seriously ill, yeah.

Did that make you pause and rethink things?

I really didn't, you know, I really didn't [*enthusiastically*] because in a generalized way I hadn't done that to myself and it was so unspecific that there was no . . . without exception there was nothing in my mind to say I did this to get that, you know? It was nonaccidental. It's not like I even needed the time to slow down and look at things. Really it was actually for no purpose except that I was down for about six weeks. But I don't remember particularly having any kind of great illuminations at that time.

Bruce Springsteen once said that without you there'd be no 'Sgt. Pepper,' no 'Pet Sounds,' no Pistols' "God Save the Queen," no U2's "Pride," etc. Does that statement take on a different dimension coming from a friend?

[*Lost for words momentarily*] Well, I mean you know you just have to go on. We can influence all kinds of people but sometimes it gets in the way, especially if you're influencing somebody, if somebody is accusing you of influencing somebody that you had no intention of interesting or influencing at all. I've never given it any mind at all really. I don't really care to really influence anybody at this time and if I have influenced anybody what can I say?

You did a press conference in Sydney for the tour with Tom Petty, and I was standing next to the late artist Brett Whitely. [The conference was held in Whitely's Surry Hills studio in Sydney.] Fond memories of him?

Oh yeah, I thought the world of Brett. I loved his artwork and I still do. He gave me a bunch of his books before he passed on and I still do have them. I don't know what the story was with Brett really.

Are you concerned that perhaps you're creating too great an expectation?

That I've created too great an expectation?

Yeah.

In what way?

Well, as you were saying previously about the generational figurehead thing and that some people can't get past that . . .

No, I don't think that's true because I have to see people every night. If I didn't go out and play maybe I'd agree with you. But my concerts are populated by people who wouldn't be there if they just were there looking at a figurehead. They just wouldn't be there. They'd come once and they wouldn't come back. But we played in Australia like I said and played in these towns I guess in '93 or '94 and I still get letters from those towns. I would hope that we play for more people this time.

Do you remember someone spilling a cup of coffee on you backstage in Sydney on that tour?

Oh, that happens all the time!

There's always talk about the peaks in people's work. With you the talk is about 'Blonde on Blonde,' 'Blood on the Tracks,' 'Infidels,' etc. Do you sense that too? Have you got a good sense of your own magic?

Well those records were made a long time ago and you know truthfully records that were made in that day and age all were good. They all had some magic to them because the technology didn't go past what the artist was doing. It was a lot easier to get excellence back in those days on a record than it is now. So as far as the records I made back then, I made records back then just like a lot of other people who were my age and we all made good records. Those records seem to cast a long shadow. But how much of it is the technology and how much of it is the talent and influence I really don't know. I know you can't make records that sound that way anymore. The high priority is technology now. It's not the artist or the art. It's the technology which is coming through. That's what makes *Time Out of Mind* . . . it doesn't take itself seriously but then again the sound is very significant to that record. If that record was made in just a trivialized way it wouldn't have sounded that way. It wouldn't have had the impact that it did. The guys that helped me make it, they went out of their way to make a record that sounds like a record played on a record player. There wasn't any wasted effort on that particular record and I don't think there will be on any more of my records.

The performance for the Pope must have been tremendously moving . . .

Well, it's all surreal you know? But yeah, it was moving. I mean, he's the Pope [*laughs*]. You know what I mean? There's only one Pope, right?

Did the irony of playing "Knockin' on Heaven's Door" strike you at the time?

No, because that's the song they wanted to hear. It seemed to be a good correspondent to the situation.

Marlon Brando once said that you and the Band were the loudest thing he'd ever heard . . .

Hmmm . . .

Do you see some sort of affinity or have you ever seen some sort of affinity with him?

Oh yeah, absolutely! I think he's brave and fearless and undaunted. The whole thing. He's one of the modern-day heroes. There's absolutely no question about that. But I think he said that a long time ago when at that time it might have been true, but it wouldn't be true today.

30. Interview with Mikal Gilmore, ROLLING STONE

DECEMBER 22, 2001

"That night in Switzerland," says Bob Dylan, "it all just came to me. All of a sudden I could sing anything. There might've been a time when I was going to quit or retire, but the next day it was like, 'I can't really retire now because I really haven't done anything yet,' you know? I want to see where this will lead me, because now I can control it all. Before, I wasn't controlling it. I was just being swept by the wind, this way or that way."

As Dylan speaks, we are seated at a small table in a comfortable hotel suite, located on the beach at Santa Monica. Dylan is dressed in the sort of country-gentleman finery he has tended to favor in recent years—a nicely stitched white Western shirt and sharp-looking black slacks with arrows embroidered at the edges of the pocket seams. Dylan has been talking about a crucial turning point in his life and art, during the time since ROLLING STONE last published a lengthy interview with him in 1992. In several of those years, Dylan produced erratic and mixed-up work—and he is the first to admit it. But increasingly, those years also featured some of the most resourceful and remarkable creativity in Dylan's forty-year recording and performing career—and that progress, it is only fair to say, was sometimes less noted than it should have been. All that changed in 1997. In that year, Dylan fell sick with a rare fungal infection that caused severe swelling around his heart. It was a painful condition that temporarily debilitated him, and it could have proved fatal. Around the same time as his illness, Dylan finished and soon released his first album of original material in seven years, *Time Out of Mind*. It was a work unlike any other that Dylan had created—a trek through the unmapped frontier that lies beyond loss and disillusion—and it was heralded as a startling work of renewal. *Time Out of Mind* went on to win the Grammy for Best Album of the Year—Dylan's first such honor in that category.

In September, Dylan released another collection of new songs, *Love and Theft*—his forty-third album. *Love and Theft* sounds at moments like Dylan is unearthing new revelations with an acerbic wit and impulsive language—in much the same way he did on his early hallmark, *Highway 61 Revisited*—though *Love and Theft* also seems to derive from ancient wellsprings of American vision and concealment, much like *John Wesley Harding* or his legendary 1967 Basement Tapes sessions with the Band. Dylan, however, bristles at such comparisons. *Love and Theft*, as he puts it, plays by its own rules.

The 1980s saw Dylan lose his focus. He mounted widely publicized and well-attended tours with Tom Petty and the Heartbreakers and the Grateful Dead—but these were tours in which Dylan seemed to be casting about for a sense of connection and intent. To many observers, Dylan gave the impression that he was adrift. In recent years, he has told the story of an event—a moment of awareness—that came to him onstage in Locarno, Switzerland. He said that a phrase struck him—"I'm determined to stand whether God will deliver me or not"—and in that moment, he realized that it was his vocation to rededicate himself to his music and its performance. Dylan didn't make any public pronouncements about this realization and how it had changed his purpose as a singer, musician and songwriter. In a low-key yet determined way, Dylan invested himself in his music's sustaining power perhaps more than ever before. As good as *Time Out of Mind* and *Love and Theft* may be, the live shows that Dylan has been playing for years with an evolving, carefully selected band (which presently consists of bassist Tony Garnier, drummer David Kemper, and guitarists Larry Campbell and Charlie Sexton), make the case that his essential art can be found onstage even more than on record. Indeed, Dylan—who turned sixty this last May—seems to have adopted a viewpoint similar to the one favored by jazz trumpeter and bandleader Miles Davis for most of his career: namely, that the truest vital experience of music resides in the moment of its performance, in the living act of its formation and the spontaneous yet hard-earned discoveries that those acts of creation yield. The next time the musicians play the same song, it is not really the same song. It is a new moment and creation, a new possibility, a newfound place on the map, soon to be left behind for the next place. These live shows are the quintessence of Bob Dylan and how he has moved into the new century, bringing with him what he values most from the music of the last century, even as night after night he takes us to unfamiliar and transfixing understandings of what we once thought we knew so well.

It was a Tuesday in September when Dylan and I sat down to discuss his recent art—two weeks to the day after the shocking attacks that destroyed New York's World Trade Center buildings. (The tragedy's date, September 11th, was also the release date for *Love and Theft*.) As we talked, Dylan and I were near the room's open balcony doors and windows, overlooking the Pacific Ocean. The Los Angeles airport is just down the highway, and every few minutes you could see an airplane in its ascent as it embarked on its journey. Once or twice, we just watched without comment, but there was a sense that nobody will ever look at the commonplace sight of a plane moving across the sky in quite the same way again. It would be unfair to Dylan to make the claim that anything in his music anticipated the horrific turn of recent events. And yet clearly he has been writing about dread realities and dangerous likelihoods for four decades now, from the end-times vision of 1963's "A Hard Rain's A-Gonna Fall" to his current remorseful statement about personal and national spirit in *Love and Theft*'s "Mississippi." Bob Dylan may no longer be the young firebrand who tore through the world with such energy and disdain in the 1960s, but he is still a songwriter, singer and literary artist of continuing power and depth. If there was any principal meaning to Dylan's early music, perhaps it was that it is hardly trouble-free for a smart, conscientious person to live in times that witness the betrayal or inversion of our best values and dreams. To live through such times with scruples and intellect intact, Dylan has declared in his music, one has to hold an honest and fearless mirror up to the face of cultural and moral disorder.

Dylan was convivial and confident as we talked on this day, but in his speech, just as in his songs and vocals, one senses that he carries a dignified knowledge of enduring mysteries that probably unsettle him every bit as much as his awareness of them distinguishes him. And in conversation, just as in his music, Bob Dylan lets go of his insights in constantly surprising and singular turns of phrase and temperament.

—

*In 1998, when you received the Grammy Award for Album of the
Year, you said something that surprised me—maybe surprised other people as
well. You said, "We didn't know what we had when we did it, but we did it
anyway." That was interesting because 'Time Out of Mind' plays as an album
made with purpose and vision, with a consistent mood and set of themes. Was
it, in fact, an album you approached with forethought, or was its seeming
cohesiveness incidental?*

What happened was, I'd been writing down couplets and verses
and things, and then putting them together at later times. I had a
lot of that—it was starting to pile up—so I thought, "Well, I got all
this—maybe, I'll try to record it." I'd had good luck with Daniel Lanois
[producer of the 1989 album *Oh Mercy*], so I called him and showed him
a lot of the songs. I also familiarized him with the way I wanted the songs
to *sound*. I think I played him some Slim Harpo recordings—early stuff
like that. He seemed pretty agreeable to it, and we set aside a certain
time and place. But I had a schedule—I only had so much time—and
we made that record, *Time Out of Mind*, that way. It was a little rougher.
. . . I wouldn't say *rougher*. . . . It was . . . I feel we were *lucky* to get that
record.

Really?

Well, I didn't go into it with the idea that this was going to be a
finished album. It got off the tracks more than a few times, and people
got frustrated. I know I did. I know Lanois did. There were myriad
musicians down there. At that point in time, I didn't have the same
band I have now. I was kind of just auditioning players here and there
for a band, but I didn't feel like I could trust them man-to-man in the
studio with unrecorded songs. So we started to use some musicians that
Lanois would choose and a couple that I had in mind: [keyboardist] Jim
Dickinson; [drummer] Jim Keltner; [guitarist] Duke Robillard. I started
just assembling people that I knew could play. They had the right soulful
kind of attitude for these songs. But we just couldn't . . . I felt extremely
frustrated, because I couldn't get any of the up-tempo songs that I
wanted.

Don't you think a song like "Cold Irons Bound" certainly has a drive to it?

Yeah, there's a real drive to it, but it isn't even close to the way I
had it envisioned. I mean, I'm satisfied with what we did. But there were
things I had to throw out because this assortment of people just couldn't
lock in on riffs and rhythms all together. I got so frustrated in the studio

that I didn't really dimensionalize the songs. I could've if I'd had the willpower. I just didn't at that time, and so you got to steer it where the event itself wants to go. I feel there was a sameness to the rhythms. It was more like that swampy, voodoo thing that Lanois is so good at. I just wish I'd been able to get more of a legitimate rhythm-oriented sense into it. I didn't feel there was any *mathematical* thing about that record at all. The one beat could've been anywhere, when instead, the singer should have been defining where the drum should be. It was tricky trying to steer that ship.

I think that's why people say *Time Out of Mind* is sort of dark and foreboding: because we locked into that one dimension in the sound. People say the record deals with mortality—*my* mortality for some reason! [*Laughs*] Well, it *doesn't* deal with my mortality. It maybe just deals with mortality in general. It's one thing that we all have in common, isn't it? But I didn't see any one critic say: "It deals with *my* mortality"—you know, his *own*. As if he's immune in some kind of way—like whoever's writing about the record has got eternal life and the singer doesn't. I found this condescending attitude toward that record revealed in the press quite frequently, but, you know, nothing you can do about that.

The language in 'Time Out of Mind' seems very stripped down, as if the songs don't have the patience or room to bear any unessential imagery.

I just come down the line too far to make any superfluous song. I mean, I'm sure I've made enough of them, or that I've got enough super-fluous lines in a lot of songs. But I've kind of passed that point. I have to impress myself *first*, and unless I'm speaking in a certain language to my own self, I don't feel anything less than that will do for the public, really.

"Highlands" strikes me as the album's most singular song. It begins in a place of isolation; it tells a story but rambles. It's poignant as hell, but it's also very funny—especially the conversation it portrays between the narrator and the waitress in the café. And by the time we get to the end of it, we don't know if we're in a place of desolation or release.

That particular song, we worked with a track that I had done at a sound check once in some hall. The assembled group of musicians we had down at the studio just couldn't get it, so I said, "Just use that origi-nal track, and I'll sing over it." It was just some old blues song I always wanted to use, and I felt that once I was able to control it, I could've written about anything with it. But you're right—I forgot that was on that record. You know, I'm not really quite sure why it seems to people that *Time Out of Mind* is a darker picture. In my mind, there's nothing dark about it. It's not like, you know, Dante's *Inferno* or something. It doesn't paint a picture of goblins and goons and grotesque-looking creatures or anything like that. I really don't understand why it is looked at as such a dark album, really. It *does* have that song "Highlands" at the end.

In the end, are you happy with 'Time Out of Mind'? After all, it was seen as not merely a return to form for you but also as a real extension of your gifts—and as your most powerful work since 1975's 'Blood on the Tracks.'

Well, you know, I never listen to my records. Once they're turned in, I'm done with them. I don't want to hear them anymore. I know the songs. I'll play them, but I don't want to hear them on a record. It sounds superficial to me to hear a record—I don't feel like it tells me anything in particular. I'm not going to learn anything from it.

It was during the final stages of the album that you were hit with a serious swelling around your heart and were laid up in the hospital. You've said that that infection was truly painful and debilitating. Did it alter your view of life in any way?

No. No, because it didn't! You can't even say something like, "Well, you were in the wrong place at the wrong time." Even that excuse didn't work. It was like I learned *nothing*. I wish I could say I put the time to good use or, you know, got highly educated in something or had some revelations about *anything*. But I can't say that any of that happened. I just laid around and then had to wait for my strength to come back.

Do you think that the proximity of your illness to the album's release helped account for why reviewers saw so many themes of mortality in 'Time Out of Mind'?

When I recorded that album, the media weren't paying any attention to me. I was totally outside of it.

True, but the album came out not long after you'd gone through the illness.

It did?

Yes. You were in the hospital in the spring of 1997, and 'Time Out of Mind' was released in autumn that same year.

OK, well, then it could've been perceived that way in the organized media. But that would just be characterizing the album, really.

I want to step back a bit, to those years preceding 'Time Out of Mind.' First, I'd like to ask you about an occasion at an earlier Grammy Awards, in 1991, when you received a Lifetime Achievement Award. At that point, America was deep into its involvement in the Gulf War. You came out onstage that night with a small band and played a severe version of "Masters of War"—a performance that remains controversial even today. Some critics found it rushed and embarrassing, others thought it was brilliant. Then, after Jack Nicholson presented you the award, you made the following comment: "My daddy [once said], 'Son, it's possible to become so defiled in this world that your own mother and father will abandon you. And if that happens, God will always believe in your own ability to mend your ways.' " I've always thought that was one of the more remarkable things I've heard you say. What was going through your mind at that time?

I don't remember the time and place my father said that to me, and maybe he didn't say it to me in that exact way. I was probably paraphrasing the whole idea, really—I'm not even sure I paraphrased in the proper context. It might've been something that just sort of popped in my head at that time. The only thing I remember about that whole episode, as long as you bring it up, was that I had a fever—like 104. I was extremely sick that night. Not only that, but I was disillusioned with the entire musical community and environment. If I remember correctly, the Grammy people called me months before then and said that they wanted to give me this Lifetime Achievement honor. Well, we all know that they give those things out when you're old—when you're nothing, a has-been. Everybody knows that, right? So I wasn't sure whether it was a compliment or an insult. I wasn't really sure about it. And then they said, "Here's what we want to do. . . ." I don't want to name these performers because you know them, but one performer was going to sing "Like a Rolling Stone." Another performer was going to sing "The Times [They] Are A-Changin'." Another was going to sing "All Along the Watchtower," and another was going to sing "It's All Over Now, Baby Blue." They were going to sing bits of all these songs, and then they were going to have somebody introduce me, and I would just collect this Lifetime Achievement Award, say a few words and go on my merry way. The performers, they told me, had all agreed to it, so there really wasn't anything for me to do except show up.

Then the Gulf War broke out. The Grammy people called and said, "Listen, we're in a tight fix. So-and-so, who was going to sing 'Times Are A-Changin',' is afraid to get on an airplane. So-and-so, who was going to sing 'Like a Rolling Stone,' doesn't want to travel because he just had another baby and he doesn't want to leave his family." That's understandable. But then so-and-so, who was going to sing "It's All Over, Baby Blue," was in Africa and didn't want to take a chance flying to New York, and so-and-so, who was going to sing "All Along the Watchtower," wasn't sure he wanted to be at any high-visibility place right then, because it may be a little dangerous. So, they said, "Could you come and sing? Could *you* fill the time?" And I said, "What about the guy who's going to introduce me [Jack Nicholson]?" They said, "He's OK. He's coming." Anyway, I got disillusioned with all the characters at that time—with their inner character and their ability to be able to keep their word and their idealism and their insecurity. All the ones that have the gall to thrust their tortured inner psyches on an outer world but can't at least be true to their word. From that point on, that's what the music business and all the people in it represented to me. I just lost all respect for them. There's a few that are decent and God-fearing and will stand up in a righteous way. But I wouldn't want to count on most of them. And maybe me singing "Masters of War" . . . I've said before that song's got nothing to do with being anti-war. It has more to do with the military industrial complex that Eisenhower was talking about. Anyway, I went up and did that, but I was sick, and I felt they put me through a whole lot of trouble over nothing. I just tried to disguise myself the best I could. That was more along the line of . . . you know, the press was finding me irrelevant then, and it couldn't have happened at a better time, really, because I wouldn't have *wanted* to have been relevant. I wouldn't have wanted to be someone that the press was examining—every move. I wouldn't have ever been able to develop again in any kind of artistic way.

But certainly you knew by playing "Masters of War" at the height of the Gulf War, it would be received a certain way.

Yeah, but I wasn't looking at it that way. I knew the lyrics of the song were holding up, and I brought maybe two or three ferocious guitar players, you know? And I always had a song for any occasion.

Truthfully, I was just disgusted in having to be there after they told me what they intended to do and then backed out. I probably shouldn't have even gone myself, and I wouldn't have gone, except the other guy [Nicholson] was true to his word. [*Taps his fingers rapidly on the tabletop*]

What about that statement you made, about the wisdom your father had shared with you? It could almost be read as a personal statement—you talking about your own life. Or was it about the world around you?

I was thinking more in terms of, like, we're living in a Machiavellian world, whether we like it or we don't. Any act that's immoral, as long as it succeeds, it's all right. To apply that type of meaning to the way I was feeling that night probably has more to do with it than any kind of conscious effort to bring out some religiosity, or any kind of biblical saying about God, one way or another. You hear a lot about God these days: God, the beneficent; God, the all-great; God, the Almighty; God, the most powerful; God, the giver of life; God, the creator of death. I mean, we're hearing about God all the time, so we better learn how to deal with it. But if we know anything about God, God is *arbitrary*. So people better be able to deal with that, too.

That's interesting, because so many people think that God is constant, you know, and unchanging.

Oh, absolutely.

But "arbitrary" would seem to imply a rather different view. Is there something about the word "arbitrary" that you would like to clarify or perhaps that I'm not understanding?

No. I mean, you can look it up in the dictionary. I don't consider myself a sophist or a cynic or a stoic or some kind of bourgeois industrialist, or whatever titles people put on people. Basically, I'm just a regular person. I don't walk around all the time out of my mind with inspiration. So what can I tell you about that? Anyway, I wasn't in a good state of mind that night. I was frustrated. It's difficult to attach yourself to the past or be paralyzed by the past in any kind of way, so I just said it and moved on. I was glad to have gotten out of there, really.

You said a moment ago that this happened during a time when you weren't being seen as relevant and didn't want to be seen as relevant. Though you would continue to tour through most of the 1990s, more than seven years would pass between albums of new songs. Some biographers have more or less referred to this as a time when you seemed adrift and confused—a time in which you seemed unhappy and disconnected from your music. What was going on during this period?

I really thought I was through making records. I didn't want to make any more. I thought, "I'll make a couple more records and just have them be folk songs, in a really simplified way—no big production or anything." Beyond that, I didn't want to record anymore. I was more concerned with what I do in personal appearances. It was clear to me I had more than enough songs to play. Forever.

See, I'd made that record with Lanois in 1988 [*Oh Mercy*]. I was already playing over a hundred shows a year at that point. I decided I would just go back to live performing, which I hadn't really thought I'd done since maybe 1966. Some performers make a lot of sacrifices to make a record—they forfeit an abundance of time and energy. I did that with Lanois back then, and it worked out rather well. But then around that same time I was making a Traveling Wilburys record, and then I started this record with Don Was, *Under the Red Sky*. All of this was happening in the same period. Looking back on it now, it seems kind of unthinkable. I would leave the Wilburys and go down to Sunset Sound and record *Under the Red Sky* simultaneously, all within a set schedule because I needed to be in Prague or someplace on a certain date. And then both records—the Wilburys record and *Under the Red Sky*—I'd just leave them hanging and see the finished product later. All those things happened at the same time, and that was when I found I'd really had it. My rational mind didn't know what to make of that. I'd really had my fill. I was going to stick to my declaration and definitely not make any records. I didn't feel the need to announce that, but I had come to that conclusion. I didn't care to record no more. I'd rather play on the road. Recording was too mental. Also, I didn't feel I was writing any of the songs that I really wanted to write. I wasn't getting the help I needed to record right, I didn't like the sound of the records. . . . I don't really remember. It was just . . . one thing leads to another, you know? I reckoned I was done with it. But then you go out and play live shows, and you *do* get thoughts, and you *do* get an inspiration here and there. So I just reluctantly started writing things down, in the way I described that led to the making of *Time Out of Mind*.

Did you ever consider just flat-out retiring?

Well, I really don't have any defined retirement plan! More than a few times I probably felt I had retired. I felt I'd had retired in 1966 and 1967. I was fulfilling my recording contracts, but outside of that I think I felt like I had retired from the cultural scene at the time.

Did you have comparable feelings at any point in the 1980s or 1990s?

Something would always come up that put the idea off. But sure, at times I felt like, "I don't want to do this anymore." Then something would always lead me to something else, which would keep me at it.

According to a couple of recent biographies, the late 1980s and early 1990s were troubling for you in other ways. Some people have claimed that these were years when you were drinking too frequently—and that your drinking was interfering with your music or was a reflection of a deeper unhappiness for you. According to these biographers, it wasn't until you quit drinking—some time in the early 1990s—that your performances and writing really rebounded.

That's completely inaccurate [*laughs*]. I can drink or not drink. I don't know why people would associate drinking or not drinking with *anything* that I do, really. I've never thought about it one way or another. For some reason there's a certain crowd—if you want to call it a crowd—that would assume certain things about me or anybody which simply aren't true. They perceive it by appearances. They might hear rumors. They might *start* rumors, but it's their own minds going to work. Therefore, if they believe a certain thing about that person, then any act that person does they would apply it to that. "Oh, he fell down—he must be drinking." Or, "He smashed his car into a tree. I guess he was hopped-up on something." But those are people who are celebrity-minded. They live in their own universe, and they try to project it outwardly, and it doesn't work. Usually, those people have a touch of insanity, and they have to be knocked down to earth. It's like you got to choose. Either there's order or there's chaos, and you got to choose. People of that nature don't seem to understand either one. And they apply it to, well, in this country, to celebrities. But I don't think any of us who could fit the description of that can pay any mind to what people think or how many books are written or any of that if we want to exist and have a certain amount of free will about what we do. I mean, these kind of people are the ones who would make laws against free will, that are contrary to free will. They're just not serious people. Unfortunately, I guess, all performers have a bunch of them hanging on. Anybody and everybody can get typecast, you know, in a second, by just doing great work. But the truth is, it's my job to drive my own car, if you know what I mean. It's not somebody else's job.

But something did seem to turn around for you in the early 1990s. You've said as much yourself. You've spoken about some epiphany that changed your purpose and commitment—some recognition that came to you onstage. You've described it as a moment when you realized that what was important was not your legend or how that weighed you down. What was important, you seemed to say, was for you to stand by your work—and that meant playing music on a regular basis, no matter who you were playing it for.

It happened—or had its beginning, anyway—when I was playing some shows with the Grateful Dead [in 1987]. They wanted to play some of my songs that I hadn't played in years and years. I had already been on a long string of dates with Tom Petty and the Heartbreakers, and night after night I was only playing maybe fifteen to twenty of the songs I had written, and I couldn't really grasp the older ones. But when I began to play with the Grateful Dead, those are the only songs they wanted to play: the ones that I wasn't playing with Petty. I really had some sort of epiphany then on how to do those songs again, using certain techniques that I had never thought about. When I went back and played with Petty again, I was using those techniques, and I found I could play anything. But then there was a show in Switzerland when the techniques failed me, and I had to come up with another one really quick. I was kind of standing on a different foundation at that point and realized, "*I could do this.*" I found out I could do it effortlessly—that I could sing night after night after night and never get tired. I could project it out differently.

Not only that, but Lonnie Johnson, the blues-jazz player, showed me a technique on the guitar in maybe 1964. I hadn't really understood it when he first showed it to me. It had to do with the mathematical order of the scale on a guitar, and how to make things happen, where it gets under somebody's skin and there's really nothing they can do about it, because it's mathematical. He didn't even play that way himself. He played mostly jazz—a kind of guitar I can't play at all, though when I think of a guitar player, I think of somebody like Eddie Lang or Charlie Christian or Freddie Green. I don't listen to many people in the rock & roll area. Anyway, he just told me, "I want to show you something. You might be able to use this some day." It's more kind of an ancient way of playing. I always wanted to use this technique, but I never was really able to do it with my own songs.

One of the things I've noticed about your shows is that starting in the 1990s they grew more and more musical. You've opened the songs up to more instrumental exploration and new textures and rhythmic shifts—like you're trying to stretch or reinvent them—and you seem very much at the heart of that. You're your own band director at this point.

Well, I don't think you've seen me play too many mindless jams.

What I do is all done with technique and certain stratagems. But they're not intellectual ones; they're designed to make people feel something. And I understand that it's not necessarily the same for everyone who hears me play and sing. Everyone is feeling a different thing. I would like to be a performer who maybe could read and write music and play the violin. Then I could design a bigger band with more comprehensive parts of harmony in different arrangements, and still have the songs evolve within that. But if anything, I do know my limitations, and so I don't try to transcend those limitations. Or if I do transcend the limitations, it's all done with the technique I was talking about. Which is to say, you can do it whether you feel good or you don't feel good, or no matter how you're feeling. It really doesn't matter. It has nothing to do with personality. It's difficult even to find the words to talk about it.

It seems that some of your most impassioned and affecting performances, from night to night, are your covers of traditional folk songs.

Folk music is where it all starts and in many ways ends. If you don't have that foundation, or if you're not knowledgeable about it and you don't know how to control that, and you don't feel historically tied to it, then what you're doing is not going to be as strong as it could be. Of course, it helps to have been born in a certain era because it would've been closer to you, or it helps to be a part of the culture when it was happening. It's not the same thing, relating to something second- or third-hand off of a record.

I think one of the best records that I've ever been even a part of was the record I made with Big Joe Williams and Victoria Spivey. Now that's a record that I hear from time to time and I don't mind listening to it. It amazes me that I was there and had done that.

In 'Invisible Republic' —Greil Marcus' book about you, the Band, the Basement Tapes sessions and the place of all that in American culture [now retitled 'The Old, Weird America: The World of Bob Dylan's Basement Tapes']—Marcus wrote about the importance of Harry Smith's legendary 'Anthology of American Folk Music' and its influence on all of your work, from your earliest to most-recent recordings.

Well, he makes way too much of that.

Why do you say that?

Because those records were around—that Harry Smith anthology—but that's not what everybody was listening to. Sure, there were all those songs. You could hear them at people's houses. I know in my case, I think Dave Van Ronk had that record. But in those days we really didn't have places to live, or places to have a lot of records. We were sort of living from this place to that—kind of a transient existence. I know I was living that way. You heard records where you could, but mostly you heard other *performers*. All those people [Marcus is] talking about, you could hear the actual people singing those ballads. You could hear Clarence Ashley, Doc Watson, Dock Boggs, the Memphis Jug Band, Furry Lewis. You could see those people live and in person. They were around. He intellectualizes it too much. Performers *did* know of that record, but it wasn't, in retrospect, the monumental iconic recordings at the time that he makes them out to be.

It wasn't like someone discovered this pot of gold somewhere. There were other records out that were on rural labels. Yazoo had records out. They weren't all compiled like they are now. In New York City, there was a place called the Folklore Center that had all the folk-music records. It was like a library, and you could listen to them there. And they had folk-music books there. Certain other towns had it, too. There was a place in Chicago called the Old Town School of Folk Music. You could find the stuff there. It wasn't the only thing that people had—that *Anthology of American Folk Music*. And the Folkways label itself had many other folk recordings of all kinds of people. They just were highly secretive. And they weren't really secretive because they were *trying* to be secretive. The people I knew—the people who were like-minded as myself—were trying to be folk musicians. That's *all* they wanted to be, that's *all* the aspirations they had. There wasn't anything monetary about it. There was no money in folk music. It was a way of life. And it was an identity which the three-buttoned-suit postwar generation of America really wasn't offering to kids my age: an identity. This music was *impossible* to get anywhere really, except in a nucleus of a major city, and a record shop might have a few recordings of the hard-core folklore music. There were other folk-music records, commercial folk-music records, like those by the Kingston Trio. I never really was an elitist. Personally, I liked the Kingston Trio. I could see the picture. But for a lot of people it was a little hard to take. Like the left-wing puritans that seemed to have a *hold* on the folk-music community, they disparaged these records. I didn't particularly want to sing any of those songs *that* way, but the Kingston Trio were probably the best commercial group going, and they seemed to know what they were doing.

What *I* was most interested in twenty-four hours a day was the rural music. But you could only hear it, like, in isolated caves [*laughs*], like, on a few bohemian streets in America at that time. The idea was to be able to master these songs. It wasn't about *writing* your own songs. That didn't even enter anybody's *mind*.

In a way, this line of talk brings us to your newest album, 'Love and Theft.' On one hand, parts of this record sound like work that might have heralded from the early forms of twentieth-century folk music we've been discussing. Its sense of timelessness and caprices reminds me of some of the songs we hear on 'The Basement Tapes' and 'John Wesley Harding' — records that emanated from your strong folk background. But 'Love and Theft' also seems to recall 'Highway 61 Revisited' and that album's delight in discovering new world-changing methods of language and sharp wit, and the way in which the music digs down deep into ancient blues structures to yield something wholly unexpected. Just as important, 'Love and Theft,' like your other albums I just mentioned, feels like a work made specifically from inside an American temperament — the America we live in now, but also the America we have left behind. Or am I reading too much into this record?

For starters, no one should really be curious or too excited about comparing this album to any of my other albums. Compare this album to the *other* albums that are out there. Compare this album to other artists who make albums. You know, comparing me to myself [*laughs*] is really like . . . I mean, you're talking to a person that feels like he's walking around in the ruins of Pompeii all the time. It's always been that way, for one reason or another. I deal with all the old stereotypes. The language and the identity I use is the one that I know only so well, and I'm not about to go on and keep doing this—comparing my new work to my old work. It creates a kind of Achilles' heel for myself. It isn't going to happen.

Maybe a better way to put it is to ask: Do you see this as an album that emanates from your experience of America at this time?

Every one of the records I've made has emanated from the entire panorama of what America is to me. America, to me, is a rising tide that lifts all ships, and I've never really sought inspiration from other types of music. My problem in writing songs has always been how to tone down the rhetoric in using the language. I don't really give it a whole lot of soulful thought. A song is a reflection of what I see all around me all the time. I'm only speaking about . . . [*Pauses*] See, I'm still back on your other question. I really don't think it's fair to compare this album to any of my past albums. I mean, I'm still the same person. You know, like Hank Williams would say, my hair's still curly, my eyes are still blue. And that's all I know.

What is your own description of what the songs on 'Love and Theft' are about?

You're putting me in a difficult position. A question like that can't be answered in the terms that you're asking. A song is just a mood that an artist is attempting to convey. To be truthful, I haven't listened to this record since it was made—since probably last spring. Actually, I don't need to hear it. I just need to look at the lyrics, and we can start from there. But I really don't know what the summation of all these songs would really represent. [*Pauses again, drumming his fingers on the table*] The whole album deals with power. If life teaches us anything, it's that there's nothing that men and women won't do to get power. The album deals with power, wealth, knowledge and salvation—the way I look at it. If it's a great album—which I hope it is—it's a great album because it deals with great themes. It speaks in a noble language. It speaks of the issues or the ideals of an age in some nation, and hopefully, it would also speak across the ages. It'd be as good tomorrow as it is today and would've been as good yesterday. That's what I was trying to make happen, because just to make another record at this point in my career . . . career, by the way, isn't how I look at what I do. *Career* is a French word. It means "carrier." It's something that takes you from one place to the other. I don't feel like what I do qualifies to be called a career. It's more of a calling.

This album holds ruminations every bit as dark as those found in 'Time Out of Mind,' but this time you put them across without the previous album's spooky musical ambience. Since you produced this album yourself, you must have wanted a different sound.

The way the record is presented is just as important as what it's presenting. Therefore, anybody—even if they'd been a great producer—would only have gotten in the way on this, and there really wasn't a lot of time. I would've loved to have somebody help me make this record, but I couldn't think of anybody on short notice. And besides, what could they do? For this particular record it wouldn't have mattered.

There's also a good deal of humor on this record—maybe more than on any record of yours since the 1960s.

Well . . .

C'mon, there are some pretty funny lines on this album—like the exchange between Romeo and Juliet in "Floater (Too Much to Ask)," and that knock-knock joke in "Po' Boy."

Yeah, funny . . . *and* dark. But still, in my own mind, not really poking fun at the principles that would guide a person's life or anything. Basically, the songs deal with what many of my songs deal with—which is business, politics and war, and maybe love interest on the side. That would be the first level you would have to appreciate them on.

In a recent interview you said that you saw this album as autobiographical.

Oh, *absolutely*. It would be autobiographical on every front. It obviously plays by its own set of rules, but a listener wouldn't really have to be aware of those rules when hearing it. But absolutely. It's not like the songs were written by some kind of Socrates, you know, some kind of buffoon, the man about town pretending to be happy [*laughs*]. There wouldn't be any of that in this record.

Both 'Time Out of Mind' and 'Love and Theft' have been received as some of the best work you've ever done. Does songwriting now feel more accessible to you than it did before?

Well, I follow the dictates of my conscience to write a song, and I don't really have a time or place I set aside. I don't really preconceive it. I couldn't tell you when I could come up with something. It just happens at odd times, here and there. It's amazing to me that I'm still able to *do* it, really. And I do them as well as I seem able to handle it. When you're young, you're probably writing stronger and a lot quicker, but in my case, I just try to use the traditional values of logic and reason no matter what age I've ever written any of my songs.

This record was released on September 11th—the same date as the terrorist attacks on the World Trade Center and the Pentagon. I've talked with several people in the time since then who have turned to 'Love and Theft' because they find something in it that matches the spirit of dread and uncertainty of our present conditions. For my part, I've kept circling around a line from "Mississippi": "Sky full of fire, pain pourin' down." Is there anything you would like to say about your reaction to the events of that day?

One of those Rudyard Kipling poems, "Gentlemen-Rankers," comes to my mind: "We have done with Hope and Honour, we are lost to Love and Truth/We are dropping down the ladder rung by rung/And the measure of our torment is the measure of our youth/God help us, for we knew the worst too young!" If anything, my mind would go to young people at a time like this. That's really the only way to put it.

You mean because of what's at stake for them right now, as we apparently go to war?

Exactly. I mean, art imposes order on life, but how much more art will there be? We don't really know. There's a secret sanctity of nature. How much more of that will there be? At the moment, the rational mind's way of thinking wouldn't really explain what's happened. You need something else, with a capital E, to explain it. It's going to have to be dealt with sooner or later, of course.

Do you see any hope for the situation we find ourselves in?

I don't really know what I could tell you. I don't consider myself an educator or an explainer. You see what it is that I do, and that's what I've always done. But it is time now for great men to come forward. With small men, no great thing can be accomplished at the moment. Those people in charge, I'm sure they've read Sun-Tzu, who wrote *The Art of War* in the sixth century. In there he says, "If you know the enemy and know yourself, you need not fear the result of a hundred battles. If you know yourself and not your enemy, for every victory gained you will suffer a defeat." And he goes on to say, "If you know neither the enemy nor yourself, you will succumb in every battle." Whoever's in charge, I'm sure they would have read that.

Things will have to change. And one of these things that will have to change: People will have to change their internal world.

31. Interview with Robert Hilburn, *The Los Angeles Times*

APRIL 4, 2004

"No, no, no," Bob Dylan says sharply when asked if aspiring songwriters should learn their craft by studying his albums, which is precisely what thousands have done for decades.

"It's only natural to pattern yourself after someone," he says, opening a door on a subject that has long been off-limits to reporters: his songwriting process. "If I wanted to be a painter, I might think about trying to be like Van Gogh, or if I was an actor, act like Laurence Olivier. If I was an architect, there's Frank Gehry.

"But you can't just copy somebody. If you like someone's work, the important thing is to be exposed to everything that person has been exposed to. Anyone who wants to be a songwriter should listen to as much folk music as they can, study the form and structure of stuff that has been around for 100 years. I go back to Stephen Foster."

For four decades, Dylan has been a grand American paradox: an artist who revolutionized popular songwriting with his nakedly personal yet challenging work but who keeps us at such distance from his private life—and his creative technique—that he didn't have to look far for the title of his recent movie: *Masked and Anonymous.*

Although fans and biographers might read his hundreds of songs as a chronicle of one man's love and loss, celebration and outrage, he doesn't revisit the stories behind the songs, per se, when he talks about his art this evening. What's more comfortable, and perhaps more interesting to him, is the way craft lets him turn life, ideas, observations and strings of poetic images into songs.

As he sits in the quiet of a grand hotel overlooking one of the city's [Amsterdam's] picturesque canals, he paints a very different picture of his evolution as a songwriter than you might expect of an artist who seemed to arrive on the pop scene in the '60s with his vision and skills fully intact. Dylan's lyrics to "Blowin' in the Wind" were printed in *Broadside*, the folk music magazine, in May 1962, the month he turned 21.

The story he tells is one of trial and error, false starts and hard work—a young man in a remote stretch of Minnesota finding such freedom in the music of folk songwriter Woody Guthrie that he felt he could spend his life just singing Guthrie songs—until he discovered his true calling through a simple twist of fate.

Dylan has often said that he never set out to change pop songwriting or society, but it's clear he was filled with the high purpose of living up to the ideals he saw in Guthrie's work. Unlike rock stars before him, his chief goal wasn't just making the charts.

"I always admired true artists who were dedicated, so I learned from them," Dylan says, rocking slowly in the hotel room chair. "Popular culture usually comes to an end very quickly. It gets thrown into the grave. I wanted to do something that stood alongside Rembrandt's paintings."

Even after all these years, his eyes still light up at the mention of Guthrie, the "Dust Bowl" poet, whose best songs, such as "This Land Is Your Land," spoke so eloquently about the gulf Guthrie saw between America's ideals and its practices.

"To me, Woody Guthrie was the be-all and end-all," says Dylan, 62, his curly hair still framing his head majestically as it did on album covers four decades ago. "Woody's songs were about everything at the same time. They were about rich and poor, black and white, the highs and lows of life, the contradictions between what they were teaching in school and what was really happening. He was saying everything in his songs that I felt but didn't know how to.

"It wasn't only the songs, though. It was his voice—it was like a stiletto—and his diction. I had never heard anybody sing like that. His guitar strumming was more intricate than it sounded. All I knew was I wanted to learn his songs."

Dylan played so much Guthrie during his early club and coffeehouse days that he was dubbed a Woody Guthrie "jukebox." So imagine the shock when someone told him another singer—Ramblin' Jack Elliott—

was doing that too. "It's like being a doctor who has spent all these years discovering penicillin and suddenly [finding out] someone else had already done it," he recalls.

A less ambitious young man might have figured no big deal—there's plenty of room for two singers who admire Guthrie. But Dylan was too independent. "I knew I had something that Jack didn't have," he says, "though it took a while before I figured out what it was."

Songwriting, he finally realized, was what could set him apart. Dylan had toyed with the idea earlier, but he felt he didn't have enough vocabulary or life experience.

Scrambling to distinguish himself on the New York club scene in 1961, though, he tried again. The first song of his own that drew attention to him was "Song to Woody," which included the lines, "Hey, hey, Woody Guthrie . . . I know that you know/All the things that I'm a-sayin' an' a-many times more."

Within two years, he had written and recorded songs, including "Girl of the North Country" and "A Hard Rain's A-Gonna Fall," that helped lift the heart of pop music from sheer entertainment to art.

'Songs Are the Star'

Dylan, whose work and personal life have been dissected in enough books to fill a library wall, seems to welcome the chance to talk about his craft, not his persona or history. It's as if he wants to demystify himself.

"To me, the performer is here and gone," he once said. "The songs are the star of the show, not me."

He also hates focusing on the past. "I'm always trying to stay right square in the moment. I don't want to get nostalgic or narcissistic as a writer or a person. I think successful people don't dwell in the past. I think only losers do."

Yet his sense of tradition is strong. He likes to think of himself as part of a brotherhood of writers whose roots are in the raw country, blues and folk strains of Guthrie, the Carter Family, Robert Johnson and scores of Scottish and English balladeers.

Over the course of the evening, he offers glimpses into how his ear and eye put pieces of songs together using everything from Beat poetry and the daily news to lessons picked up from contemporaries.

He is so committed to talking about his craft that he has a guitar at his side in case he wants to demonstrate a point. When his road manager knocks on the door after 90 minutes to see if everything is OK, Dylan waves him off. After three hours, he volunteers to get together again after the next night's concert.

"There are so many ways you can go at something in a song," he says. "One thing is to give life to inanimate objects. Johnny Cash is good at that. He's got the line that goes, 'A freighter said, "She's been here, but she's gone, boy, she's gone." ' That's great. 'A freighter says ' "She's been here." ' That's high art. If you do that once in a song, you usually turn it on its head right then and there."

The process he describes is more workaday than capturing lightning in a bottle. In working on "Like a Rolling Stone," he says, "I'm not thinking about what I want to say, I'm just thinking 'Is this OK for the meter?' "

But there's an undeniable element of mystery too. "It's like a ghost is writing a song like that. It gives you the song and it goes away, it goes away. You don't know what it means. Except the ghost picked me to write the song."

Some listeners over the years have complained that Dylan's songs are too ambiguous—that they seem to be simply an exercise in narcissistic wordplay. But most critics say Dylan's sometimes competing images are his greatest strength.

Few in American pop have consistently written lines as hauntingly beautiful and richly challenging as his "Just Like a Woman," a song from the mid-'60s. Dylan stares impassively at a lyric sheet for "Just Like a Woman" when it is handed to him. As is true of so many of his works, the song seems to be about many things at once.

"I'm not good at defining things," he says. "Even if I could tell you what the song was about I wouldn't. It's up to the listener to figure out what it means to him."

As he stares at the page in the quiet of the room, however, he budges a little. "This is a very broad song. A line like, 'Breaks just like a little girl' is a metaphor. It's like a lot of blues-based songs. Someone may be talking about a woman, but they're not really talking about a woman at all. You can say a lot if you use metaphors."

After another pause, he adds: "It's a city song. It's like looking at something extremely powerful, say the shadow of a church or something like that. I don't think in lateral terms as a writer. That's a fault of a lot of the old Broadway writers. . . . They are so lateral. There's no circular thing, nothing to be learned from the song, nothing to inspire you. I always try to turn a song on its head. Otherwise, I figure I'm wasting the listener's time."

Discovering Folk Music

Dylan's pop sensibilities were shaped long before he made his journey east in the winter of 1960–61. Growing up in the icy isolation of Hibbing, Minn., Dylan, who was still Robert Allen Zimmerman then, found comfort in the country, blues and early rock 'n' roll that he heard at night on a Louisiana radio station whose signal came in strong and clear. It was worlds away from the local Hibbing station, which leaned toward mainstream pop like Perry Como, Frankie Laine and Doris Day.

Dylan has respect for many of the pre-rock songwriters, citing Cole Porter, whom he describes as a "fearless" rhymer, and Porter's "Don't Fence Me In" as a favorite. But he didn't feel most of the pre-rock writers were speaking to him.

"When you listened to [Porter's] songs and the Gershwins' and Rodgers and Hammerstein, who wrote some great songs, they were writing for their generation and it just didn't feel like mine," he says. "I realized at some point that the important thing isn't just how you write songs, but your subject matter, your point of view."

The music that did speak to him as a teenager in the '50s was rock 'n' roll—especially Elvis Presley. "When I got into rock 'n' roll, I didn't even think I had any other option or alternative," he says. "It showed me where my future was, just like some people know they are going to be doctors or lawyers or shortstop for the New York Yankees."

He became a student of what he heard.

"Chuck Berry wrote amazing songs that spun words together in a remarkably complex way," he says. "Buddy Holly's songs were much more simplified, but what I got out of Buddy was that you can take influences from anywhere. Like his 'That'll Be the Day.' I read somewhere that it was a line he heard in a movie, and I started realizing you can take things from everyday life that you hear people say.

"That I still find true. You can go anywhere in daily life and have your ears open and hear something, either something someone says to you or something you hear across the room. If it has resonance, you can use it in a song."

After rock took on a blander tone in the late '50s, Dylan looked for new inspiration. He began listening to the Kingston Trio, who helped popularize folk music with polished versions of "Tom Dooley" and "A Worried Man." Most folk purists felt the group was more "pop" than authentic, but Dylan, new to folk, responded to the messages in the songs.

He worked his way through such other folk heroes as Odetta and Leadbelly before fixating on Guthrie. Trading his electric guitar for an acoustic one, he spent months in Minneapolis, performing in clubs, preparing himself for the trip east.

Going to New York rather than rival music center Los Angeles was a given, he says, "because everything I knew came out of New York. I listened to the Yankees games on the radio, and the Giants and the Dodgers. All the radio programs, like 'The Fat Man,' the NBC chimes—would be from New York. So were all the record companies. It seemed like New York was the capital of the world."

Devouring Poetry

Dylan pursued his muse in New York with an appetite for anything he felt would help him improve his craft, whether it was learning old blues and folk songs or soaking up literature.

"I had read a lot of poetry by the time I wrote a lot of those early songs," he volunteers. "I was into the hard-core poets. I read them the way some people read Stephen King. I had also seen a lot of it growing up. Poe's stuff knocked me out in more ways than I could name. Byron and Keats and all those guys. John Donne.

"Byron's stuff goes on and on and on and you don't know half the things he's talking about or half the people he's addressing. But you could appreciate the language."

He found himself side by side with the Beat poets. "The idea that poetry was spoken in the streets and spoken publicly, you couldn't help but be excited by that," he says. "There would always be a poet in the clubs and you'd hear the rhymes, and [Allen] Ginsberg and [Gregory] Corso—those guys were highly influential."

Dylan once said he wrote songs so fast in the '60s that he didn't want to go to sleep at night because he was afraid he might miss one. Similarly, he soaked up influences so rapidly that it was hard to turn off the light at night. Why not read more?

"Someone gave me a book of François Villon poems and he was writing about hard-core street stuff and making it rhyme," Dylan says, still conveying the excitement of tapping into inspiration from 15th century France. "It was pretty staggering, and it made you wonder why you couldn't do the same thing in a song.

"I'd see Villon talking about visiting a prostitute and I would turn it around. I won't visit a prostitute, I'll talk about rescuing a prostitute.

Again, it's turning stuff on its head, like 'vice is salvation and virtue will lead to ruin.' "

When you hear Dylan still marveling at lines such as the one above from Machiavelli or Shakespeare's "fair is foul and foul is fair," you can see why he would pepper his own songs with phrases that forever ask us to question our assumptions—classic lines such as "There's no success like failure and failure's no success at all," from 1965's "Love Minus Zero/No Limit."

As always, he's quick to give credit to the tradition.

"I didn't invent this, you know," he stresses. "Robert Johnson would sing some song and out of nowhere there would be some kind of Confucius saying that would make you go, 'Wow, where did that come from?' It's important to always turn things around in some fashion."

Exploring His Themes

Some writers sit down every day for two or three hours, at least, to write, whether they are in the mood or not. Others wait for inspiration. Dylan scoffs at the discipline of daily writing.

"Oh, I'm not that serious a songwriter," he says, a smile on his lips. "Songs don't just come to me. They'll usually brew for a while, and you'll learn that it's important to keep the pieces until they are completely formed and glued together."

He sometimes writes on a typewriter but usually picks up a pen because he says he can write faster than he can type. "I don't spend a lot of time going over songs," Dylan says. "I'll sometimes make changes, but the early songs, for instance, were mostly all first drafts."

He doesn't insist that his rhymes be perfect. "What I do that a lot of other writers don't do is take a concept and line I really want to get into a song and if I can't figure out for the life of me how to simplify it, I'll just take it all—lock, stock and barrel—and figure out how to sing it so it fits the rhyming scheme. I would prefer to do that rather than bust it down or lose it because I can't rhyme it."

Themes, he says, have never been a problem. When he started out, the Korean War had just ended. "That was a heavy cloud over everyone's head," he says. "The communist thing was still big, and the civil rights movement was coming on. So there was lots to write about.

"But I never set out to write politics. I didn't want to be a political moralist. There were people who just did that. Phil Ochs focused on political things, but there are many sides to us, and I wanted to follow them all. We can feel very generous one day and very selfish the next hour."

Dylan found subject matter in newspapers. He points to 1964's "The Lonesome Death of Hattie Carroll," the story of a wealthy Baltimore man who was given only a six-month sentence for killing a maid with a cane. "I just let the story tell itself in that song," he says. "Who wouldn't be offended by some guy beating an old woman to death and just getting a slap on the wrist?"

Other times, he was reacting to his own anxieties.

"A Hard Rain's A-Gonna Fall" helped define his place in pop with an apocalyptic tale of a society being torn apart on many levels. The song has captured the imagination of listeners for generations, and like most of Dylan's songs, it has lyrics rich and poetic enough to defy age. Dylan scholars have often said the song was inspired by the Cuban missile crisis.

"All I remember about the missile crisis is there were bulletins coming across on the radio, people listening in bars and cafes, and the scariest thing was that cities, like Houston and Atlanta, would have to be evacuated. That was pretty heavy.

"Someone pointed out it was written before the missile crisis, but it doesn't really matter where a song comes from. It just matters where it takes you."

His Constant Changes

Dylan's career path hasn't been smooth. During an unprecedented creative spree that resulted in three landmark albums (*Bringing It All Back Home*, *Highway 61 Revisited* and *Blonde on Blonde*) being released in 15 months, Dylan reconnected with the rock 'n' roll of his youth. Impressed by the energy he felt in the Beatles and desiring to speak in the musical language of his generation, he declared his independence from folk by going electric at the Newport Folk Festival in 1965.

His music soon became a new standard of rock achievement, influencing not only his contemporaries, including the Beatles, but almost everyone to follow.

The pressure on him was soon so intense that he went underground for a while in 1966, not fully resuming his career until the mid-'70s when he did a celebrated tour with the Band and then recorded one of his most hailed albums, *Blood on the Tracks*. By the end of the decade, he confused some old fans by turning to brimstone gospel music.

There were gems throughout the '70s and '80s, but Dylan seemed for much of the '90s to be tired of songwriting, or, maybe, just tired of always being measured against the standards he set in the '60s.

In the early '90s he seemed to find comfort only in the rhythm of the road, losing himself in the troubadour tradition, not even wanting to talk about songwriting or his future. "Maybe I've written enough songs," he said then. "Maybe it's someone else's turn."

Somehow, however, all those shows reignited the songwriting spark—as demonstrated in his Grammy-winning *Time Out of Mind* album in 1997; the bittersweet song from the movie *Wonder Boys*, "Things Have Changed," that won an Oscar in 2001 for best original song; and his heralded 2001 album, *Love and Theft*. He spent much of last year working on a series of autobiographical chronicles. The first installment is due this fall from Simon & Schuster.

But nowhere, perhaps, is Dylan's regained passion more evident than in his live show, where he has switched primarily from guitar to electric keyboard and now leads his four-piece band with the intensity of a young punk auteur.

Dylan—who has lived in Southern California since he and ex-wife Sara Lowndes moved to Malibu in the mid-'70s with their five children— was in Amsterdam to headline two sold-out concerts at a 6,000-seat hall. He does more than 100 shows a year.

The audience on the chilly winter night after our first conversation is divided among people Dylan's age who have been following his career since the '60s and young people drawn to him by his classic body of work, and they call out for new songs, not just the classics.

Refiguring the Melodies

Back at the hotel afterward, Dylan looks about as satisfied as a man with his restless creative spirit can be.

It's nearly 2 a.m. by now and another pot of coffee cools. He rubs his hand through his curly hair. After all these hours, I realize I haven't asked the most obvious question: Which comes first, the words or the music?

Dylan leans over and picks up the acoustic guitar.

"Well, you have to understand that I'm not a melodist," he says. "My songs are either based on old Protestant hymns or Carter Family songs or variations of the blues form.

"What happens is, I'll take a song I know and simply start playing it in my head. That's the way I meditate. A lot of people will look at a crack on the wall and meditate, or count sheep or angels or money or something, and it's a proven fact that it'll help them relax. I don't meditate on any of that stuff. I meditate on a song.

"I'll be playing Bob Nolan's 'Tumbling Tumbleweeds,' for instance, in my head constantly—while I'm driving a car or talking to a person or sitting around or whatever. People will think they are talking to me and I'm talking back, but I'm not. I'm listening to the song in my head. At a certain point, some of the words will change and I'll start writing a song."

He's slowly strumming the guitar, but it's hard to pick out the tune.

"I wrote 'Blowin' in the Wind' in 10 minutes, just put words to an old spiritual, probably something I learned from Carter Family records. That's the folk music tradition. You use what's been handed down. 'The Times They Are A-Changin'' is probably from an old Scottish folk song."

As he keeps playing, the song starts sounding vaguely familiar.

I want to know about "Subterranean Homesick Blues," one of his most radical songs. The 1965 number fused folk and blues in a way that made everyone who heard it listen to it over and over. John Lennon once said the song was so captivating on every level that it made him wonder how he could ever compete with it.

The lyrics, again, were about a society in revolution, a tale of drugs and misuse of authority and trying to figure out everything when little seemed to make sense:

> Johnny's in the basement
> Mixing up the medicine
> I'm on the pavement
> Thinking about the government

The music too reflected the paranoia of the time—roaring out of the speakers at the time with a cannonball force.

Where did that come from?

Without pause, Dylan says, almost with a wink, that the inspiration dates to his teens. "It's from Chuck Berry, a bit of 'Too Much Monkey Business' and some of the scat songs of the '40s."

As the music from the guitar gets louder, you realize Dylan is playing one of the most famous songs of the 20th century, Irving Berlin's "Blue Skies."

You look into his eyes for a sign.

Is he writing a new song as we speak?

"No," he says with a smile. "I'm just showing you what I do."

Contributors

Jay Cocks wrote this piece as an undergraduate at Kenyon College in Gambier, Ohio. He went on to write *The Age of Innocence* and *Gangs of New York* for Martin Scorsese.

John Cohen is a filmmaker, musician, and photographer. He was a member of the New Lost City Ramblers and worked with photographer Robert Frank on the legendary Beat Generation film *Pull My Daisy*. He directed *The High and Lonesome Sound*, a portrait of rural Kentucky and musician Roscoe Holcomb. *Young Bob: John Cohen's Early Photographs of Bob Dylan* was published in 2003.

Jonathan Cott has been a contributing editor to ROLLING STONE since its inception. He is the author of sixteen books including *Dylan, Conversations With Glenn Gould, Stockhausen: Conversations With the Composer*, and *Back to a Shadow in the Night: Music Writings and Interviews 1968–2001*.

Toby Creswell is a former editor of both ROLLING STONE *Australia* and *Juice* magazines.

Susan Edmiston is a writer and coauthor of *Literary New York: A History and Guide*.

Murray Engleheart is an Australian rock critic. He has written for numerous publications including *Guitar World, Beat Magazine, Drum Media,* and *Uncut.*

Nora Ephron is the noted essayist, novelist, and screenwriter of such films as *Sleepless in Seattle, When Harry Met Sally . . .* , and *Silkwood.*

Mikal Gilmore is the former music editor for *L.A. Weekly* and *The Los Angeles Herald Examiner.* In 2000 he published the critically praised *Shot in the Heart.*

Ralph J. Gleason was a highly influential jazz and pop-music critic, as well as a cofounder of ROLLING STONE. He served as pop-music critic at the *San Francisco Chronicle* beginning in the late forties and was one of the first to champion Miles Davis, Bob Dylan, and numerous Bay Area acts such as the Grateful Dead and Jefferson Airplane. He published three books during his lifetime and was nominated for two Grammys. He died in 1975 at the age of 58.

Cynthia Gooding is a folk singer and was an interviewer and regular program presenter of "Folksinger's Choice" on WBAI – FM in the 1960's.

Joseph Haas was for many years a Michigan publisher and journalist.

Bruce Heiman was a radio interviewer for KMEX in Tucson, Arizona, in 1979.

Nat Hentoff is a self-described "Jewish atheist civil-libertarian pro-lifer" as well as being a noted jazz aficionado. He wrote the liner notes to *The Freewheelin' Bob Dylan* and is the author of *The Jazz Life, Boston Boy,* and *The Nat Hentoff Reader.*

Robert Hilburn is the pop music editor at *The Los Angeles Times.* He has written books about Bruce Springsteen and Michael Jackson.

Karen Hughes was a young journalist who was granted two interviews with Dylan after a chance encounter with him at an Australian stop during his 1978 world tour.

Bert Kleinman, a veteran of commercial radio programming, is currently the senior managing consultant for Radio Sawa—an Arab language radio station in the Middle East.

Kurt Loder is a contributing editor at Rolling Stone as well as the lead anchor for MTV News. He cowrote *I, Tina* with Tina Turner.

Artie Mogull, who died in 2004, was a record executive who held executive positions at Warner Bros. Records, Capitol Records, and MCA Records.

Jon Pareles is currently the pop music editor for *The New York Times*. He has written for *Crawdaddy*, *The Village Voice*, and Rolling Stone.

Paul J. Robbins was a journalist for the *L.A. Free Press* in the 1970s.

Ron Rosenbaum is a journalist whose work regularly appears in *The New York Times*, *Esquire*, *The New Yorker*, and *Vanity Fair*. He is the author of *Explaining Hitler: The Search for the Origins of his Evil* and *Those Who Forget the Past: The Question of Anti-Semitism*.

Robert Shelton is widely credited with helping launch Bob Dylan's career after writing a glowing review of his 1961 Gerde's gig for *The New York Times*. In 1986 he published a Dylan book entitled *No Direction Home*. He died in 1995 at the age of 69.

Sam Shepard is a noted playwright and actor. He won a Pulitzer Prize in 1979 for his play *Buried Child*. He cowrote the song "Brownsville Girl" with Bob Dylan in 1986. In *A Short Life of Trouble*, he taped an interview with Dylan and transformed it into a remarkable playlet.

Studs Terkel is the author of twelve books of oral history, including *Hope Dies Last*, *Working*, and the Pulitzer Prize–winning *The Good War*. A member of the Academy of Arts and Letters, he is a recipient of a Presidential National Humanities Medal, the National Book Foundation Medal for Distinguished Contribution to American Letters, a George Polk Career Award, and the National Book Critics Ivan Sandrof Lifetime Achievement Award. Throughout the second half of the twentieth century, he hosted a legendary daily radio program on WFMT in Chicago, presenting listeners with a singular take on an eclectic range of music, from classical, opera, and jazz to gospel, blues, folk, and rock.

Happy Traum is the former editor of *Sing Out!* magazine. He has played and recorded with Bob Dylan, Eric Andersen, Allen Ginsberg, Levon Helm, Rick Danko, Richard Manuel, and many others in addition to cutting several of his own solo albums. He has also published more than a dozen guitar instructional manuals.

A.J. Weberman, who coined the word *Dylanology*, is currently attempting to solve the JFK assassination conspiracy.

Jann S. Wenner is the editor and publisher of ROLLING STONE and the chairman of Wenner Media.

Paul Zollo was the editor of *SongTalk* magazine from 1987 to 1997. He is currently the senior editor at *American Songwriter*. He is the author of *Songwriters on Songwriting*. He recently published a book entitled *Conversations With Tom Petty*.

Permissions

We gratefully acknowledge everyone who gave permission for written material to appear in this book. We have made every effort to trace and contact copyright holders. If an error or omission is brought to our notice we will be pleased to correct the situation in future editions of this book. For further information, please contact the publisher.

Radio interview with Studs Terkel, WFMT (Chicago), May 1963: Reprinted by permission of Granta Books from *And They All Sang* copyright © 2005 by Studs Terkel.

"The Crackin', Shakin', Breakin', Sounds," Nat Hentoff, *The New Yorker*, October 24, 1964: Copyright © 1964 Nat Hentoff. Used by permission of the author.

Interview with Jay Cocks, *The Kenyon Collegian*, November 20, 1964: Used by permission of *The Kenyon Collegian*.

Interview with Nora Ephron and Susan Edmiston, *Positively Tie Dream*, August 1965: Copyright © 1965 by Nora Ephron and Susan Edmiston. Used by permission of Nora Ephron.

Interview with Robert Shelton, from *No Direction Home*, March 1966: Copyright © 1986 by Robert Shelton. Reprinted by permission of Hodder & Stoughton Publishers.

Lyric credits:

Acknowledgments

Thanks to the following persons who made this book possible: Jann S. Wenner, Robert Wallace, John Gruber, Corey Seymour, Nina Pearlman, Andrew Greene, Mayapriya Long, Stephen Doyle, August Heffner, Brian Chojnowski, David Malley, Tom Maloney, Kate Rockland, Frederick Kennedy, Robert Legault, William Goodman, Evelyn Bernal, Maureen Lamberti, Meredith Phares, Christine Calabrese, and Theresa Sanchez.